The CARTOON INTRODUCTION to PHILOSOPHY

ALSO AVAILABLE FROM HILL AND WANG

THE CARTOON INTRODUCTION TO ECONOMICS: VOLUME ONE: MICROECONOMICS
THE CARTOON INTRODUCTION TO ECONOMICS: VOLUME TWO: MACROECONOMICS
THE CARTOON INTRODUCTION TO STATISTICS

The CARTOON INTRODUCTION to PHILOSOPHY

Written by Michael F. Patton and Kevin Cannon

Illustrated by Kevin Cannon

A NOVEL GRAPHIC FROM HILL AND WANG
A DIVISION OF FARRAR, STRAUS AND GIROUX
NEW YORK

HILL AND WANG
A DIVISION OF FARRAR, STRAUS AND GIROUX
18 WEST 18TH STREET, NEW YORK 10011

PRINTED IN THE UNITED STATES OF AMERICA
FIRST EDITION, 2015

LIBRARY OF CONGRESS CATALOGING-IN-PUBLICATION DATA
PATTON, MICHAEL F., 1961- AUTHOR.
    THE CARTOON INTRODUCTION TO PHILOSOPHY / WRITTEN BY MICHAEL F. PATTON AND KEVIN CANNON ;
  ILLUSTRATED BY KEVIN CANNON -- FIRST EDITION.
      PAGES   CM
    ISBN 978-0-8090-3362-1 (PAPERBACK) -- ISBN 978-1-4299-4522-6 (E-BOOK)
    1. PHILOSOPHY -- INTRODUCTIONS -- COMIC BOOKS, STRIPS, ETC.   I. CANNON, KEVIN, ILLUSTRATOR.
  II. TITLE.

BD21 .P27 2015
100 -- DC23
                                                        2014029343

DESIGNED BY KEVIN CANNON

HILL AND WANG BOOKS MAY BE PURCHASED FOR EDUCATIONAL, BUSINESS, OR PROMOTIONAL
USE. FOR INFORMATION ON BULK PURCHASES, PLEASE CONTACT THE MACMILLAN CORPORATE
AND PREMIUM SALES DEPARTMENT AT 1-800-221-7945, EXTENSION 5442, OR WRITE TO
SPECIALMARKETS@MACMILLAN.COM.

WWW.FSGBOOKS.COM
WWW.TWITTER.COM/FSGBOOKS • WWW.FACEBOOK.COM/FSGBOOKS

10 9 8 7 6 5 4 3 2 1

TO CHERYL STEINBACH PATTON, WHO GIVES ME
SO MUCH MORE THAN THE WORLD TAKES AWAY

-- *MICHAEL F. PATTON*

FOR R.A.

-- *KEVIN CANNON*

ACKNOWLEDGMENTS

I WOULD LIKE TO THANK DAVID CHALMERS FOR SUGGESTING ME
AS A PINCH AUTHOR AND TO ACKNOWLEDGE THE INDIFFERENCE
OF MY CATS, THE SUPPORT OF MY WIFE, AND COMMENTS AND
ENCOURAGEMENT FROM MANY OTHER FRIENDS AND COLLEAGUES,
INCLUDING TORIN ALTER AND ESPECIALLY STEFAN FORRESTER.

-- *MICHAEL F. PATTON*

FIRST AND FOREMOST, I'D LIKE TO THANK MY PARTNER IN CRIME
ZANDER CANNON (NO RELATION), WHOSE ENTHUSIASM MADE THIS
BOOK POSSIBLE. ALSO, ZANDER AND JAMIE SCHUMACHER AND KATE
CANNON READ EARLY DRAFTS OF THE BOOK AND GAVE VALUABLE
FEEDBACK, AND FOR THAT I AM GRATEFUL. FINALLY, A HUGE THANKS
TO MY PRODUCTION ASSISTANT, ATHENA CURRIER, WHOSE TALENT
AND ATTENTION TO DETAIL ARE UNMATCHED.

-- *KEVIN CANNON*

BOTH OF US WOULD LIKE TO EXTEND THANKS TO HILL AND WANG'S
THOMAS LEBIEN FOR SPEARHEADING THIS PROJECT, AND TO AMANDA
MOON FOR MAKING THIS BOOK WHAT IT IS TODAY, AND TO THE
NUMEROUS MEN AND WOMEN WHO WORKED ON THIS BOOK BEHIND
THE SCENES.

-- *MICHAEL AND KEVIN*

"Upon those who
step into the same rivers,
different and again different
waters flow."

-- Heraclitus

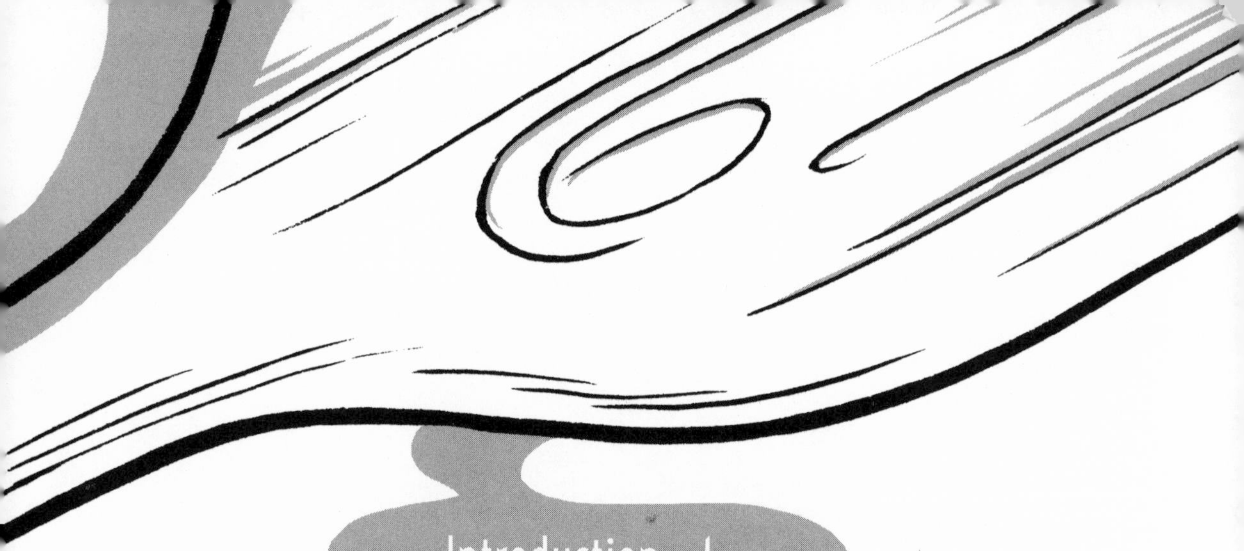

INTRODUCTION

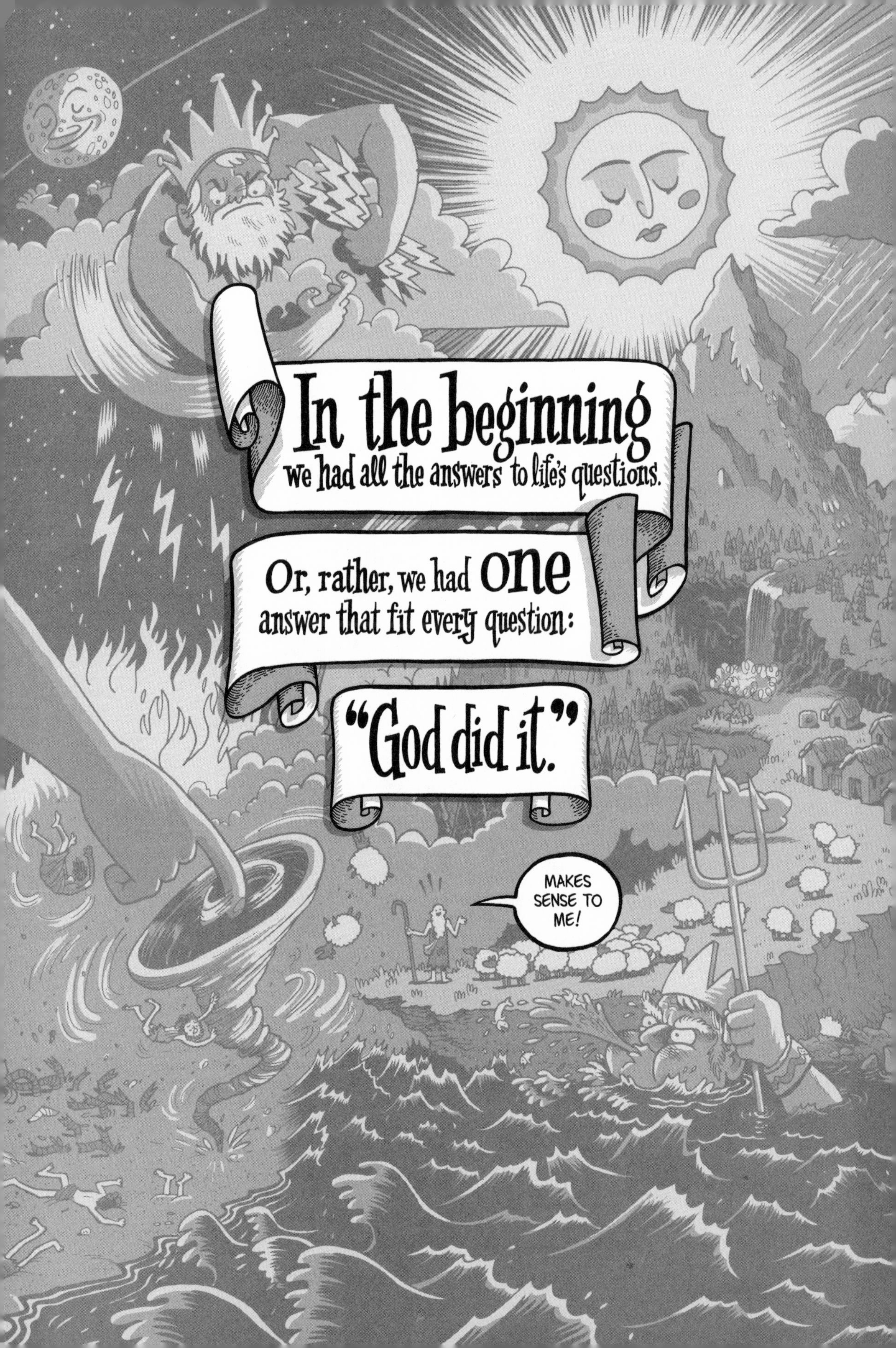
In the beginning
we had all the answers to life's questions.
Or, rather, we had one answer that fit every question:
"God did it."
MAKES SENSE TO ME!

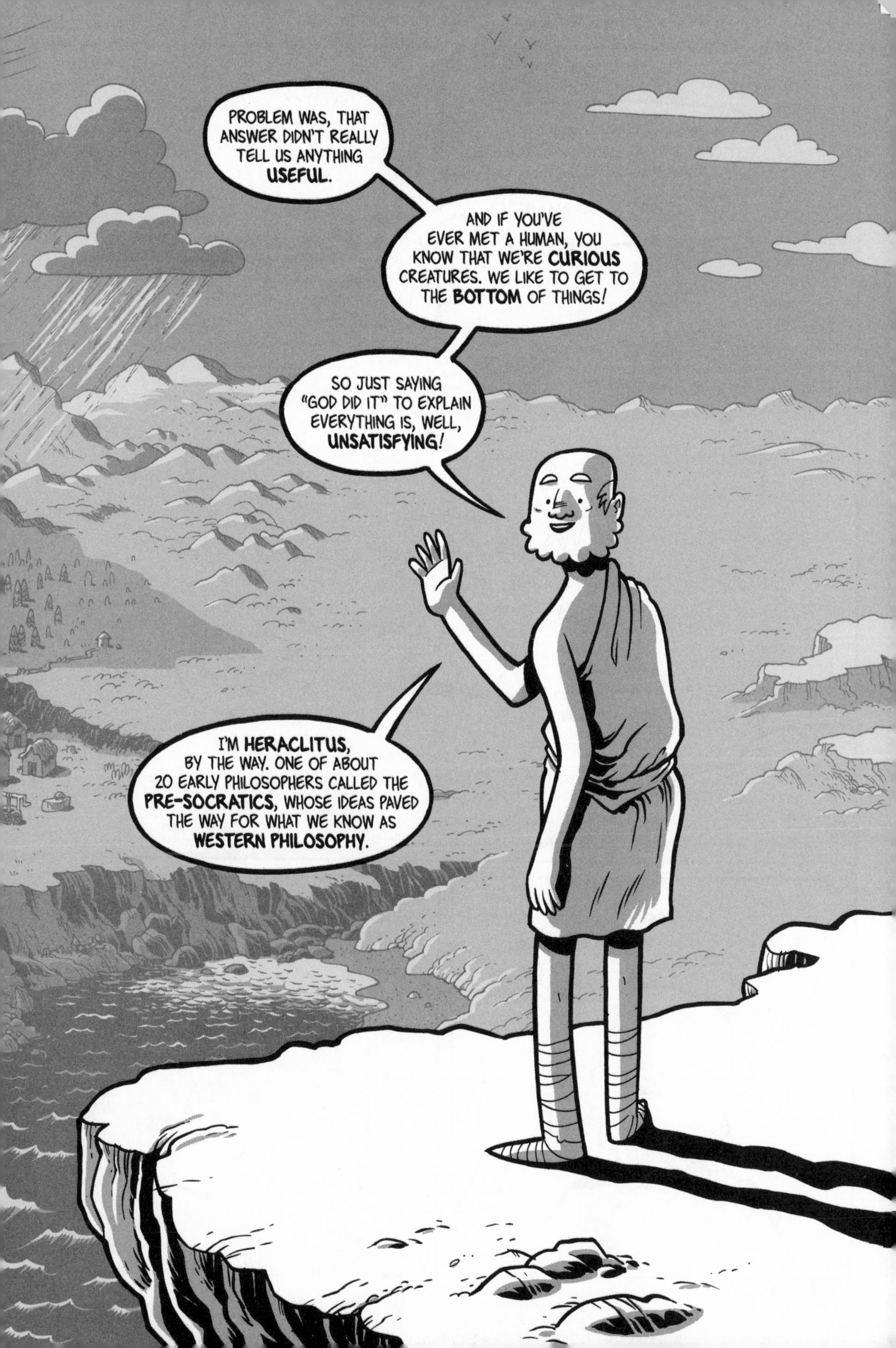
PROBLEM WAS, THAT ANSWER DIDN'T REALLY TELL US ANYTHING **USEFUL**.
AND IF YOU'VE EVER MET A HUMAN, YOU KNOW THAT WE'RE **CURIOUS** CREATURES. WE LIKE TO GET TO THE **BOTTOM** OF THINGS!
SO JUST SAYING "GOD DID IT" TO EXPLAIN EVERYTHING IS, WELL, **UNSATISFYING**!
I'M **HERACLITUS**, BY THE WAY. ONE OF ABOUT 20 EARLY PHILOSOPHERS CALLED THE **PRE-SOCRATICS**, WHOSE IDEAS PAVED THE WAY FOR WHAT WE KNOW AS **WESTERN PHILOSOPHY**.

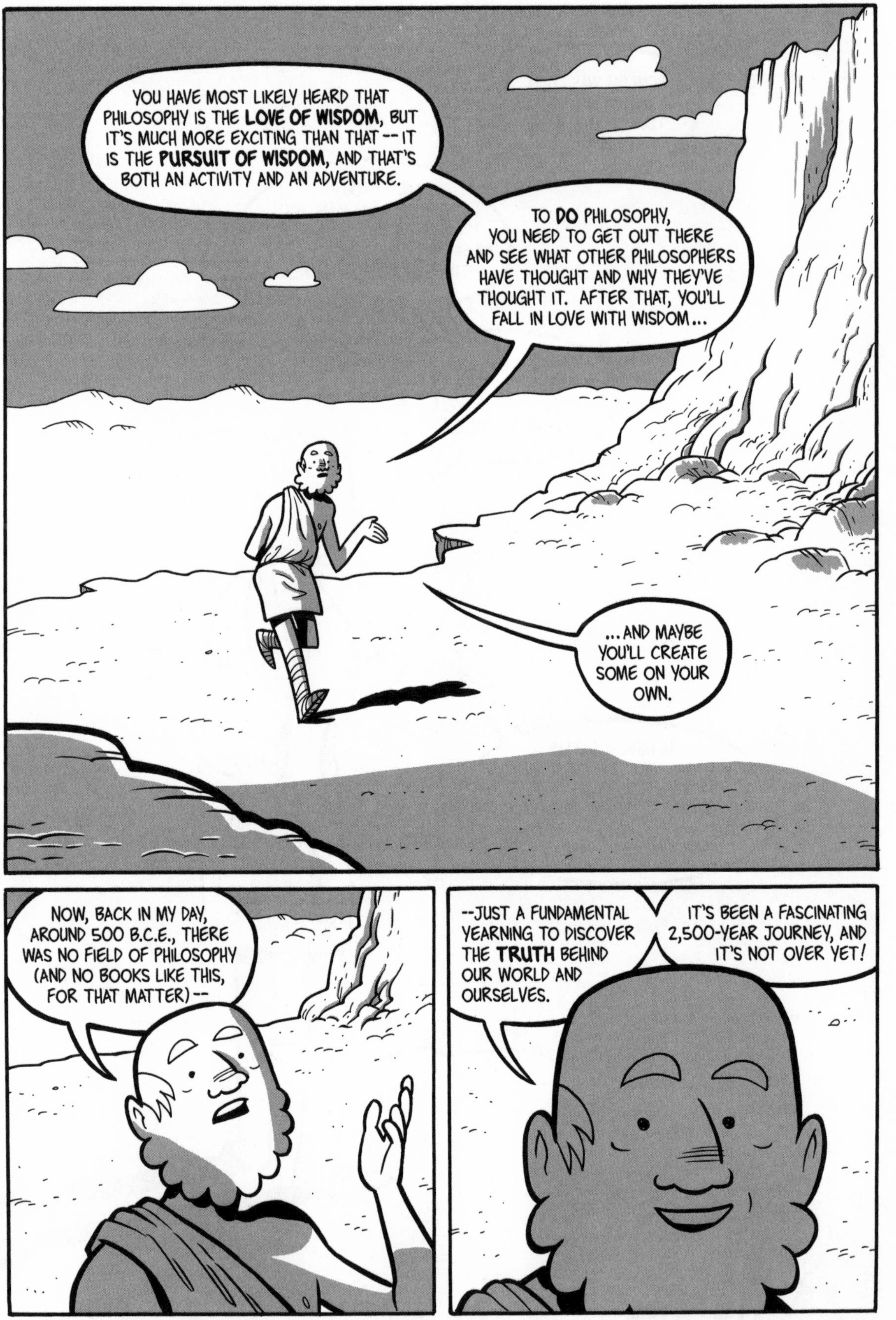
YOU HAVE MOST LIKELY HEARD THAT PHILOSOPHY IS THE **LOVE OF WISDOM**, BUT IT'S MUCH MORE EXCITING THAN THAT -- IT IS THE **PURSUIT OF WISDOM**, AND THAT'S BOTH AN ACTIVITY AND AN ADVENTURE.
TO **DO** PHILOSOPHY, YOU NEED TO GET OUT THERE AND SEE WHAT OTHER PHILOSOPHERS HAVE THOUGHT AND WHY THEY'VE THOUGHT IT. AFTER THAT, YOU'LL FALL IN LOVE WITH WISDOM...
...AND MAYBE YOU'LL CREATE SOME ON YOUR OWN.
NOW, BACK IN MY DAY, AROUND 500 B.C.E., THERE WAS NO FIELD OF PHILOSOPHY (AND NO BOOKS LIKE THIS, FOR THAT MATTER)--
--JUST A FUNDAMENTAL YEARNING TO DISCOVER THE **TRUTH** BEHIND OUR WORLD AND OURSELVES.
IT'S BEEN A FASCINATING 2,500-YEAR JOURNEY, AND IT'S NOT OVER YET!

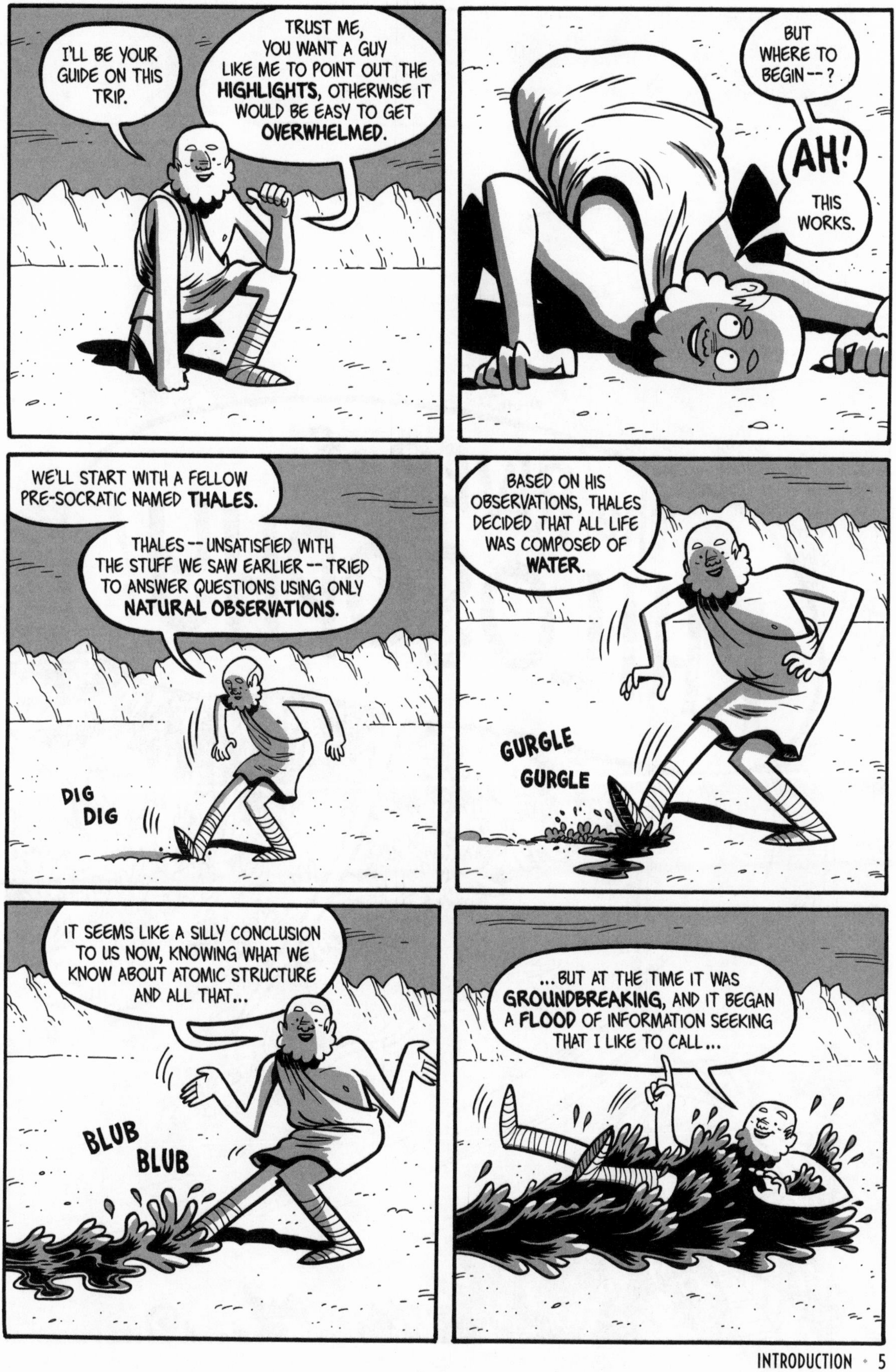
I'LL BE YOUR GUIDE ON THIS TRIP.
TRUST ME, YOU WANT A GUY LIKE ME TO POINT OUT THE **HIGHLIGHTS**, OTHERWISE IT WOULD BE EASY TO GET **OVERWHELMED**.
BUT WHERE TO BEGIN--?
AH!
THIS WORKS.
WE'LL START WITH A FELLOW PRE-SOCRATIC NAMED **THALES**.
THALES--UNSATISFIED WITH THE STUFF WE SAW EARLIER--TRIED TO ANSWER QUESTIONS USING ONLY **NATURAL OBSERVATIONS**.
DIG
DIG
BASED ON HIS OBSERVATIONS, THALES DECIDED THAT ALL LIFE WAS COMPOSED OF **WATER**.
GURGLE
GURGLE
IT SEEMS LIKE A SILLY CONCLUSION TO US NOW, KNOWING WHAT WE KNOW ABOUT ATOMIC STRUCTURE AND ALL THAT...
BLUB
BLUB
...BUT AT THE TIME IT WAS **GROUNDBREAKING**, AND IT BEGAN A **FLOOD** OF INFORMATION SEEKING THAT I LIKE TO CALL...

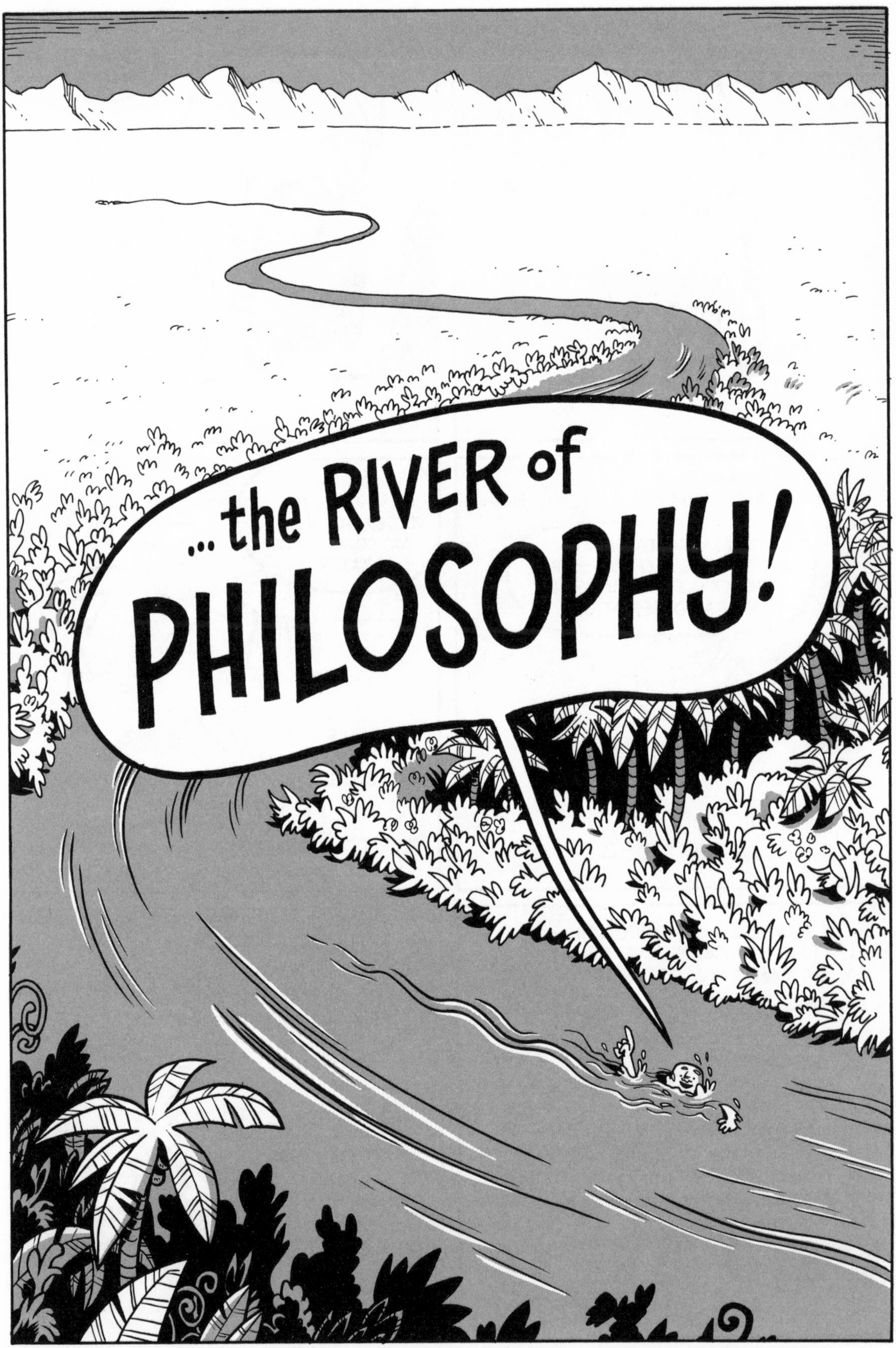
... the RIVER of PHILOSOPHY!

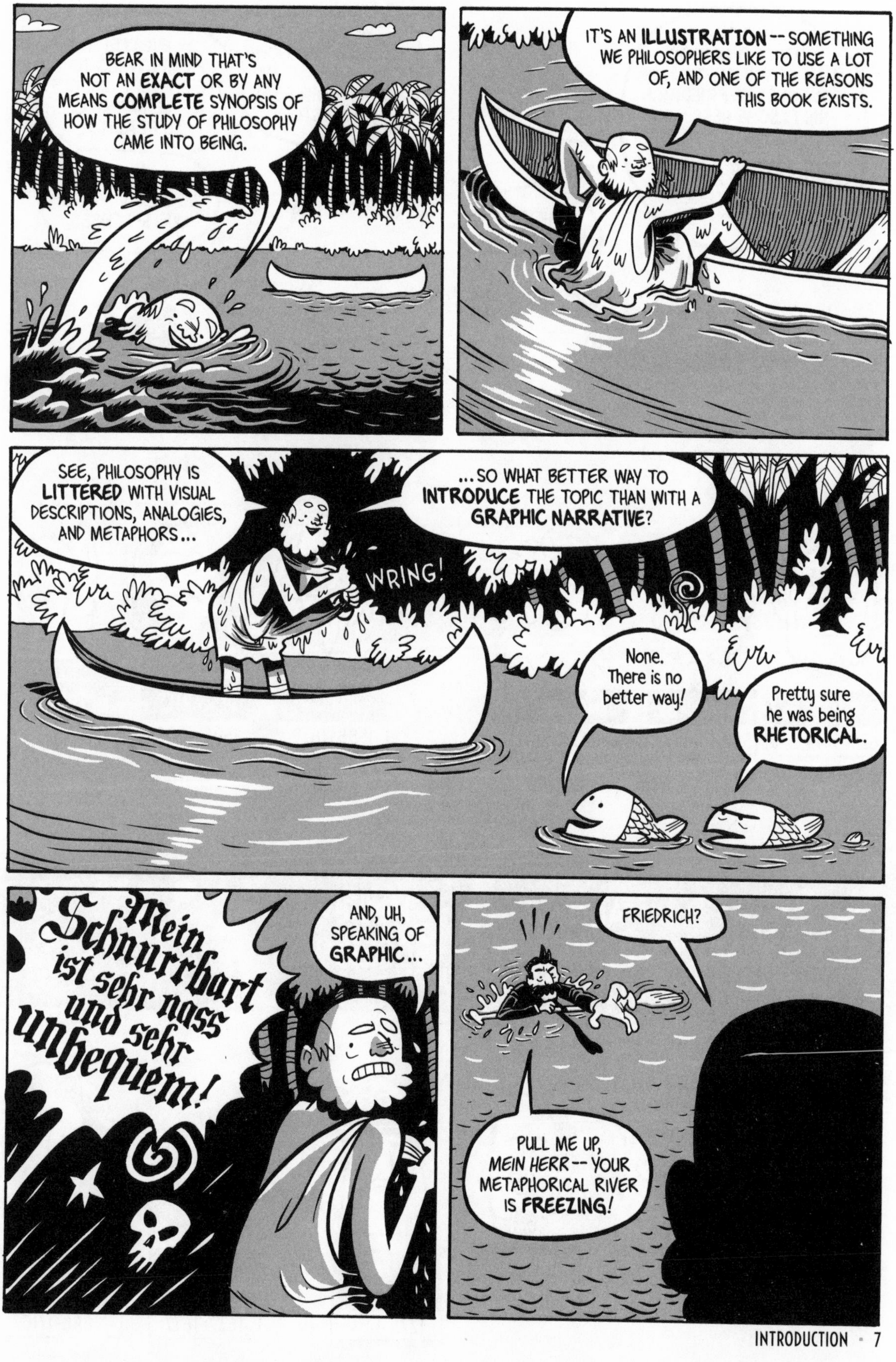
BEAR IN MIND THAT'S NOT AN EXACT OR BY ANY MEANS COMPLETE SYNOPSIS OF HOW THE STUDY OF PHILOSOPHY CAME INTO BEING.
IT'S AN ILLUSTRATION -- SOMETHING WE PHILOSOPHERS LIKE TO USE A LOT OF, AND ONE OF THE REASONS THIS BOOK EXISTS.
SEE, PHILOSOPHY IS LITTERED WITH VISUAL DESCRIPTIONS, ANALOGIES, AND METAPHORS...
...SO WHAT BETTER WAY TO INTRODUCE THE TOPIC THAN WITH A GRAPHIC NARRATIVE?
WRING!
None. There is no better way!
Pretty sure he was being RHETORICAL.
Mein Schnurrbart ist sehr nass und sehr unbequem!
AND, UH, SPEAKING OF GRAPHIC...
FRIEDRICH?
PULL ME UP, MEIN HERR -- YOUR METAPHORICAL RIVER IS FREEZING!

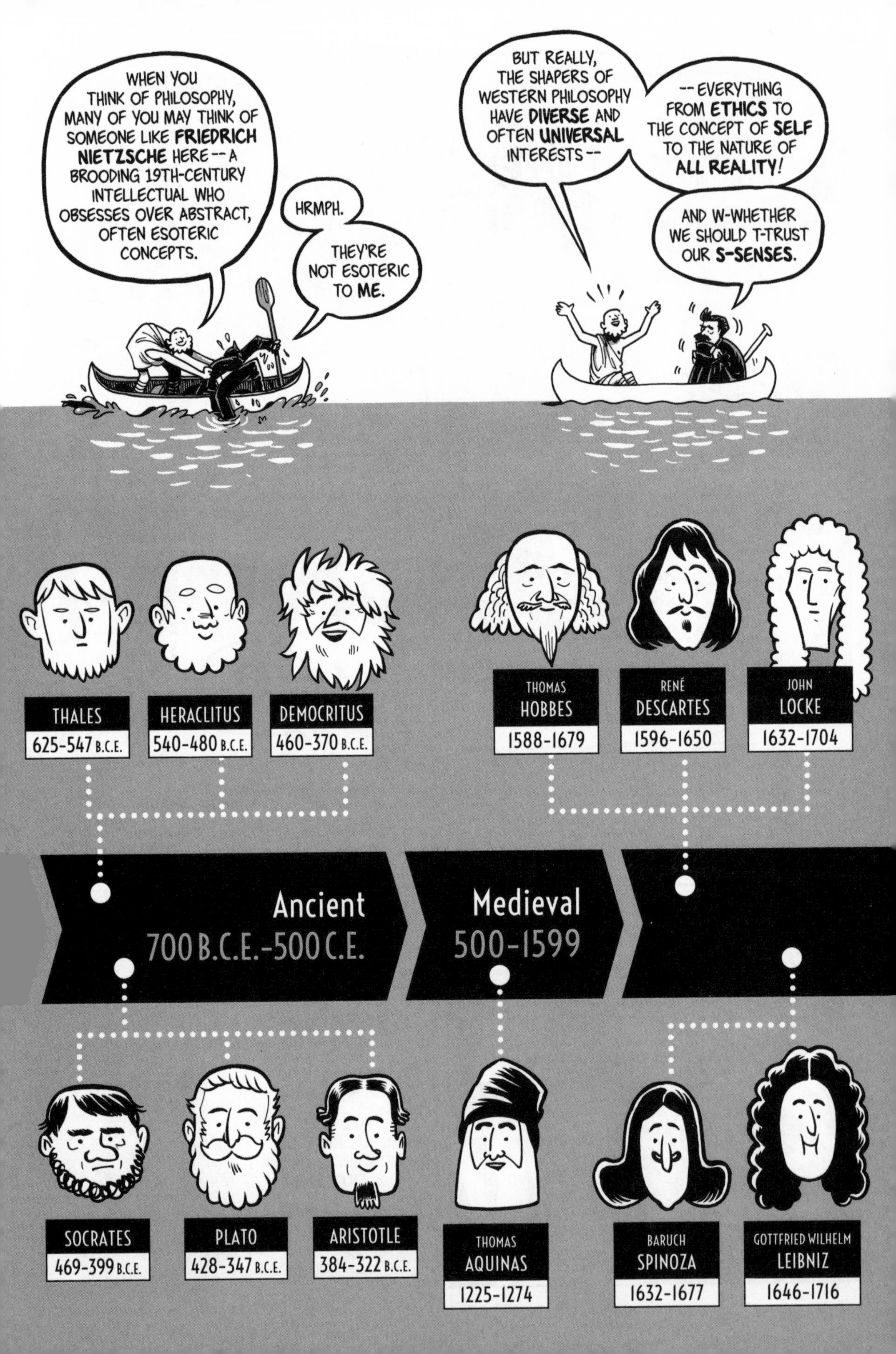

WHEN YOU THINK OF PHILOSOPHY, MANY OF YOU MAY THINK OF SOMEONE LIKE FRIEDRICH NIETZSCHE HERE -- A BROODING 19TH-CENTURY INTELLECTUAL WHO OBSESSES OVER ABSTRACT, OFTEN ESOTERIC CONCEPTS.
HRMPH.
THEY'RE NOT ESOTERIC TO ME.
BUT REALLY, THE SHAPERS OF WESTERN PHILOSOPHY HAVE DIVERSE AND OFTEN UNIVERSAL INTERESTS --
-- EVERYTHING FROM ETHICS TO THE CONCEPT OF SELF TO THE NATURE OF ALL REALITY!
AND W-WHETHER WE SHOULD T-TRUST OUR S-SENSES.
THALES 625-547 B.C.E.
HERACLITUS 540-480 B.C.E.
DEMOCRITUS 460-370 B.C.E.
THOMAS HOBBES 1588-1679
RENÉ DESCARTES 1596-1650
JOHN LOCKE 1632-1704
Ancient 700 B.C.E.-500 C.E.
Medieval 500-1599
SOCRATES 469-399 B.C.E.
PLATO 428-347 B.C.E.
ARISTOTLE 384-322 B.C.E.
THOMAS AQUINAS 1225-1274
BARUCH SPINOZA 1632-1677
GOTTFRIED WILHELM LEIBNIZ 1646-1716

KIND OF HEAVY ON THE **GUYS**, DON'T YOU THINK?

YEAH, IT'S TRUE THAT WHILE WOMEN HAVE MADE GREAT CONTRIBUTIONS TO THE FIELD, THEY ARE WOEFULLY UNDERREPRESENTED IN THE ACCEPTED **CANON**.

GIVEN OUR BRIEF WINDOW HERE, WE'RE GOING TO FOCUS ONLY ON CANON PHILOSOPHERS, THUS THE TESTOSTERONE-HEAVY LINEUP YOU SEE BELOW.

WRING

?

KEEP THIS TIME LINE **HANDY**, BY THE WAY.

OUR TOUR WILL BE COVERING THE **BIG IDEAS** IN WESTERN PHILOSOPHY, AND TO DO THAT EFFECTIVELY WE'LL BE MEETING THINKERS FROM **ALL** ERAS, AND NOT NECESSARILY IN ANY SORT OF **LINEAR** FASHION.

YOU'VE REALLY CAPTURED THE LOOK OF MY SCHNURRBART.

| GEORGE **BERKELEY** |
| 1685-1753 |

| JULIEN OFFRAY DE **LA METTRIE** |
| 1709-1751 |

| DAVID **HUME** |
| 1711-1776 |

| CHARLES ROBERT **DARWIN** |
| 1809-1882 |

| FRIEDRICH WILHELM **NIETZSCHE** |
| 1844-1900 |

Early Modern 1600-1800

19th Century

20th Century

| IMMANUEL **KANT** |
| 1724-1804 |

| WILLIAM **PALEY** |
| 1743-1805 |

| JEREMY **BENTHAM** |
| 1748-1832 |

| JOHN STUART **MILL** |
| 1806-1873 |

| ALAN **TURING** |
| 1912-1954 |

| DAVID **CHALMERS** |
| 1966- |

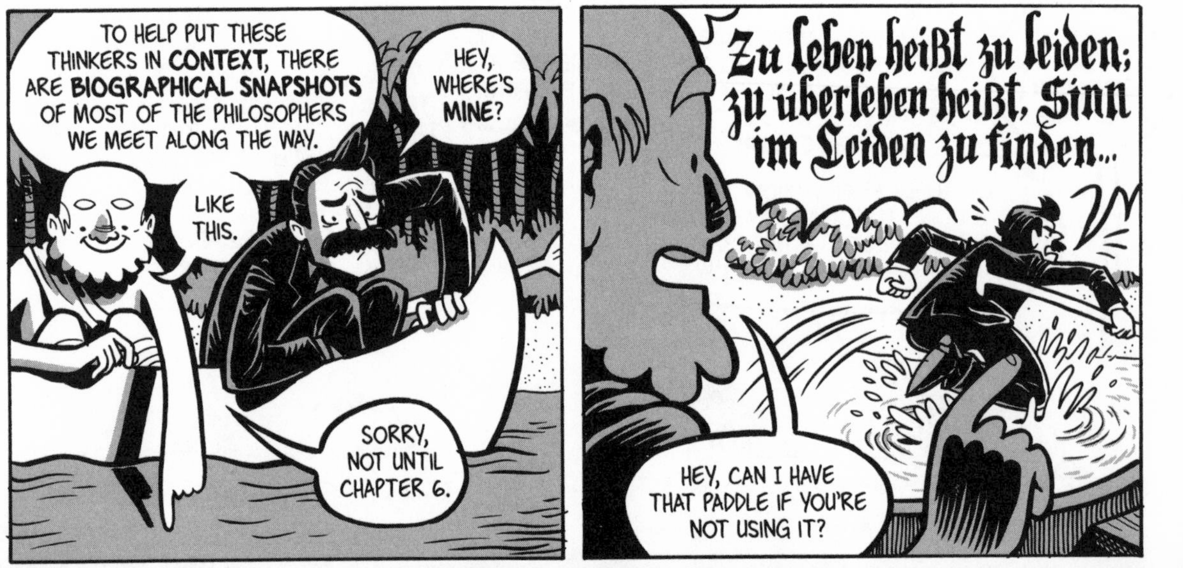
TO HELP PUT THESE THINKERS IN **CONTEXT**, THERE ARE **BIOGRAPHICAL SNAPSHOTS** OF MOST OF THE PHILOSOPHERS WE MEET ALONG THE WAY.
HEY, WHERE'S **MINE**?
LIKE THIS.
SORRY, NOT UNTIL CHAPTER 6.
Zu leben heißt zu leiden; zu überleben heißt, Sinn im Leiden zu finden...
HEY, CAN I HAVE THAT PADDLE IF YOU'RE NOT USING IT?

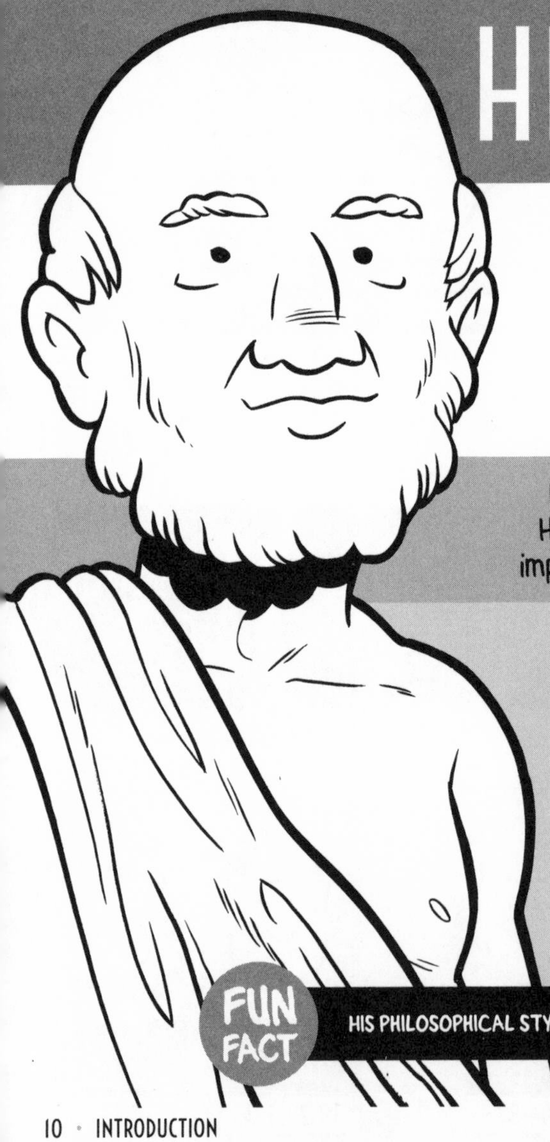

HERACLITUS

b. 540
d. 480
B.C.E.

"The sun is new every day."

-- cited by Aristotle in *Metaphysics* (350 B.C.E.) and others

Heraclitus was a pre-Socratic Greek philosopher. He is known for his emphasis on change and impermanence rather than on stability in the world.

MOST FAMOUS WORK:

Known primarily through the discussions of his work by later writers. Only fragments of his own work remain.

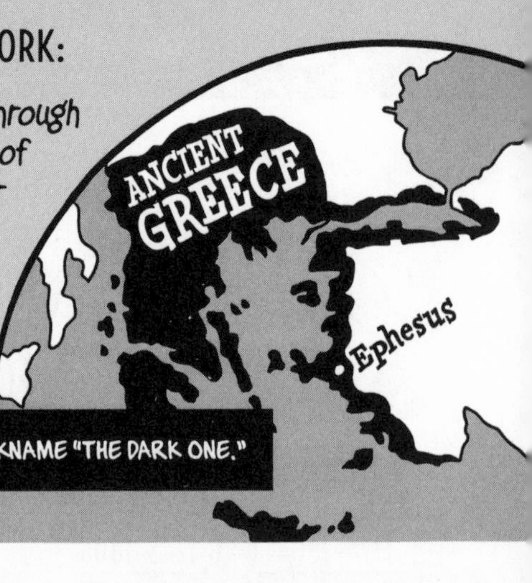
ANCIENT GREECE
Ephesus

FUN FACT HIS PHILOSOPHICAL STYLE EARNED HIM THE NICKNAME "THE DARK ONE."

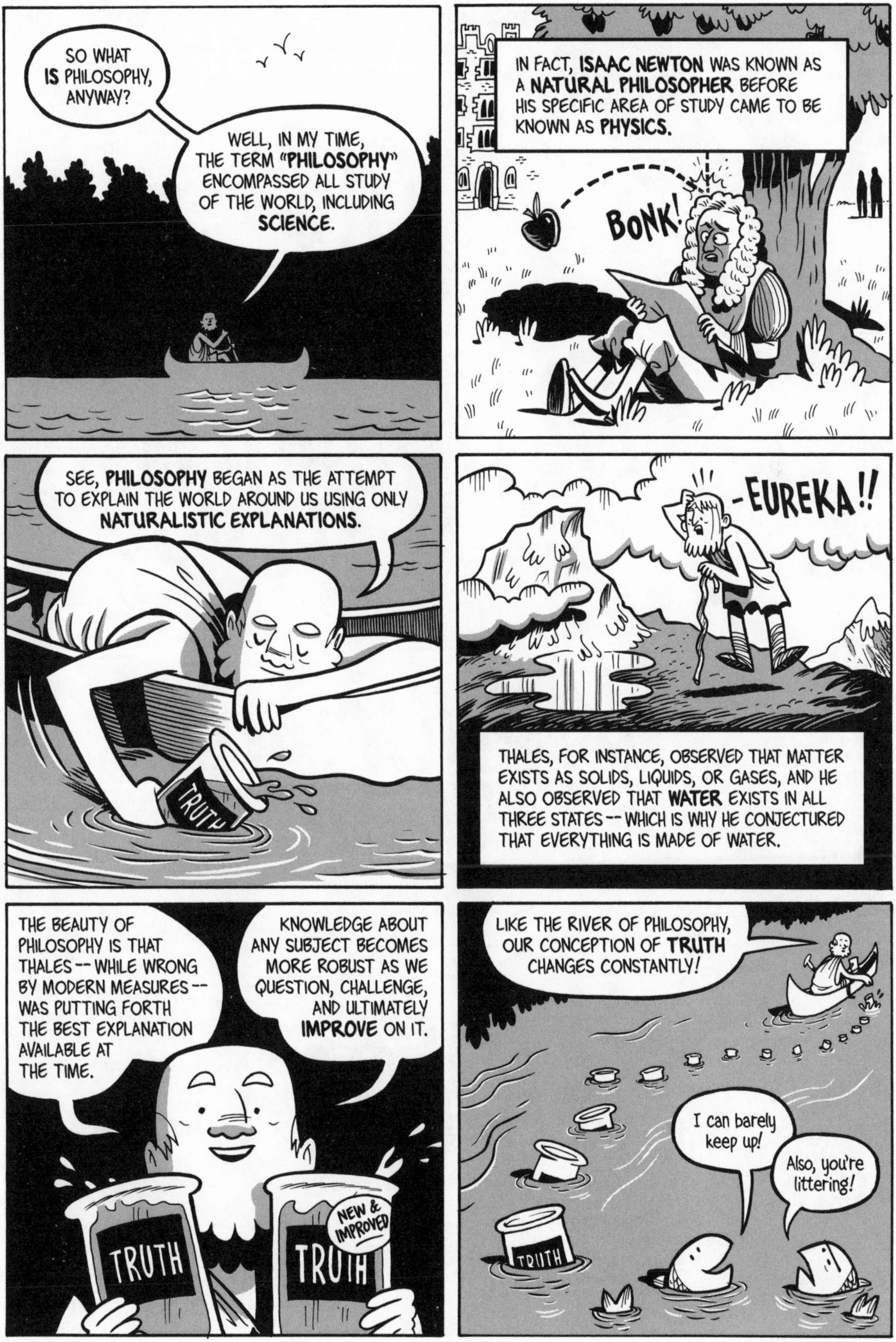
SO WHAT IS PHILOSOPHY, ANYWAY?
WELL, IN MY TIME, THE TERM "PHILOSOPHY" ENCOMPASSED ALL STUDY OF THE WORLD, INCLUDING SCIENCE.
IN FACT, ISAAC NEWTON WAS KNOWN AS A NATURAL PHILOSOPHER BEFORE HIS SPECIFIC AREA OF STUDY CAME TO BE KNOWN AS PHYSICS.
BONK!
SEE, PHILOSOPHY BEGAN AS THE ATTEMPT TO EXPLAIN THE WORLD AROUND US USING ONLY NATURALISTIC EXPLANATIONS.
TRUTH
-EUREKA!!
THALES, FOR INSTANCE, OBSERVED THAT MATTER EXISTS AS SOLIDS, LIQUIDS, OR GASES, AND HE ALSO OBSERVED THAT WATER EXISTS IN ALL THREE STATES -- WHICH IS WHY HE CONJECTURED THAT EVERYTHING IS MADE OF WATER.
THE BEAUTY OF PHILOSOPHY IS THAT THALES -- WHILE WRONG BY MODERN MEASURES -- WAS PUTTING FORTH THE BEST EXPLANATION AVAILABLE AT THE TIME.
KNOWLEDGE ABOUT ANY SUBJECT BECOMES MORE ROBUST AS WE QUESTION, CHALLENGE, AND ULTIMATELY IMPROVE ON IT.
TRUTH
NEW & IMPROVED
TRUTH
LIKE THE RIVER OF PHILOSOPHY, OUR CONCEPTION OF TRUTH CHANGES CONSTANTLY!
I can barely keep up!
Also, you're littering!
TRUTH

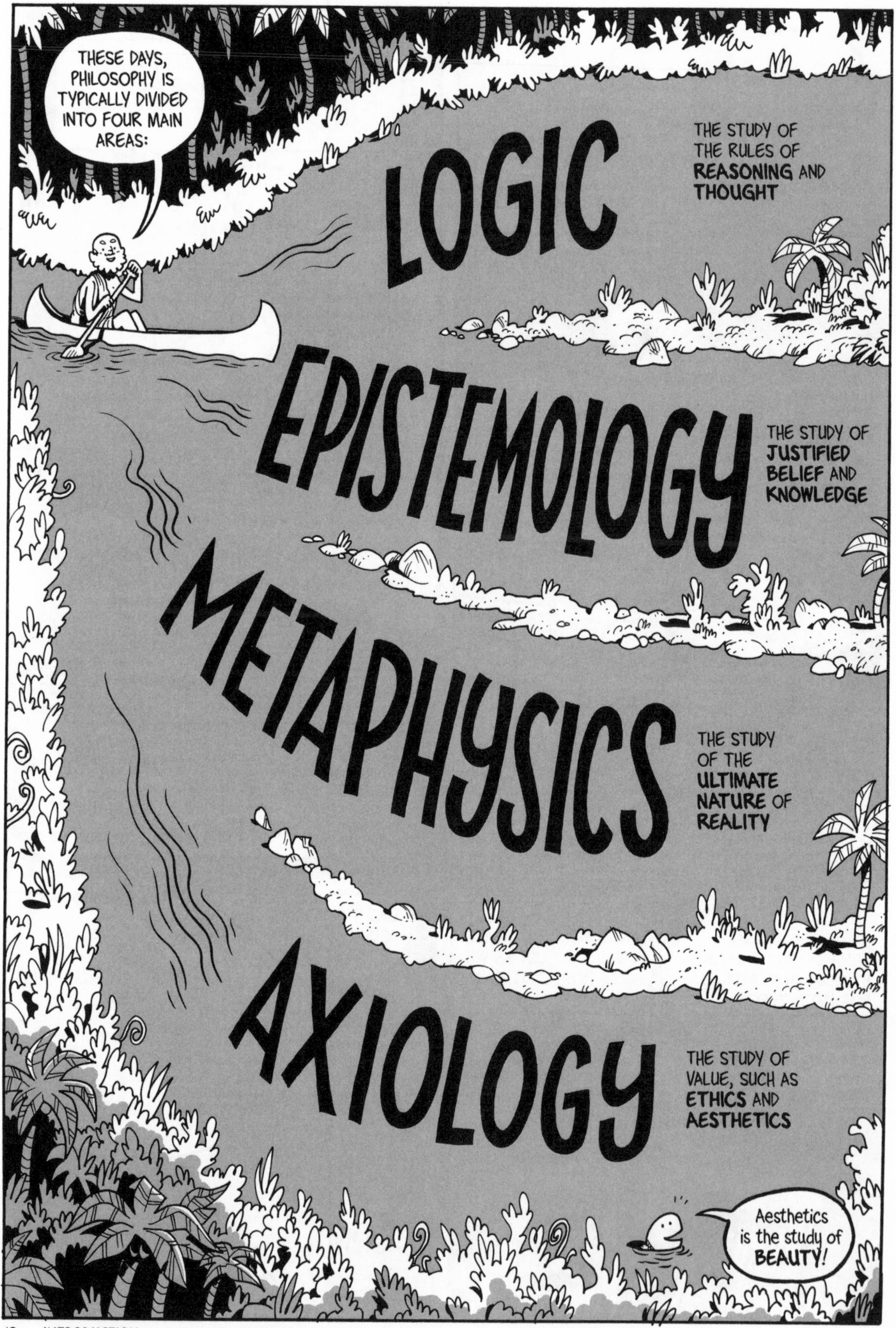
THESE DAYS, PHILOSOPHY IS TYPICALLY DIVIDED INTO FOUR MAIN AREAS:
LOGIC
THE STUDY OF THE RULES OF REASONING AND THOUGHT
EPISTEMOLOGY
THE STUDY OF JUSTIFIED BELIEF AND KNOWLEDGE
METAPHYSICS
THE STUDY OF THE ULTIMATE NATURE OF REALITY
AXIOLOGY
THE STUDY OF VALUE, SUCH AS ETHICS AND AESTHETICS
Aesthetics is the study of BEAUTY!

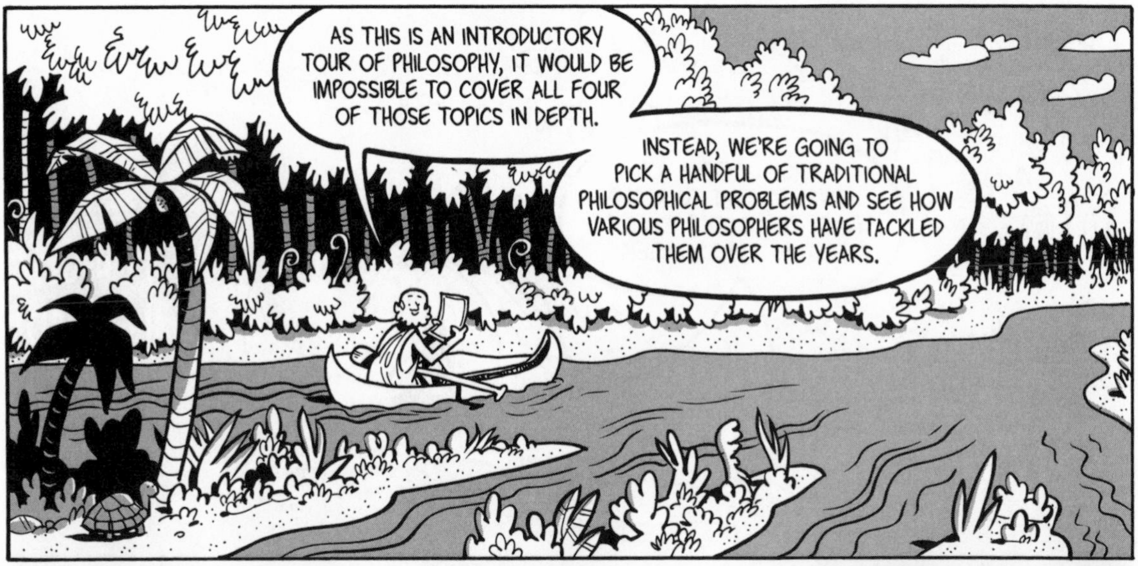
AS THIS IS AN INTRODUCTORY TOUR OF PHILOSOPHY, IT WOULD BE IMPOSSIBLE TO COVER ALL FOUR OF THOSE TOPICS IN DEPTH.
INSTEAD, WE'RE GOING TO PICK A HANDFUL OF TRADITIONAL PHILOSOPHICAL PROBLEMS AND SEE HOW VARIOUS PHILOSOPHERS HAVE TACKLED THEM OVER THE YEARS.

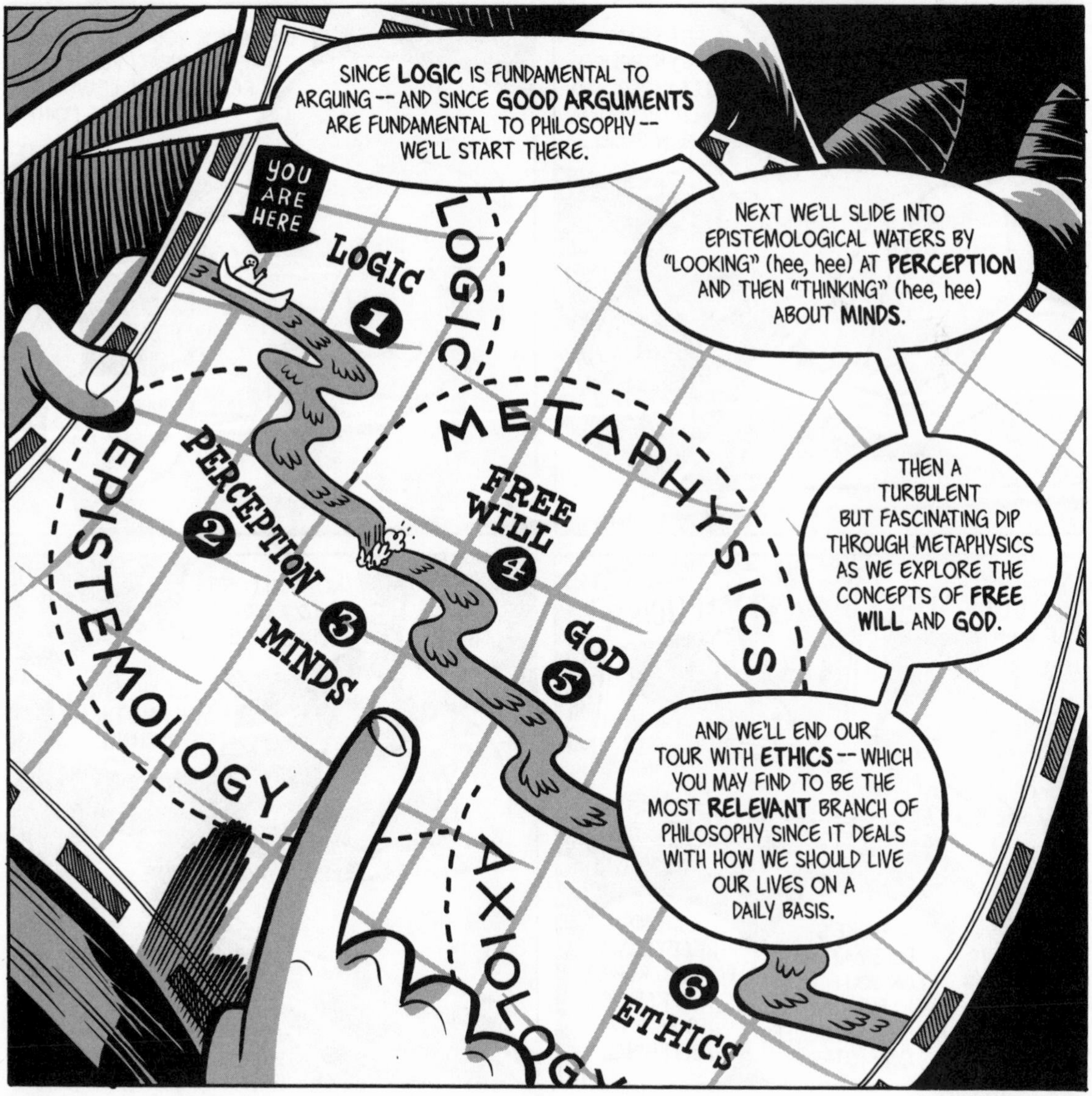
SINCE **LOGIC** IS FUNDAMENTAL TO ARGUING -- AND SINCE **GOOD ARGUMENTS** ARE FUNDAMENTAL TO PHILOSOPHY -- WE'LL START THERE.
YOU ARE HERE
LOGIC
1
LOGIC
NEXT WE'LL SLIDE INTO EPISTEMOLOGICAL WATERS BY "LOOKING" (hee, hee) AT **PERCEPTION** AND THEN "THINKING" (hee, hee) ABOUT **MINDS.**
EPISTEMOLOGY
PERCEPTION
2
MINDS
3
METAPHYSICS
FREE WILL
4
GOD
5
THEN A TURBULENT BUT FASCINATING DIP THROUGH METAPHYSICS AS WE EXPLORE THE CONCEPTS OF **FREE WILL** AND **GOD.**
AND WE'LL END OUR TOUR WITH **ETHICS** -- WHICH YOU MAY FIND TO BE THE MOST **RELEVANT** BRANCH OF PHILOSOPHY SINCE IT DEALS WITH HOW WE SHOULD LIVE OUR LIVES ON A DAILY BASIS.
AXIOLOGY
6
ETHICS

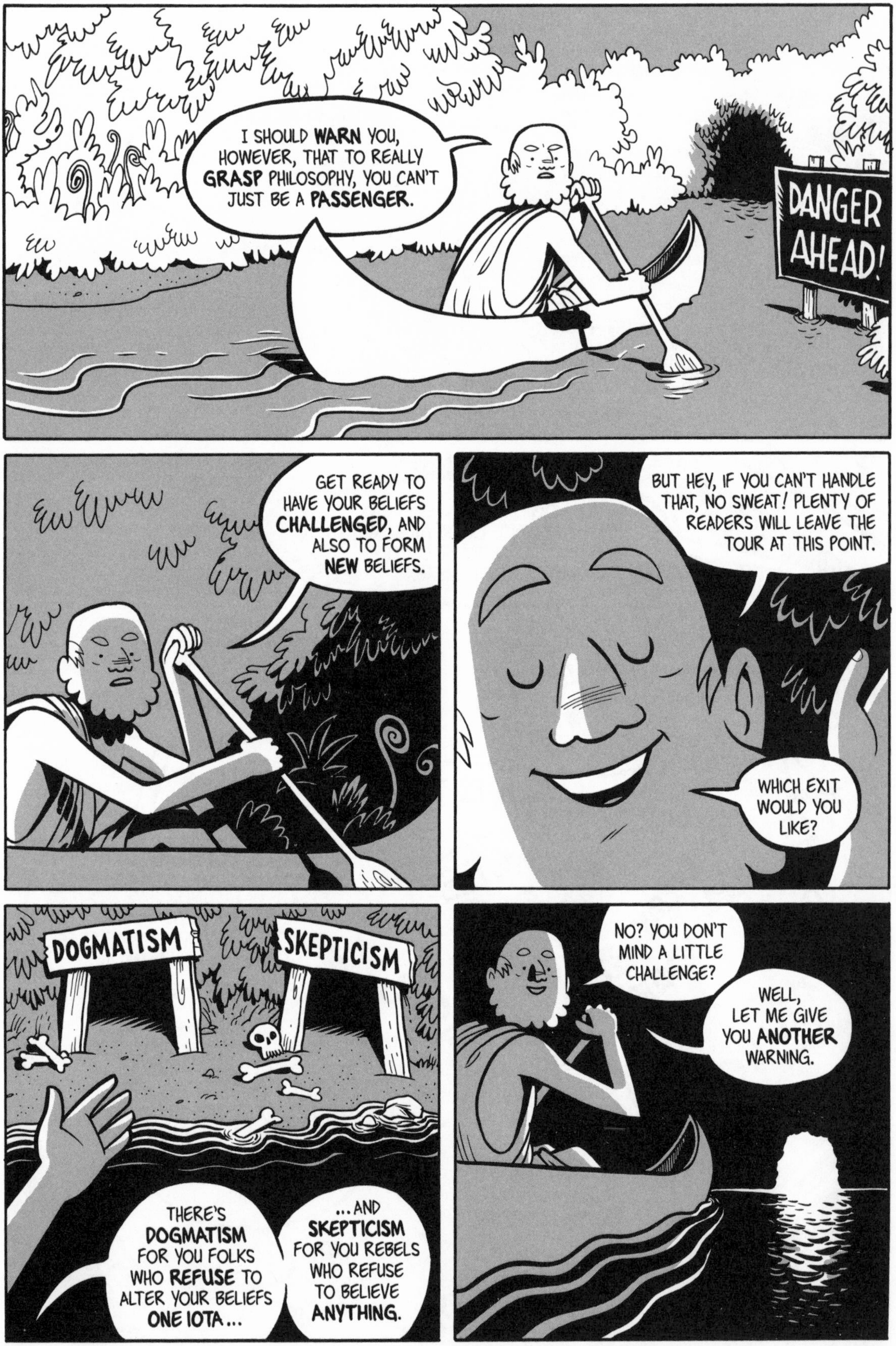
I SHOULD WARN YOU, HOWEVER, THAT TO REALLY GRASP PHILOSOPHY, YOU CAN'T JUST BE A PASSENGER.
DANGER AHEAD!
GET READY TO HAVE YOUR BELIEFS CHALLENGED, AND ALSO TO FORM NEW BELIEFS.
BUT HEY, IF YOU CAN'T HANDLE THAT, NO SWEAT! PLENTY OF READERS WILL LEAVE THE TOUR AT THIS POINT.
WHICH EXIT WOULD YOU LIKE?
DOGMATISM
SKEPTICISM
THERE'S DOGMATISM FOR YOU FOLKS WHO REFUSE TO ALTER YOUR BELIEFS ONE IOTA...
...AND SKEPTICISM FOR YOU REBELS WHO REFUSE TO BELIEVE ANYTHING.
NO? YOU DON'T MIND A LITTLE CHALLENGE?
WELL, LET ME GIVE YOU ANOTHER WARNING.

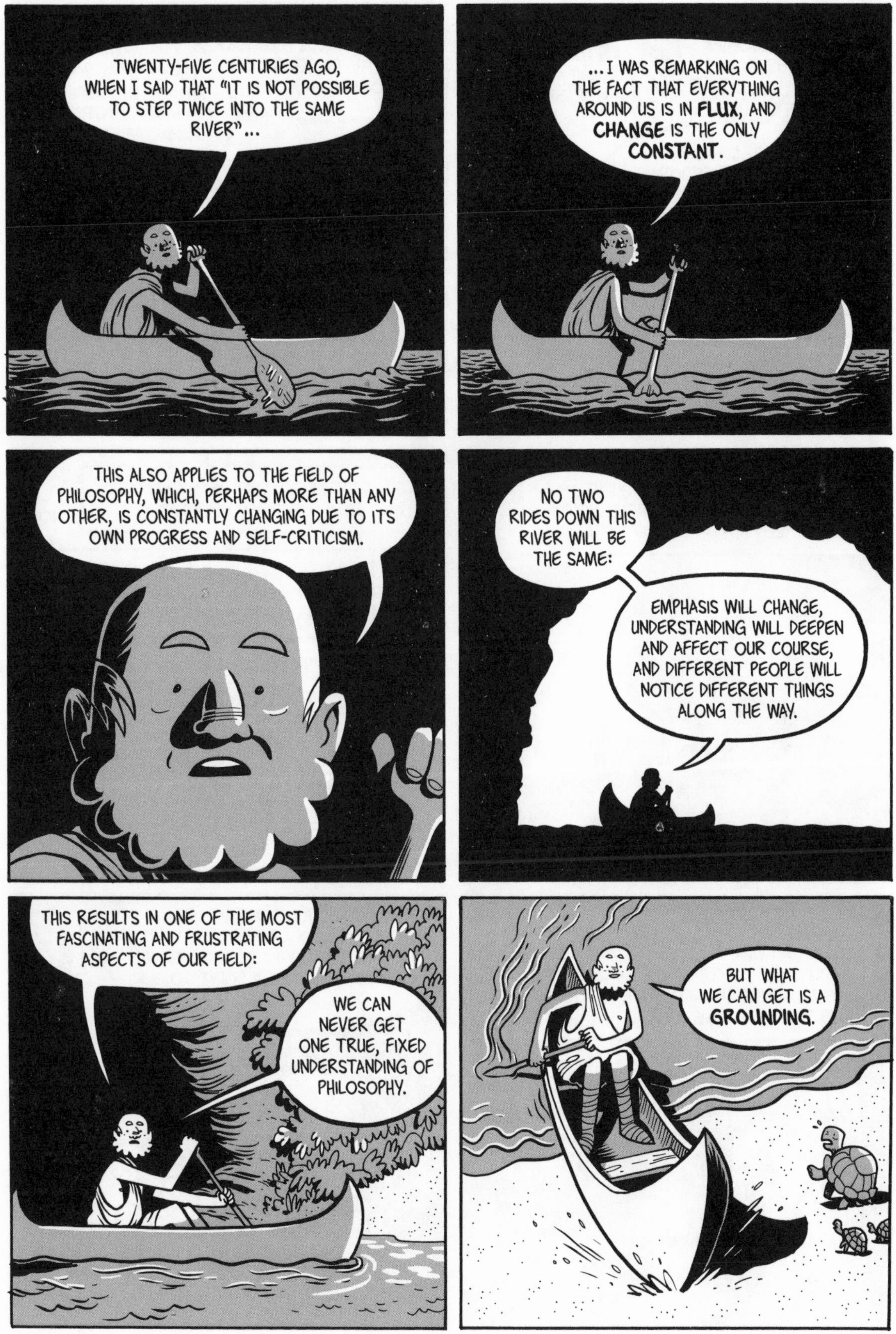
TWENTY-FIVE CENTURIES AGO, WHEN I SAID THAT "IT IS NOT POSSIBLE TO STEP TWICE INTO THE SAME RIVER"...
...I WAS REMARKING ON THE FACT THAT EVERYTHING AROUND US IS IN **FLUX**, AND **CHANGE** IS THE ONLY **CONSTANT**.
THIS ALSO APPLIES TO THE FIELD OF PHILOSOPHY, WHICH, PERHAPS MORE THAN ANY OTHER, IS CONSTANTLY CHANGING DUE TO ITS OWN PROGRESS AND SELF-CRITICISM.
NO TWO RIDES DOWN THIS RIVER WILL BE THE SAME:
EMPHASIS WILL CHANGE, UNDERSTANDING WILL DEEPEN AND AFFECT OUR COURSE, AND DIFFERENT PEOPLE WILL NOTICE DIFFERENT THINGS ALONG THE WAY.
THIS RESULTS IN ONE OF THE MOST FASCINATING AND FRUSTRATING ASPECTS OF OUR FIELD:
WE CAN NEVER GET ONE TRUE, FIXED UNDERSTANDING OF PHILOSOPHY.
BUT WHAT WE CAN GET IS A **GROUNDING**.

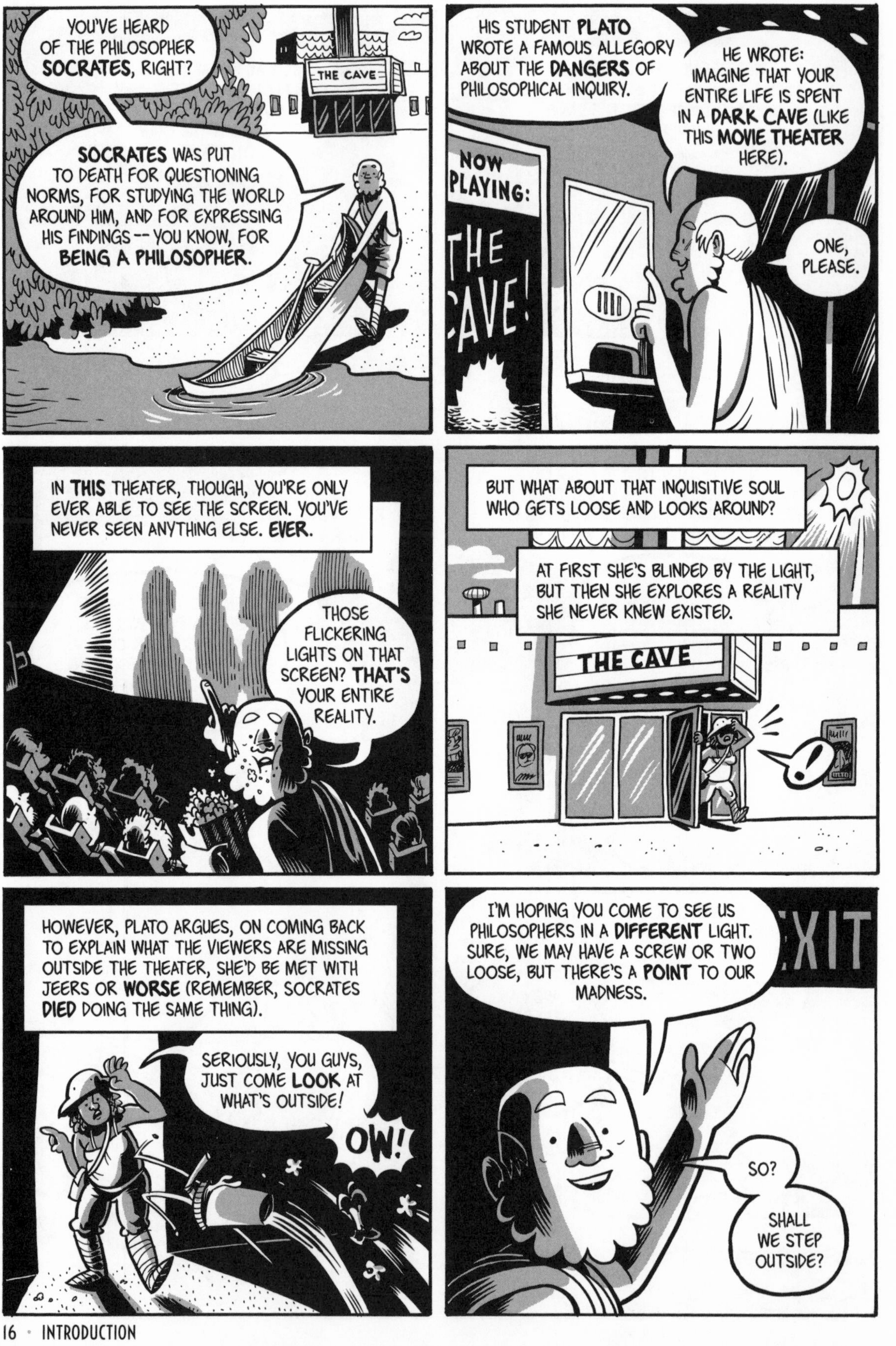
YOU'VE HEARD OF THE PHILOSOPHER **SOCRATES**, RIGHT?
THE CAVE
SOCRATES WAS PUT TO DEATH FOR QUESTIONING NORMS, FOR STUDYING THE WORLD AROUND HIM, AND FOR EXPRESSING HIS FINDINGS -- YOU KNOW, FOR **BEING A PHILOSOPHER**.
HIS STUDENT **PLATO** WROTE A FAMOUS ALLEGORY ABOUT THE **DANGERS** OF PHILOSOPHICAL INQUIRY.
HE WROTE: IMAGINE THAT YOUR ENTIRE LIFE IS SPENT IN A **DARK CAVE** (LIKE THIS **MOVIE THEATER** HERE).
NOW PLAYING:
THE CAVE!
ONE, PLEASE.
IN **THIS** THEATER, THOUGH, YOU'RE ONLY EVER ABLE TO SEE THE SCREEN. YOU'VE NEVER SEEN ANYTHING ELSE. **EVER**.
THOSE FLICKERING LIGHTS ON THAT SCREEN? **THAT'S** YOUR ENTIRE REALITY.
BUT WHAT ABOUT THAT INQUISITIVE SOUL WHO GETS LOOSE AND LOOKS AROUND?
AT FIRST SHE'S BLINDED BY THE LIGHT, BUT THEN SHE EXPLORES A REALITY SHE NEVER KNEW EXISTED.
THE CAVE
!
HOWEVER, PLATO ARGUES, ON COMING BACK TO EXPLAIN WHAT THE VIEWERS ARE MISSING OUTSIDE THE THEATER, SHE'D BE MET WITH JEERS OR **WORSE** (REMEMBER, SOCRATES **DIED** DOING THE SAME THING).
SERIOUSLY, YOU GUYS, JUST COME **LOOK** AT WHAT'S OUTSIDE!
OW!
I'M HOPING YOU COME TO SEE US PHILOSOPHERS IN A **DIFFERENT** LIGHT. SURE, WE MAY HAVE A SCREW OR TWO LOOSE, BUT THERE'S A **POINT** TO OUR MADNESS.
EXIT
SO?
SHALL WE STEP OUTSIDE?

chapter I

LOGIC

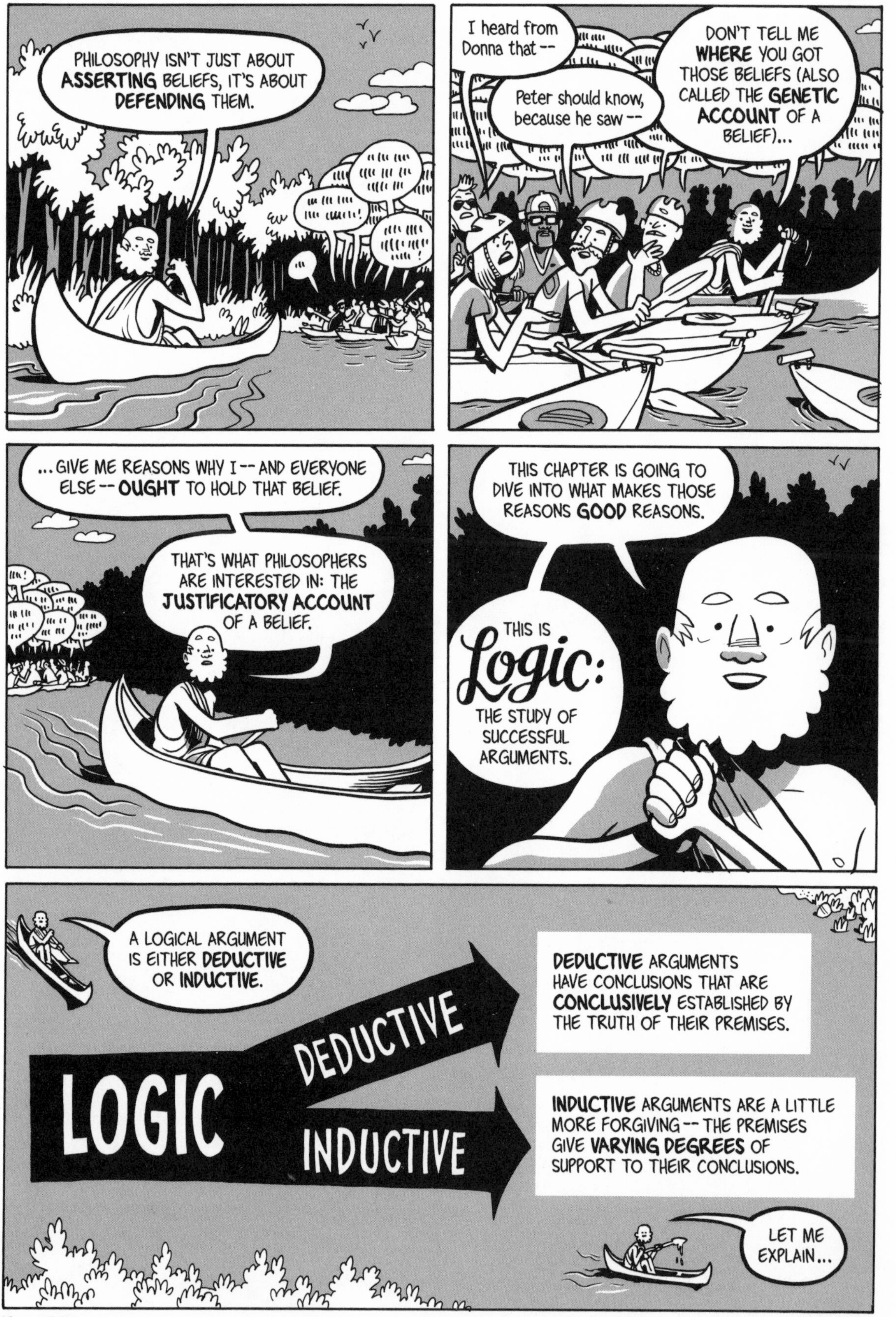
PHILOSOPHY ISN'T JUST ABOUT ASSERTING BELIEFS, IT'S ABOUT DEFENDING THEM.
I heard from Donna that --
Peter should know, because he saw --
DON'T TELL ME WHERE YOU GOT THOSE BELIEFS (ALSO CALLED THE GENETIC ACCOUNT OF A BELIEF)...
... GIVE ME REASONS WHY I -- AND EVERYONE ELSE -- OUGHT TO HOLD THAT BELIEF.
THAT'S WHAT PHILOSOPHERS ARE INTERESTED IN: THE JUSTIFICATORY ACCOUNT OF A BELIEF.
THIS CHAPTER IS GOING TO DIVE INTO WHAT MAKES THOSE REASONS GOOD REASONS.
THIS IS Logic: THE STUDY OF SUCCESSFUL ARGUMENTS.
A LOGICAL ARGUMENT IS EITHER DEDUCTIVE OR INDUCTIVE.
LOGIC
DEDUCTIVE
INDUCTIVE
DEDUCTIVE ARGUMENTS HAVE CONCLUSIONS THAT ARE CONCLUSIVELY ESTABLISHED BY THE TRUTH OF THEIR PREMISES.
INDUCTIVE ARGUMENTS ARE A LITTLE MORE FORGIVING -- THE PREMISES GIVE VARYING DEGREES OF SUPPORT TO THEIR CONCLUSIONS.
LET ME EXPLAIN...

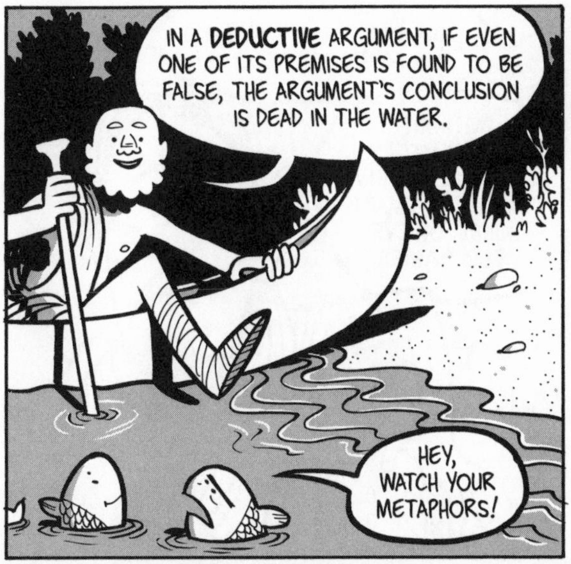
IN A DEDUCTIVE ARGUMENT, IF EVEN ONE OF ITS PREMISES IS FOUND TO BE FALSE, THE ARGUMENT'S CONCLUSION IS DEAD IN THE WATER.
HEY, WATCH YOUR METAPHORS!

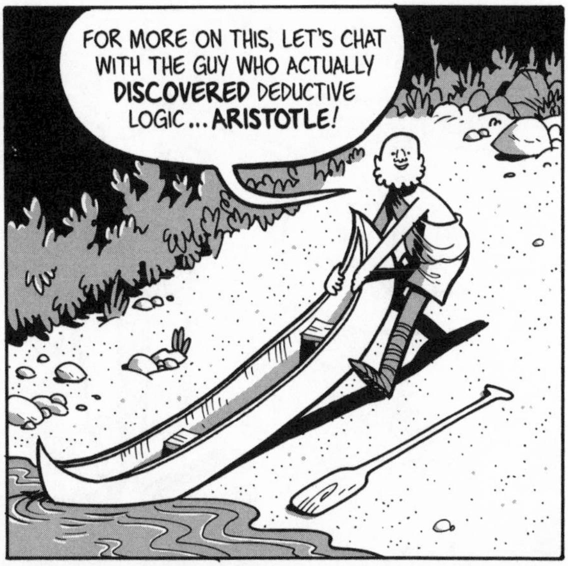
FOR MORE ON THIS, LET'S CHAT WITH THE GUY WHO ACTUALLY DISCOVERED DEDUCTIVE LOGIC... ARISTOTLE!

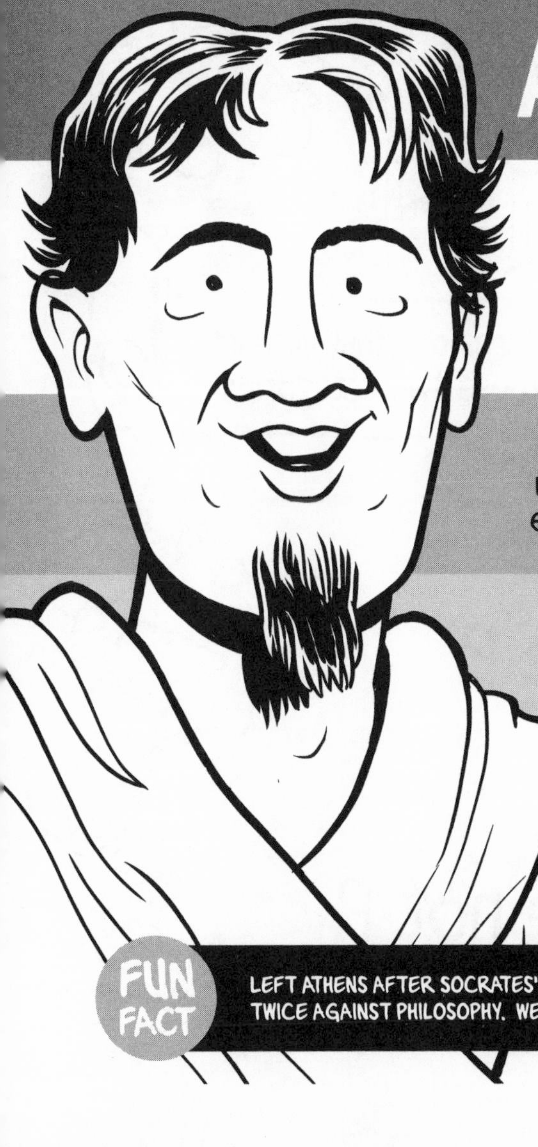

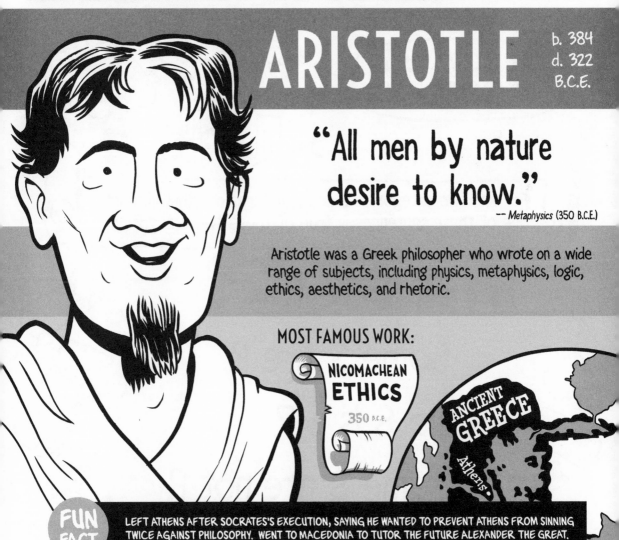

ARISTOTLE

b. 384
d. 322
B.C.E.

"All men by nature desire to know."

-- *Metaphysics* (350 B.C.E.)

Aristotle was a Greek philosopher who wrote on a wide range of subjects, including physics, metaphysics, logic, ethics, aesthetics, and rhetoric.

MOST FAMOUS WORK:

NICOMACHEAN ETHICS
350 B.C.E.

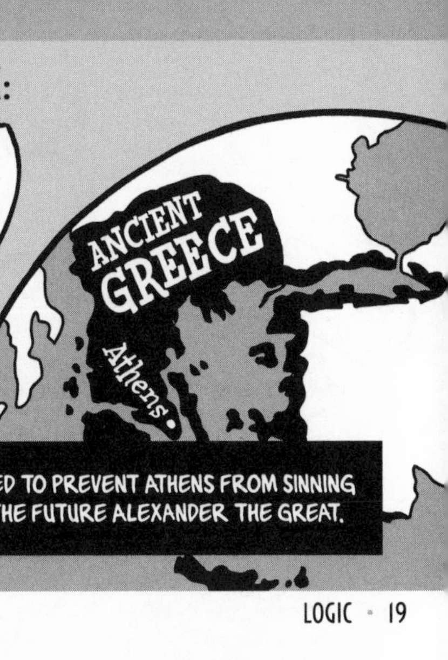
ANCIENT
GREECE
Athens

FUN FACT LEFT ATHENS AFTER SOCRATES'S EXECUTION, SAYING HE WANTED TO PREVENT ATHENS FROM SINNING TWICE AGAINST PHILOSOPHY. WENT TO MACEDONIA TO TUTOR THE FUTURE ALEXANDER THE GREAT.

HI, FOLKS, I AM INDEED ARISTOTLE...
...AND YES, AS HERACLITUS MENTIONED, I DISCOVERED **LOGIC**, WHICH IS THE FOUNDATION OF RIGOROUS **MATH**!
LIBRARY OF ALEXANDRIA
WAIT, DON'T WALK AWAY! IT'S NOT AS BAD AS IT SOUNDS!
WITHOUT LOGIC AND MATH YOU ALSO WOULDN'T HAVE COMPUTERS, SMART-PHONES, OR EVEN **VIDEO GAMES**!

WHAT I DISCOVERED IS THAT **ALL RELATIONSHIPS** BETWEEN TYPES OF THINGS CAN BE EXPRESSED IN FOUR EASY-TO-REMEMBER SENTENCES.

For any two categories **S** and **P**, it turns out that at least one of these sentences is true of those two categories:

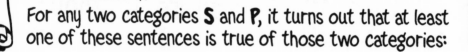

All S are P.

Some S are P.

No S is a P.

Some S are not P.

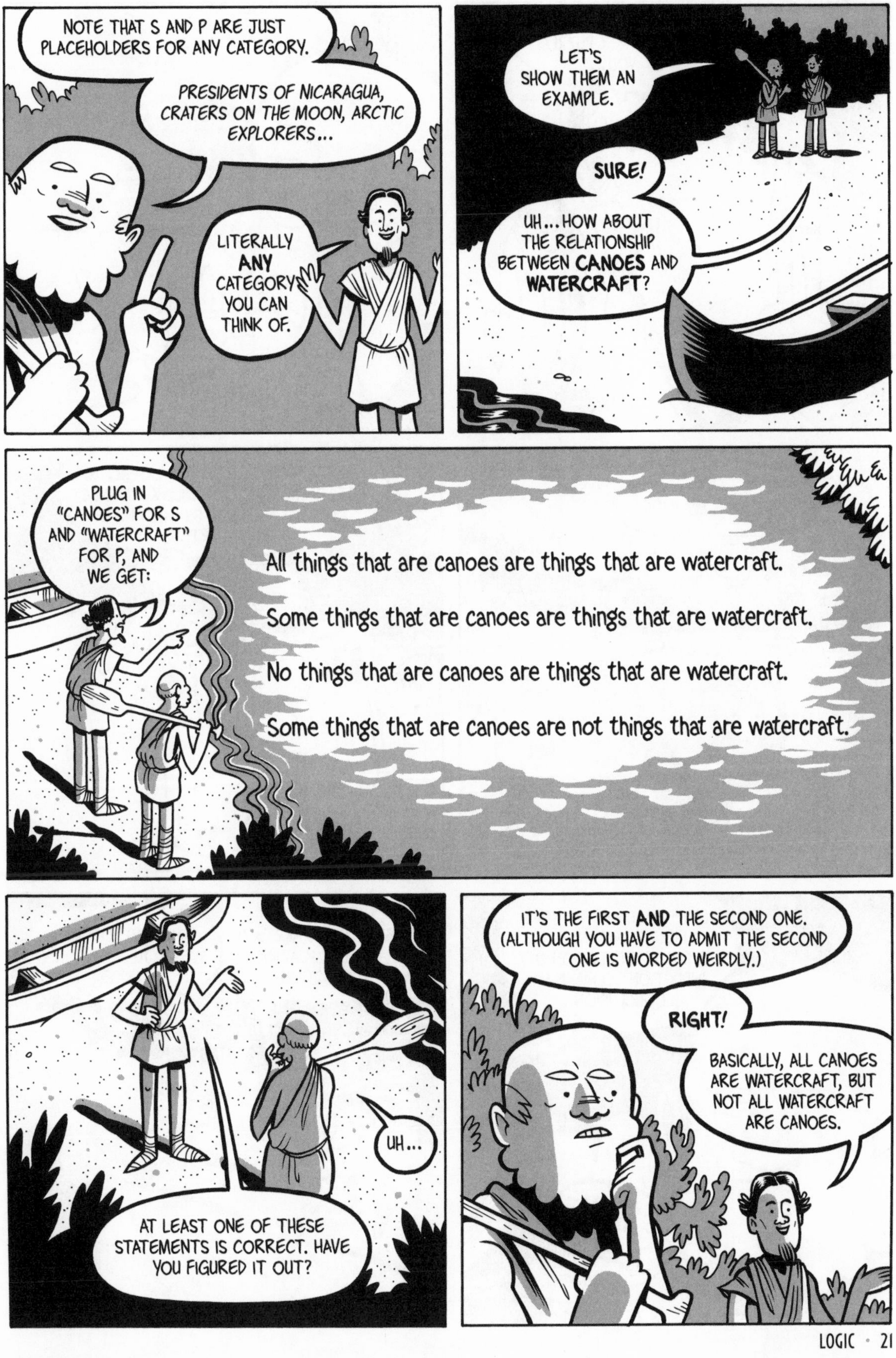
NOTE THAT S AND P ARE JUST PLACEHOLDERS FOR ANY CATEGORY.
PRESIDENTS OF NICARAGUA, CRATERS ON THE MOON, ARCTIC EXPLORERS...
LITERALLY **ANY** CATEGORY YOU CAN THINK OF.
LET'S SHOW THEM AN EXAMPLE.
SURE!
UH...HOW ABOUT THE RELATIONSHIP BETWEEN **CANOES** AND **WATERCRAFT**?
PLUG IN "CANOES" FOR S AND "WATERCRAFT" FOR P, AND WE GET:
All things that are canoes are things that are watercraft.
Some things that are canoes are things that are watercraft.
No things that are canoes are things that are watercraft.
Some things that are canoes are not things that are watercraft.
AT LEAST ONE OF THESE STATEMENTS IS CORRECT. HAVE YOU FIGURED IT OUT?
UH...
IT'S THE FIRST **AND** THE SECOND ONE. (ALTHOUGH YOU HAVE TO ADMIT THE SECOND ONE IS WORDED WEIRDLY.)
RIGHT!
BASICALLY, ALL CANOES ARE WATERCRAFT, BUT NOT ALL WATERCRAFT ARE CANOES.

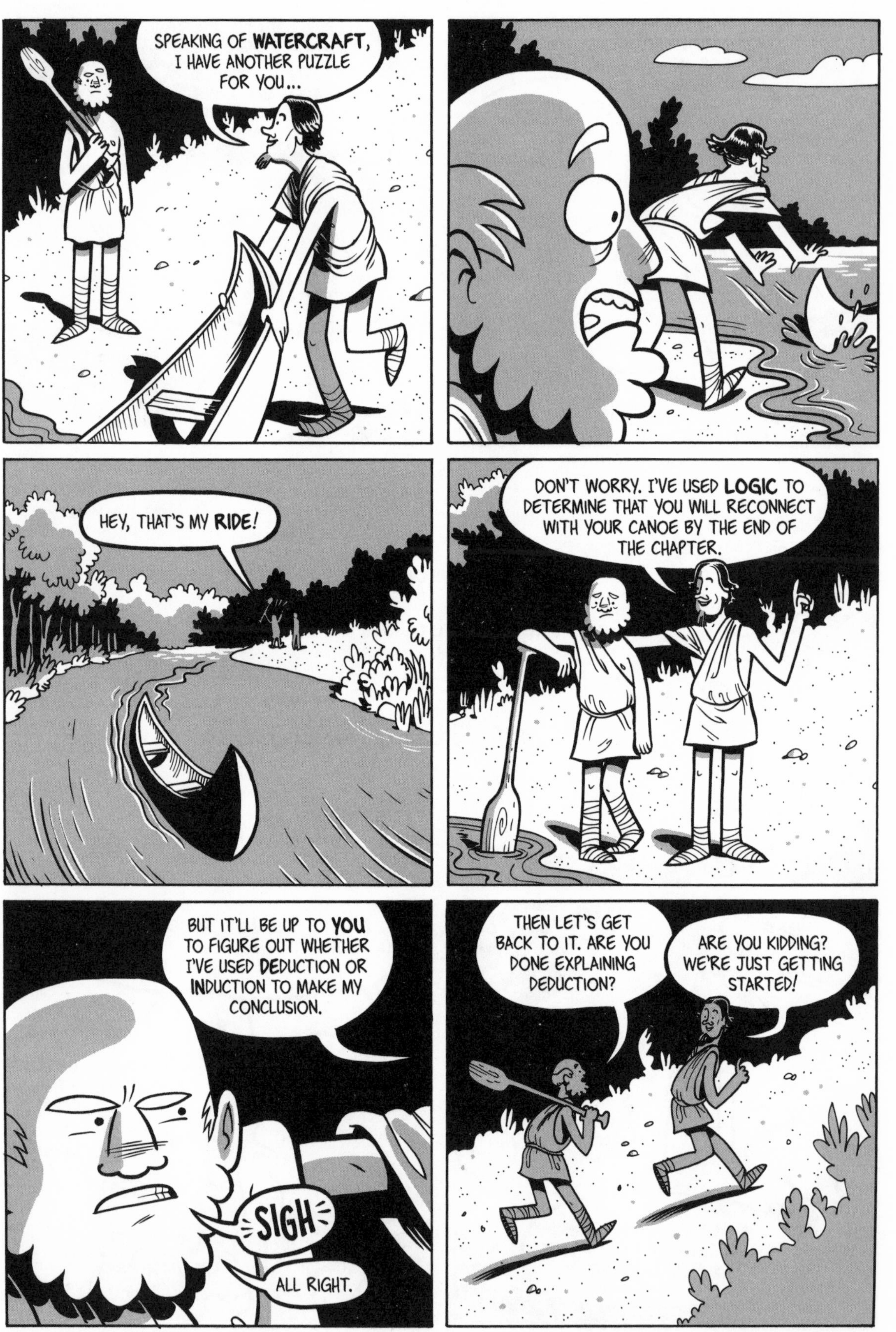
SPEAKING OF WATERCRAFT, I HAVE ANOTHER PUZZLE FOR YOU...
HEY, THAT'S MY RIDE!
DON'T WORRY. I'VE USED LOGIC TO DETERMINE THAT YOU WILL RECONNECT WITH YOUR CANOE BY THE END OF THE CHAPTER.
BUT IT'LL BE UP TO YOU TO FIGURE OUT WHETHER I'VE USED DEDUCTION OR INDUCTION TO MAKE MY CONCLUSION.
SIGH
ALL RIGHT.
THEN LET'S GET BACK TO IT. ARE YOU DONE EXPLAINING DEDUCTION?
ARE YOU KIDDING? WE'RE JUST GETTING STARTED!

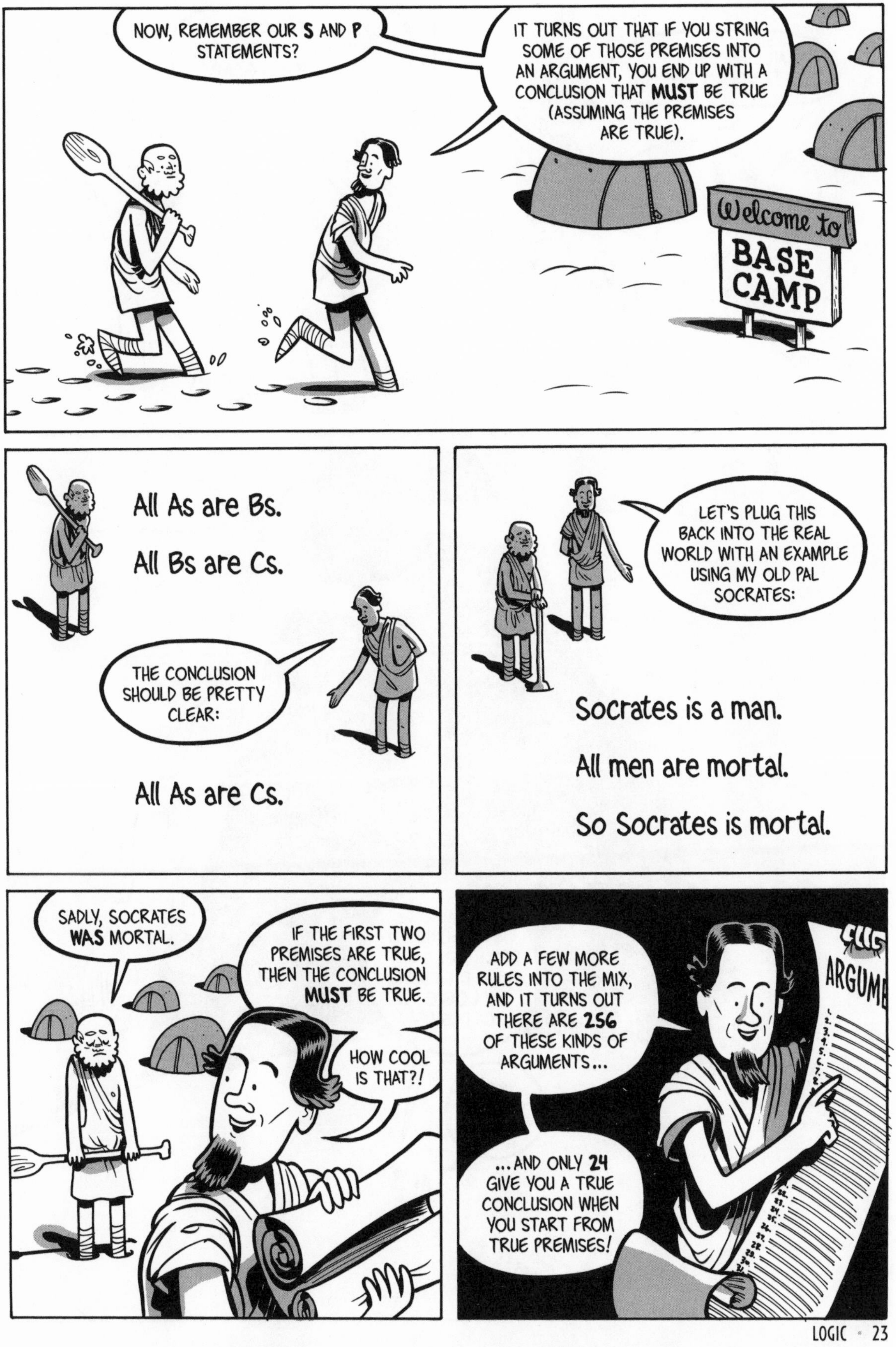
NOW, REMEMBER OUR S AND P STATEMENTS?
IT TURNS OUT THAT IF YOU STRING SOME OF THOSE PREMISES INTO AN ARGUMENT, YOU END UP WITH A CONCLUSION THAT MUST BE TRUE (ASSUMING THE PREMISES ARE TRUE).
Welcome to BASE CAMP
All As are Bs.
All Bs are Cs.
THE CONCLUSION SHOULD BE PRETTY CLEAR:
All As are Cs.
LET'S PLUG THIS BACK INTO THE REAL WORLD WITH AN EXAMPLE USING MY OLD PAL SOCRATES:
Socrates is a man.
All men are mortal.
So Socrates is mortal.
SADLY, SOCRATES WAS MORTAL.
IF THE FIRST TWO PREMISES ARE TRUE, THEN THE CONCLUSION MUST BE TRUE.
HOW COOL IS THAT?!
ADD A FEW MORE RULES INTO THE MIX, AND IT TURNS OUT THERE ARE 256 OF THESE KINDS OF ARGUMENTS...
...AND ONLY 24 GIVE YOU A TRUE CONCLUSION WHEN YOU START FROM TRUE PREMISES!

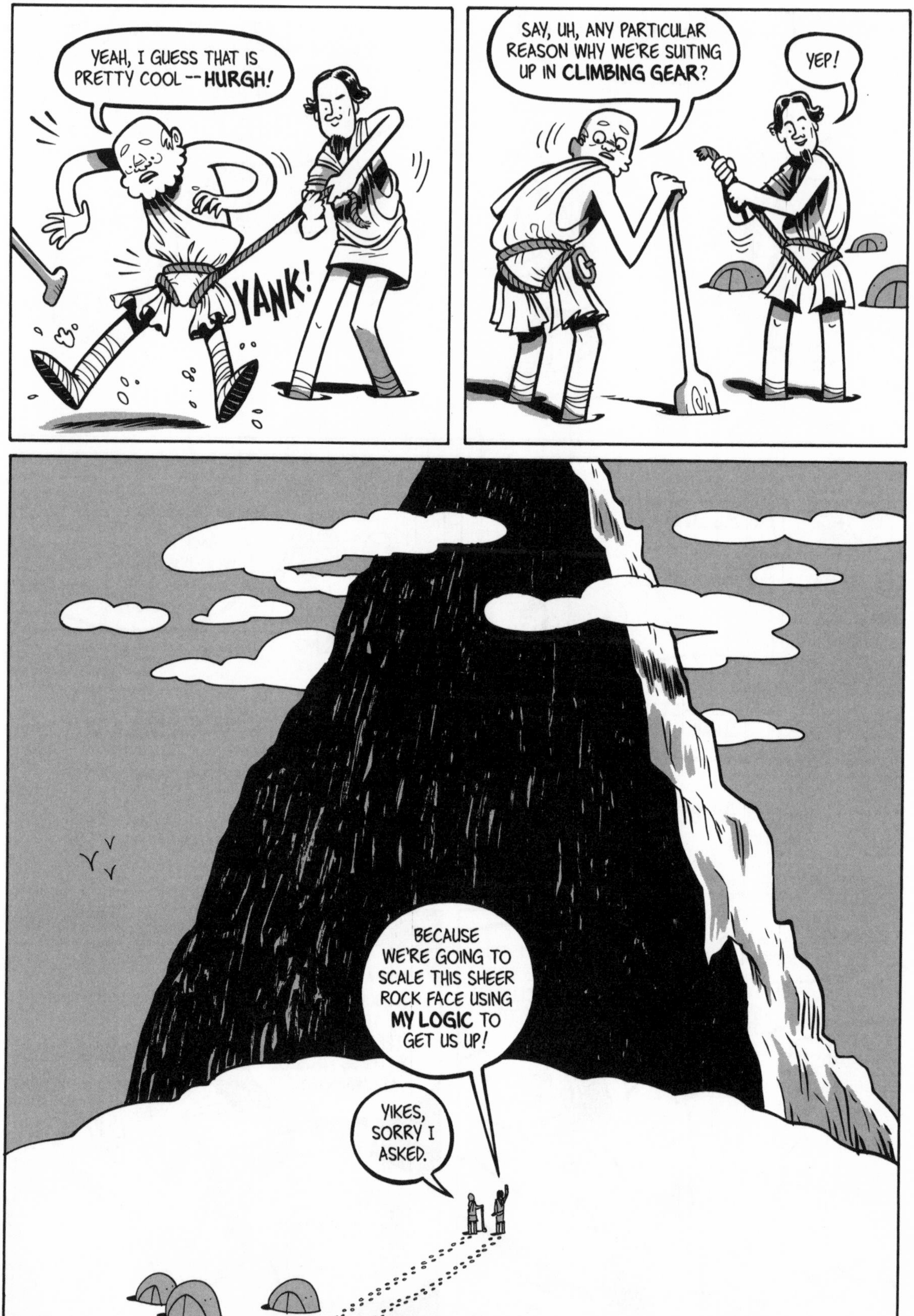
YEAH, I GUESS THAT IS PRETTY COOL--**HURGH**!
YANK!
SAY, UH, ANY PARTICULAR REASON WHY WE'RE SUITING UP IN **CLIMBING GEAR**?
YEP!
BECAUSE WE'RE GOING TO SCALE THIS SHEER ROCK FACE USING **MY LOGIC** TO GET US UP!
YIKES, SORRY I ASKED.

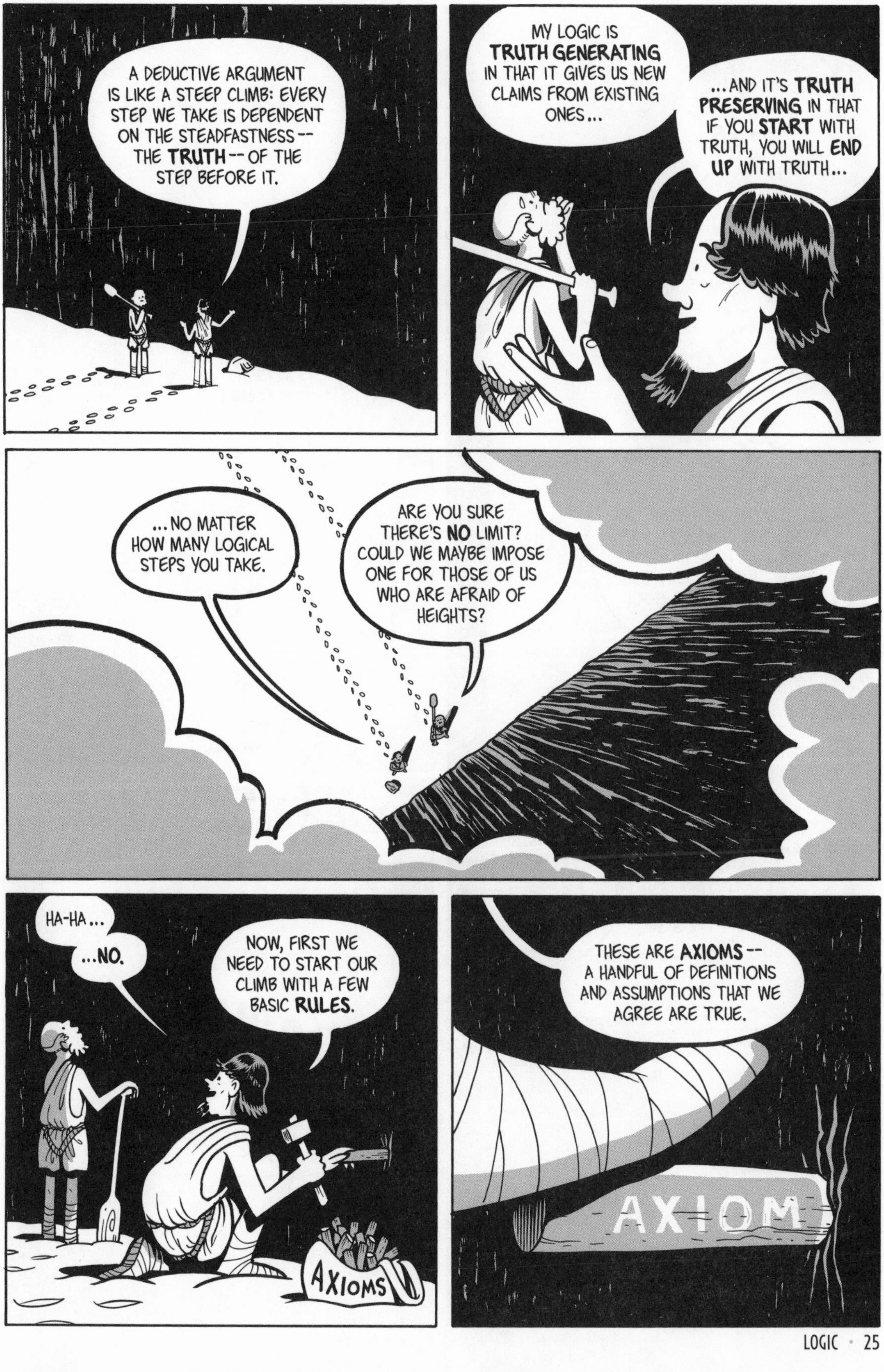
A DEDUCTIVE ARGUMENT IS LIKE A STEEP CLIMB: EVERY STEP WE TAKE IS DEPENDENT ON THE STEADFASTNESS-- THE **TRUTH**--OF THE STEP BEFORE IT.
MY LOGIC IS **TRUTH GENERATING** IN THAT IT GIVES US NEW CLAIMS FROM EXISTING ONES...
...AND IT'S **TRUTH PRESERVING** IN THAT IF YOU **START** WITH TRUTH, YOU WILL **END UP** WITH TRUTH...
...NO MATTER HOW MANY LOGICAL STEPS YOU TAKE.
ARE YOU SURE THERE'S **NO** LIMIT? COULD WE MAYBE IMPOSE ONE FOR THOSE OF US WHO ARE AFRAID OF HEIGHTS?
HA-HA...
...**NO.**
NOW, FIRST WE NEED TO START OUR CLIMB WITH A FEW BASIC **RULES**.
AXIOMS
THESE ARE **AXIOMS**-- A HANDFUL OF DEFINITIONS AND ASSUMPTIONS THAT WE AGREE ARE TRUE.
AXIOM

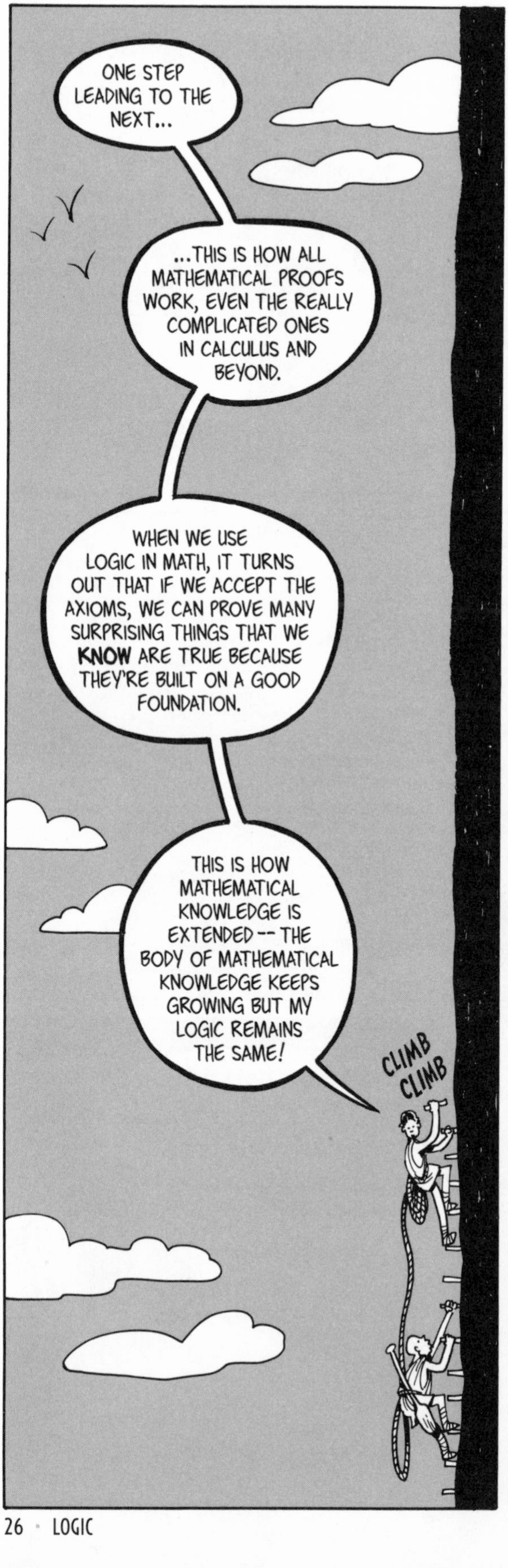
ONE STEP LEADING TO THE NEXT...
...THIS IS HOW ALL MATHEMATICAL PROOFS WORK, EVEN THE REALLY COMPLICATED ONES IN CALCULUS AND BEYOND.
WHEN WE USE LOGIC IN MATH, IT TURNS OUT THAT IF WE ACCEPT THE AXIOMS, WE CAN PROVE MANY SURPRISING THINGS THAT WE **KNOW** ARE TRUE BECAUSE THEY'RE BUILT ON A GOOD FOUNDATION.
THIS IS HOW MATHEMATICAL KNOWLEDGE IS EXTENDED -- THE BODY OF MATHEMATICAL KNOWLEDGE KEEPS GROWING BUT MY LOGIC REMAINS THE SAME!
CLIMB CLIMB

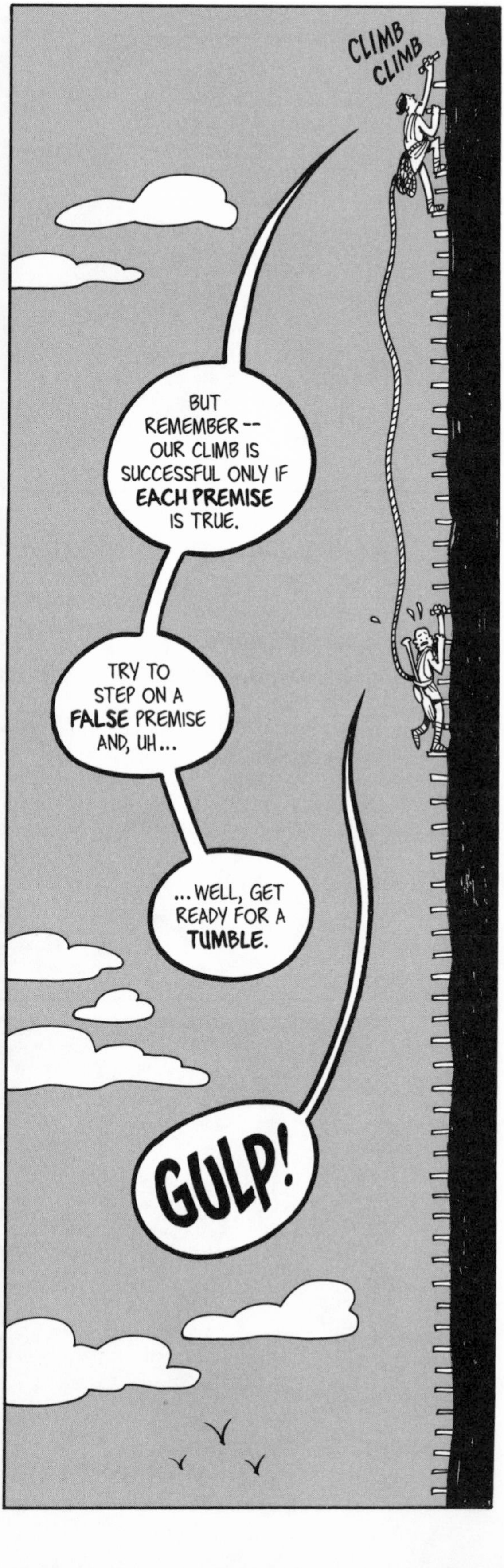
CLIMB CLIMB
BUT REMEMBER -- OUR CLIMB IS SUCCESSFUL ONLY IF **EACH PREMISE** IS TRUE.
TRY TO STEP ON A **FALSE** PREMISE AND, UH...
...WELL, GET READY FOR A **TUMBLE**.
GULP!

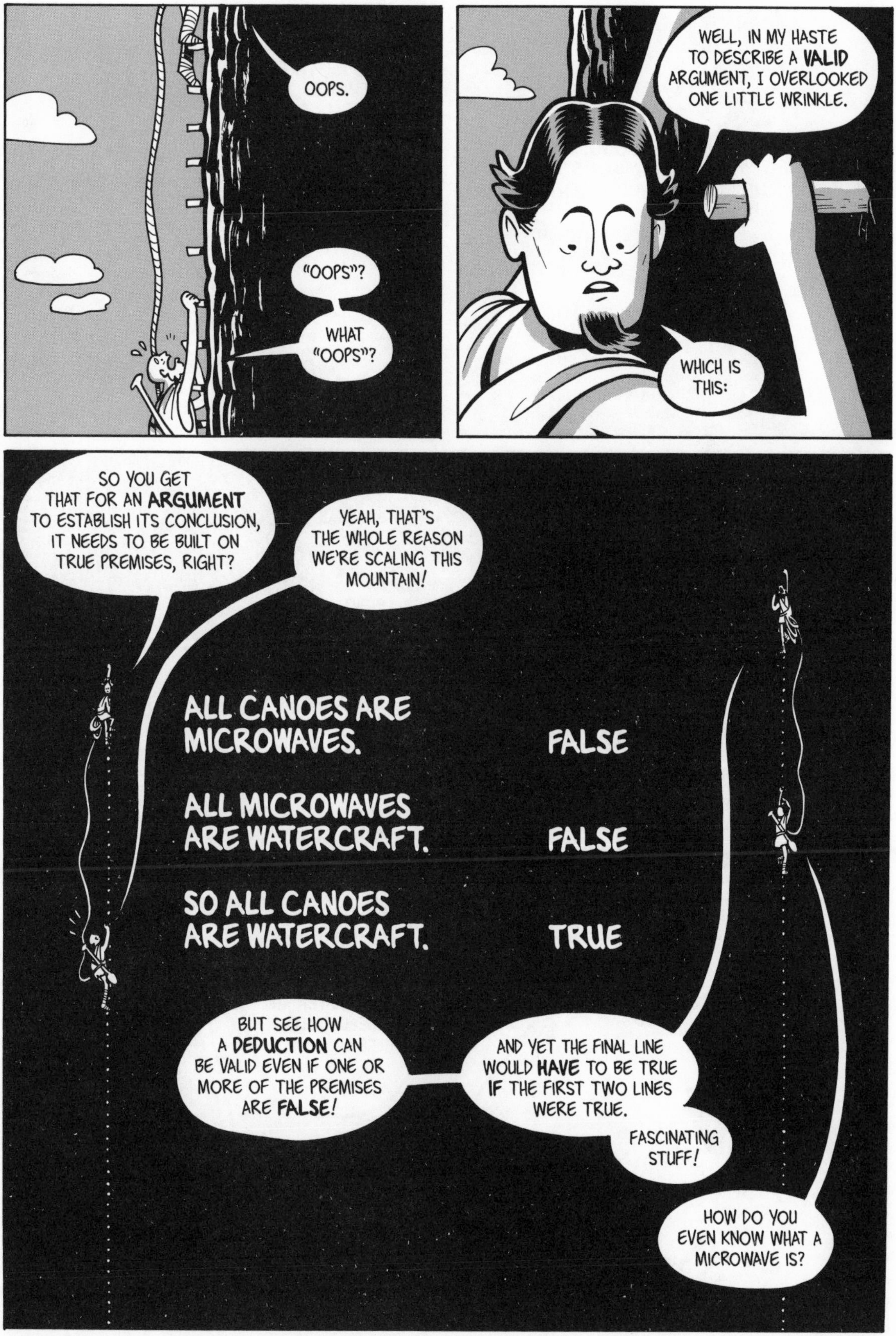

OOPS.

"OOPS"?

WHAT "OOPS"?

WELL, IN MY HASTE TO DESCRIBE A **VALID** ARGUMENT, I OVERLOOKED ONE LITTLE WRINKLE.

WHICH IS THIS:

SO YOU GET THAT FOR AN **ARGUMENT** TO ESTABLISH ITS CONCLUSION, IT NEEDS TO BE BUILT ON TRUE PREMISES, RIGHT?

YEAH, THAT'S THE WHOLE REASON WE'RE SCALING THIS MOUNTAIN!

ALL CANOES ARE MICROWAVES.	FALSE
ALL MICROWAVES ARE WATERCRAFT.	FALSE
SO ALL CANOES ARE WATERCRAFT.	TRUE

BUT SEE HOW A **DEDUCTION** CAN BE VALID EVEN IF ONE OR MORE OF THE PREMISES ARE **FALSE**!

AND YET THE FINAL LINE WOULD **HAVE** TO BE TRUE IF THE FIRST TWO LINES WERE TRUE.

FASCINATING STUFF!

HOW DO YOU EVEN KNOW WHAT A MICROWAVE IS?

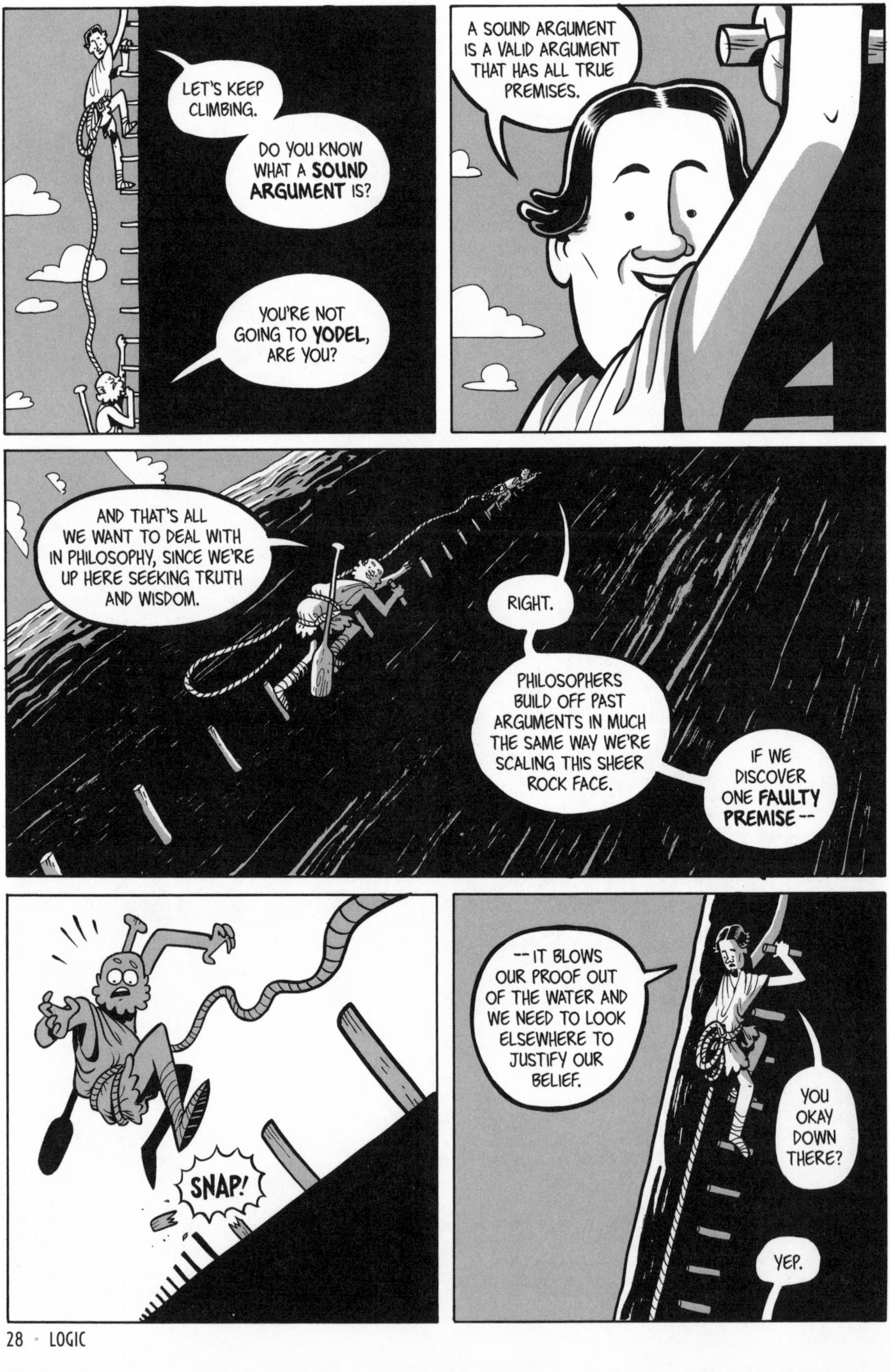
LET'S KEEP CLIMBING.
DO YOU KNOW WHAT A **SOUND ARGUMENT** IS?
YOU'RE NOT GOING TO **YODEL**, ARE YOU?
A SOUND ARGUMENT IS A VALID ARGUMENT THAT HAS ALL TRUE PREMISES.
AND THAT'S ALL WE WANT TO DEAL WITH IN PHILOSOPHY, SINCE WE'RE UP HERE SEEKING TRUTH AND WISDOM.
RIGHT.
PHILOSOPHERS BUILD OFF PAST ARGUMENTS IN MUCH THE SAME WAY WE'RE SCALING THIS SHEER ROCK FACE.
IF WE DISCOVER ONE **FAULTY PREMISE** --
SNAP!
-- IT BLOWS OUR PROOF OUT OF THE WATER AND WE NEED TO LOOK ELSEWHERE TO JUSTIFY OUR BELIEF.
YOU OKAY DOWN THERE?
YEP.

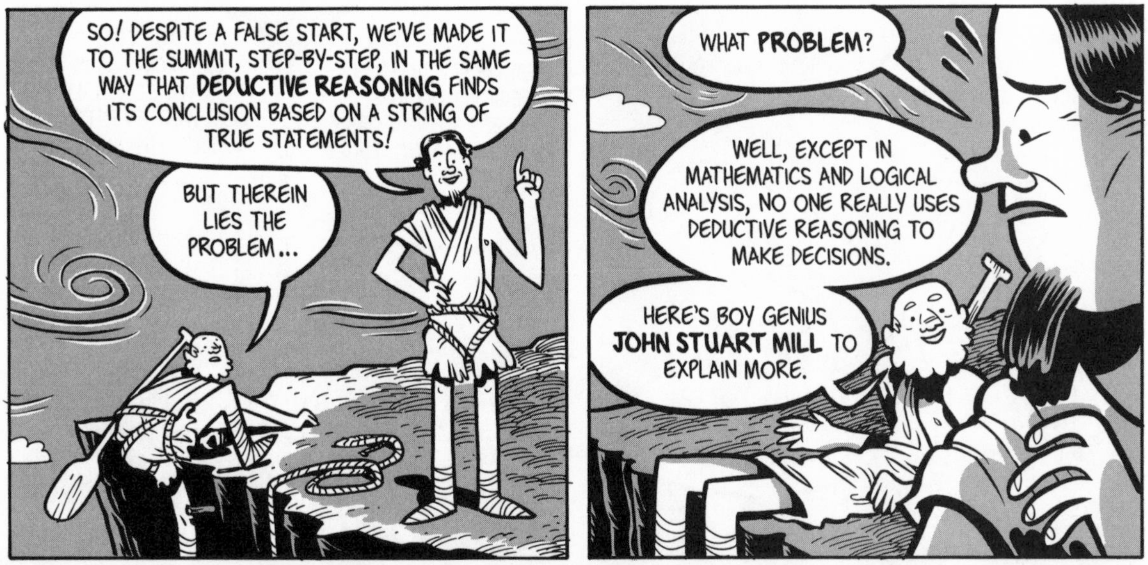
SO! DESPITE A FALSE START, WE'VE MADE IT TO THE SUMMIT, STEP-BY-STEP, IN THE SAME WAY THAT **DEDUCTIVE REASONING** FINDS ITS CONCLUSION BASED ON A STRING OF TRUE STATEMENTS!
BUT THEREIN LIES THE PROBLEM...
WHAT **PROBLEM**?
WELL, EXCEPT IN MATHEMATICS AND LOGICAL ANALYSIS, NO ONE REALLY USES DEDUCTIVE REASONING TO MAKE DECISIONS.
HERE'S BOY GENIUS **JOHN STUART MILL** TO EXPLAIN MORE.

JOHN STUART MILL

b. 1806
d. 1873
C.E.

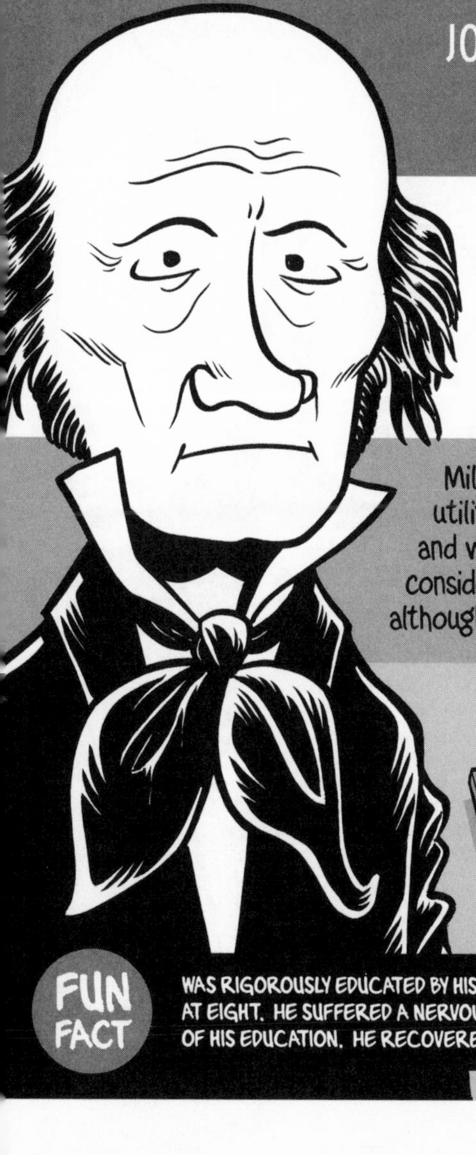

"It is better to be a human dissatisfied than a pig satisfied; better to be Socrates dissatisfied than a fool satisfied."

-- *Utilitarianism*

Mill was a British empiricist who further developed Bentham's utilitarian ethics, wrote about deductive and inductive logic, and wrote very influential books on political philosophy. He is considered by some to have had one of the highest IQs in history, although he, of course, never took an IQ test.

MOST FAMOUS WORK:

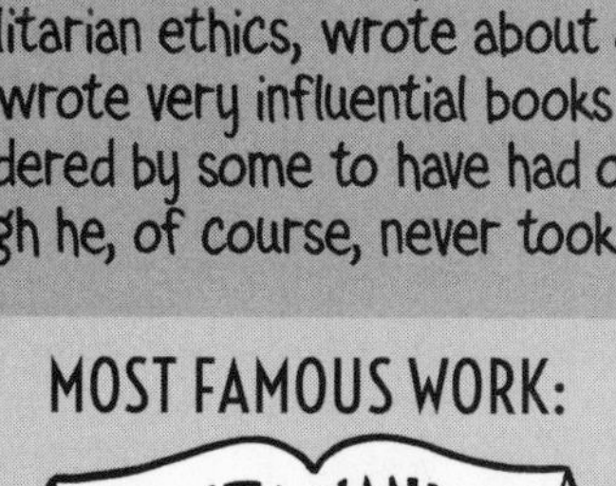
UTILITARIANISM
1863

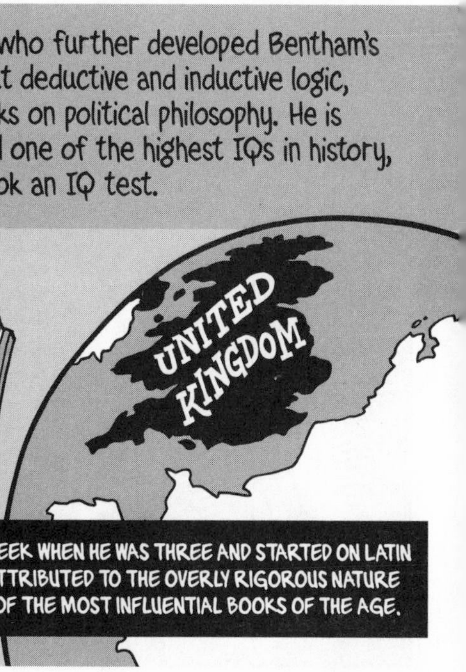
UNITED KINGDOM

FUN FACT WAS RIGOROUSLY EDUCATED BY HIS FATHER. HE BEGAN STUDYING GREEK WHEN HE WAS THREE AND STARTED ON LATIN AT EIGHT. HE SUFFERED A NERVOUS BREAKDOWN AT 20, WHICH HE ATTRIBUTED TO THE OVERLY RIGOROUS NATURE OF HIS EDUCATION. HE RECOVERED AND WENT ON TO WRITE SOME OF THE MOST INFLUENTIAL BOOKS OF THE AGE.

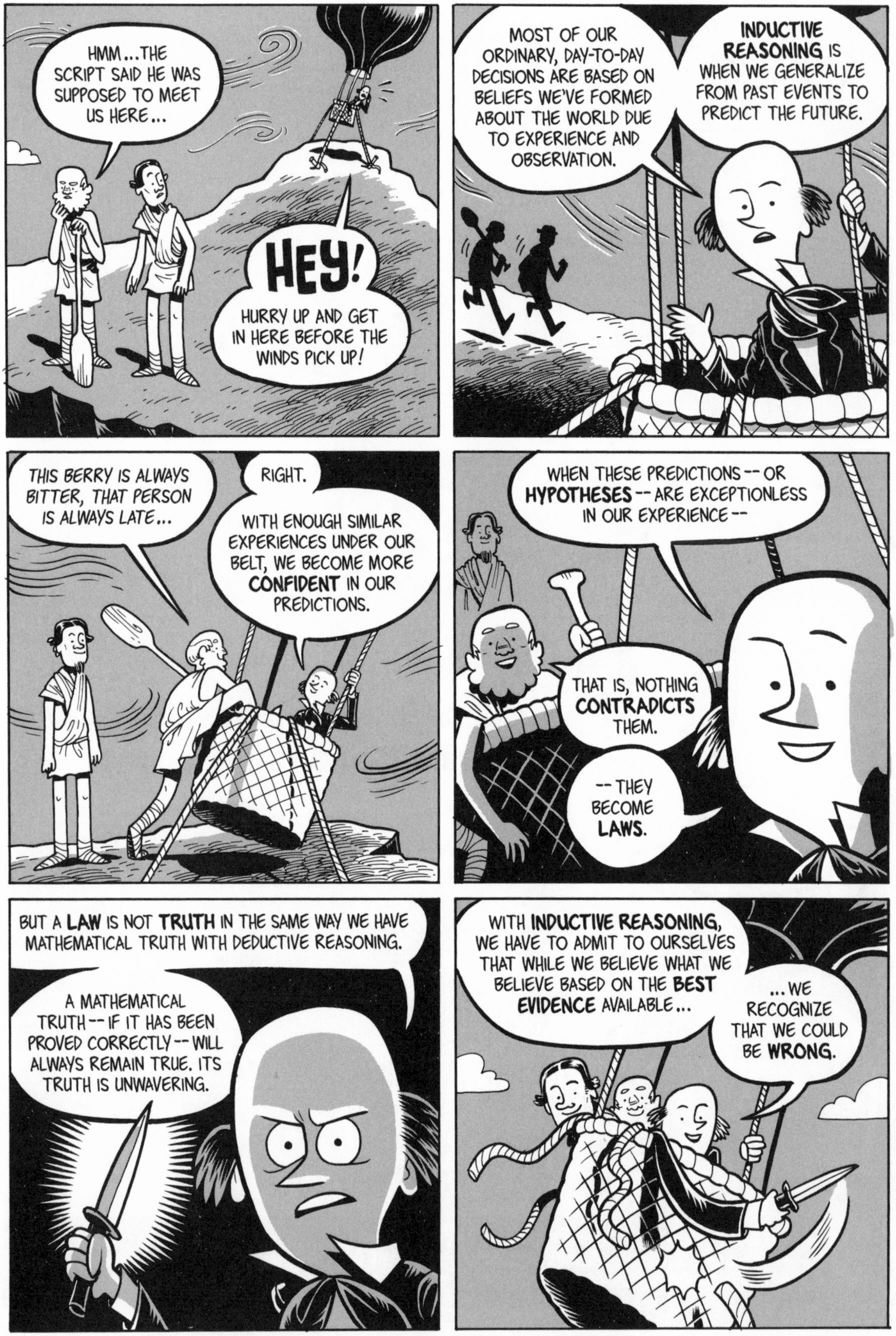
HMM...THE SCRIPT SAID HE WAS SUPPOSED TO MEET US HERE...
HEY!
HURRY UP AND GET IN HERE BEFORE THE WINDS PICK UP!
MOST OF OUR ORDINARY, DAY-TO-DAY DECISIONS ARE BASED ON BELIEFS WE'VE FORMED ABOUT THE WORLD DUE TO EXPERIENCE AND OBSERVATION.
INDUCTIVE REASONING IS WHEN WE GENERALIZE FROM PAST EVENTS TO PREDICT THE FUTURE.
THIS BERRY IS ALWAYS BITTER, THAT PERSON IS ALWAYS LATE...
RIGHT.
WITH ENOUGH SIMILAR EXPERIENCES UNDER OUR BELT, WE BECOME MORE **CONFIDENT** IN OUR PREDICTIONS.
WHEN THESE PREDICTIONS -- OR **HYPOTHESES** -- ARE EXCEPTIONLESS IN OUR EXPERIENCE --
THAT IS, NOTHING **CONTRADICTS** THEM.
-- THEY BECOME **LAWS.**
BUT A **LAW** IS NOT **TRUTH** IN THE SAME WAY WE HAVE MATHEMATICAL TRUTH WITH DEDUCTIVE REASONING.
A MATHEMATICAL TRUTH -- IF IT HAS BEEN PROVED CORRECTLY -- WILL ALWAYS REMAIN TRUE. ITS TRUTH IS UNWAVERING.
WITH **INDUCTIVE REASONING,** WE HAVE TO ADMIT TO OURSELVES THAT WHILE WE BELIEVE WHAT WE BELIEVE BASED ON THE **BEST EVIDENCE** AVAILABLE...
...WE RECOGNIZE THAT WE COULD BE **WRONG.**

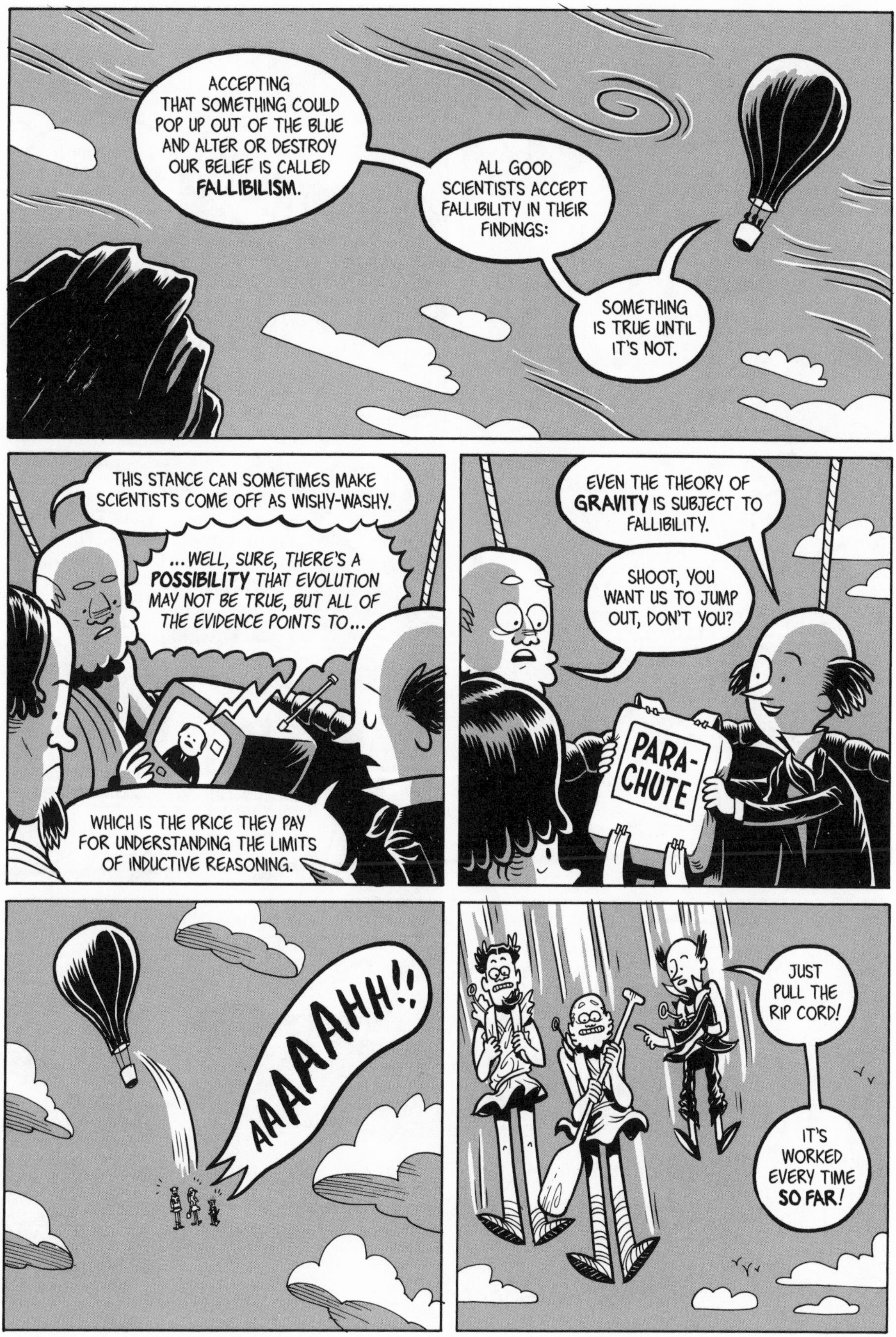
ACCEPTING THAT SOMETHING COULD POP UP OUT OF THE BLUE AND ALTER OR DESTROY OUR BELIEF IS CALLED **FALLIBILISM**.
ALL GOOD SCIENTISTS ACCEPT FALLIBILITY IN THEIR FINDINGS:
SOMETHING IS TRUE UNTIL IT'S NOT.
THIS STANCE CAN SOMETIMES MAKE SCIENTISTS COME OFF AS WISHY-WASHY.
...WELL, SURE, THERE'S A **POSSIBILITY** THAT EVOLUTION MAY NOT BE TRUE, BUT ALL OF THE EVIDENCE POINTS TO...
WHICH IS THE PRICE THEY PAY FOR UNDERSTANDING THE LIMITS OF INDUCTIVE REASONING.
EVEN THE THEORY OF **GRAVITY** IS SUBJECT TO FALLIBILITY.
SHOOT, YOU WANT US TO JUMP OUT, DON'T YOU?
PARA-CHUTE
AAAAAHH!!
JUST PULL THE RIP CORD!
IT'S WORKED EVERY TIME **SO FAR**!

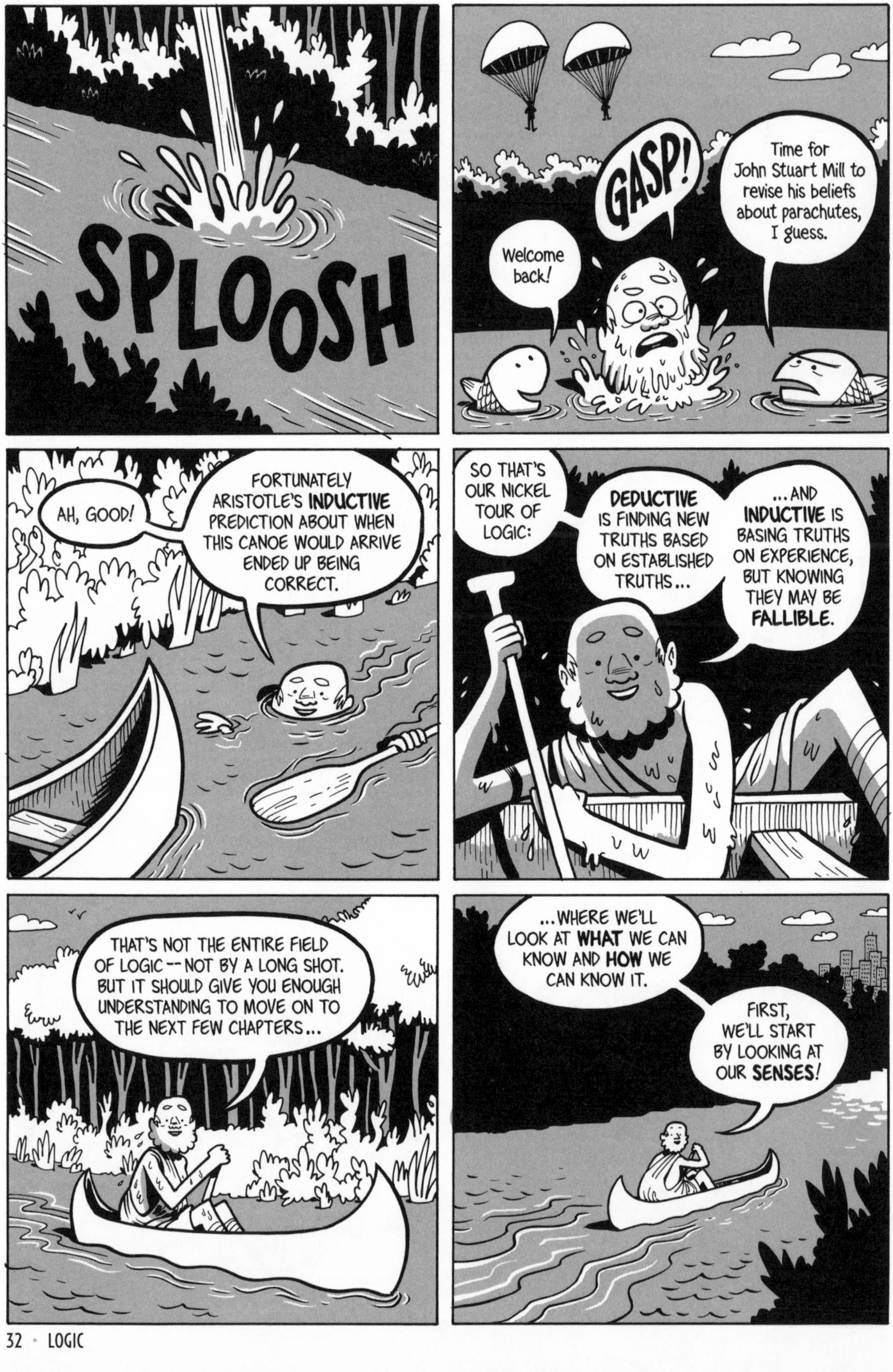
SPLOOSH
GASP!
Welcome back!
Time for John Stuart Mill to revise his beliefs about parachutes, I guess.
AH, GOOD!
FORTUNATELY ARISTOTLE'S **INDUCTIVE** PREDICTION ABOUT WHEN THIS CANOE WOULD ARRIVE ENDED UP BEING CORRECT.
SO THAT'S OUR NICKEL TOUR OF LOGIC:
DEDUCTIVE IS FINDING NEW TRUTHS BASED ON ESTABLISHED TRUTHS...
...AND **INDUCTIVE** IS BASING TRUTHS ON EXPERIENCE, BUT KNOWING THEY MAY BE **FALLIBLE.**
THAT'S NOT THE ENTIRE FIELD OF LOGIC--NOT BY A LONG SHOT. BUT IT SHOULD GIVE YOU ENOUGH UNDERSTANDING TO MOVE ON TO THE NEXT FEW CHAPTERS...
...WHERE WE'LL LOOK AT **WHAT** WE CAN KNOW AND **HOW** WE CAN KNOW IT.
FIRST, WE'LL START BY LOOKING AT OUR **SENSES**!

chapter 2
PERCEPTION

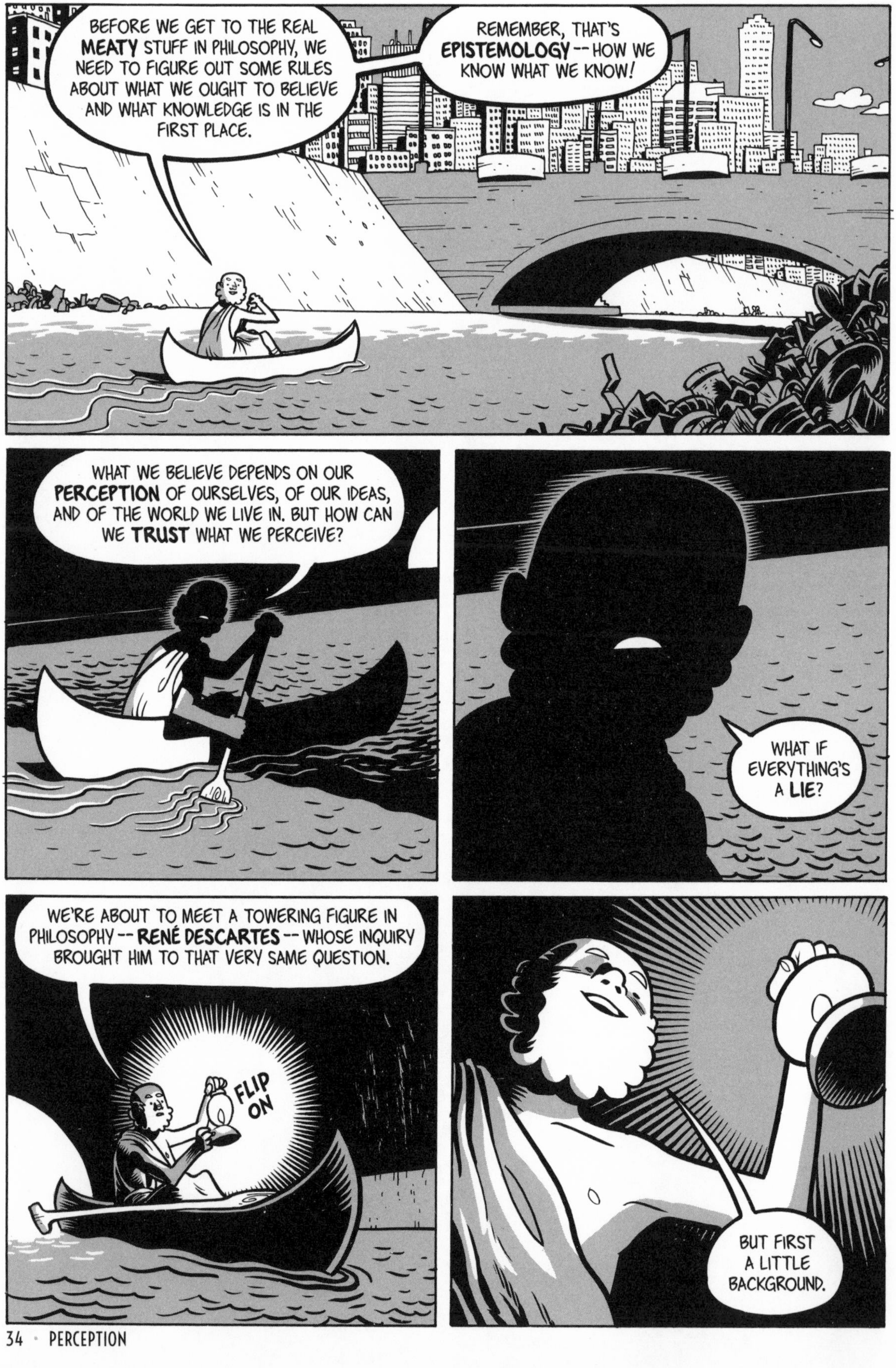
BEFORE WE GET TO THE REAL MEATY STUFF IN PHILOSOPHY, WE NEED TO FIGURE OUT SOME RULES ABOUT WHAT WE OUGHT TO BELIEVE AND WHAT KNOWLEDGE IS IN THE FIRST PLACE.
REMEMBER, THAT'S EPISTEMOLOGY -- HOW WE KNOW WHAT WE KNOW!
WHAT WE BELIEVE DEPENDS ON OUR PERCEPTION OF OURSELVES, OF OUR IDEAS, AND OF THE WORLD WE LIVE IN. BUT HOW CAN WE TRUST WHAT WE PERCEIVE?
WHAT IF EVERYTHING'S A LIE?
WE'RE ABOUT TO MEET A TOWERING FIGURE IN PHILOSOPHY -- RENÉ DESCARTES -- WHOSE INQUIRY BROUGHT HIM TO THAT VERY SAME QUESTION.
FLIP ON
BUT FIRST A LITTLE BACKGROUND.

FOR CENTURIES, THE WEST WAS CONTROLLED BY THE CATHOLIC CHURCH AND THE TEACHINGS OF ITS FAVORITE PHILOSOPHER, ARISTOTLE.

CHURCH (BFFs) ARISTOTLE

BUT IN THE FIRST QUARTER OF THE 16th CENTURY SOME REAL RIVALS EMERGED. IN 1517 MARTIN LUTHER NAILED HIS **95 THESES** TO THE DOOR OF THE CASTLE CHURCH IN WITTENBERG, AND IN 1532 THE FRENCHMAN JOHN CALVIN PROPOSED **HIS** IDEAS.

95

THE STAGE WAS SET FOR ANOTHER FRENCHMAN, DESCARTES -- A **SKEPTIC** -- TO START QUESTIONING THE CHURCH'S TEACHINGS.

Hmm...

DESCARTES (A COOL GUY)

BUT THE CATHOLIC CHURCH WAS STILL POWERFUL -- THEY USED THE THREAT OF TORTURE TO FORCE GALILEO TO RECANT HIS ENDORSEMENT OF THE HELIOCENTRIC SOLAR SYSTEM -- SO DESCARTES TROD CAREFULLY.

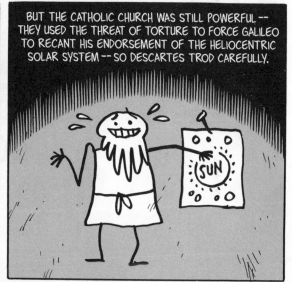

SUN

INSTEAD OF JUST SAYING THAT ARISTOTLE WAS WRONG, DESCARTES ASKED:

SPRAY!

HOW CAN ANYONE KNOW IF **ANYTHING** IS RIGHT IN THE FIRST PLACE?

HE -- OH NO!

FREEZE!

THAT'S **VANDALISM**, FRENCHIE! I'M PUTTIN' YOU UNDER ARREST!

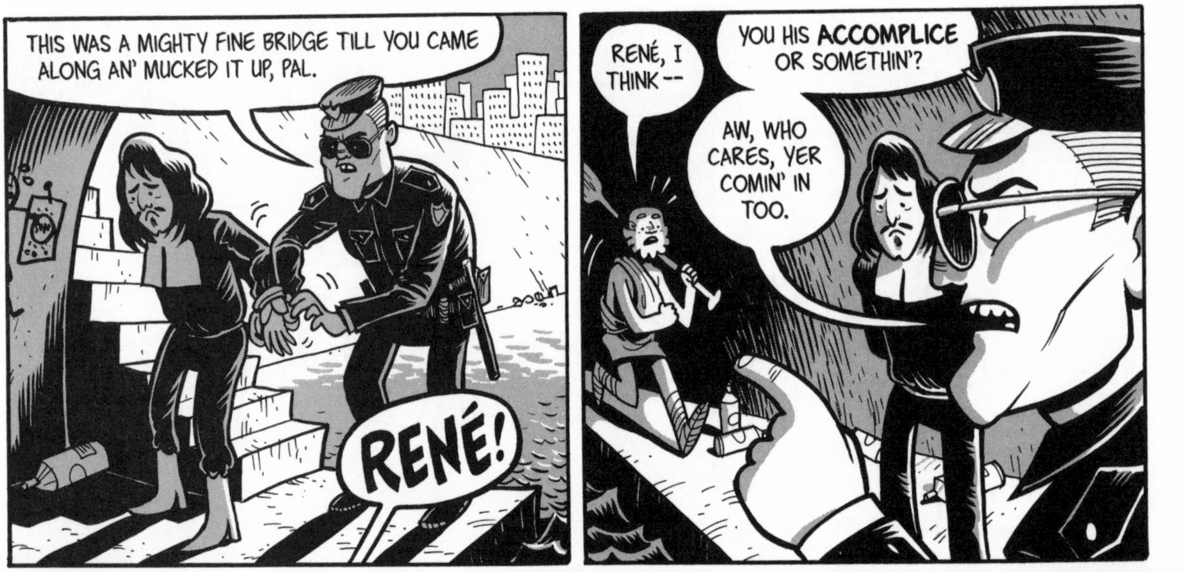
THIS WAS A MIGHTY FINE BRIDGE TILL YOU CAME ALONG AN' MUCKED IT UP, PAL.
RENÉ!
RENÉ, I THINK --
YOU HIS **ACCOMPLICE** OR SOMETHIN'?
AW, WHO CARES, YER COMIN' IN TOO.

RENÉ DESCARTES

b. 1596
d. 1650
C.E.

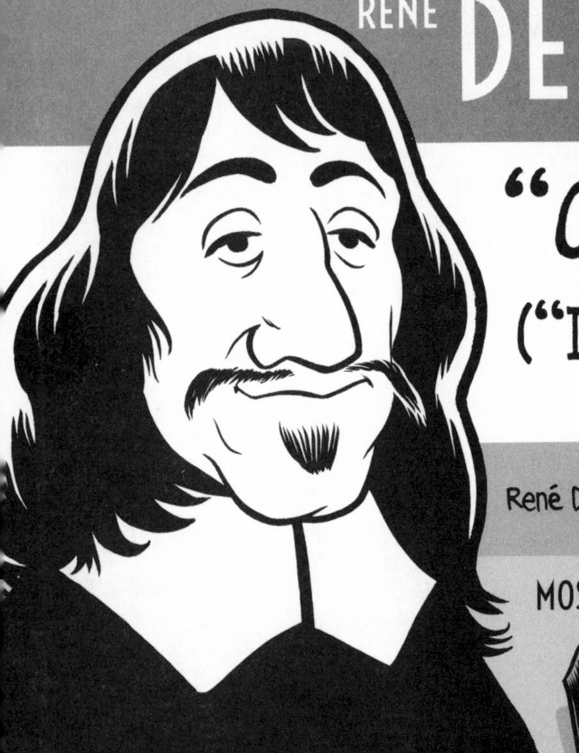

"Cogito, ergo sum."

("I think, therefore I am.")

-- *Meditations on First Philosophy*

René Descartes was a French philosopher and mathematician.

MOST FAMOUS WORK:

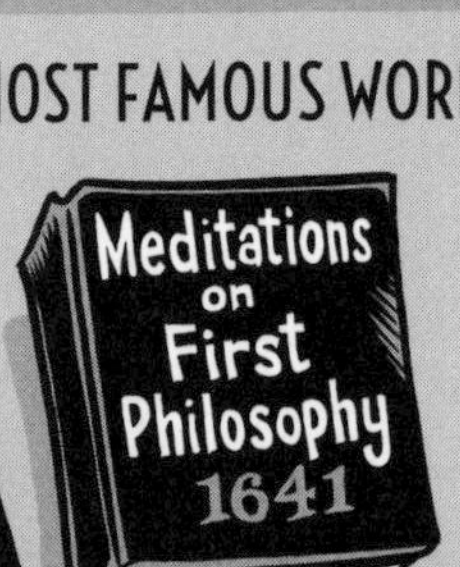
Meditations
on
First
Philosophy
1641

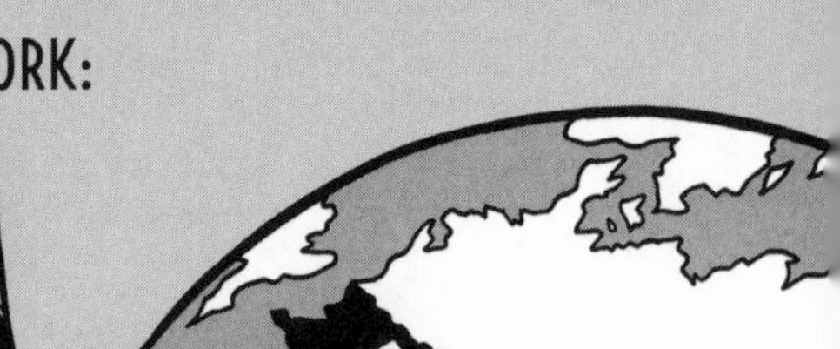
FRANCE

FUN FACT HE ALLEGEDLY NEVER LEFT BED BEFORE 11 A.M. BUT INVENTED ANALYTIC GEOMETRY AND THE CARTESIAN COORDINATE SYSTEM, AND DISCOVERED SOME BASIC LAWS OF OPTICS. HE WAS A TUTOR OF QUEEN CHRISTINA OF SWEDEN.

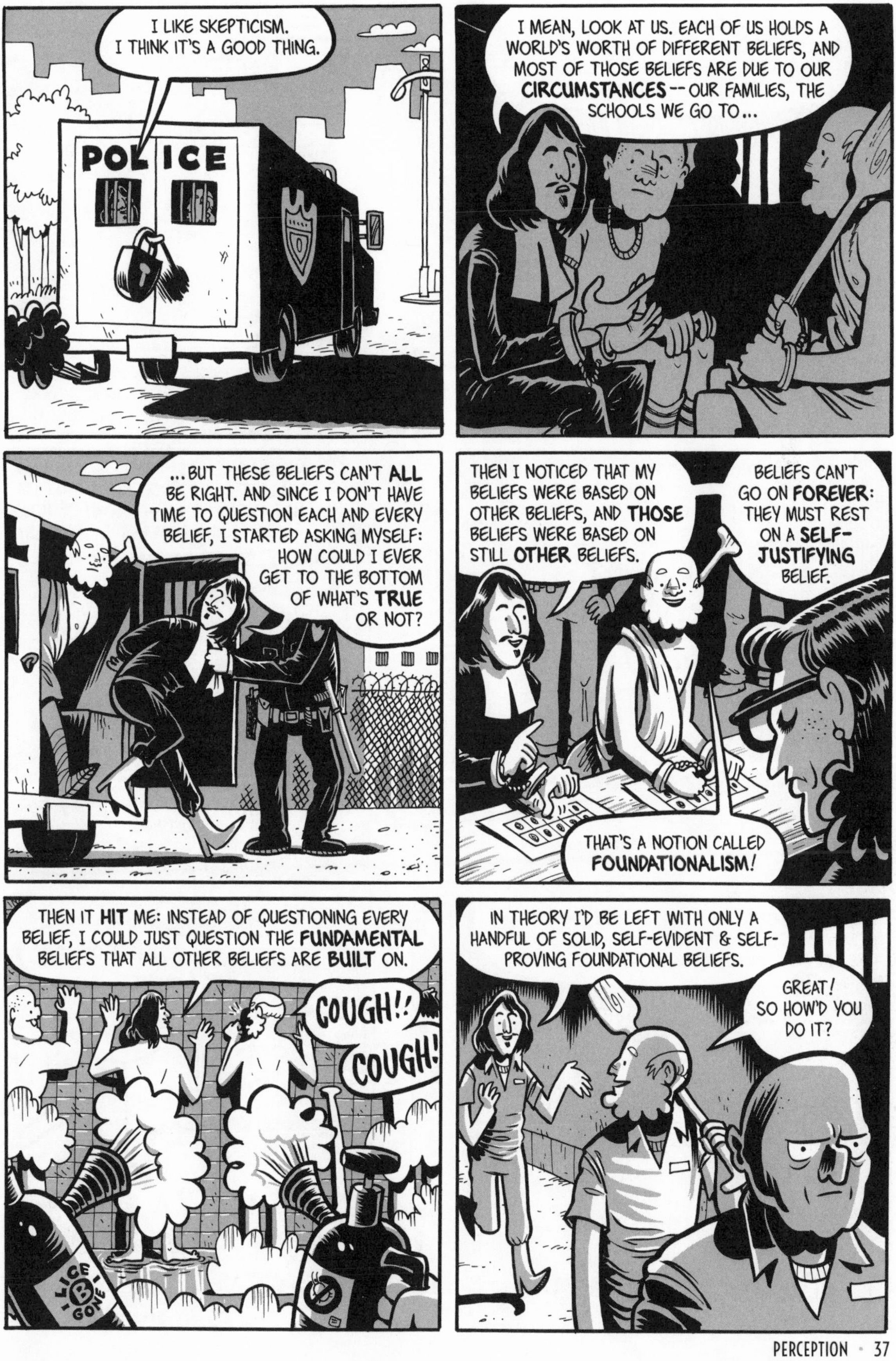
I LIKE SKEPTICISM. I THINK IT'S A GOOD THING.
POLICE
I MEAN, LOOK AT US. EACH OF US HOLDS A WORLD'S WORTH OF DIFFERENT BELIEFS, AND MOST OF THOSE BELIEFS ARE DUE TO OUR **CIRCUMSTANCES** -- OUR FAMILIES, THE SCHOOLS WE GO TO...
...BUT THESE BELIEFS CAN'T **ALL** BE RIGHT. AND SINCE I DON'T HAVE TIME TO QUESTION EACH AND EVERY BELIEF, I STARTED ASKING MYSELF: HOW COULD I EVER GET TO THE BOTTOM OF WHAT'S **TRUE** OR NOT?
THEN I NOTICED THAT MY BELIEFS WERE BASED ON OTHER BELIEFS, AND **THOSE** BELIEFS WERE BASED ON STILL **OTHER** BELIEFS.
BELIEFS CAN'T GO ON **FOREVER**: THEY MUST REST ON A **SELF-JUSTIFYING** BELIEF.
THAT'S A NOTION CALLED **FOUNDATIONALISM**!
THEN IT **HIT** ME: INSTEAD OF QUESTIONING EVERY BELIEF, I COULD JUST QUESTION THE **FUNDAMENTAL** BELIEFS THAT ALL OTHER BELIEFS ARE **BUILT** ON.
COUGH!!
COUGH!
LICE B GONE
IN THEORY I'D BE LEFT WITH ONLY A HANDFUL OF SOLID, SELF-EVIDENT & SELF-PROVING FOUNDATIONAL BELIEFS.
GREAT! SO HOW'D YOU DO IT?

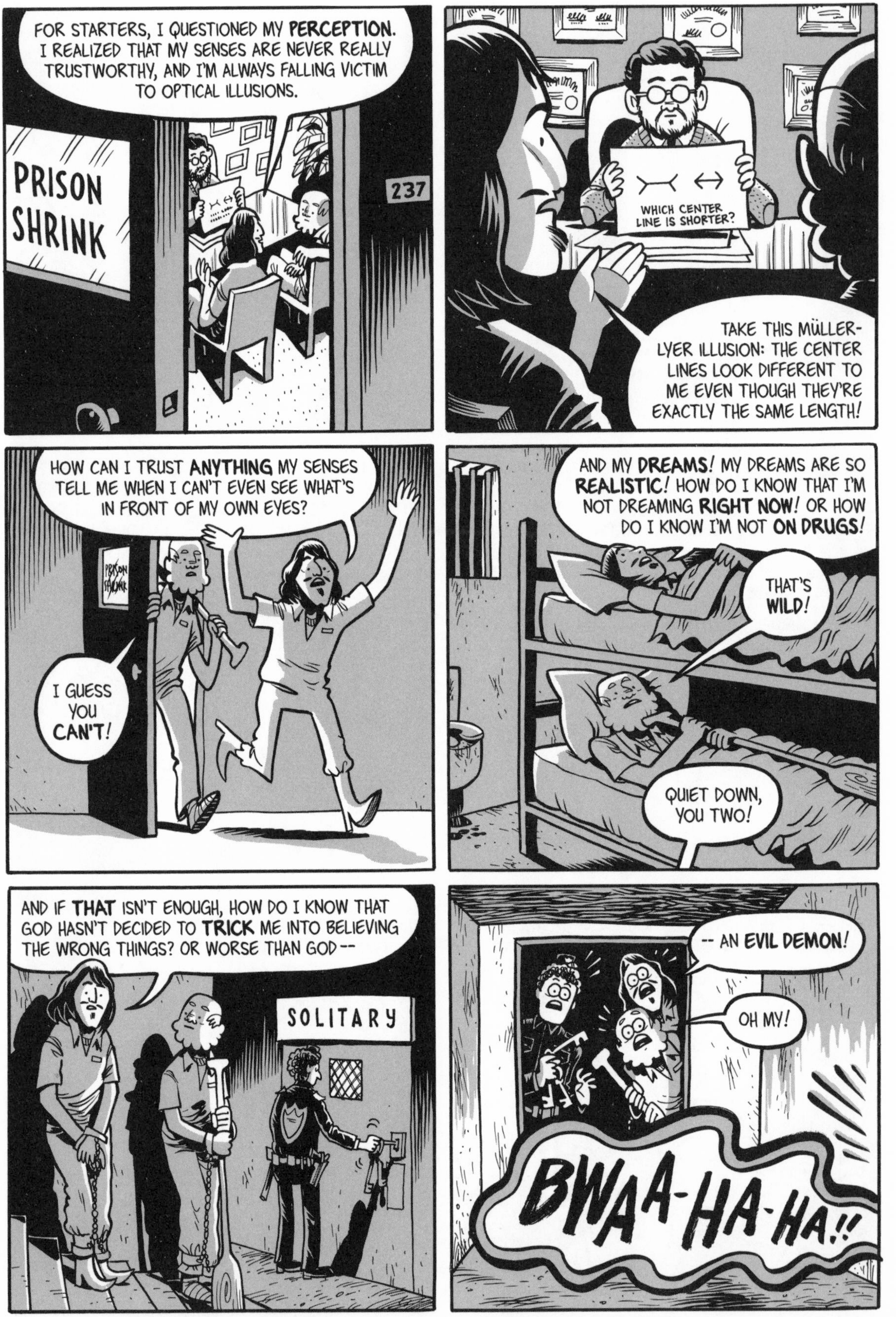
FOR STARTERS, I QUESTIONED MY **PERCEPTION**. I REALIZED THAT MY SENSES ARE NEVER REALLY TRUSTWORTHY, AND I'M ALWAYS FALLING VICTIM TO OPTICAL ILLUSIONS.
PRISON SHRINK
237
WHICH CENTER LINE IS SHORTER?
TAKE THIS MÜLLER-LYER ILLUSION: THE CENTER LINES LOOK DIFFERENT TO ME EVEN THOUGH THEY'RE EXACTLY THE SAME LENGTH!
HOW CAN I TRUST **ANYTHING** MY SENSES TELL ME WHEN I CAN'T EVEN SEE WHAT'S IN FRONT OF MY OWN EYES?
I GUESS YOU **CAN'T**!
AND MY **DREAMS**! MY DREAMS ARE SO **REALISTIC**! HOW DO I KNOW THAT I'M NOT DREAMING **RIGHT NOW**! OR HOW DO I KNOW I'M NOT **ON DRUGS**!
THAT'S **WILD**!
QUIET DOWN, YOU TWO!
AND IF **THAT** ISN'T ENOUGH, HOW DO I KNOW THAT GOD HASN'T DECIDED TO **TRICK** ME INTO BELIEVING THE WRONG THINGS? OR WORSE THAN GOD--
SOLITARY
-- AN **EVIL DEMON**!
OH MY!
BWAA-HA-HA!!

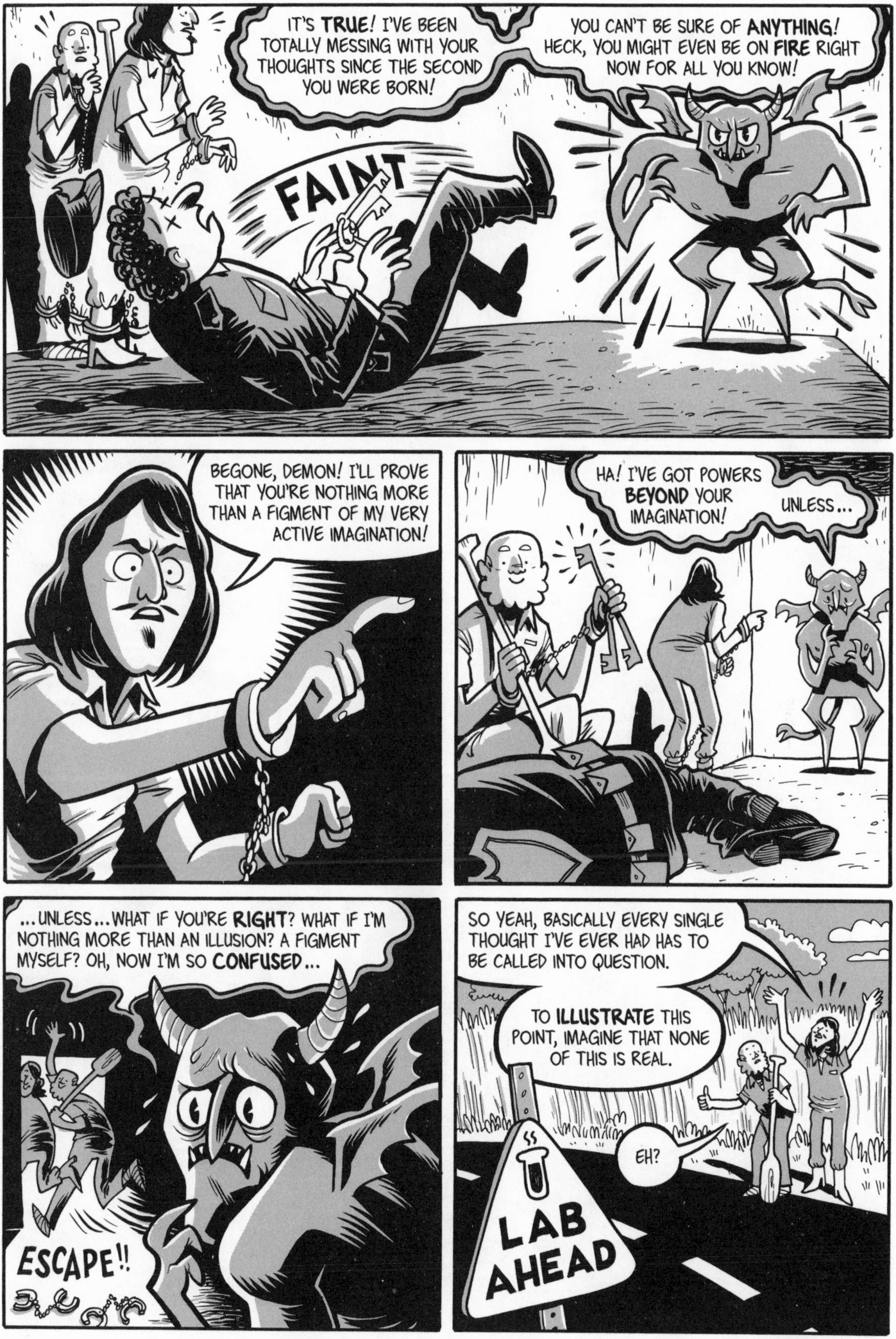
IT'S TRUE! I'VE BEEN TOTALLY MESSING WITH YOUR THOUGHTS SINCE THE SECOND YOU WERE BORN!
YOU CAN'T BE SURE OF ANYTHING! HECK, YOU MIGHT EVEN BE ON FIRE RIGHT NOW FOR ALL YOU KNOW!
FAINT
BEGONE, DEMON! I'LL PROVE THAT YOU'RE NOTHING MORE THAN A FIGMENT OF MY VERY ACTIVE IMAGINATION!
HA! I'VE GOT POWERS BEYOND YOUR IMAGINATION!
UNLESS...
...UNLESS...WHAT IF YOU'RE RIGHT? WHAT IF I'M NOTHING MORE THAN AN ILLUSION? A FIGMENT MYSELF? OH, NOW I'M SO CONFUSED...
ESCAPE!!
SO YEAH, BASICALLY EVERY SINGLE THOUGHT I'VE EVER HAD HAS TO BE CALLED INTO QUESTION.
TO ILLUSTRATE THIS POINT, IMAGINE THAT NONE OF THIS IS REAL.
EH?
LAB AHEAD

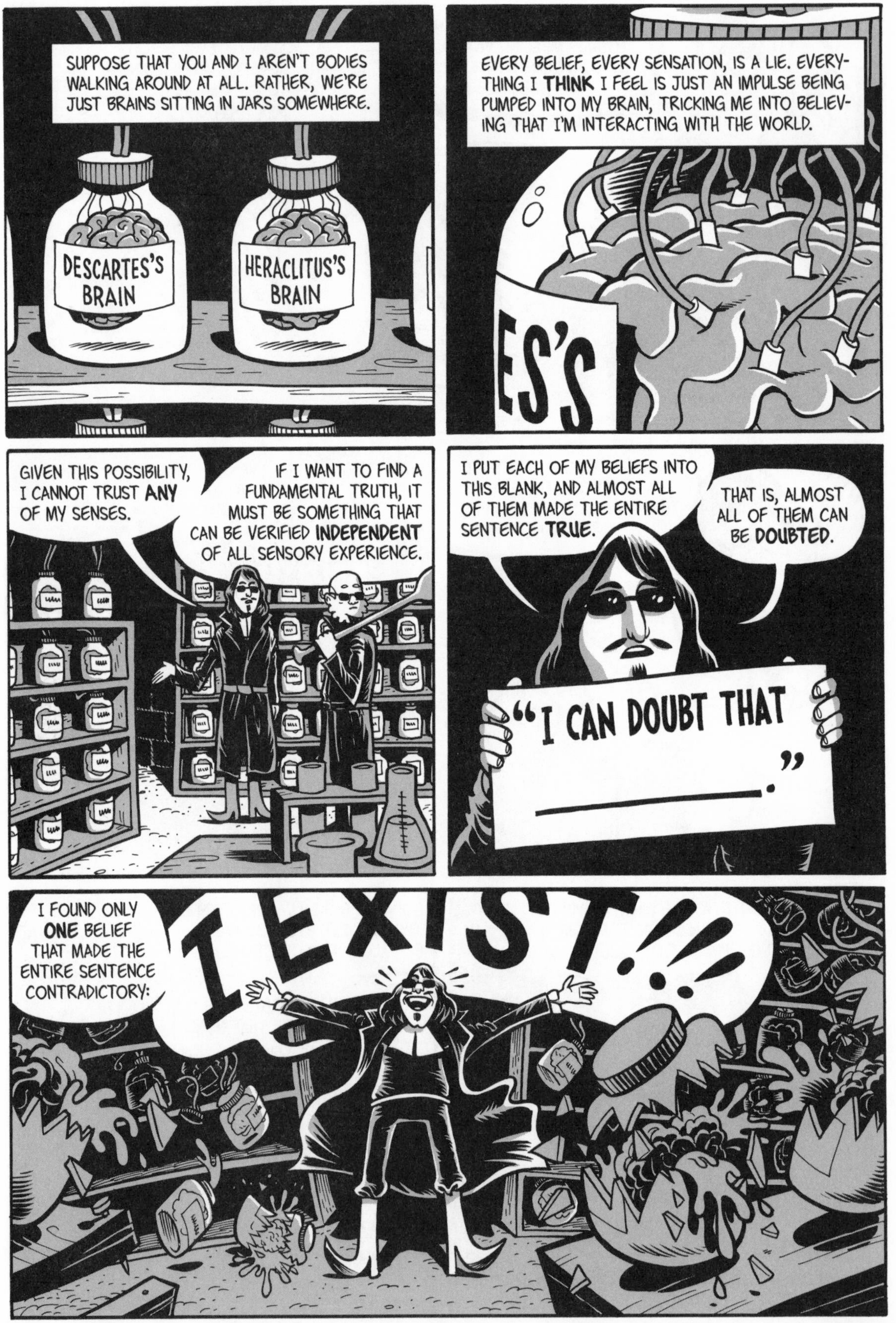
SUPPOSE THAT YOU AND I AREN'T BODIES WALKING AROUND AT ALL. RATHER, WE'RE JUST BRAINS SITTING IN JARS SOMEWHERE.
DESCARTES'S BRAIN
HERACLITUS'S BRAIN
EVERY BELIEF, EVERY SENSATION, IS A LIE. EVERYTHING I **THINK** I FEEL IS JUST AN IMPULSE BEING PUMPED INTO MY BRAIN, TRICKING ME INTO BELIEVING THAT I'M INTERACTING WITH THE WORLD.
ES'S
GIVEN THIS POSSIBILITY, I CANNOT TRUST **ANY** OF MY SENSES.
IF I WANT TO FIND A FUNDAMENTAL TRUTH, IT MUST BE SOMETHING THAT CAN BE VERIFIED **INDEPENDENT** OF ALL SENSORY EXPERIENCE.
I PUT EACH OF MY BELIEFS INTO THIS BLANK, AND ALMOST ALL OF THEM MADE THE ENTIRE SENTENCE **TRUE**.
THAT IS, ALMOST ALL OF THEM CAN BE **DOUBTED**.
"I CAN DOUBT THAT ________."
I FOUND ONLY **ONE** BELIEF THAT MADE THE ENTIRE SENTENCE CONTRADICTORY:
I EXIST!!!

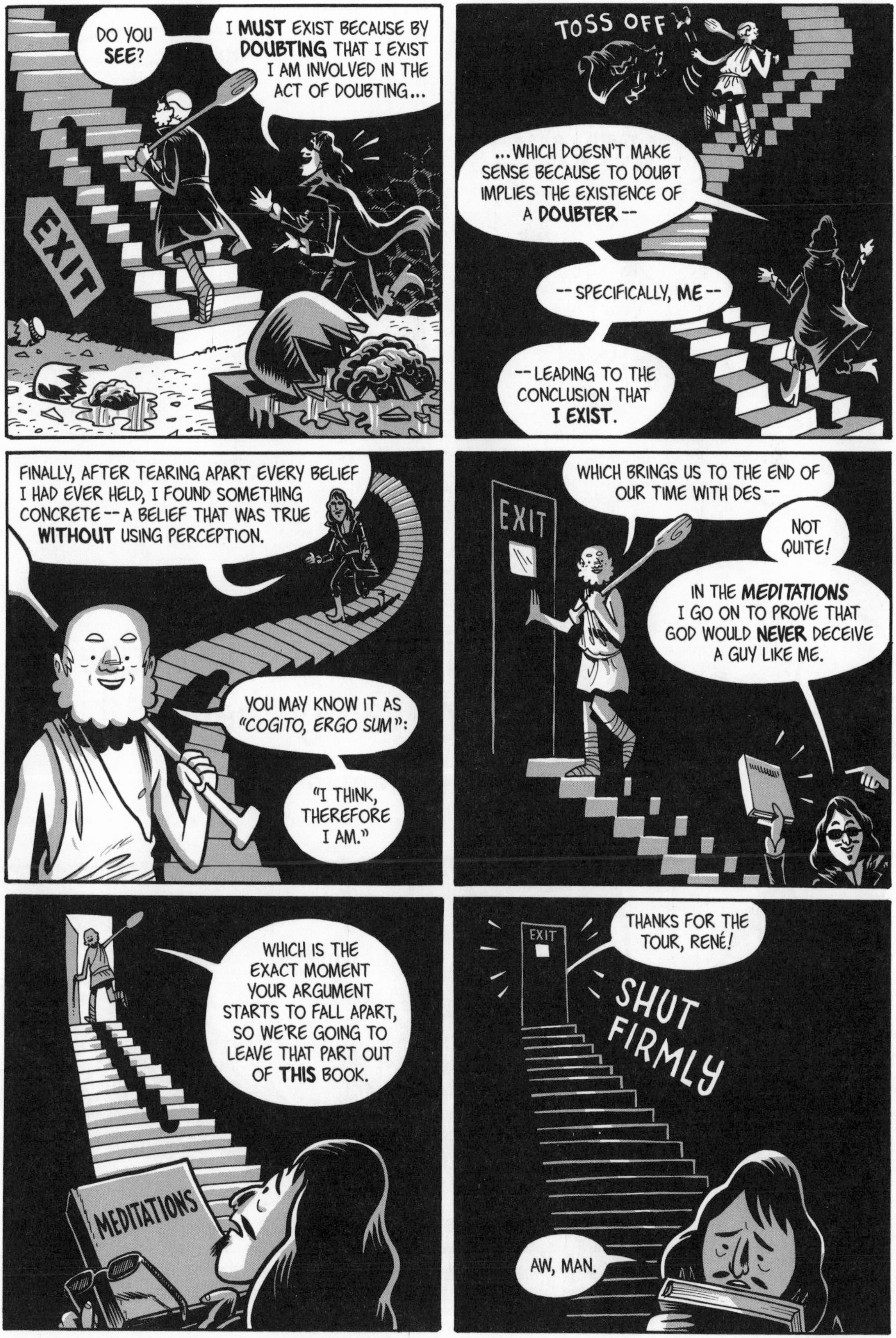

DO YOU **SEE**?
I **MUST** EXIST BECAUSE BY **DOUBTING** THAT I EXIST I AM INVOLVED IN THE ACT OF DOUBTING...
EXIT
TOSS OFF
...WHICH DOESN'T MAKE SENSE BECAUSE TO DOUBT IMPLIES THE EXISTENCE OF A **DOUBTER** --
-- SPECIFICALLY, **ME** --
-- LEADING TO THE CONCLUSION THAT **I EXIST**.
FINALLY, AFTER TEARING APART EVERY BELIEF I HAD EVER HELD, I FOUND SOMETHING CONCRETE -- A BELIEF THAT WAS TRUE **WITHOUT** USING PERCEPTION.
YOU MAY KNOW IT AS "COGITO, ERGO SUM":
"I THINK, THEREFORE I AM."
EXIT
WHICH BRINGS US TO THE END OF OUR TIME WITH DES --
NOT QUITE!
IN THE ***MEDITATIONS*** I GO ON TO PROVE THAT GOD WOULD **NEVER** DECEIVE A GUY LIKE ME.
WHICH IS THE EXACT MOMENT YOUR ARGUMENT STARTS TO FALL APART, SO WE'RE GOING TO LEAVE THAT PART OUT OF **THIS** BOOK.
MEDITATIONS
EXIT
THANKS FOR THE TOUR, RENÉ!
SHUT FIRMLY
AW, MAN.

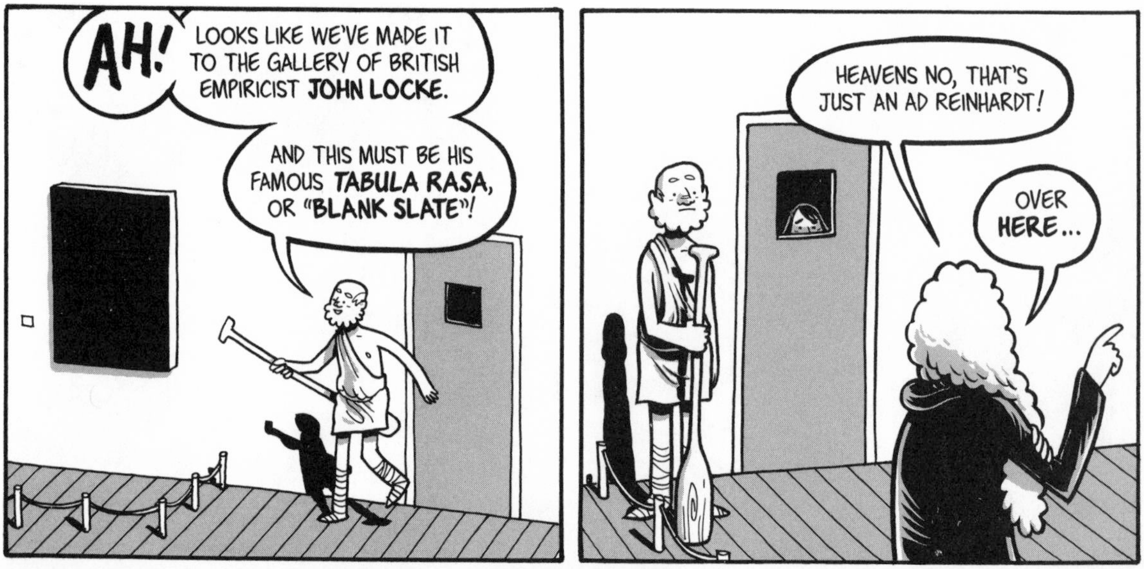
AH!
LOOKS LIKE WE'VE MADE IT TO THE GALLERY OF BRITISH EMPIRICIST **JOHN LOCKE**.
AND THIS MUST BE HIS FAMOUS ***TABULA RASA***, OR "**BLANK SLATE**"!
HEAVENS NO, THAT'S JUST AN AD REINHARDT!
OVER **HERE**...

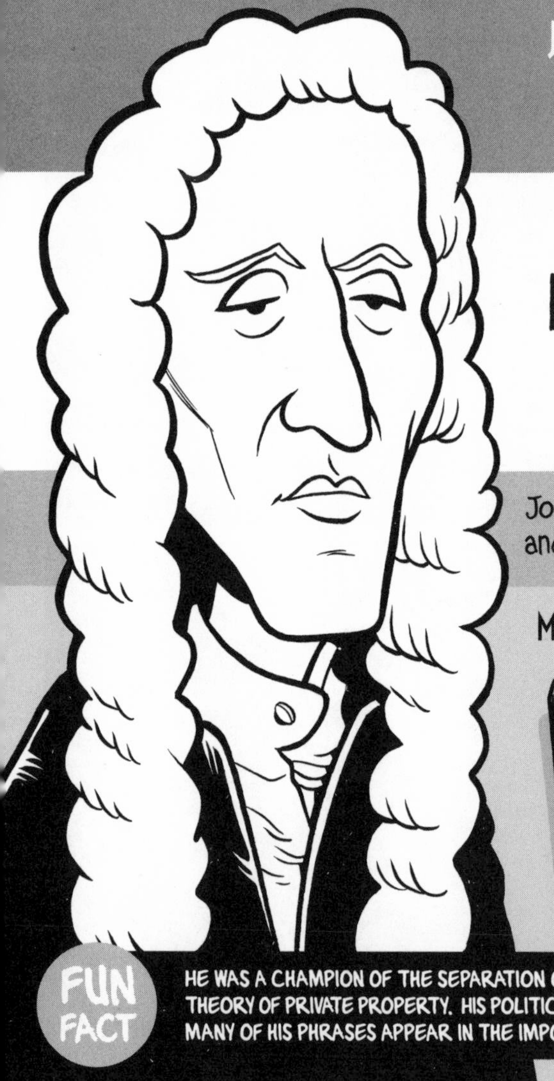

JOHN LOCKE

b. 1632
d. 1704
C.E.

"No man's knowledge here can go beyond his experience."

-- *An Essay Concerning Human Understanding*

John Locke was an English philosopher whose empiricism and politics remain influential.

MOST FAMOUS WORK:

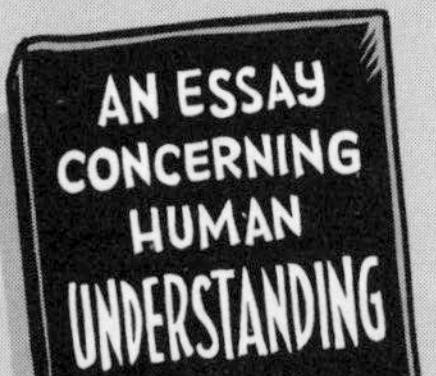
AN ESSAY CONCERNING HUMAN UNDERSTANDING
1689

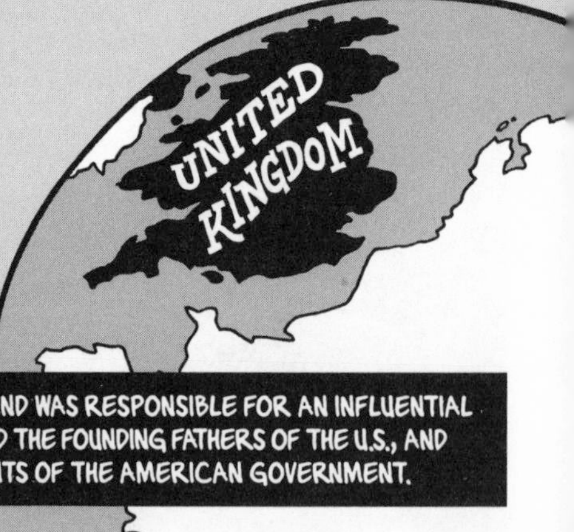
UNITED KINGDOM

FUN FACT

HE WAS A CHAMPION OF THE SEPARATION OF CHURCH AND STATE AND WAS RESPONSIBLE FOR AN INFLUENTIAL THEORY OF PRIVATE PROPERTY. HIS POLITICAL WRITINGS INFLUENCED THE FOUNDING FATHERS OF THE U.S., AND MANY OF HIS PHRASES APPEAR IN THE IMPORTANT EARLY DOCUMENTS OF THE AMERICAN GOVERNMENT.

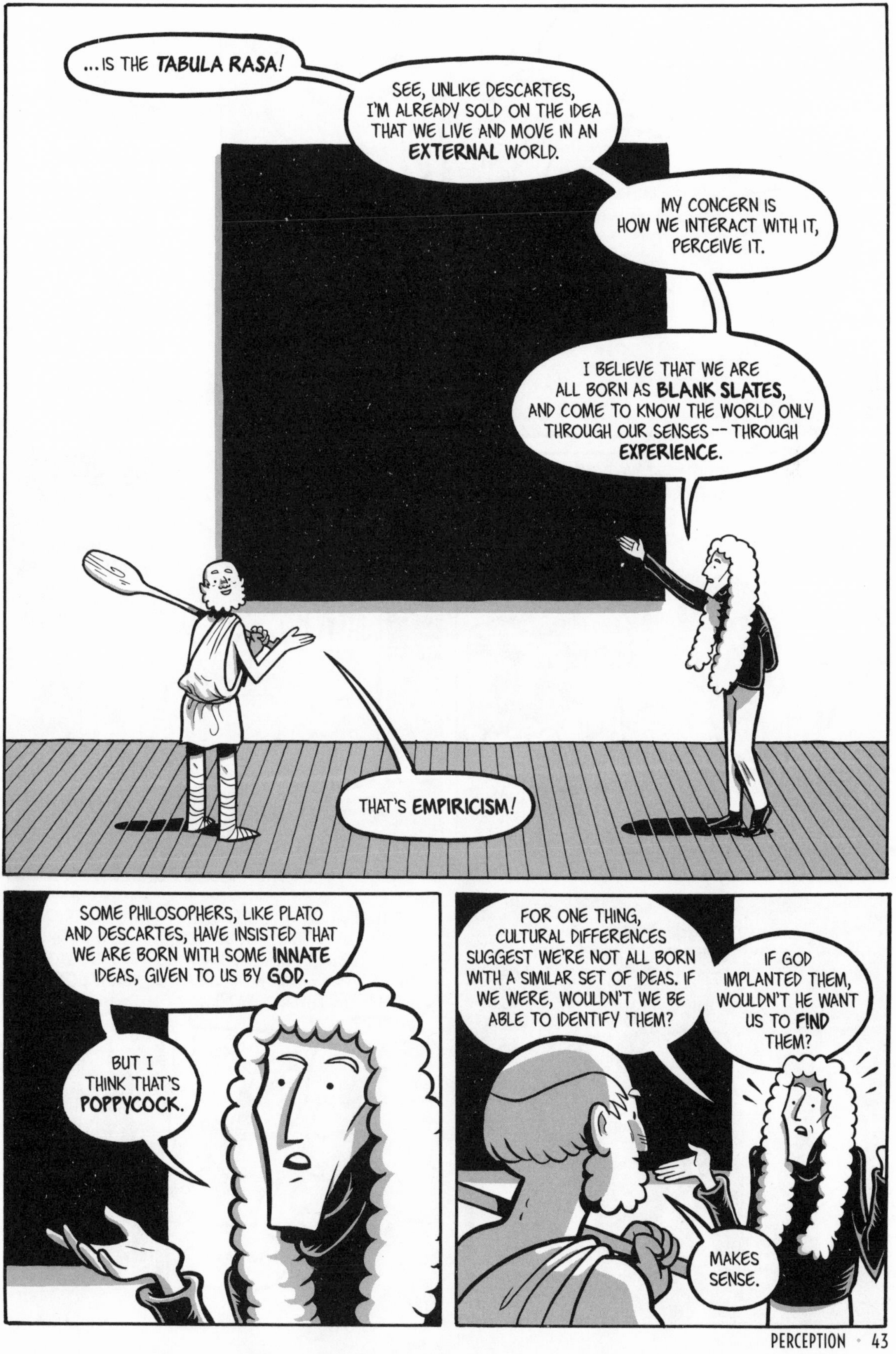
...IS THE **TABULA RASA**!
SEE, UNLIKE DESCARTES, I'M ALREADY SOLD ON THE IDEA THAT WE LIVE AND MOVE IN AN **EXTERNAL** WORLD.
MY CONCERN IS HOW WE INTERACT WITH IT, PERCEIVE IT.
I BELIEVE THAT WE ARE ALL BORN AS **BLANK SLATES**, AND COME TO KNOW THE WORLD ONLY THROUGH OUR SENSES -- THROUGH **EXPERIENCE**.
THAT'S **EMPIRICISM**!
SOME PHILOSOPHERS, LIKE PLATO AND DESCARTES, HAVE INSISTED THAT WE ARE BORN WITH SOME **INNATE** IDEAS, GIVEN TO US BY **GOD**.
BUT I THINK THAT'S **POPPYCOCK**.
FOR ONE THING, CULTURAL DIFFERENCES SUGGEST WE'RE NOT ALL BORN WITH A SIMILAR SET OF IDEAS. IF WE WERE, WOULDN'T WE BE ABLE TO IDENTIFY THEM?
IF GOD IMPLANTED THEM, WOULDN'T HE WANT US TO **FIND** THEM?
MAKES SENSE.

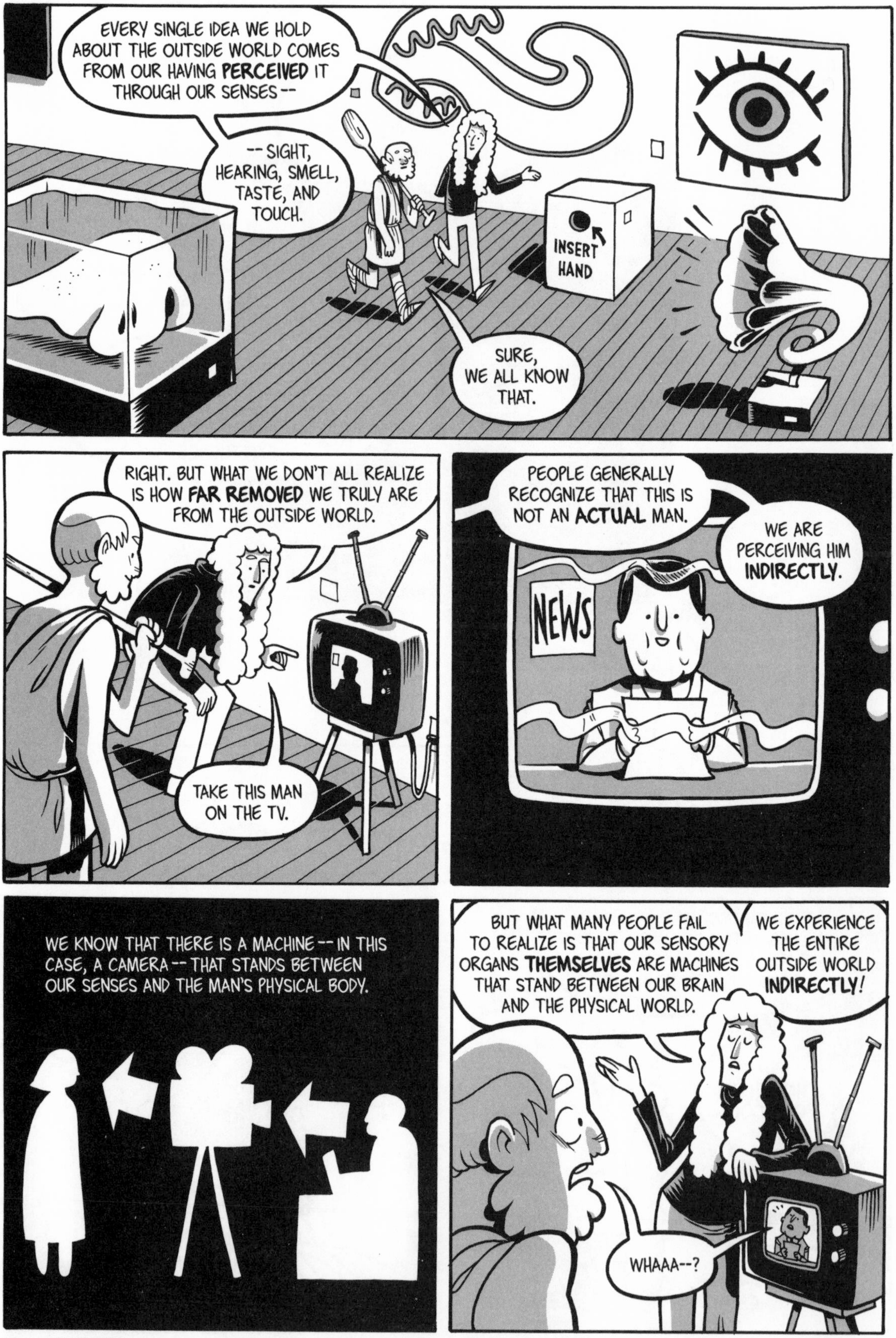
EVERY SINGLE IDEA WE HOLD ABOUT THE OUTSIDE WORLD COMES FROM OUR HAVING PERCEIVED IT THROUGH OUR SENSES--
--SIGHT, HEARING, SMELL, TASTE, AND TOUCH.
INSERT HAND
SURE, WE ALL KNOW THAT.
RIGHT. BUT WHAT WE DON'T ALL REALIZE IS HOW FAR REMOVED WE TRULY ARE FROM THE OUTSIDE WORLD.
TAKE THIS MAN ON THE TV.
PEOPLE GENERALLY RECOGNIZE THAT THIS IS NOT AN ACTUAL MAN.
WE ARE PERCEIVING HIM INDIRECTLY.
NEWS
WE KNOW THAT THERE IS A MACHINE--IN THIS CASE, A CAMERA--THAT STANDS BETWEEN OUR SENSES AND THE MAN'S PHYSICAL BODY.
BUT WHAT MANY PEOPLE FAIL TO REALIZE IS THAT OUR SENSORY ORGANS THEMSELVES ARE MACHINES THAT STAND BETWEEN OUR BRAIN AND THE PHYSICAL WORLD.
WE EXPERIENCE THE ENTIRE OUTSIDE WORLD INDIRECTLY!
WHAAA--?

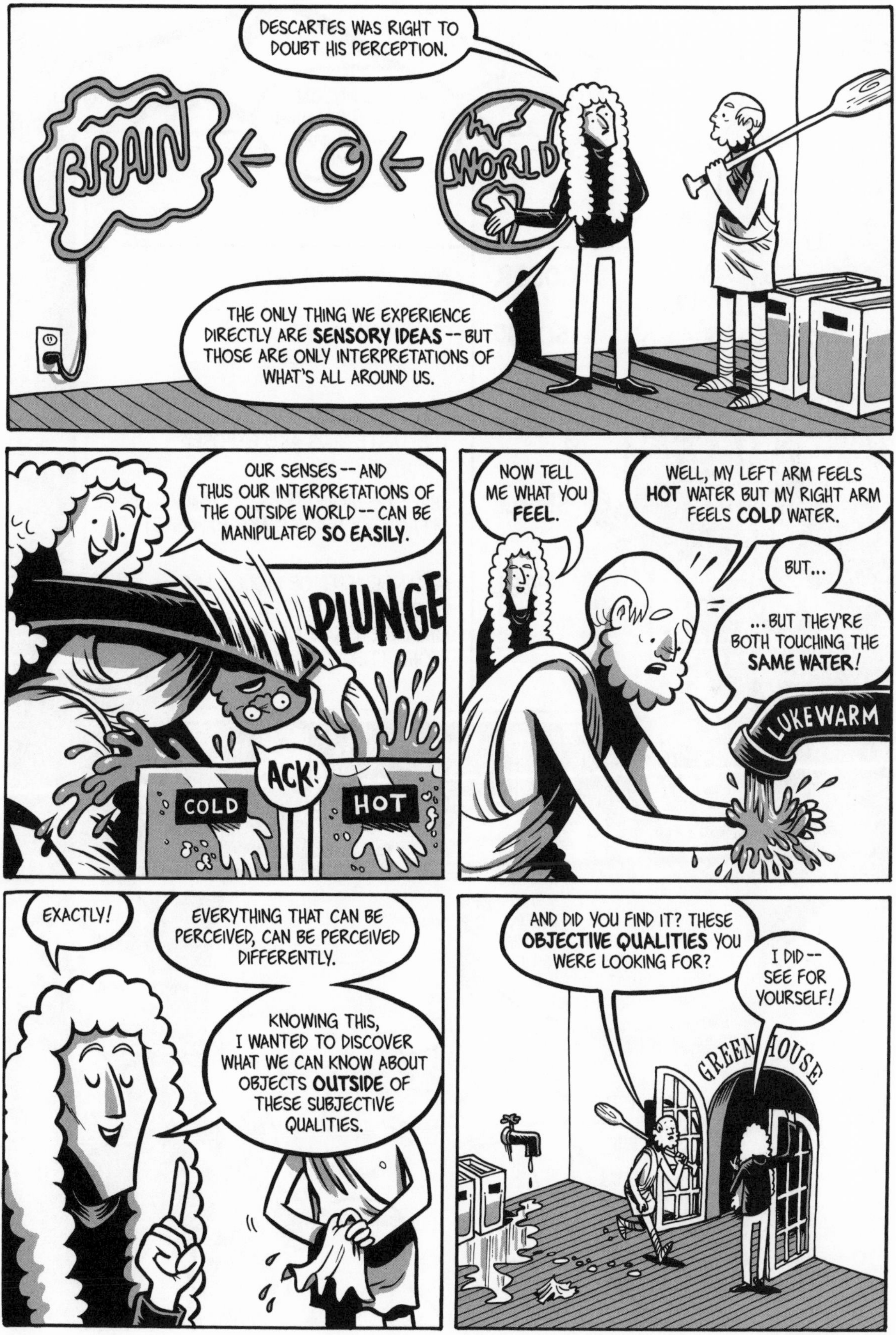
DESCARTES WAS RIGHT TO DOUBT HIS PERCEPTION.
BRAIN
WORLD
THE ONLY THING WE EXPERIENCE DIRECTLY ARE **SENSORY IDEAS** -- BUT THOSE ARE ONLY INTERPRETATIONS OF WHAT'S ALL AROUND US.
OUR SENSES -- AND THUS OUR INTERPRETATIONS OF THE OUTSIDE WORLD -- CAN BE MANIPULATED **SO EASILY**.
PLUNGE
ACK!
COLD
HOT
NOW TELL ME WHAT YOU **FEEL**.
WELL, MY LEFT ARM FEELS **HOT** WATER BUT MY RIGHT ARM FEELS **COLD** WATER.
BUT...
...BUT THEY'RE BOTH TOUCHING THE **SAME WATER**!
LUKEWARM
EXACTLY!
EVERYTHING THAT CAN BE PERCEIVED, CAN BE PERCEIVED DIFFERENTLY.
KNOWING THIS, I WANTED TO DISCOVER WHAT WE CAN KNOW ABOUT OBJECTS **OUTSIDE** OF THESE SUBJECTIVE QUALITIES.
AND DID YOU FIND IT? THESE **OBJECTIVE QUALITIES** YOU WERE LOOKING FOR?
I DID -- SEE FOR YOURSELF!
GREENHOUSE

THE SENSORY IDEAS IN **COLUMN ONE** CAN AND WILL BE EXPERIENCED DIFFERENTLY BY DIFFERENT PEOPLE, DIFFERENT SPECIES, ETC.

BUT THE PHYSICAL REALITIES IN **COLUMN TWO** WILL REMAIN THE SAME.

Column 1	Column 2
COLOR	WAVELENGTHS OF LIGHT
SOUND	FREQUENCY OF AIR PRESSURE CHANGES
TASTE	SHAPE OF MOLECULES TO WHICH THE TASTE BUDS ARE EXPOSED
SMELL	SHAPE OF MOLECULES TO WHICH THE OLFACTORY NERVES ARE EXPOSED
FEEL	ARRANGEMENT OF MOLECULES INTO SURFACE SHAPES; KINETIC ENERGY OF ATOMS (TEMPERATURE)

THIS FLOWER, FOR INSTANCE, HAS AN ATOMIC STRUCTURE THAT MAKES IT REFLECT VISIBLE LIGHT WITH A WAVELENGTH OF 475 NANOMETERS.

WE CALL THIS ONE OF THE FLOWER'S **PRIMARY** QUALITIES.

HMM.

ALL I SEE IS **BLUE!**

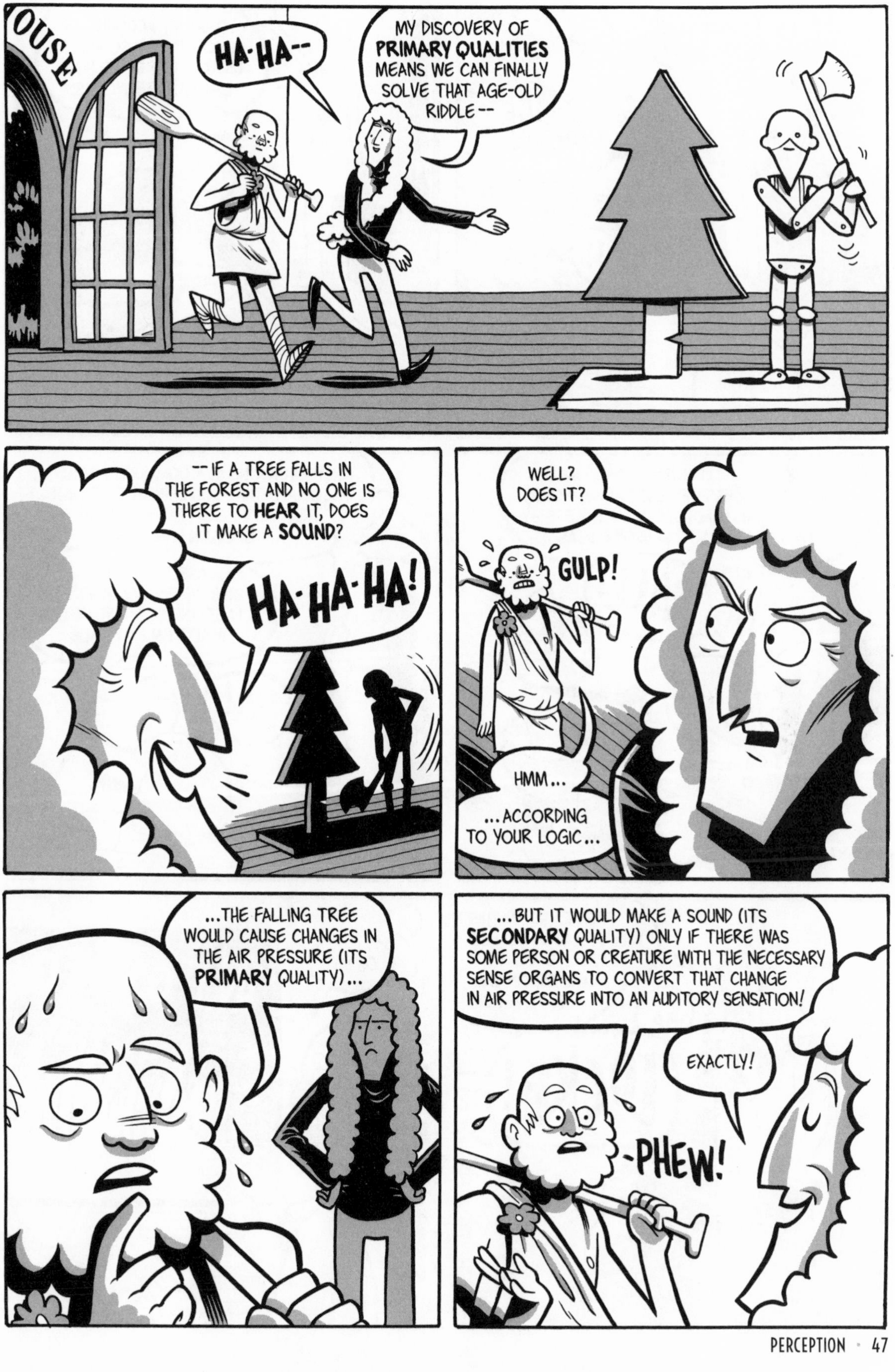
OUSE
HA-HA--
MY DISCOVERY OF PRIMARY QUALITIES MEANS WE CAN FINALLY SOLVE THAT AGE-OLD RIDDLE--
--IF A TREE FALLS IN THE FOREST AND NO ONE IS THERE TO HEAR IT, DOES IT MAKE A SOUND?
HA-HA-HA!
WELL? DOES IT?
GULP!
HMM...
...ACCORDING TO YOUR LOGIC...
...THE FALLING TREE WOULD CAUSE CHANGES IN THE AIR PRESSURE (ITS PRIMARY QUALITY)...
...BUT IT WOULD MAKE A SOUND (ITS SECONDARY QUALITY) ONLY IF THERE WAS SOME PERSON OR CREATURE WITH THE NECESSARY SENSE ORGANS TO CONVERT THAT CHANGE IN AIR PRESSURE INTO AN AUDITORY SENSATION!
EXACTLY!
-PHEW!

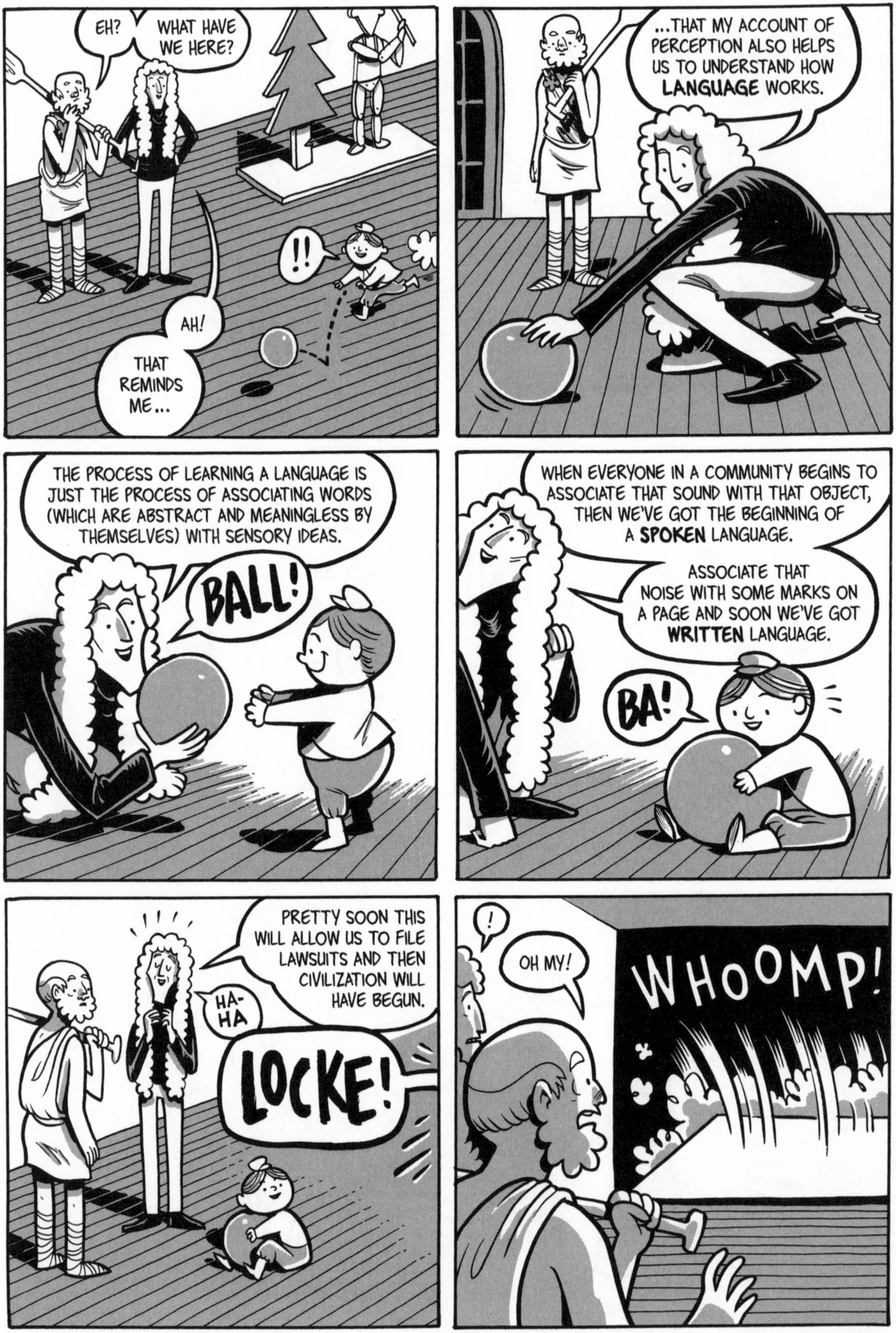
EH?
WHAT HAVE WE HERE?
!!
AH!
THAT REMINDS ME...
...THAT MY ACCOUNT OF PERCEPTION ALSO HELPS US TO UNDERSTAND HOW LANGUAGE WORKS.
THE PROCESS OF LEARNING A LANGUAGE IS JUST THE PROCESS OF ASSOCIATING WORDS (WHICH ARE ABSTRACT AND MEANINGLESS BY THEMSELVES) WITH SENSORY IDEAS.
BALL!
WHEN EVERYONE IN A COMMUNITY BEGINS TO ASSOCIATE THAT SOUND WITH THAT OBJECT, THEN WE'VE GOT THE BEGINNING OF A SPOKEN LANGUAGE.
ASSOCIATE THAT NOISE WITH SOME MARKS ON A PAGE AND SOON WE'VE GOT WRITTEN LANGUAGE.
BA!
PRETTY SOON THIS WILL ALLOW US TO FILE LAWSUITS AND THEN CIVILIZATION WILL HAVE BEGUN.
HA-HA
LOCKE!
!
OH MY!
WHOOMP!

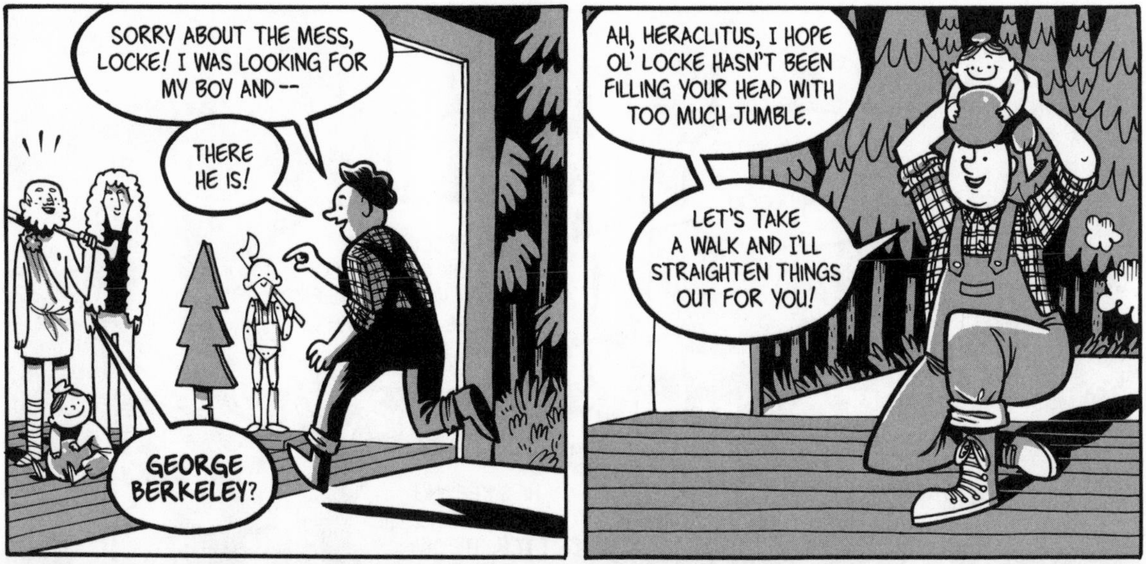
SORRY ABOUT THE MESS, LOCKE! I WAS LOOKING FOR MY BOY AND --
THERE HE IS!
GEORGE BERKELEY?
AH, HERACLITUS, I HOPE OL' LOCKE HASN'T BEEN FILLING YOUR HEAD WITH TOO MUCH JUMBLE.
LET'S TAKE A WALK AND I'LL STRAIGHTEN THINGS OUT FOR YOU!

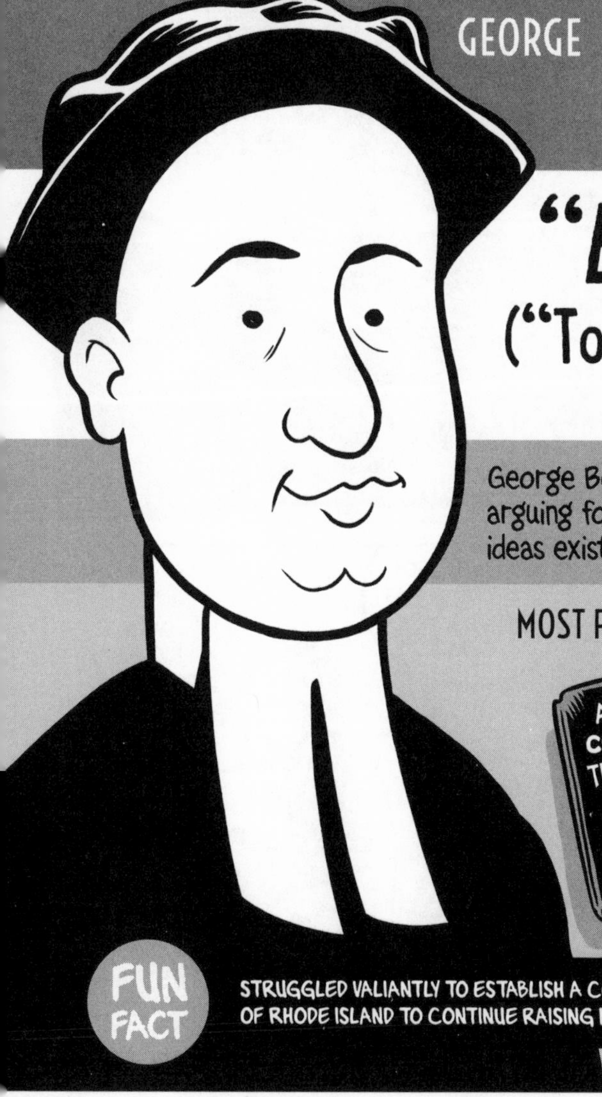

GEORGE BERKELEY

b. 1685
d. 1753
C.E.

"*Esse est percipi.*"
("To be is to be perceived.")

-- *A Treatise Concerning the Principles of Human Knowledge*

George Berkeley was an Anglo-Irish philosopher known for arguing for idealism -- the doctrine that only minds and ideas exist -- on the basic assumptions of empiricism.

MOST FAMOUS WORK:

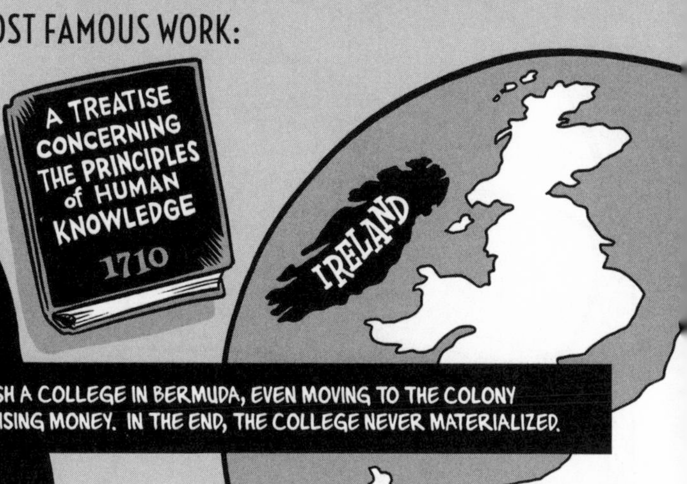
A TREATISE CONCERNING THE PRINCIPLES of HUMAN KNOWLEDGE
1710
IRELAND

FUN FACT STRUGGLED VALIANTLY TO ESTABLISH A COLLEGE IN BERMUDA, EVEN MOVING TO THE COLONY OF RHODE ISLAND TO CONTINUE RAISING MONEY. IN THE END, THE COLLEGE NEVER MATERIALIZED.

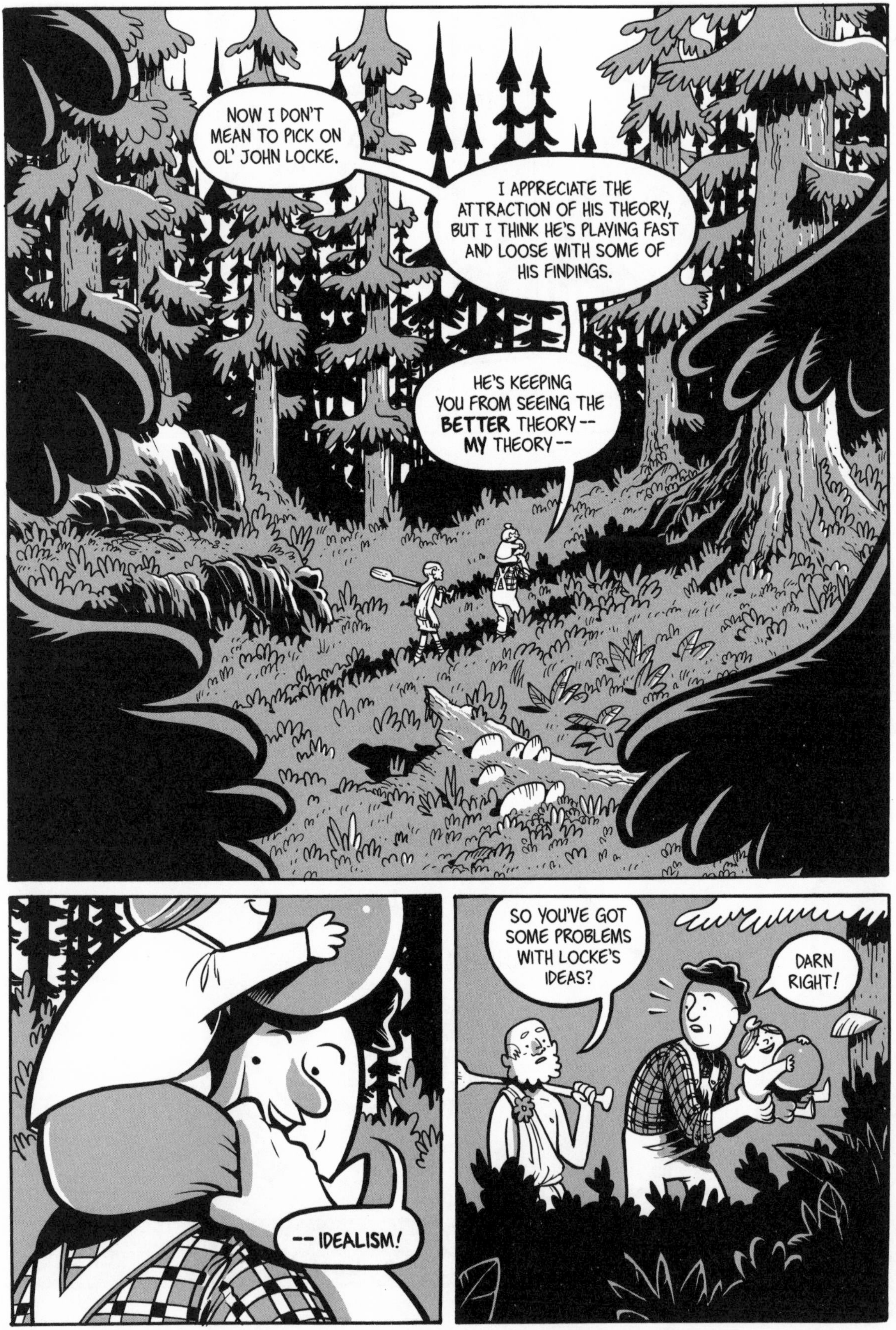
NOW I DON'T MEAN TO PICK ON OL' JOHN LOCKE.
I APPRECIATE THE ATTRACTION OF HIS THEORY, BUT I THINK HE'S PLAYING FAST AND LOOSE WITH SOME OF HIS FINDINGS.
HE'S KEEPING YOU FROM SEEING THE **BETTER** THEORY -- **MY** THEORY --
-- IDEALISM!
SO YOU'VE GOT SOME PROBLEMS WITH LOCKE'S IDEAS?
DARN RIGHT!

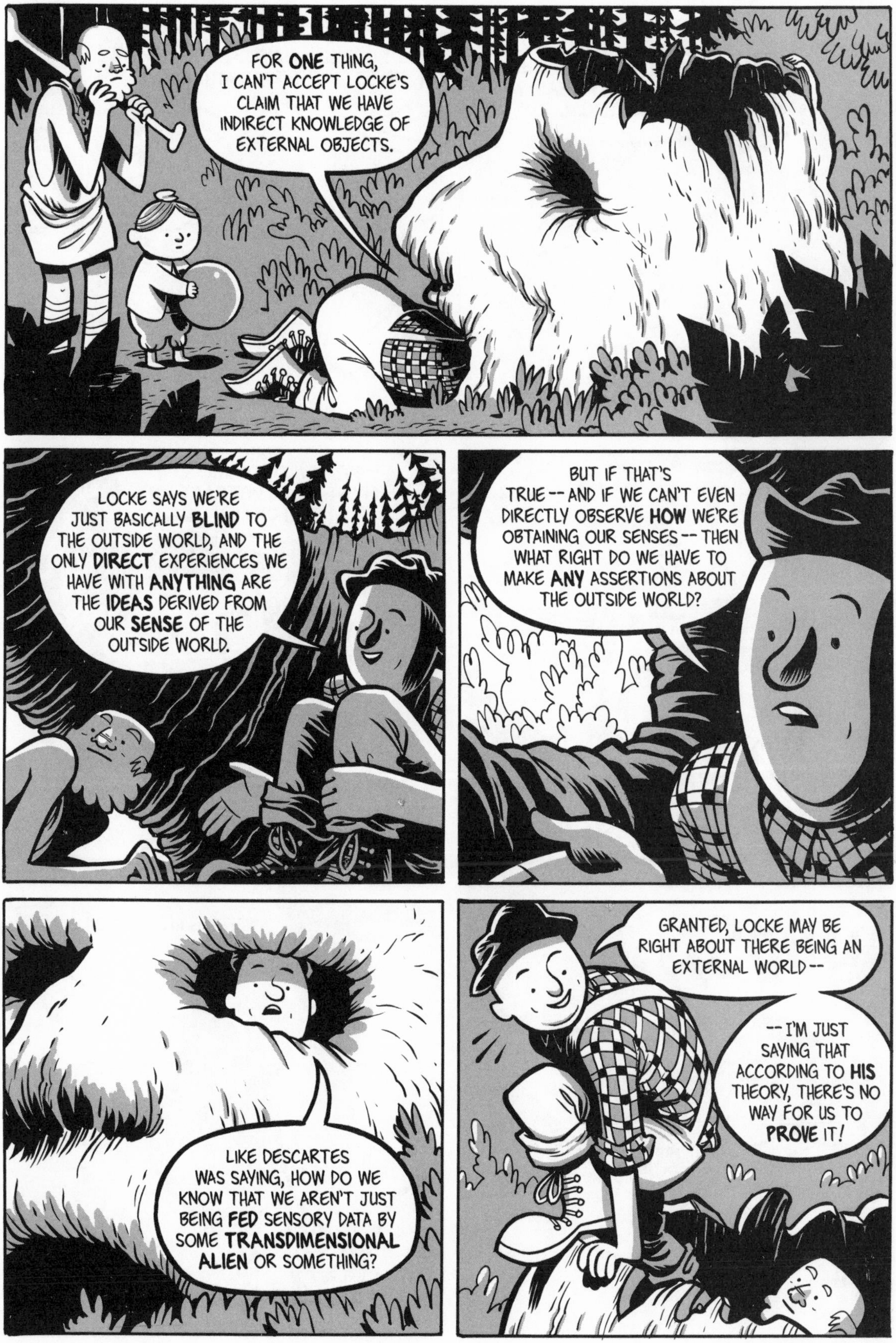

FOR **ONE** THING, I CAN'T ACCEPT LOCKE'S CLAIM THAT WE HAVE INDIRECT KNOWLEDGE OF EXTERNAL OBJECTS.
LOCKE SAYS WE'RE JUST BASICALLY **BLIND** TO THE OUTSIDE WORLD, AND THE ONLY **DIRECT** EXPERIENCES WE HAVE WITH **ANYTHING** ARE THE **IDEAS** DERIVED FROM OUR **SENSE** OF THE OUTSIDE WORLD.
BUT IF THAT'S TRUE--AND IF WE CAN'T EVEN DIRECTLY OBSERVE **HOW** WE'RE OBTAINING OUR SENSES--THEN WHAT RIGHT DO WE HAVE TO MAKE **ANY** ASSERTIONS ABOUT THE OUTSIDE WORLD?
LIKE DESCARTES WAS SAYING, HOW DO WE KNOW THAT WE AREN'T JUST BEING **FED** SENSORY DATA BY SOME **TRANSDIMENSIONAL ALIEN** OR SOMETHING?
GRANTED, LOCKE MAY BE RIGHT ABOUT THERE BEING AN EXTERNAL WORLD--
--I'M JUST SAYING THAT ACCORDING TO **HIS** THEORY, THERE'S NO WAY FOR US TO **PROVE** IT!

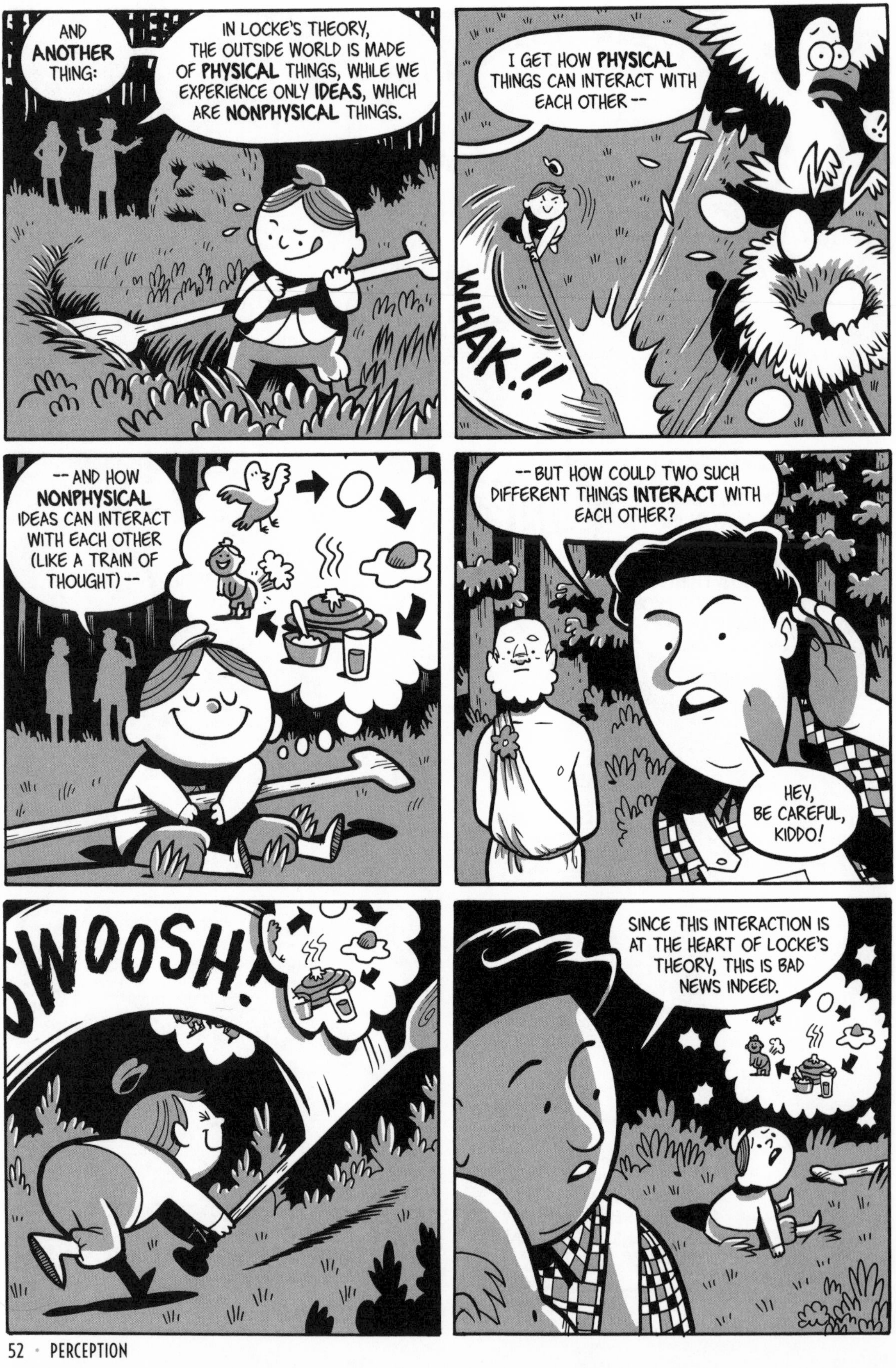
AND ANOTHER THING:
IN LOCKE'S THEORY, THE OUTSIDE WORLD IS MADE OF PHYSICAL THINGS, WHILE WE EXPERIENCE ONLY IDEAS, WHICH ARE NONPHYSICAL THINGS.
I GET HOW PHYSICAL THINGS CAN INTERACT WITH EACH OTHER --
WHAK.!!
-- AND HOW NONPHYSICAL IDEAS CAN INTERACT WITH EACH OTHER (LIKE A TRAIN OF THOUGHT) --
-- BUT HOW COULD TWO SUCH DIFFERENT THINGS INTERACT WITH EACH OTHER?
HEY, BE CAREFUL, KIDDO!
SWOOSH!
SINCE THIS INTERACTION IS AT THE HEART OF LOCKE'S THEORY, THIS IS BAD NEWS INDEED.

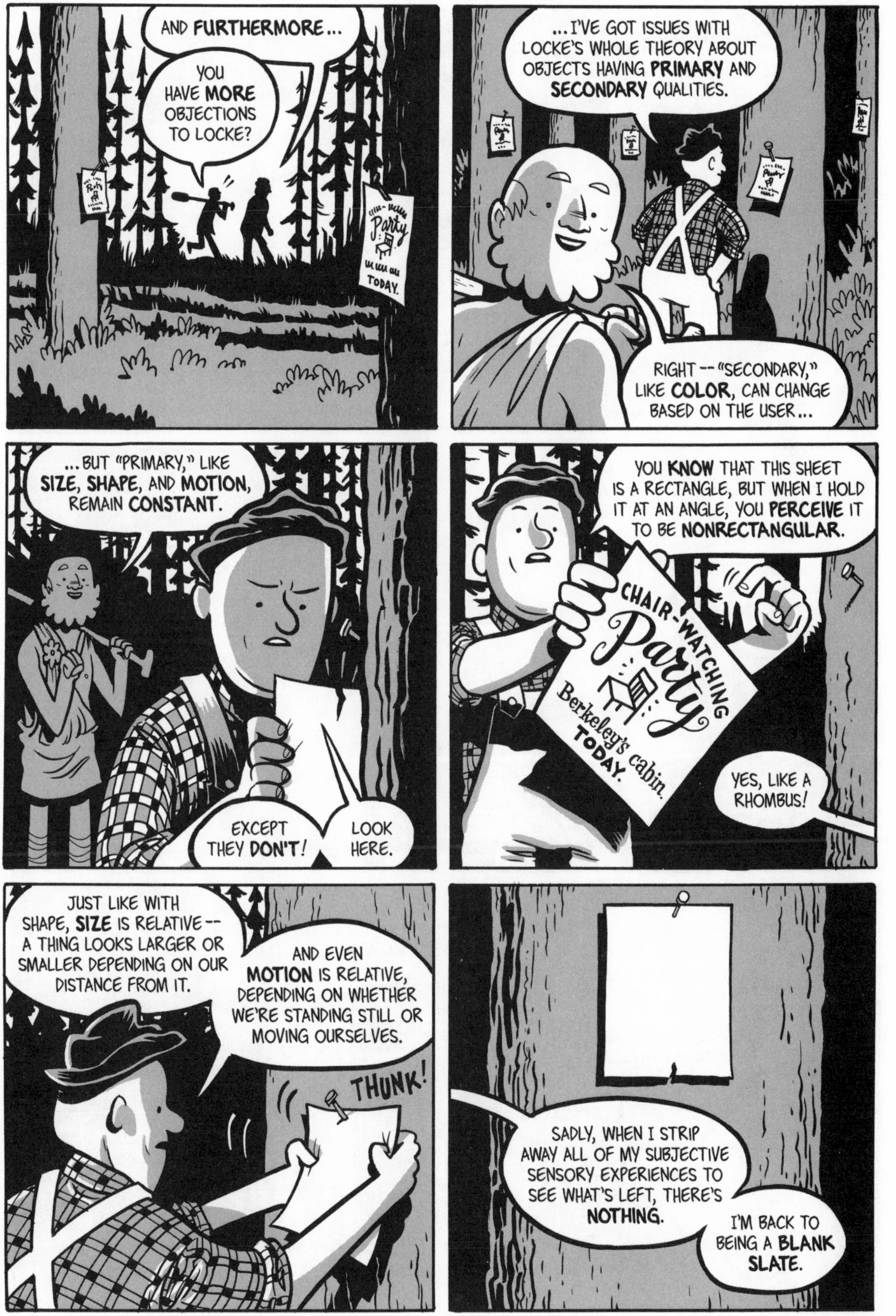
AND FURTHERMORE...
YOU HAVE MORE OBJECTIONS TO LOCKE?
Party
TODAY.
...I'VE GOT ISSUES WITH LOCKE'S WHOLE THEORY ABOUT OBJECTS HAVING PRIMARY AND SECONDARY QUALITIES.
RIGHT -- "SECONDARY," LIKE COLOR, CAN CHANGE BASED ON THE USER...
...BUT "PRIMARY," LIKE SIZE, SHAPE, AND MOTION, REMAIN CONSTANT.
EXCEPT THEY DON'T!
LOOK HERE.
YOU KNOW THAT THIS SHEET IS A RECTANGLE, BUT WHEN I HOLD IT AT AN ANGLE, YOU PERCEIVE IT TO BE NONRECTANGULAR.
CHAIR-WATCHING Party
Berkeley's cabin.
TODAY.
YES, LIKE A RHOMBUS!
JUST LIKE WITH SHAPE, SIZE IS RELATIVE -- A THING LOOKS LARGER OR SMALLER DEPENDING ON OUR DISTANCE FROM IT.
AND EVEN MOTION IS RELATIVE, DEPENDING ON WHETHER WE'RE STANDING STILL OR MOVING OURSELVES.
THUNK!
SADLY, WHEN I STRIP AWAY ALL OF MY SUBJECTIVE SENSORY EXPERIENCES TO SEE WHAT'S LEFT, THERE'S NOTHING.
I'M BACK TO BEING A BLANK SLATE.

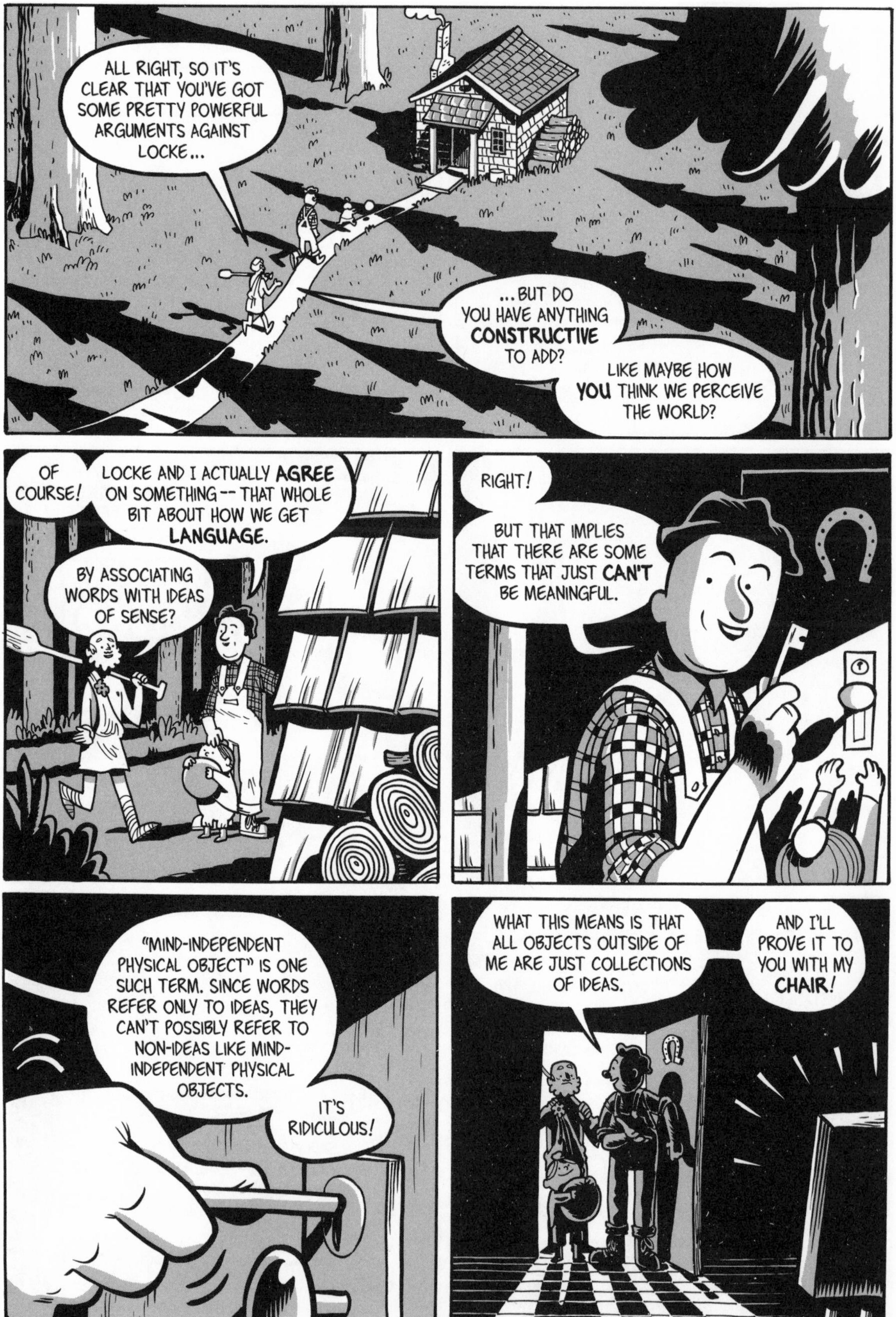
ALL RIGHT, SO IT'S CLEAR THAT YOU'VE GOT SOME PRETTY POWERFUL ARGUMENTS AGAINST LOCKE...
...BUT DO YOU HAVE ANYTHING **CONSTRUCTIVE** TO ADD?
LIKE MAYBE HOW **YOU** THINK WE PERCEIVE THE WORLD?
OF COURSE!
LOCKE AND I ACTUALLY **AGREE** ON SOMETHING -- THAT WHOLE BIT ABOUT HOW WE GET **LANGUAGE**.
BY ASSOCIATING WORDS WITH IDEAS OF SENSE?
RIGHT!
BUT THAT IMPLIES THAT THERE ARE SOME TERMS THAT JUST **CAN'T** BE MEANINGFUL.
"MIND-INDEPENDENT PHYSICAL OBJECT" IS ONE SUCH TERM. SINCE WORDS REFER ONLY TO IDEAS, THEY CAN'T POSSIBLY REFER TO NON-IDEAS LIKE MIND-INDEPENDENT PHYSICAL OBJECTS.
IT'S RIDICULOUS!
WHAT THIS MEANS IS THAT ALL OBJECTS OUTSIDE OF ME ARE JUST COLLECTIONS OF IDEAS.
AND I'LL PROVE IT TO YOU WITH MY **CHAIR**!

GO AHEAD, SIT DOWN.

THIS CHAIR DOES NOT EXIST AS A LOCKEAN OBJECT, BUT IS MERELY A COLLECTION OF IDEAS GATHERED THROUGH YOUR SENSES.

UH, ARE YOU SURE THAT --?

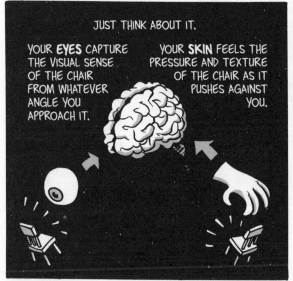

JUST THINK ABOUT IT.

YOUR **EYES** CAPTURE THE VISUAL SENSE OF THE CHAIR FROM WHATEVER ANGLE YOU APPROACH IT.

YOUR **SKIN** FEELS THE PRESSURE AND TEXTURE OF THE CHAIR AS IT PUSHES AGAINST YOU.

HEY, UH, WE'RE HERE FOR THE CHAIR-WATCHING PARTY?

KNOCK KNOC

YEP, JUST A MINUTE!

BERKELEY, YOU'RE SAYING THAT THIS CHAIR IS JUST A BUNCH OF **IDEAS**?

BUT THIS CHAIR EXISTS IN THIS ROOM WHETHER I'M HERE TO OBSERVE IT OR NOT!

THAT'S WHERE YOU'RE **WRONG** AND I'LL **PROVE** IT!

COME ON IN, BOYS!

?

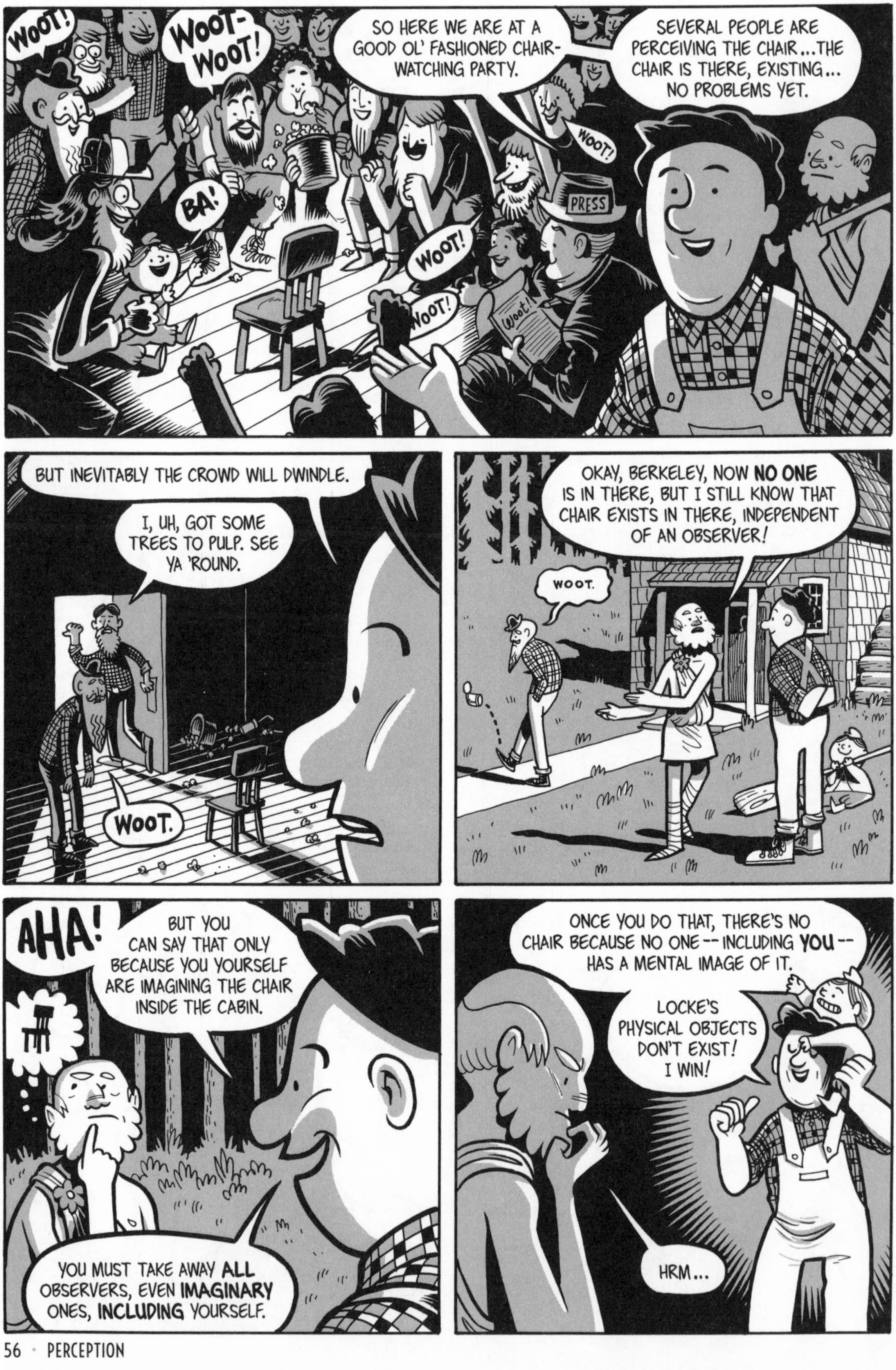
WOOT!
WOOT-WOOT!
SO HERE WE ARE AT A GOOD OL' FASHIONED CHAIR-WATCHING PARTY.
SEVERAL PEOPLE ARE PERCEIVING THE CHAIR...THE CHAIR IS THERE, EXISTING... NO PROBLEMS YET.
WOOT!
PRESS
BA!
WOOT!
WOOT!
Woot!
BUT INEVITABLY THE CROWD WILL DWINDLE.
I, UH, GOT SOME TREES TO PULP. SEE YA 'ROUND.
WOOT.
OKAY, BERKELEY, NOW **NO ONE** IS IN THERE, BUT I STILL KNOW THAT CHAIR EXISTS IN THERE, INDEPENDENT OF AN OBSERVER!
WOOT.
AHA!
BUT YOU CAN SAY THAT ONLY BECAUSE YOU YOURSELF ARE IMAGINING THE CHAIR INSIDE THE CABIN.
YOU MUST TAKE AWAY **ALL** OBSERVERS, EVEN **IMAGINARY** ONES, **INCLUDING** YOURSELF.
ONCE YOU DO THAT, THERE'S NO CHAIR BECAUSE NO ONE -- INCLUDING **YOU** -- HAS A MENTAL IMAGE OF IT.
LOCKE'S PHYSICAL OBJECTS DON'T EXIST! I WIN!
HRM...

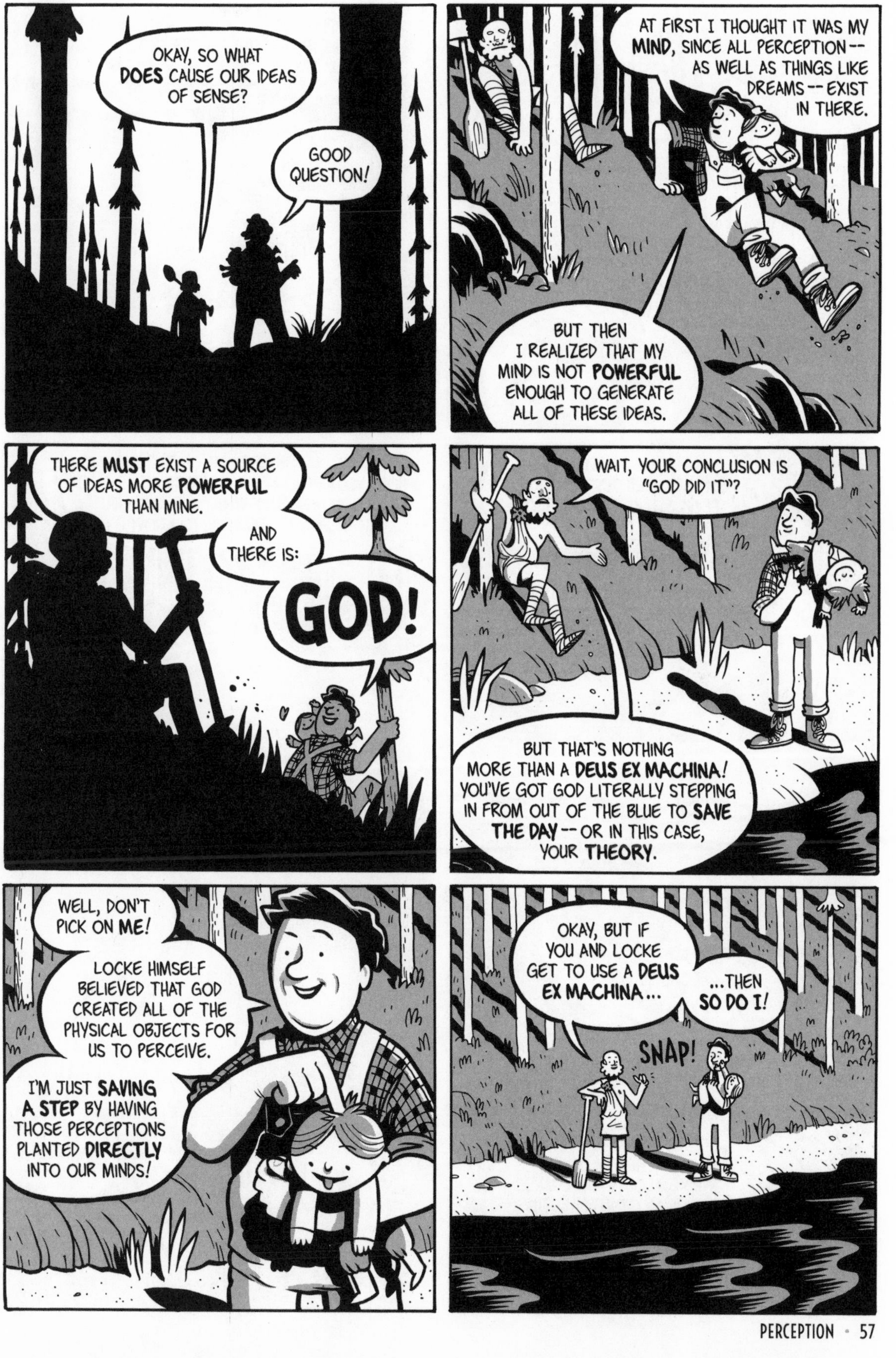
OKAY, SO WHAT **DOES** CAUSE OUR IDEAS OF SENSE?
GOOD QUESTION!
AT FIRST I THOUGHT IT WAS MY **MIND**, SINCE ALL PERCEPTION -- AS WELL AS THINGS LIKE DREAMS -- EXIST IN THERE.
BUT THEN I REALIZED THAT MY MIND IS NOT **POWERFUL** ENOUGH TO GENERATE ALL OF THESE IDEAS.
THERE **MUST** EXIST A SOURCE OF IDEAS MORE **POWERFUL** THAN MINE.
AND THERE IS:
GOD!
WAIT, YOUR CONCLUSION IS "GOD DID IT"?
BUT THAT'S NOTHING MORE THAN A **DEUS EX MACHINA**! YOU'VE GOT GOD LITERALLY STEPPING IN FROM OUT OF THE BLUE TO **SAVE THE DAY** -- OR IN THIS CASE, YOUR **THEORY**.
WELL, DON'T PICK ON **ME**!
LOCKE HIMSELF BELIEVED THAT GOD CREATED ALL OF THE PHYSICAL OBJECTS FOR US TO PERCEIVE.
I'M JUST **SAVING A STEP** BY HAVING THOSE PERCEPTIONS PLANTED **DIRECTLY** INTO OUR MINDS!
OKAY, BUT IF YOU AND LOCKE GET TO USE A **DEUS EX MACHINA**...
...THEN **SO DO I**!
SNAP!

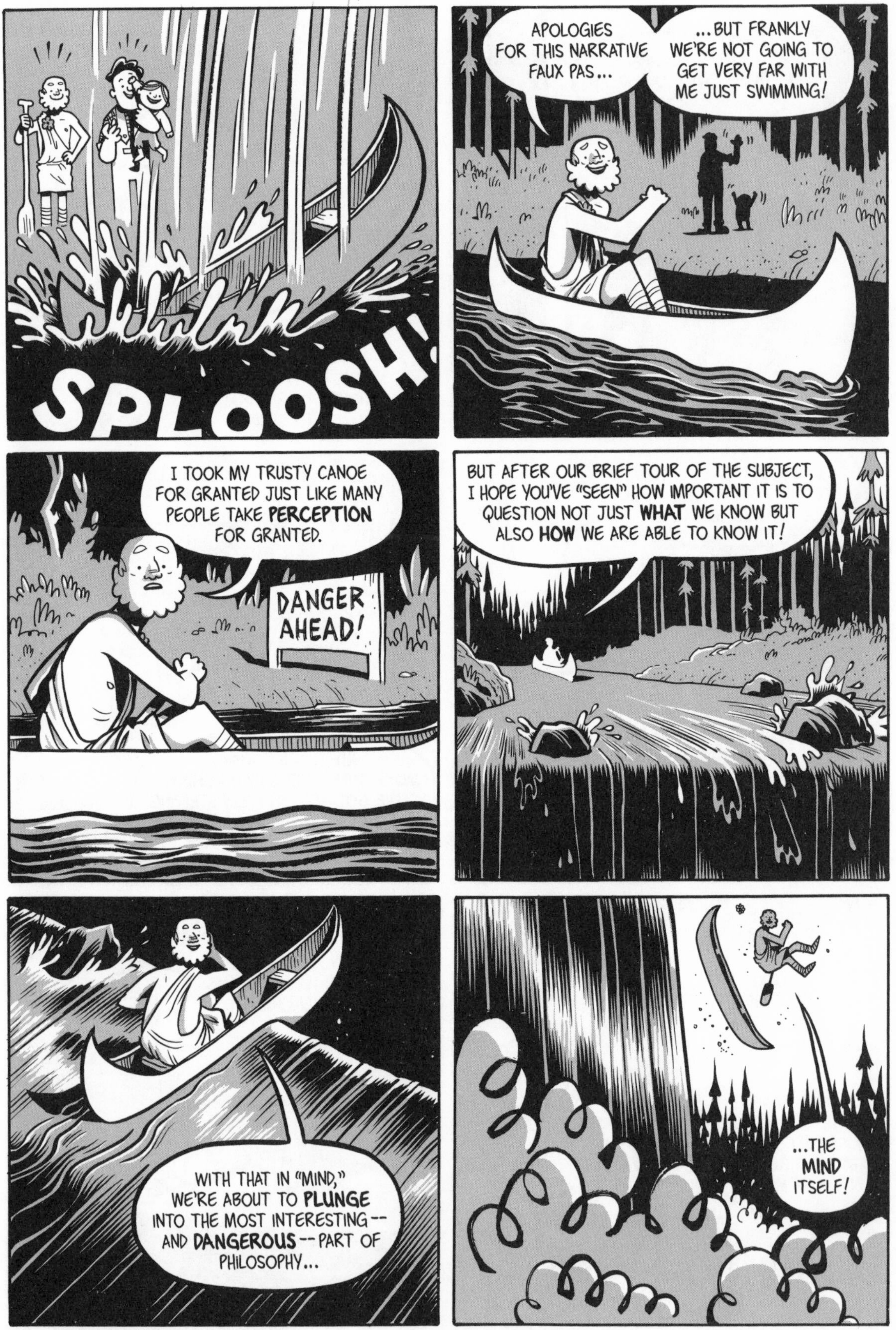
SPLOOSH!
APOLOGIES FOR THIS NARRATIVE FAUX PAS...
...BUT FRANKLY WE'RE NOT GOING TO GET VERY FAR WITH ME JUST SWIMMING!
I TOOK MY TRUSTY CANOE FOR GRANTED JUST LIKE MANY PEOPLE TAKE **PERCEPTION** FOR GRANTED.
DANGER AHEAD!
BUT AFTER OUR BRIEF TOUR OF THE SUBJECT, I HOPE YOU'VE "SEEN" HOW IMPORTANT IT IS TO QUESTION NOT JUST **WHAT** WE KNOW BUT ALSO **HOW** WE ARE ABLE TO KNOW IT!
WITH THAT IN "MIND," WE'RE ABOUT TO **PLUNGE** INTO THE MOST INTERESTING-- AND **DANGEROUS**--PART OF PHILOSOPHY...
...THE **MIND** ITSELF!

chapter 3
MINDS

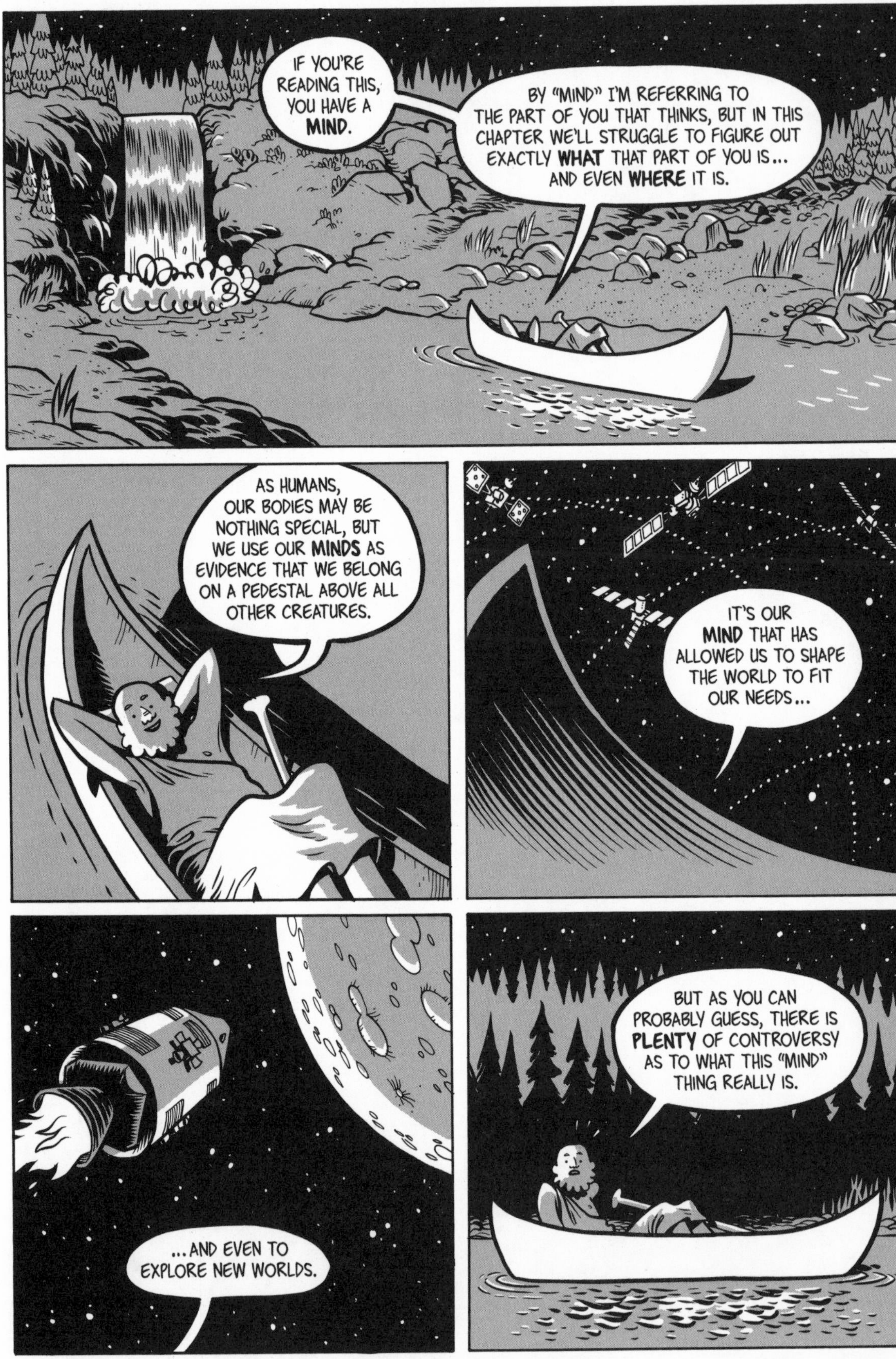
IF YOU'RE READING THIS, YOU HAVE A **MIND**.
BY "MIND" I'M REFERRING TO THE PART OF YOU THAT THINKS, BUT IN THIS CHAPTER WE'LL STRUGGLE TO FIGURE OUT EXACTLY **WHAT** THAT PART OF YOU IS... AND EVEN **WHERE** IT IS.
AS HUMANS, OUR BODIES MAY BE NOTHING SPECIAL, BUT WE USE OUR **MINDS** AS EVIDENCE THAT WE BELONG ON A PEDESTAL ABOVE ALL OTHER CREATURES.
IT'S OUR **MIND** THAT HAS ALLOWED US TO SHAPE THE WORLD TO FIT OUR NEEDS...
...AND EVEN TO EXPLORE NEW WORLDS.
BUT AS YOU CAN PROBABLY GUESS, THERE IS **PLENTY** OF CONTROVERSY AS TO WHAT THIS "MIND" THING REALLY IS.

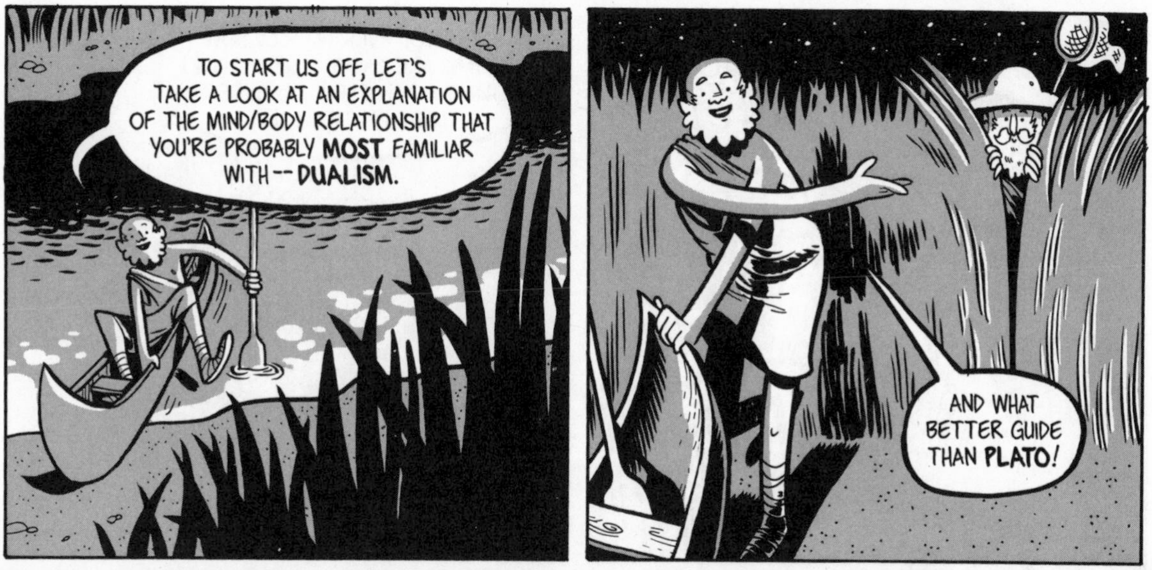
TO START US OFF, LET'S TAKE A LOOK AT AN EXPLANATION OF THE MIND/BODY RELATIONSHIP THAT YOU'RE PROBABLY **MOST** FAMILIAR WITH -- **DUALISM.**
AND WHAT BETTER GUIDE THAN **PLATO!**

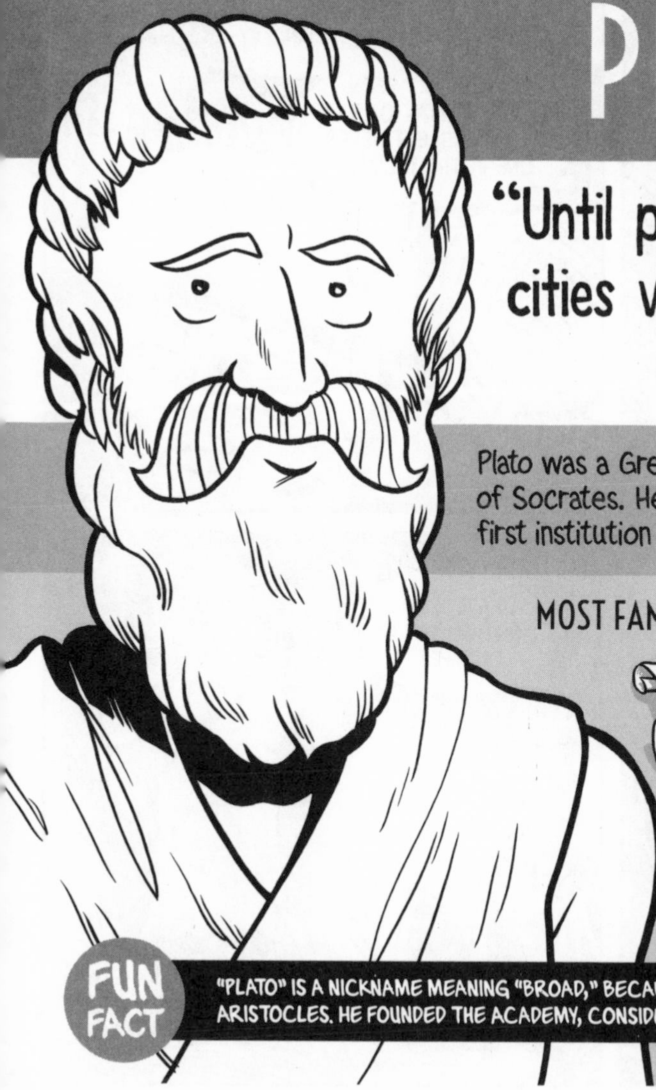

PLATO

b. 428
d. 347
B.C.E.

"Until philosophers are kings... cities will have no rest from their evils."

-- *Republic*

Plato was a Greek philosopher, mathematician, and student of Socrates. He also founded the Academy in Athens, the first institution of higher learning in the Western world.

MOST FAMOUS WORK:

REPUBLIC
360 B.C.E.

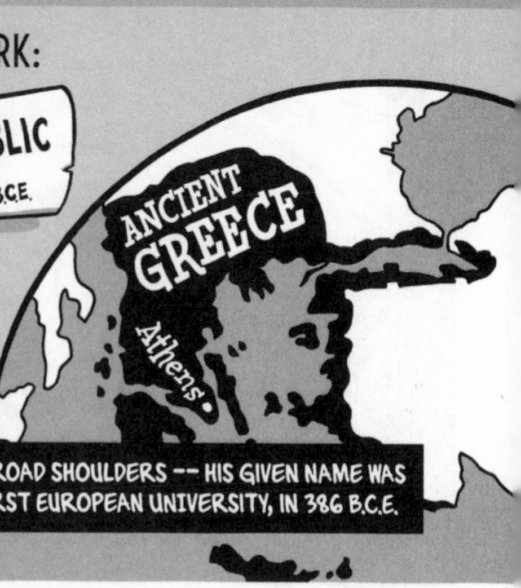
ANCIENT
GREECE
Athens

FUN FACT "PLATO" IS A NICKNAME MEANING "BROAD," BECAUSE OF HIS BROAD SHOULDERS -- HIS GIVEN NAME WAS ARISTOCLES. HE FOUNDED THE ACADEMY, CONSIDERED THE FIRST EUROPEAN UNIVERSITY, IN 386 B.C.E.

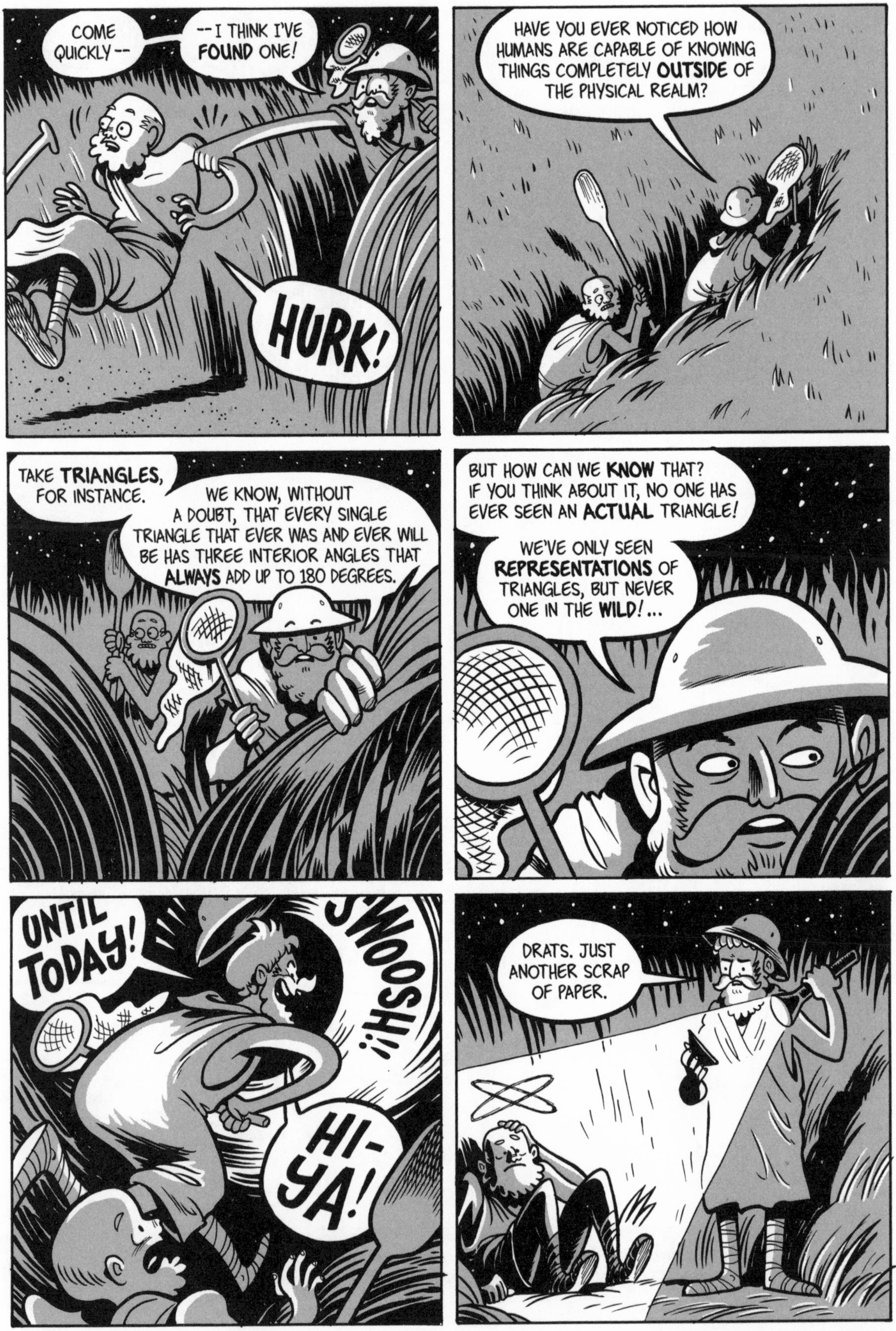
COME QUICKLY--
--I THINK I'VE FOUND ONE!
HURK!
HAVE YOU EVER NOTICED HOW HUMANS ARE CAPABLE OF KNOWING THINGS COMPLETELY OUTSIDE OF THE PHYSICAL REALM?
TAKE TRIANGLES, FOR INSTANCE.
WE KNOW, WITHOUT A DOUBT, THAT EVERY SINGLE TRIANGLE THAT EVER WAS AND EVER WILL BE HAS THREE INTERIOR ANGLES THAT ALWAYS ADD UP TO 180 DEGREES.
BUT HOW CAN WE KNOW THAT? IF YOU THINK ABOUT IT, NO ONE HAS EVER SEEN AN ACTUAL TRIANGLE!
WE'VE ONLY SEEN REPRESENTATIONS OF TRIANGLES, BUT NEVER ONE IN THE WILD!...
UNTIL TODAY!
SWOOSH!!
HI-YA!
DRATS. JUST ANOTHER SCRAP OF PAPER.

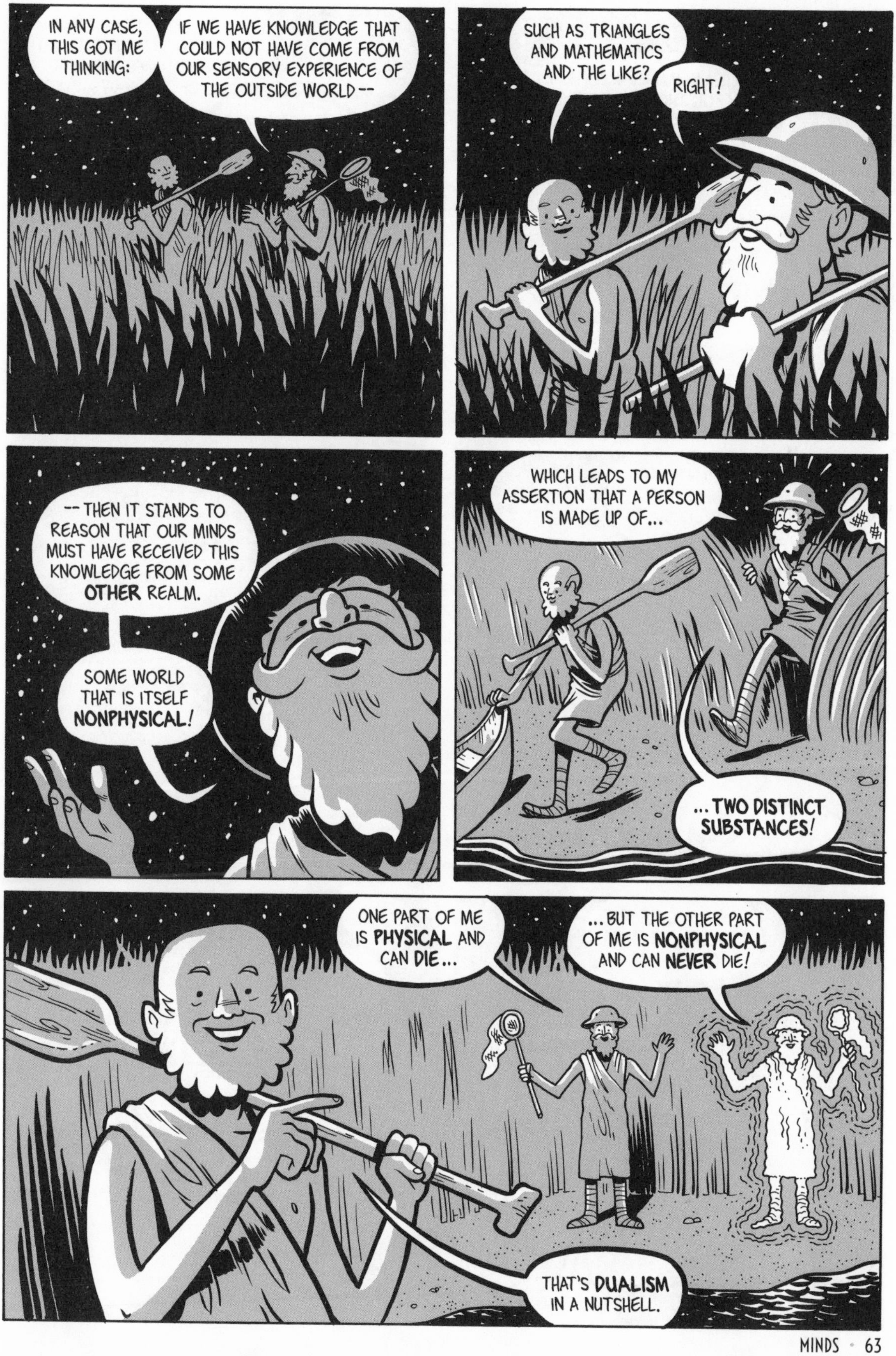
IN ANY CASE, THIS GOT ME THINKING:
IF WE HAVE KNOWLEDGE THAT COULD NOT HAVE COME FROM OUR SENSORY EXPERIENCE OF THE OUTSIDE WORLD--
SUCH AS TRIANGLES AND MATHEMATICS AND THE LIKE?
RIGHT!
--THEN IT STANDS TO REASON THAT OUR MINDS MUST HAVE RECEIVED THIS KNOWLEDGE FROM SOME **OTHER** REALM.
SOME WORLD THAT IS ITSELF **NONPHYSICAL**!
WHICH LEADS TO MY ASSERTION THAT A PERSON IS MADE UP OF...
...**TWO DISTINCT SUBSTANCES**!
ONE PART OF ME IS **PHYSICAL** AND CAN **DIE**...
...BUT THE OTHER PART OF ME IS **NONPHYSICAL** AND CAN **NEVER** DIE!
THAT'S **DUALISM** IN A NUTSHELL.

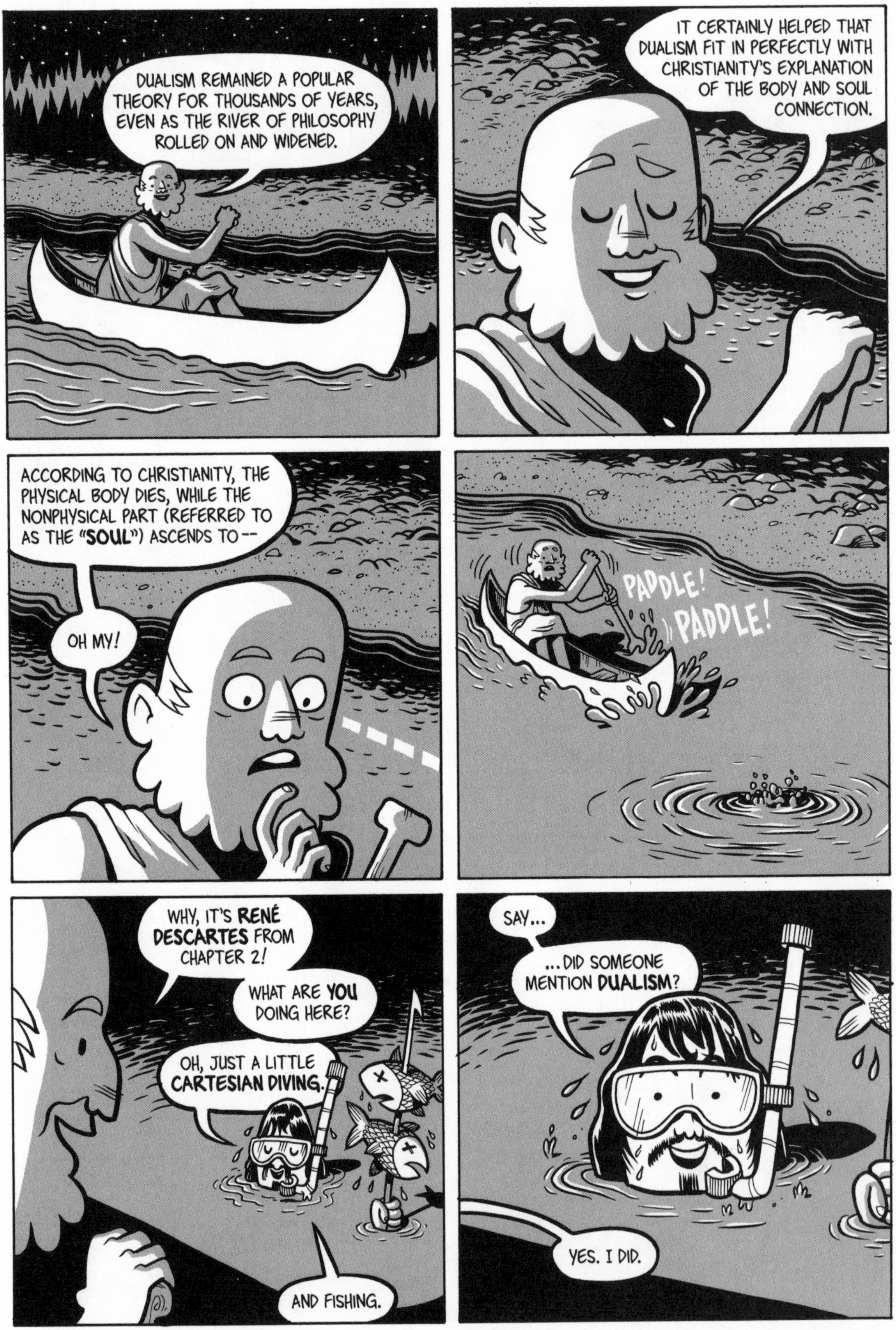
DUALISM REMAINED A POPULAR THEORY FOR THOUSANDS OF YEARS, EVEN AS THE RIVER OF PHILOSOPHY ROLLED ON AND WIDENED.
IT CERTAINLY HELPED THAT DUALISM FIT IN PERFECTLY WITH CHRISTIANITY'S EXPLANATION OF THE BODY AND SOUL CONNECTION.
ACCORDING TO CHRISTIANITY, THE PHYSICAL BODY DIES, WHILE THE NONPHYSICAL PART (REFERRED TO AS THE "SOUL") ASCENDS TO--
OH MY!
PADDLE!
PADDLE!
WHY, IT'S RENÉ DESCARTES FROM CHAPTER 2!
WHAT ARE YOU DOING HERE?
OH, JUST A LITTLE CARTESIAN DIVING.
AND FISHING.
SAY...
...DID SOMEONE MENTION DUALISM?
YES. I DID.

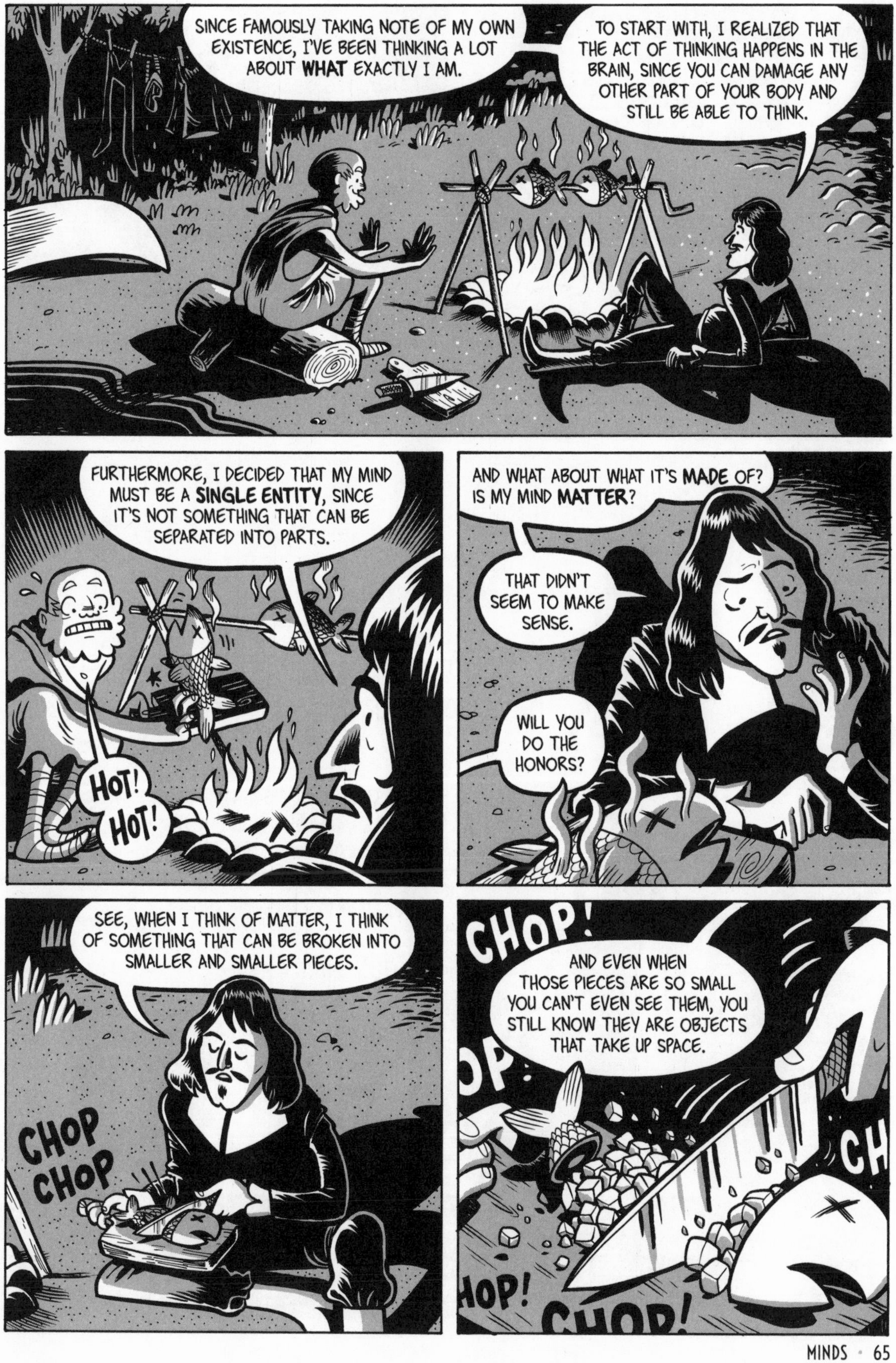
SINCE FAMOUSLY TAKING NOTE OF MY OWN EXISTENCE, I'VE BEEN THINKING A LOT ABOUT **WHAT** EXACTLY I AM.
TO START WITH, I REALIZED THAT THE ACT OF THINKING HAPPENS IN THE BRAIN, SINCE YOU CAN DAMAGE ANY OTHER PART OF YOUR BODY AND STILL BE ABLE TO THINK.
FURTHERMORE, I DECIDED THAT MY MIND MUST BE A **SINGLE ENTITY**, SINCE IT'S NOT SOMETHING THAT CAN BE SEPARATED INTO PARTS.
HOT! HOT!
AND WHAT ABOUT WHAT IT'S **MADE** OF? IS MY MIND **MATTER**?
THAT DIDN'T SEEM TO MAKE SENSE.
WILL YOU DO THE HONORS?
SEE, WHEN I THINK OF MATTER, I THINK OF SOMETHING THAT CAN BE BROKEN INTO SMALLER AND SMALLER PIECES.
CHOP CHOP
CHOP!
AND EVEN WHEN THOSE PIECES ARE SO SMALL YOU CAN'T EVEN SEE THEM, YOU STILL KNOW THEY ARE OBJECTS THAT TAKE UP SPACE.

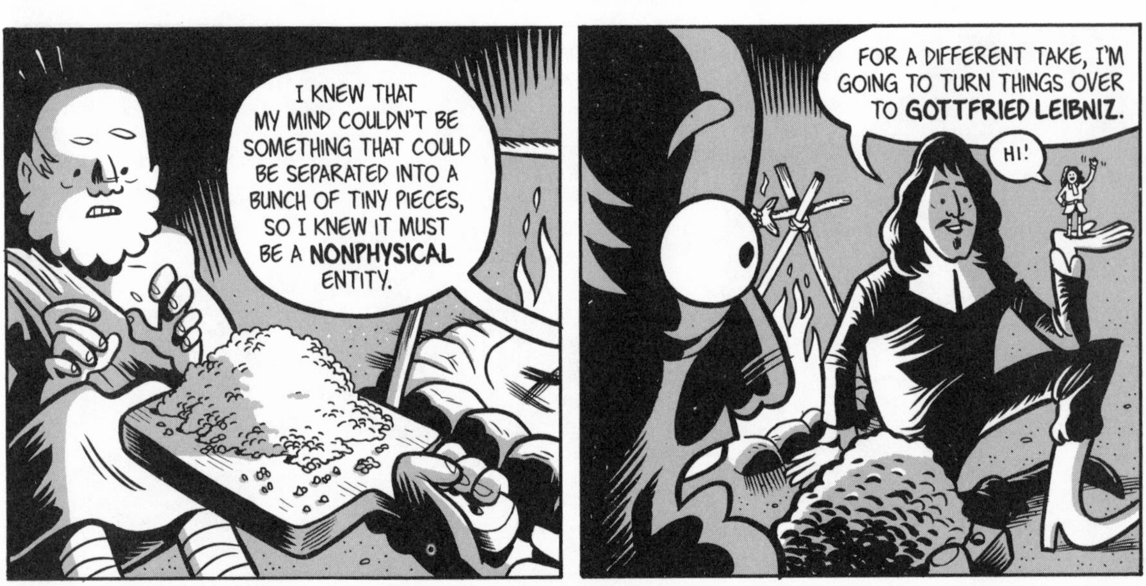
I KNEW THAT MY MIND COULDN'T BE SOMETHING THAT COULD BE SEPARATED INTO A BUNCH OF TINY PIECES, SO I KNEW IT MUST BE A **NONPHYSICAL** ENTITY.
FOR A DIFFERENT TAKE, I'M GOING TO TURN THINGS OVER TO **GOTTFRIED LEIBNIZ.**
HI!

GOTTFRIED WILHELM LEIBNIZ

b. 1646
d. 1716
C.E.

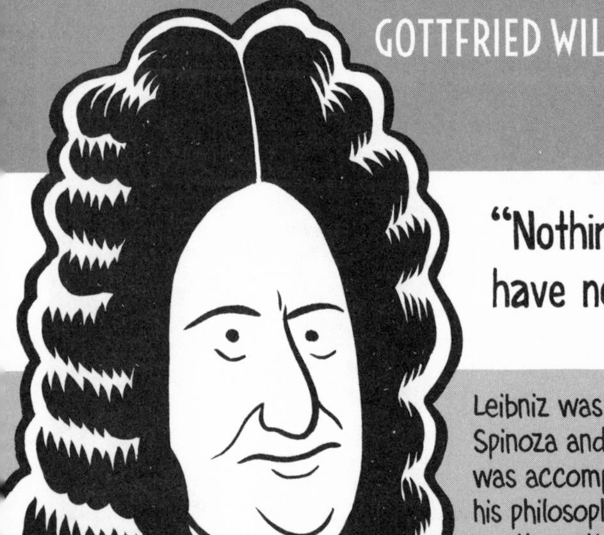

"Nothing can be taught us of which we have not already in our minds the idea."

-- *Discourse on Metaphysics*

Leibniz was one of the "big three" rationalists along with Spinoza and Descartes, and like many of his peers, he was accomplished in a number of fields. In addition to his philosophical output, he made major contributions to mathematics, logic, and mechanical computation.

MOST FAMOUS WORK:

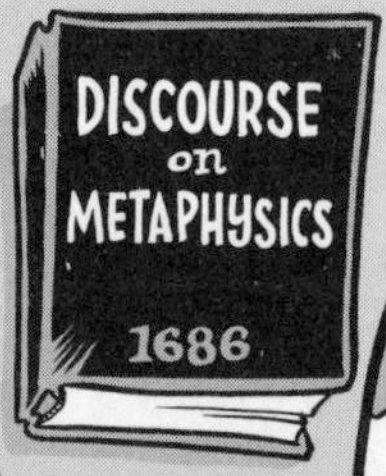
DISCOURSE
on
METAPHYSICS
1686

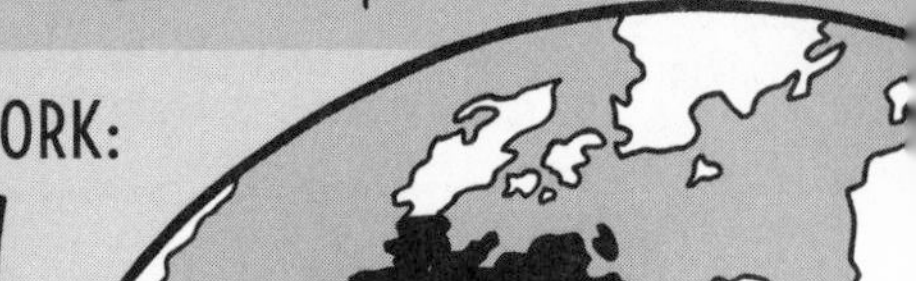
GERMANY

FUN FACT

IN ADDITION TO HIS MANY PHILOSOPHICAL CONTRIBUTIONS TO METAPHYSICS AND LOGIC, AMONG OTHER AREAS, LEIBNIZ DEVELOPED CALCULUS, AS DID ISAAC NEWTON. THOUGH LEIBNIZ PUBLISHED HIS ACCOUNT FIRST, NEWTON REACHED HIS CONCLUSIONS FIRST. A GREAT CONTROVERSY ABOUT WHO DESERVED CREDIT RAGED IN EUROPE FOR YEARS, BUT THESE DAYS THEY ARE CONSIDERED TO HAVE COME TO THE DISCOVERY INDEPENDENTLY.

WAIT -- **THAT'S** LEIBNIZ?

GUTEN TAG, HERACLITUS!

GREAT FISH, BY THE WAY.

I'M GOING TO NEED SOME EXTRA ENERGY FOR WHERE **I'M** GOING.

CHEW CHEW

AND WHERE EXACTLY ARE --

JUMP IN!

ACK!!

DESCARTES AND I MAY DISAGREE ON **PLENTY**, BUT WE DO AGREE ON THE IDEA THAT THE **BODY** AND **MIND** ARE SEPARATE, AS HE'S BEEN DESCRIBING.

BON VOYAGE!

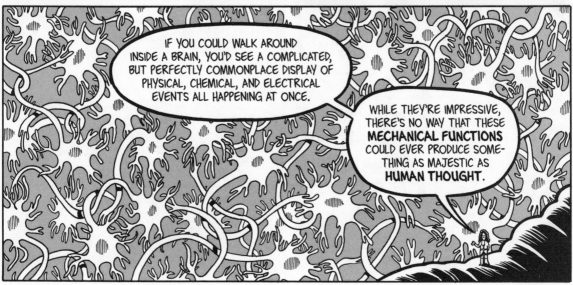

IF YOU COULD WALK AROUND INSIDE A BRAIN, YOU'D SEE A COMPLICATED, BUT PERFECTLY COMMONPLACE DISPLAY OF PHYSICAL, CHEMICAL, AND ELECTRICAL EVENTS ALL HAPPENING AT ONCE.

WHILE THEY'RE IMPRESSIVE, THERE'S NO WAY THAT THESE **MECHANICAL FUNCTIONS** COULD EVER PRODUCE SOMETHING AS MAJESTIC AS **HUMAN THOUGHT**.

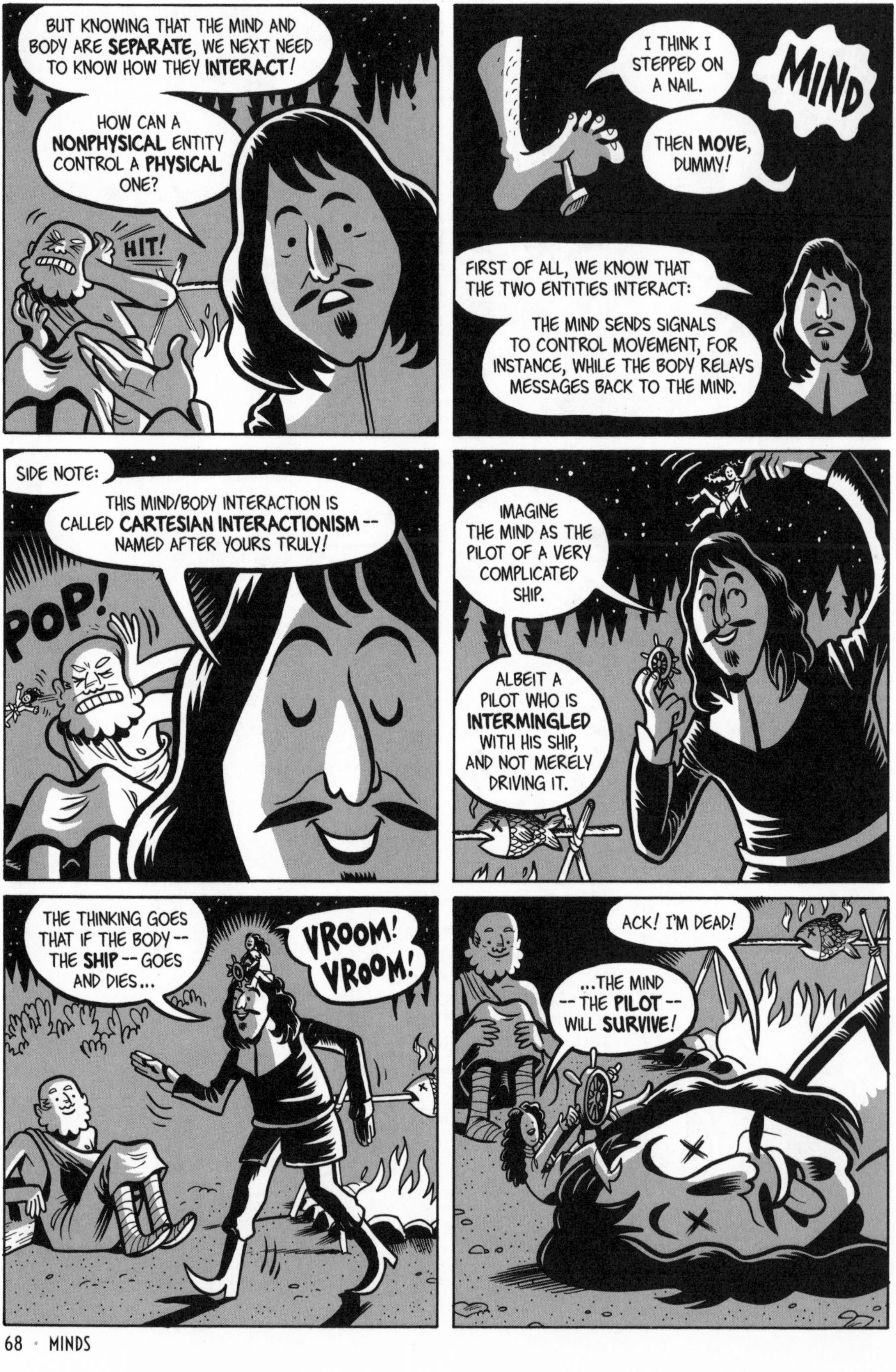
BUT KNOWING THAT THE MIND AND BODY ARE SEPARATE, WE NEXT NEED TO KNOW HOW THEY INTERACT!
HOW CAN A NONPHYSICAL ENTITY CONTROL A PHYSICAL ONE?
HIT!
I THINK I STEPPED ON A NAIL.
MIND
THEN MOVE, DUMMY!
FIRST OF ALL, WE KNOW THAT THE TWO ENTITIES INTERACT:
THE MIND SENDS SIGNALS TO CONTROL MOVEMENT, FOR INSTANCE, WHILE THE BODY RELAYS MESSAGES BACK TO THE MIND.
SIDE NOTE:
THIS MIND/BODY INTERACTION IS CALLED CARTESIAN INTERACTIONISM -- NAMED AFTER YOURS TRULY!
POP!
IMAGINE THE MIND AS THE PILOT OF A VERY COMPLICATED SHIP.
ALBEIT A PILOT WHO IS INTERMINGLED WITH HIS SHIP, AND NOT MERELY DRIVING IT.
THE THINKING GOES THAT IF THE BODY -- THE SHIP -- GOES AND DIES...
VROOM! VROOM!
ACK! I'M DEAD!
...THE MIND -- THE PILOT -- WILL SURVIVE!

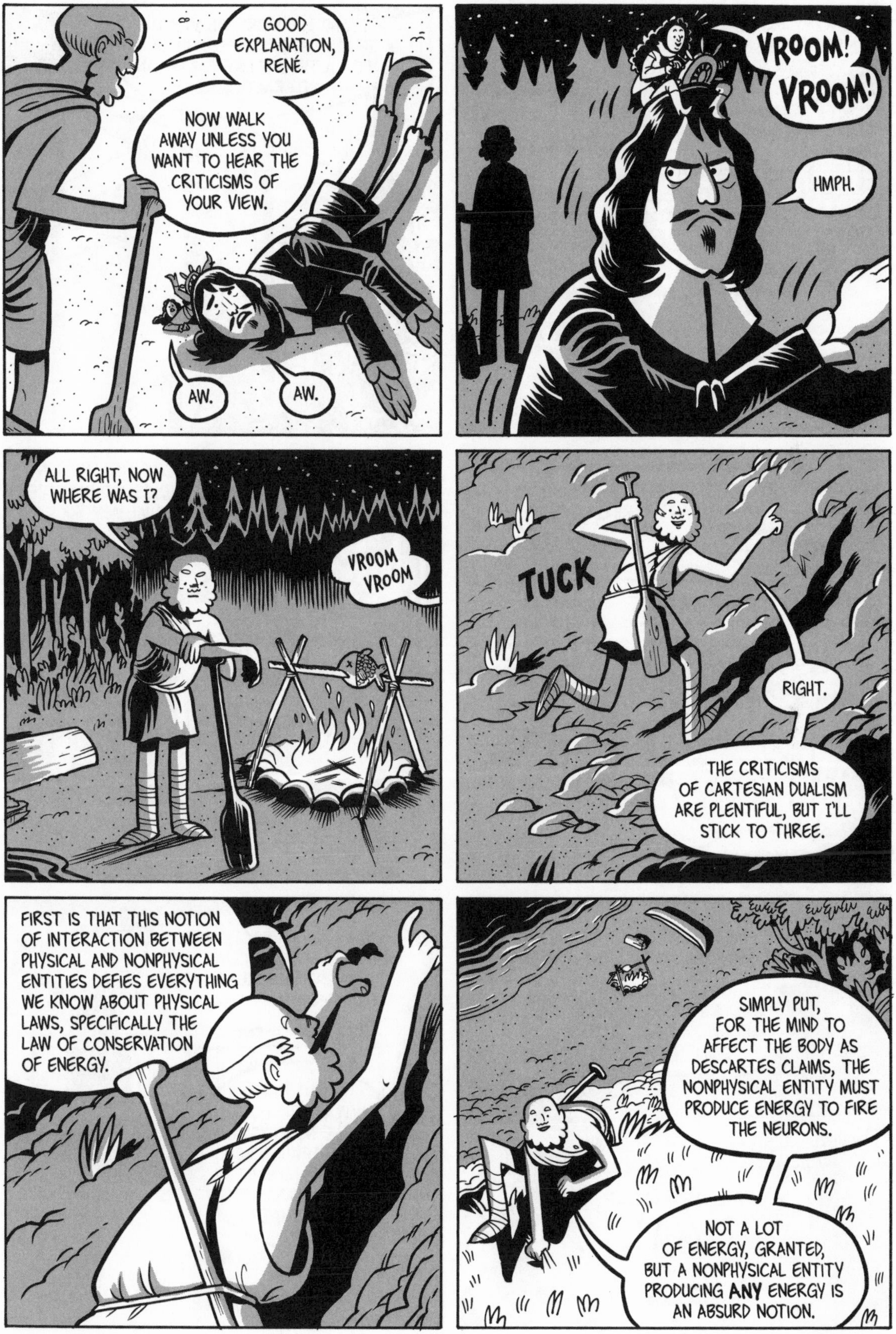

GOOD EXPLANATION, RENÉ.
NOW WALK AWAY UNLESS YOU WANT TO HEAR THE CRITICISMS OF YOUR VIEW.
AW.
AW.
VROOM! VROOM!
HMPH.
ALL RIGHT, NOW WHERE WAS I?
VROOM VROOM
TUCK
RIGHT.
THE CRITICISMS OF CARTESIAN DUALISM ARE PLENTIFUL, BUT I'LL STICK TO THREE.
FIRST IS THAT THIS NOTION OF INTERACTION BETWEEN PHYSICAL AND NONPHYSICAL ENTITIES DEFIES EVERYTHING WE KNOW ABOUT PHYSICAL LAWS, SPECIFICALLY THE LAW OF CONSERVATION OF ENERGY.
SIMPLY PUT, FOR THE MIND TO AFFECT THE BODY AS DESCARTES CLAIMS, THE NONPHYSICAL ENTITY MUST PRODUCE ENERGY TO FIRE THE NEURONS.
NOT A LOT OF ENERGY, GRANTED, BUT A NONPHYSICAL ENTITY PRODUCING **ANY** ENERGY IS AN ABSURD NOTION.

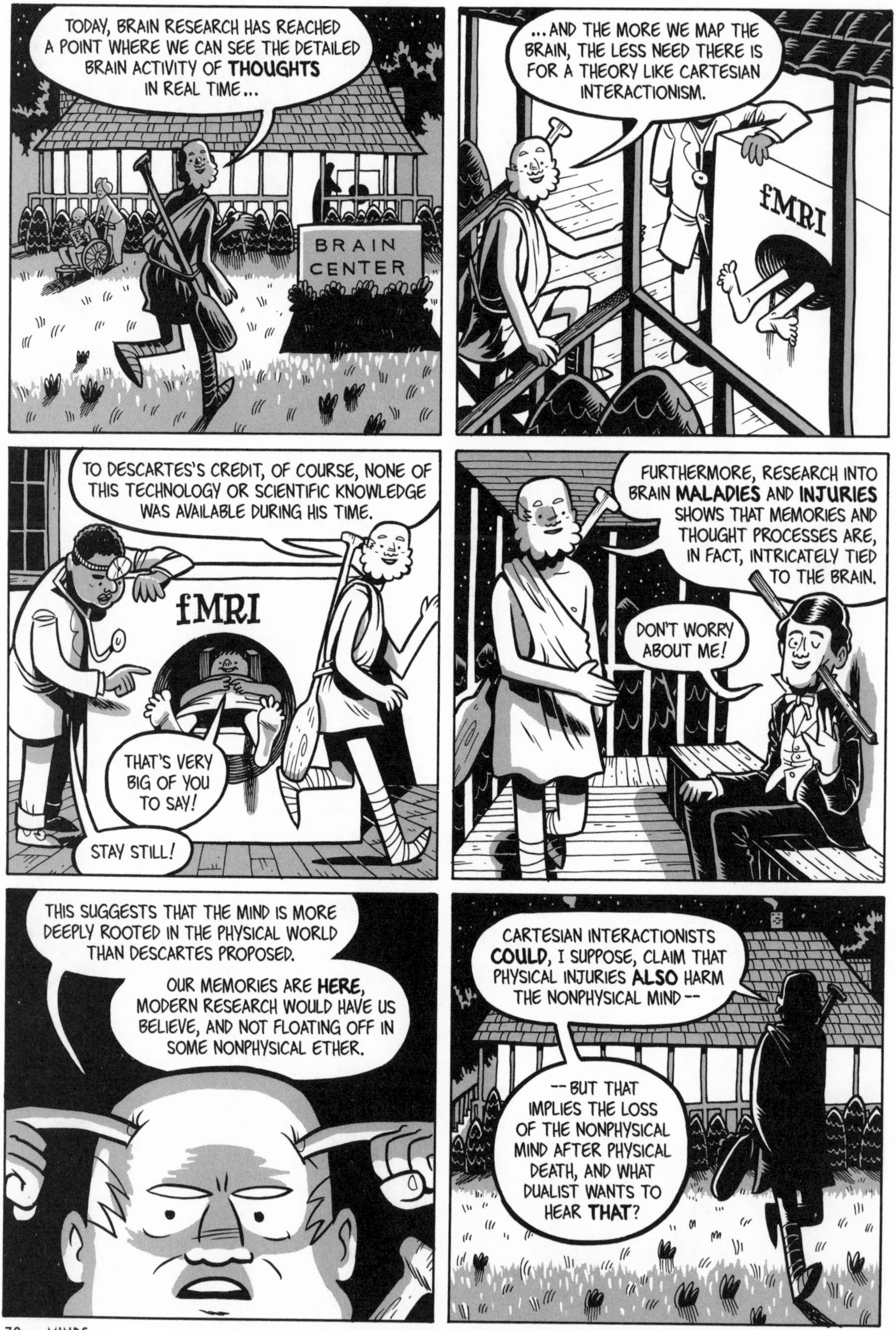
TODAY, BRAIN RESEARCH HAS REACHED A POINT WHERE WE CAN SEE THE DETAILED BRAIN ACTIVITY OF **THOUGHTS** IN REAL TIME...
BRAIN CENTER
...AND THE MORE WE MAP THE BRAIN, THE LESS NEED THERE IS FOR A THEORY LIKE CARTESIAN INTERACTIONISM.
fMRI
TO DESCARTES'S CREDIT, OF COURSE, NONE OF THIS TECHNOLOGY OR SCIENTIFIC KNOWLEDGE WAS AVAILABLE DURING HIS TIME.
fMRI
THAT'S VERY BIG OF YOU TO SAY!
STAY STILL!
FURTHERMORE, RESEARCH INTO BRAIN **MALADIES** AND **INJURIES** SHOWS THAT MEMORIES AND THOUGHT PROCESSES ARE, IN FACT, INTRICATELY TIED TO THE BRAIN.
DON'T WORRY ABOUT ME!
THIS SUGGESTS THAT THE MIND IS MORE DEEPLY ROOTED IN THE PHYSICAL WORLD THAN DESCARTES PROPOSED.
OUR MEMORIES ARE **HERE**, MODERN RESEARCH WOULD HAVE US BELIEVE, AND NOT FLOATING OFF IN SOME NONPHYSICAL ETHER.
CARTESIAN INTERACTIONISTS **COULD**, I SUPPOSE, CLAIM THAT PHYSICAL INJURIES **ALSO** HARM THE NONPHYSICAL MIND--
--BUT THAT IMPLIES THE LOSS OF THE NONPHYSICAL MIND AFTER PHYSICAL DEATH, AND WHAT DUALIST WANTS TO HEAR **THAT**?

FINALLY, OF COURSE, WE HAVE THE **LOCATION** PROBLEM.

DUALISTS CLAIM THAT THE INTERACTION BETWEEN THE PHYSICAL BODY AND THE NONPHYSICAL MIND HAPPENS SOMEWHERE IN THE BRAIN, BUT **WHERE**?

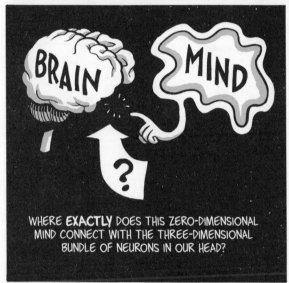

WHERE **EXACTLY** DOES THIS ZERO-DIMENSIONAL MIND CONNECT WITH THE THREE-DIMENSIONAL BUNDLE OF NEURONS IN OUR HEAD?

BUT ENOUGH PICKING ON RENÉ.

I THINK IT'S "TIME" TO GIVE LEIBNIZ THE FLOOR AGAIN.

THANK YOU, HERACLITUS.

AND THANKS FOR NOT MENTIONING THAT I'VE PUT ON A LITTLE WEIGHT SINCE THE LAST TIME WE MET.

I'M EXCITED TO ANNOUNCE THAT I'VE FOUND A **SOLUTION** TO THE PESKY PROBLEMS OF CARTESIAN INTERACTIONISM --

-- BY COMPLETELY AVOIDING IT!

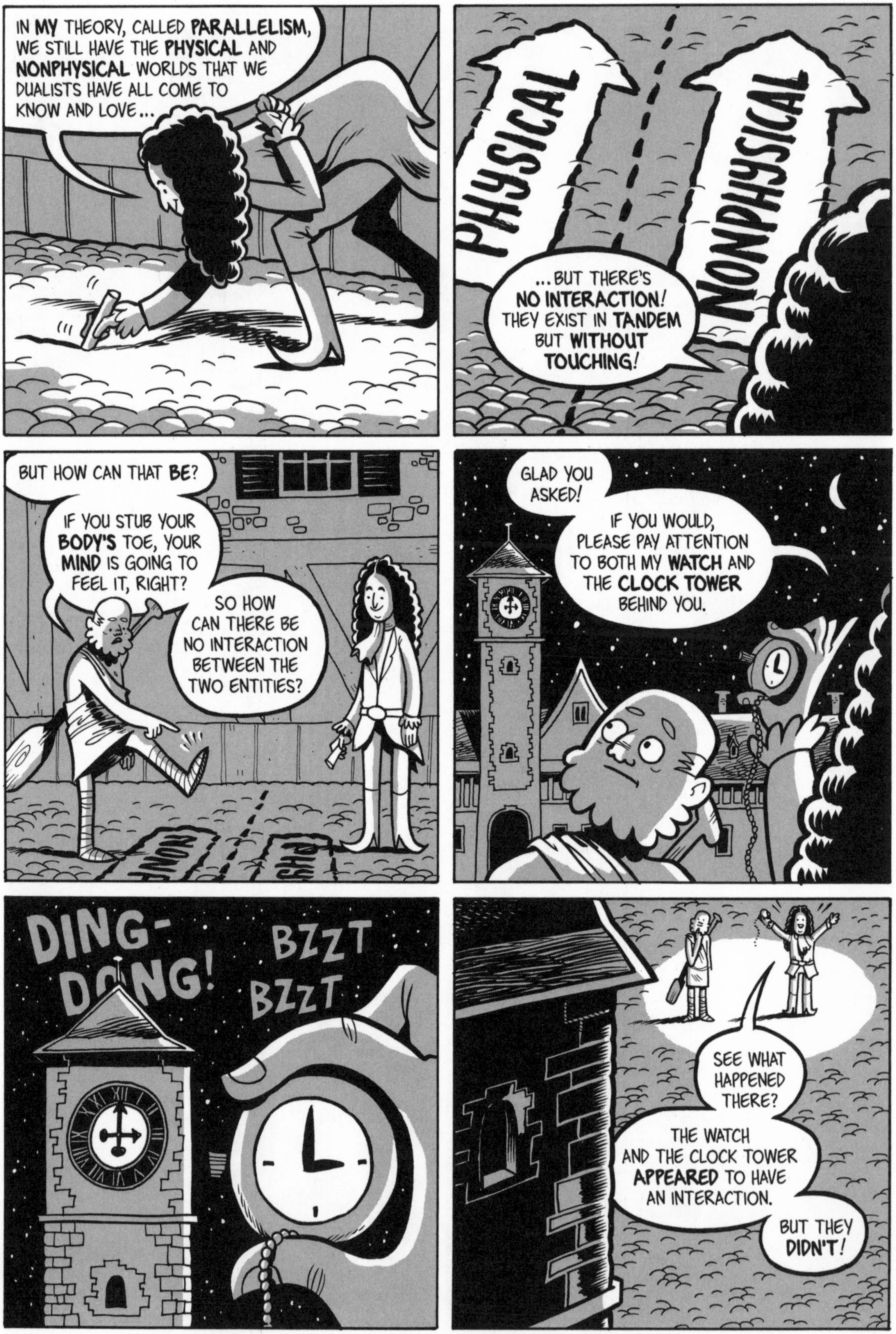
IN MY THEORY, CALLED PARALLELISM, WE STILL HAVE THE PHYSICAL AND NONPHYSICAL WORLDS THAT WE DUALISTS HAVE ALL COME TO KNOW AND LOVE...
PHYSICAL
NONPHYSICAL
...BUT THERE'S NO INTERACTION! THEY EXIST IN TANDEM BUT WITHOUT TOUCHING!
BUT HOW CAN THAT BE?
IF YOU STUB YOUR BODY'S TOE, YOUR MIND IS GOING TO FEEL IT, RIGHT?
SO HOW CAN THERE BE NO INTERACTION BETWEEN THE TWO ENTITIES?
GLAD YOU ASKED!
IF YOU WOULD, PLEASE PAY ATTENTION TO BOTH MY WATCH AND THE CLOCK TOWER BEHIND YOU.
DING-DONG!
BZZT BZZT
SEE WHAT HAPPENED THERE?
THE WATCH AND THE CLOCK TOWER APPEARED TO HAVE AN INTERACTION.
BUT THEY DIDN'T!

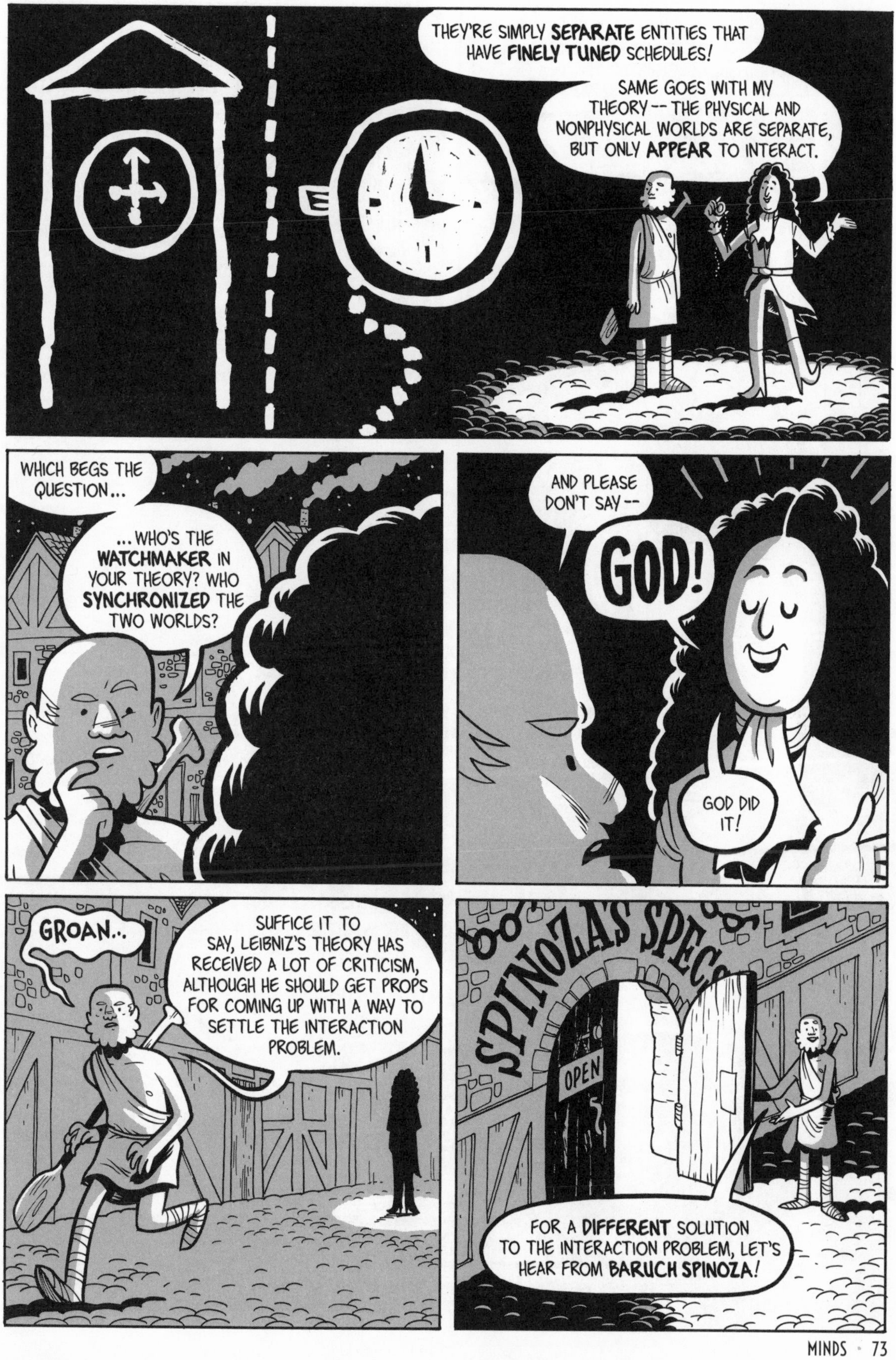
THEY'RE SIMPLY SEPARATE ENTITIES THAT HAVE FINELY TUNED SCHEDULES!
SAME GOES WITH MY THEORY -- THE PHYSICAL AND NONPHYSICAL WORLDS ARE SEPARATE, BUT ONLY APPEAR TO INTERACT.
WHICH BEGS THE QUESTION...
...WHO'S THE WATCHMAKER IN YOUR THEORY? WHO SYNCHRONIZED THE TWO WORLDS?
AND PLEASE DON'T SAY --
GOD!
GOD DID IT!
GROAN...
SUFFICE IT TO SAY, LEIBNIZ'S THEORY HAS RECEIVED A LOT OF CRITICISM, ALTHOUGH HE SHOULD GET PROPS FOR COMING UP WITH A WAY TO SETTLE THE INTERACTION PROBLEM.
SPINOZA'S SPEC
OPEN
FOR A DIFFERENT SOLUTION TO THE INTERACTION PROBLEM, LET'S HEAR FROM BARUCH SPINOZA!

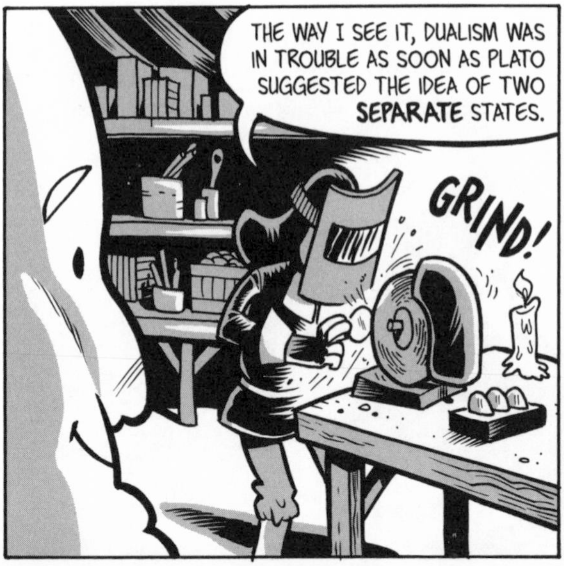
THE WAY I SEE IT, DUALISM WAS IN TROUBLE AS SOON AS PLATO SUGGESTED THE IDEA OF TWO **SEPARATE** STATES.
GRIND!

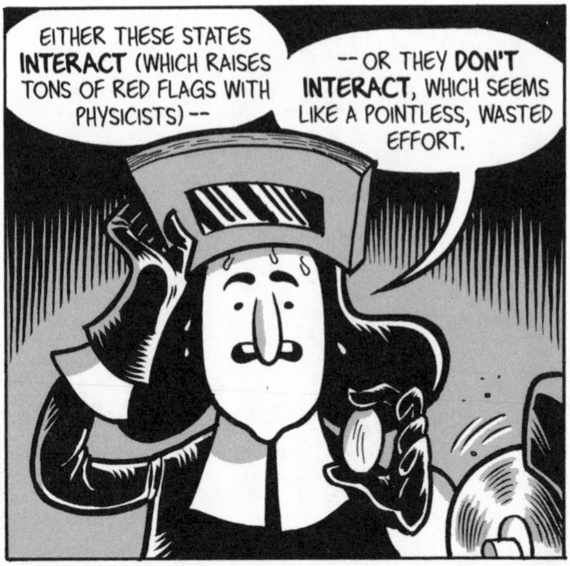
EITHER THESE STATES **INTERACT** (WHICH RAISES TONS OF RED FLAGS WITH PHYSICISTS) --
-- OR THEY **DON'T INTERACT**, WHICH SEEMS LIKE A POINTLESS, WASTED EFFORT.

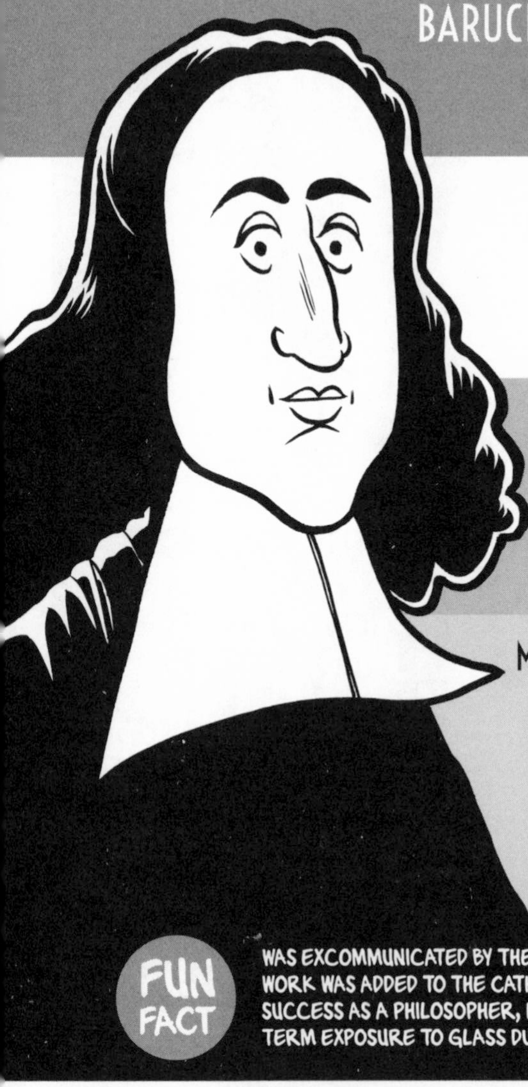

BARUCH SPINOZA

b. 1632
d. 1677
C.E.

"We feel and experience ourselves to be eternal."

-- *Ethics, Demonstrated in Geometrical Order*

Spinoza was one of the "big three" rationalists along with Leibniz and Descartes. His philosophical writings angered religious authorities by implying that the doctrine of pantheism (God is identical with the universe) is true, along with many other unorthodox conclusions.

MOST FAMOUS WORK:

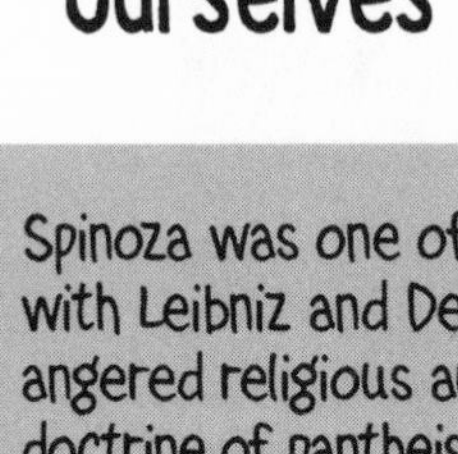
ETHICS,
DEMONSTRATED IN
GEOMETRICAL
ORDER
1665

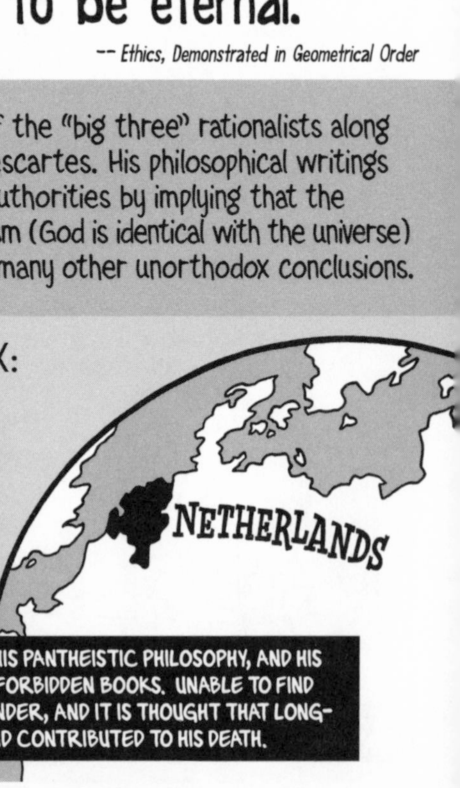
NETHERLANDS

FUN FACT

WAS EXCOMMUNICATED BY THE JEWISH COMMUNITY FOR HIS PANTHEISTIC PHILOSOPHY, AND HIS WORK WAS ADDED TO THE CATHOLIC CHURCH'S INDEX OF FORBIDDEN BOOKS. UNABLE TO FIND SUCCESS AS A PHILOSOPHER, HE WORKED AS A LENS GRINDER, AND IT IS THOUGHT THAT LONG-TERM EXPOSURE TO GLASS DUST DAMAGED HIS LUNGS AND CONTRIBUTED TO HIS DEATH.

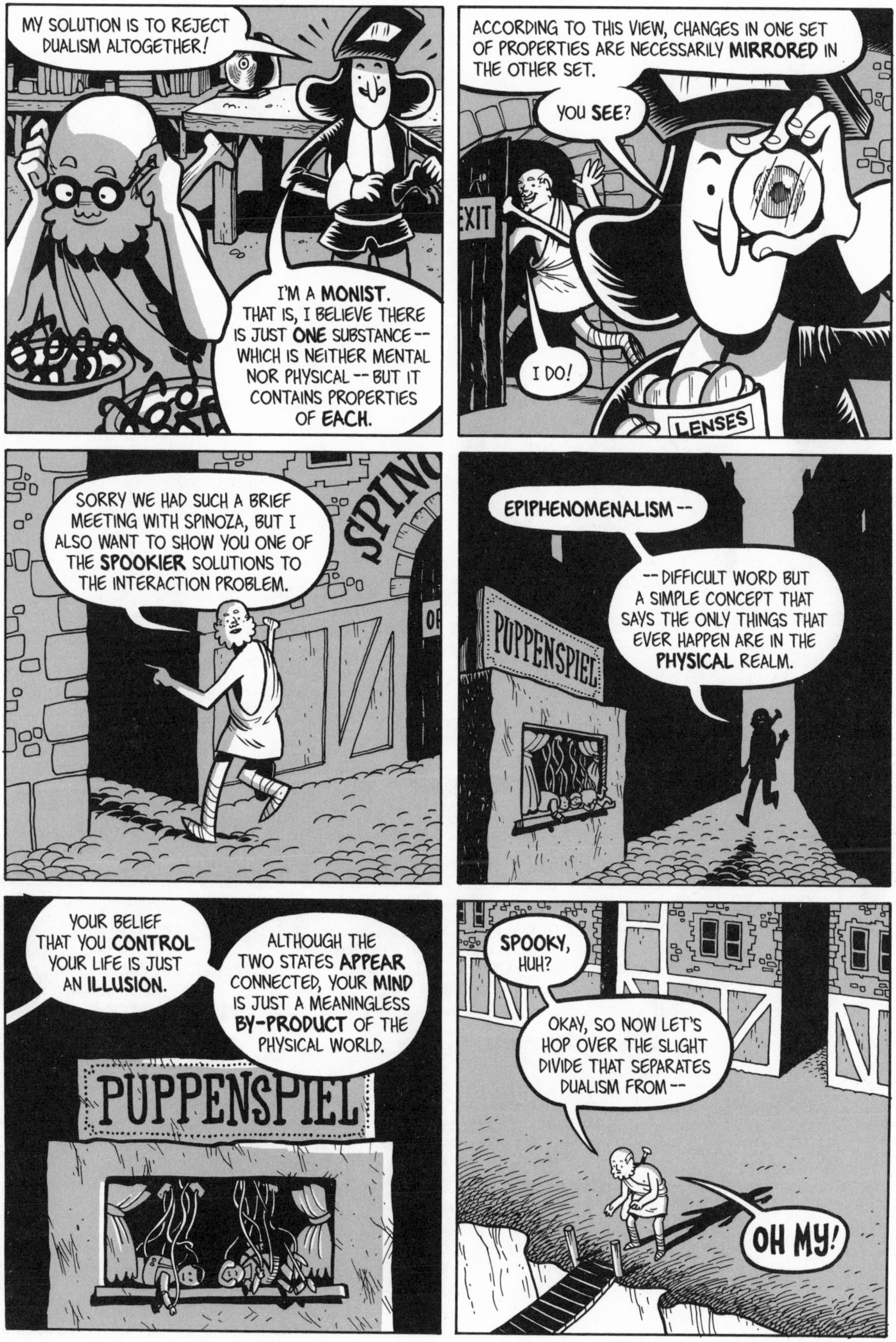

MY SOLUTION IS TO REJECT DUALISM ALTOGETHER!
I'M A MONIST. THAT IS, I BELIEVE THERE IS JUST ONE SUBSTANCE -- WHICH IS NEITHER MENTAL NOR PHYSICAL -- BUT IT CONTAINS PROPERTIES OF EACH.
ACCORDING TO THIS VIEW, CHANGES IN ONE SET OF PROPERTIES ARE NECESSARILY MIRRORED IN THE OTHER SET.
YOU SEE?
I DO!
EXIT
LENSES
SORRY WE HAD SUCH A BRIEF MEETING WITH SPINOZA, BUT I ALSO WANT TO SHOW YOU ONE OF THE SPOOKIER SOLUTIONS TO THE INTERACTION PROBLEM.
EPIPHENOMENALISM --
-- DIFFICULT WORD BUT A SIMPLE CONCEPT THAT SAYS THE ONLY THINGS THAT EVER HAPPEN ARE IN THE PHYSICAL REALM.
PUPPENSPIEL
YOUR BELIEF THAT YOU CONTROL YOUR LIFE IS JUST AN ILLUSION.
ALTHOUGH THE TWO STATES APPEAR CONNECTED, YOUR MIND IS JUST A MEANINGLESS BY-PRODUCT OF THE PHYSICAL WORLD.
PUPPENSPIEL
SPOOKY, HUH?
OKAY, SO NOW LET'S HOP OVER THE SLIGHT DIVIDE THAT SEPARATES DUALISM FROM --
OH MY!

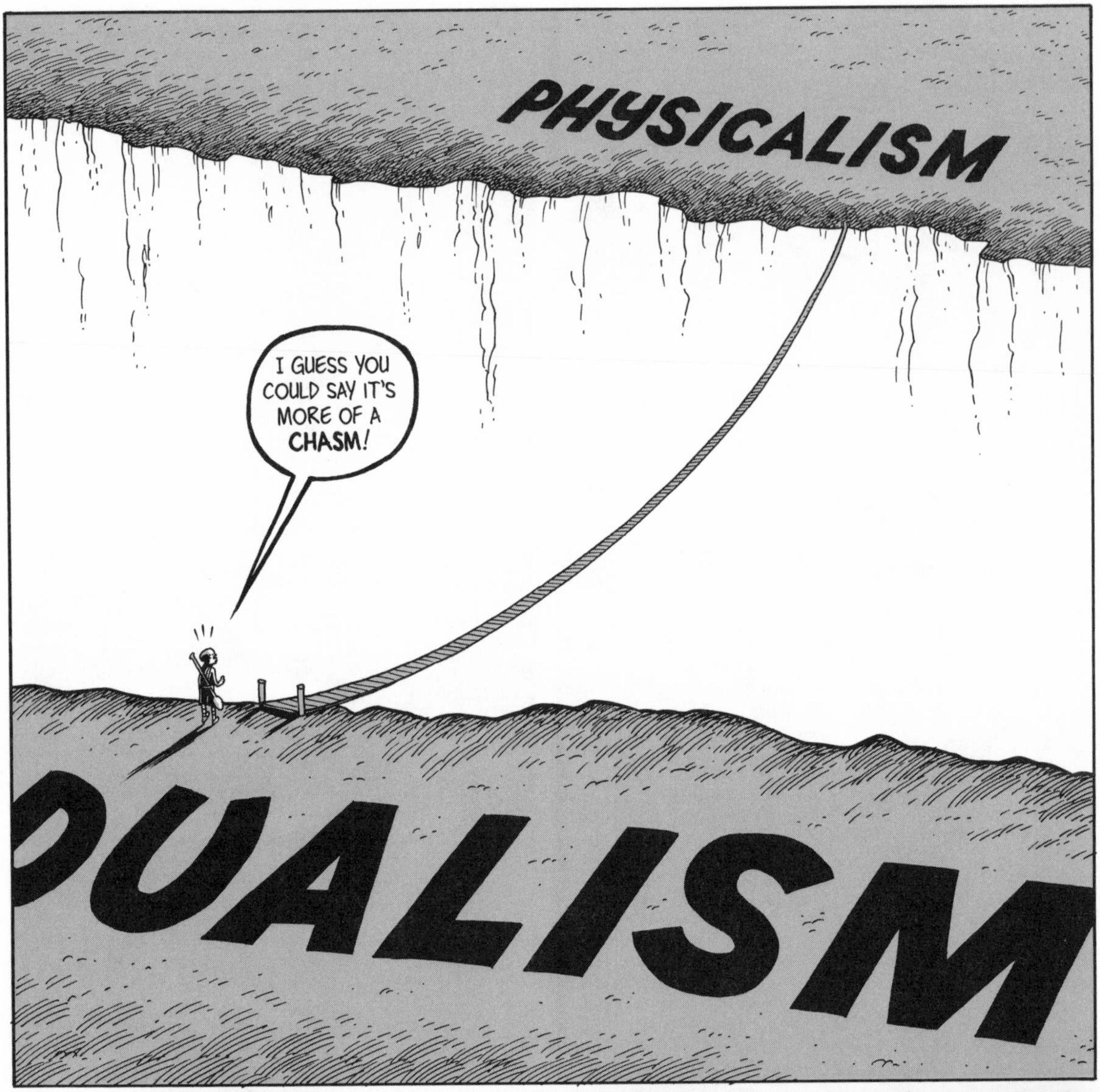
PHYSICALISM
I GUESS YOU COULD SAY IT'S MORE OF A CHASM!
DUALISM

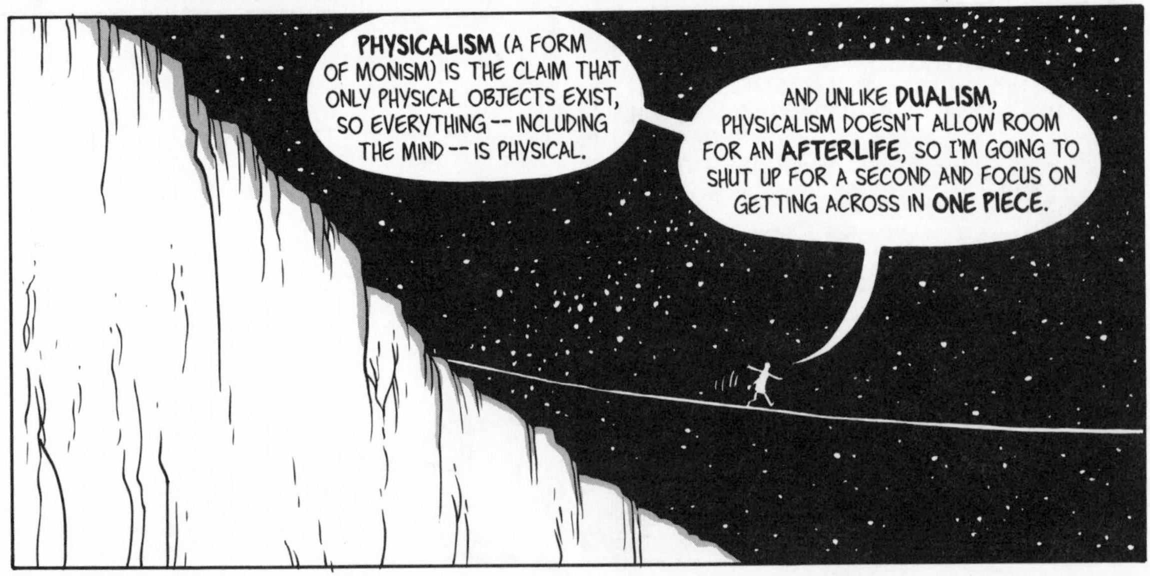
PHYSICALISM (A FORM OF MONISM) IS THE CLAIM THAT ONLY PHYSICAL OBJECTS EXIST, SO EVERYTHING -- INCLUDING THE MIND -- IS PHYSICAL.
AND UNLIKE DUALISM, PHYSICALISM DOESN'T ALLOW ROOM FOR AN AFTERLIFE, SO I'M GOING TO SHUT UP FOR A SECOND AND FOCUS ON GETTING ACROSS IN ONE PIECE.

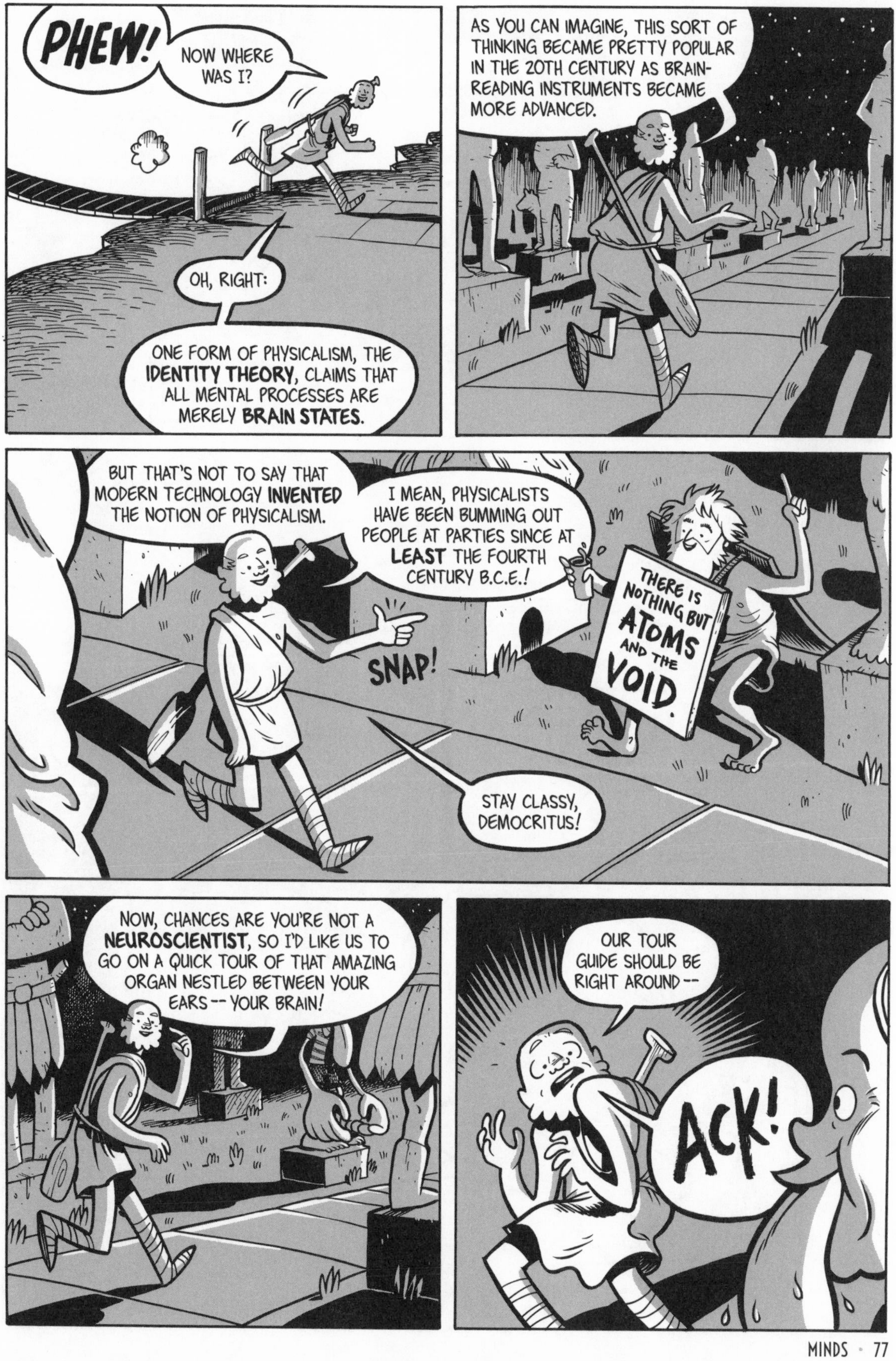
PHEW!
NOW WHERE WAS I?
OH, RIGHT:
ONE FORM OF PHYSICALISM, THE IDENTITY THEORY, CLAIMS THAT ALL MENTAL PROCESSES ARE MERELY BRAIN STATES.
AS YOU CAN IMAGINE, THIS SORT OF THINKING BECAME PRETTY POPULAR IN THE 20TH CENTURY AS BRAIN-READING INSTRUMENTS BECAME MORE ADVANCED.
BUT THAT'S NOT TO SAY THAT MODERN TECHNOLOGY INVENTED THE NOTION OF PHYSICALISM.
I MEAN, PHYSICALISTS HAVE BEEN BUMMING OUT PEOPLE AT PARTIES SINCE AT LEAST THE FOURTH CENTURY B.C.E.!
THERE IS NOTHING BUT ATOMS AND THE VOID.
SNAP!
STAY CLASSY, DEMOCRITUS!
NOW, CHANCES ARE YOU'RE NOT A NEUROSCIENTIST, SO I'D LIKE US TO GO ON A QUICK TOUR OF THAT AMAZING ORGAN NESTLED BETWEEN YOUR EARS -- YOUR BRAIN!
OUR TOUR GUIDE SHOULD BE RIGHT AROUND --
ACK!

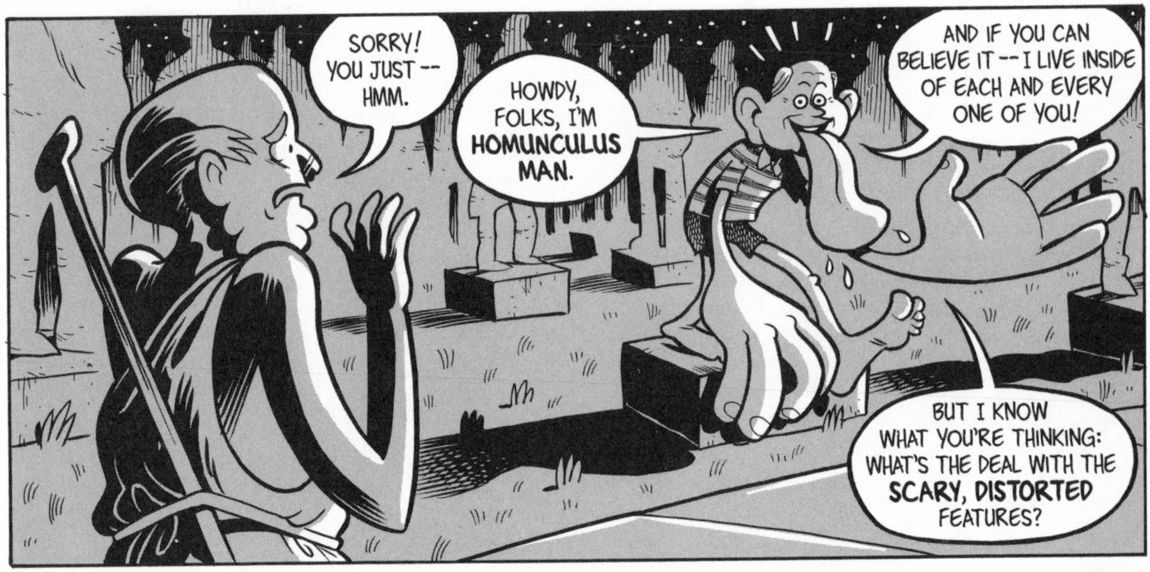
SORRY! YOU JUST -- HMM.
HOWDY, FOLKS, I'M **HOMUNCULUS MAN.**
AND IF YOU CAN BELIEVE IT -- I LIVE INSIDE OF EACH AND EVERY ONE OF YOU!
BUT I KNOW WHAT YOU'RE THINKING: WHAT'S THE DEAL WITH THE **SCARY, DISTORTED** FEATURES?

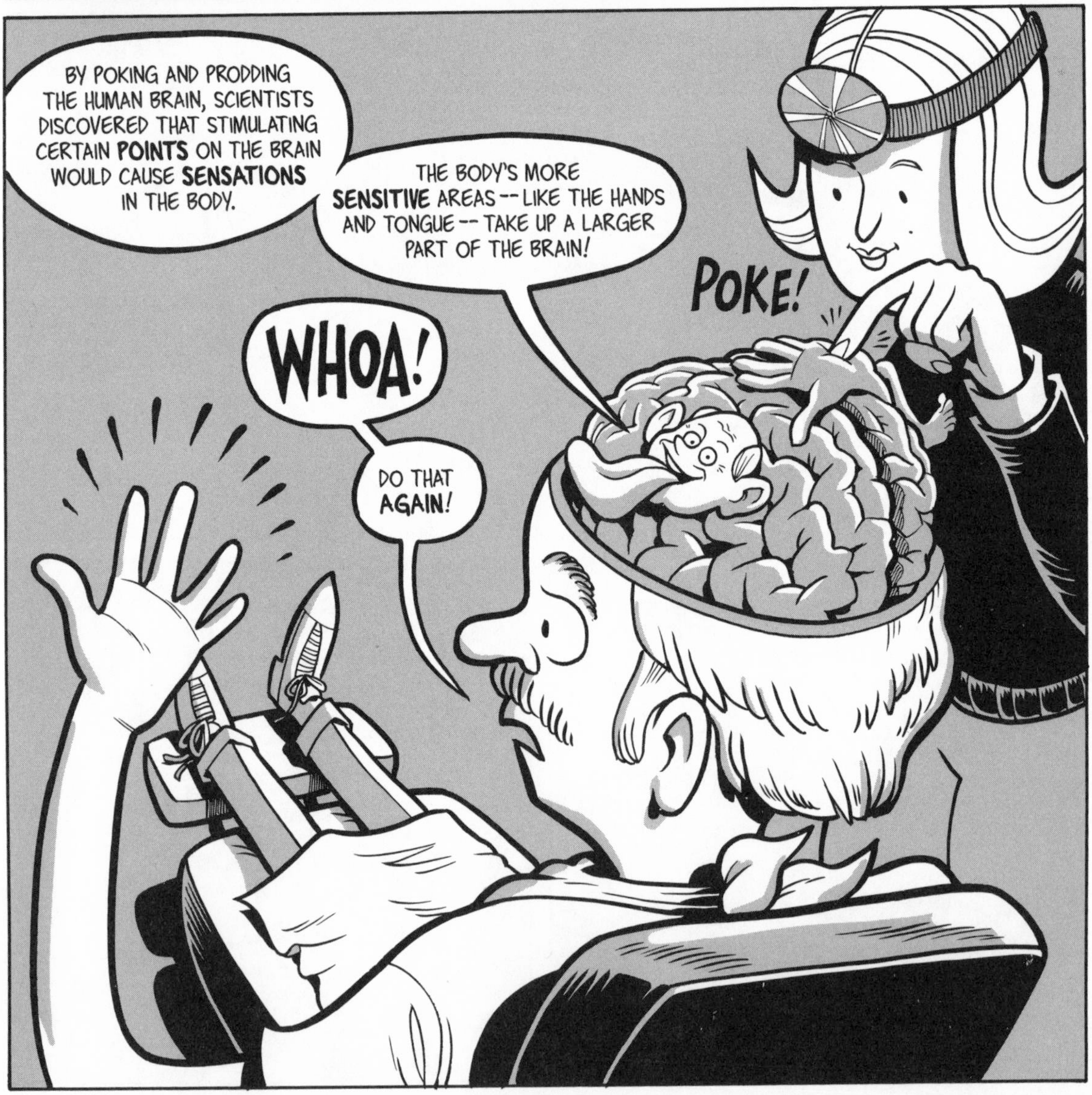
BY POKING AND PRODDING THE HUMAN BRAIN, SCIENTISTS DISCOVERED THAT STIMULATING CERTAIN **POINTS** ON THE BRAIN WOULD CAUSE **SENSATIONS** IN THE BODY.
THE BODY'S MORE **SENSITIVE** AREAS -- LIKE THE HANDS AND TONGUE -- TAKE UP A LARGER PART OF THE BRAIN!
POKE!
WHOA!
DO THAT **AGAIN**!

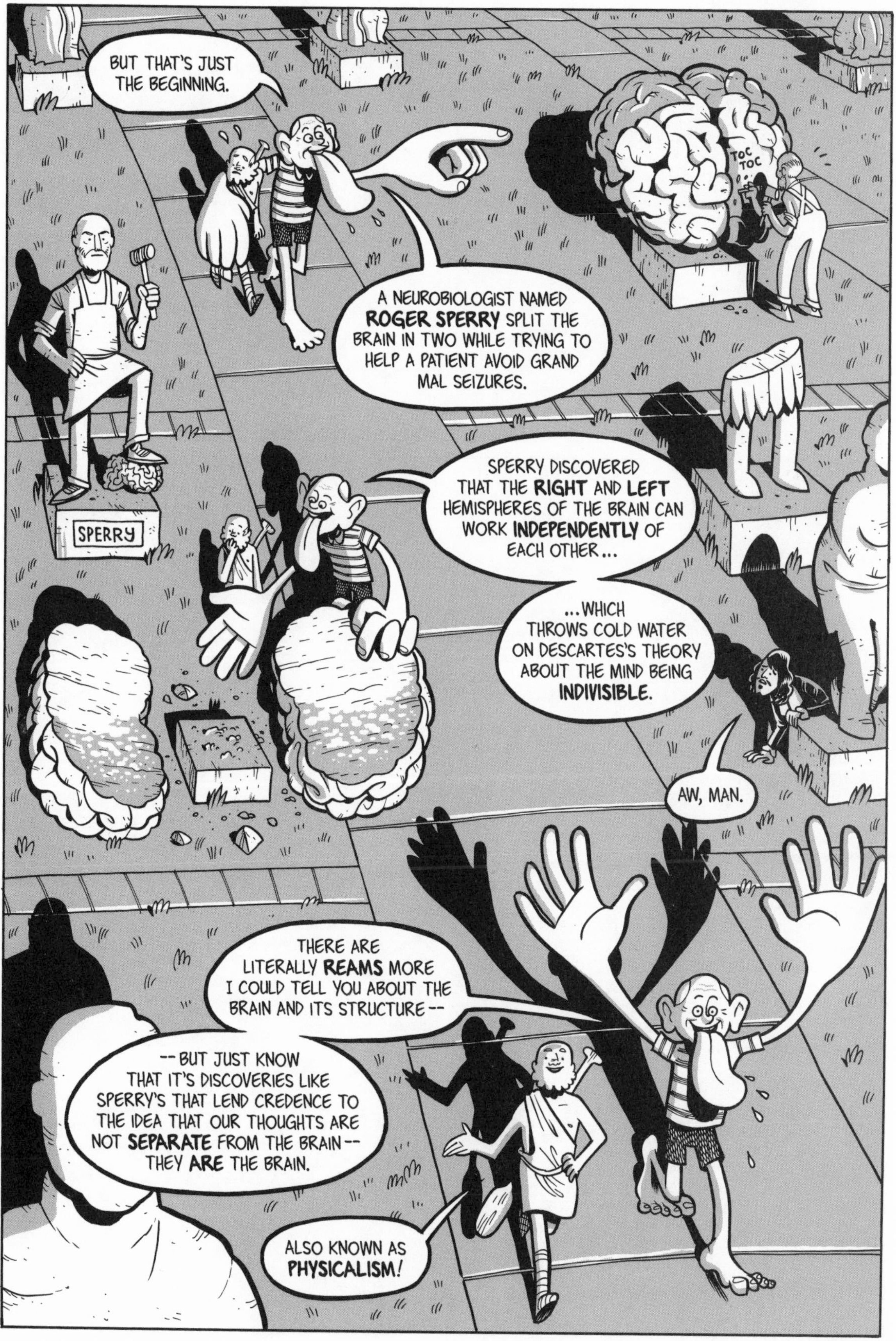
BUT THAT'S JUST THE BEGINNING.
TOC TOC
A NEUROBIOLOGIST NAMED **ROGER SPERRY** SPLIT THE BRAIN IN TWO WHILE TRYING TO HELP A PATIENT AVOID GRAND MAL SEIZURES.
SPERRY
SPERRY DISCOVERED THAT THE **RIGHT** AND **LEFT** HEMISPHERES OF THE BRAIN CAN WORK **INDEPENDENTLY** OF EACH OTHER...
...WHICH THROWS COLD WATER ON DESCARTES'S THEORY ABOUT THE MIND BEING **INDIVISIBLE**.
AW, MAN.
THERE ARE LITERALLY **REAMS** MORE I COULD TELL YOU ABOUT THE BRAIN AND ITS STRUCTURE--
--BUT JUST KNOW THAT IT'S DISCOVERIES LIKE SPERRY'S THAT LEND CREDENCE TO THE IDEA THAT OUR THOUGHTS ARE NOT **SEPARATE** FROM THE BRAIN-- THEY **ARE** THE BRAIN.
ALSO KNOWN AS **PHYSICALISM**!

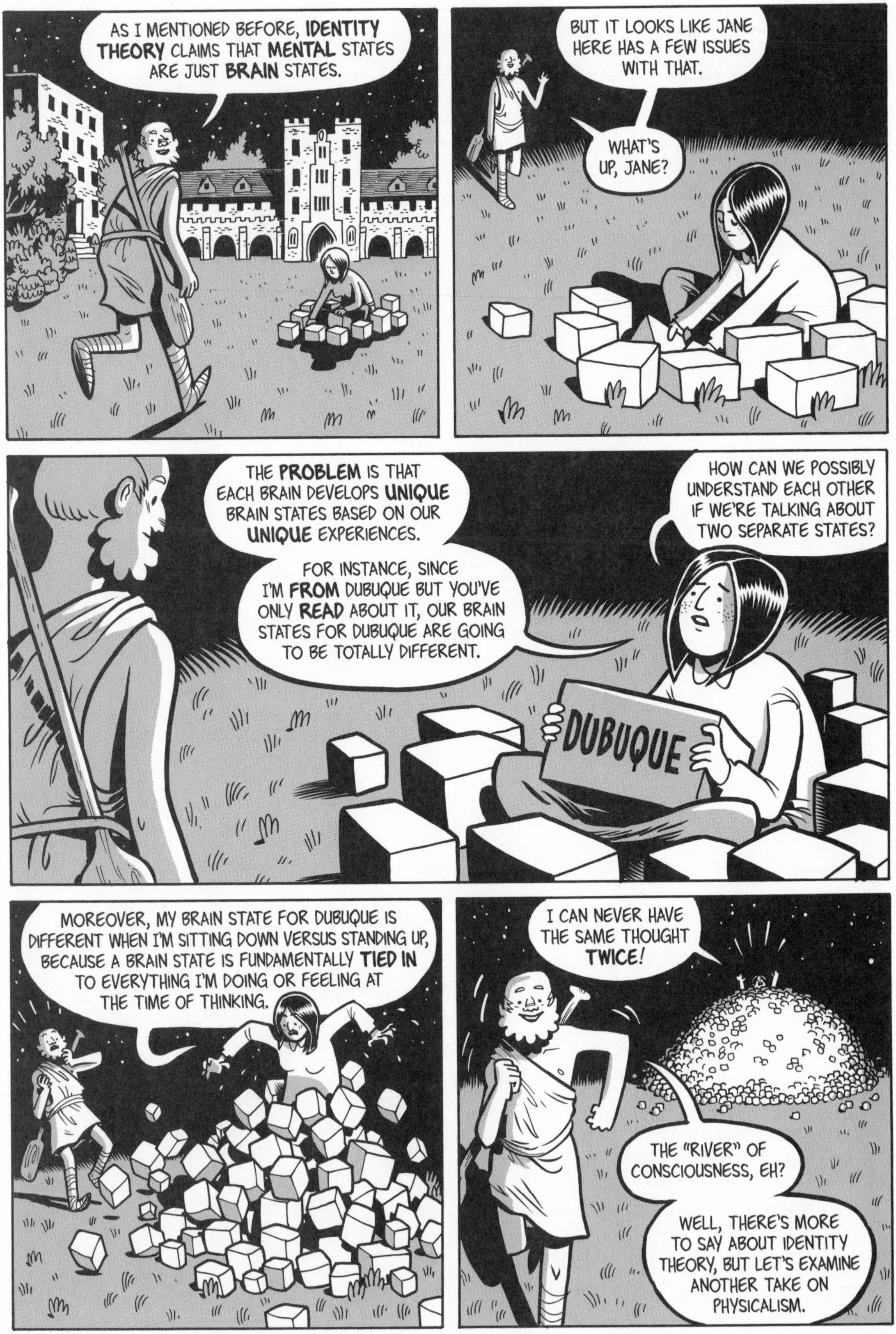
AS I MENTIONED BEFORE, **IDENTITY THEORY** CLAIMS THAT **MENTAL** STATES ARE JUST **BRAIN** STATES.
BUT IT LOOKS LIKE JANE HERE HAS A FEW ISSUES WITH THAT.
WHAT'S UP, JANE?
THE **PROBLEM** IS THAT EACH BRAIN DEVELOPS **UNIQUE** BRAIN STATES BASED ON OUR **UNIQUE** EXPERIENCES.
FOR INSTANCE, SINCE I'M **FROM** DUBUQUE BUT YOU'VE ONLY **READ** ABOUT IT, OUR BRAIN STATES FOR DUBUQUE ARE GOING TO BE TOTALLY DIFFERENT.
HOW CAN WE POSSIBLY UNDERSTAND EACH OTHER IF WE'RE TALKING ABOUT TWO SEPARATE STATES?
DUBUQUE
MOREOVER, MY BRAIN STATE FOR DUBUQUE IS DIFFERENT WHEN I'M SITTING DOWN VERSUS STANDING UP, BECAUSE A BRAIN STATE IS FUNDAMENTALLY **TIED IN** TO EVERYTHING I'M DOING OR FEELING AT THE TIME OF THINKING.
I CAN NEVER HAVE THE SAME THOUGHT **TWICE**!
THE "RIVER" OF CONSCIOUSNESS, EH?
WELL, THERE'S MORE TO SAY ABOUT IDENTITY THEORY, BUT LET'S EXAMINE ANOTHER TAKE ON PHYSICALISM.

JOE?

OKAY, SO WHEN I PLUG MONEY INTO A VENDING MACHINE, ALL I CARE ABOUT IS THE **RESULT**.

SPECIFICALLY, AN ICE-COLD **ZOOP COLA** WITH JUST A **HINT** OF LIME.

I DON'T CARE ABOUT WHAT'S HAPPENING **BEHIND THE SCENES**.

THERE COULD BE ALIEN TECHNOLOGY BEHIND THERE...

...OR A TINY PERSON SORTING THE CANS...

...I REALLY DON'T CARE.

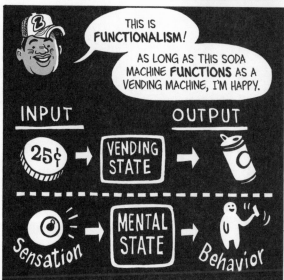

THIS IS **FUNCTIONALISM**!

AS LONG AS THIS SODA MACHINE **FUNCTIONS** AS A VENDING MACHINE, I'M HAPPY.

INPUT — OUTPUT

25¢ → VENDING STATE → [can]

Sensation → MENTAL STATE → Behavior

MMM...

AND AS LONG AS I'M SIPPING A CAN OF REFRESHING **ZOOP COLA** --

UH, JOE, THAT'S NOT A REAL BRAND. YOU'RE NOT GETTING ANY PRODUCT ENDORSEMENT KICKBACKS FROM THIS SPOT.

RUB RUB

AW, MAN.

NOTE THAT SINCE FUNCTIONALISM DOESN'T CONCERN ITSELF WITH THE MENTAL STATES **BEHIND** THE INPUTS AND OUTPUTS -- AND BECAUSE WHAT'S BEHIND MAY BE **NONPHYSICAL** -- THE THEORY IS CONSISTENT WITH **DUALISM**.

BUT ENOUGH ABOUT **PHYSICALISM**.

IT'S TIME TO ASK THE **TOUGHEST** QUESTION OF ALL...

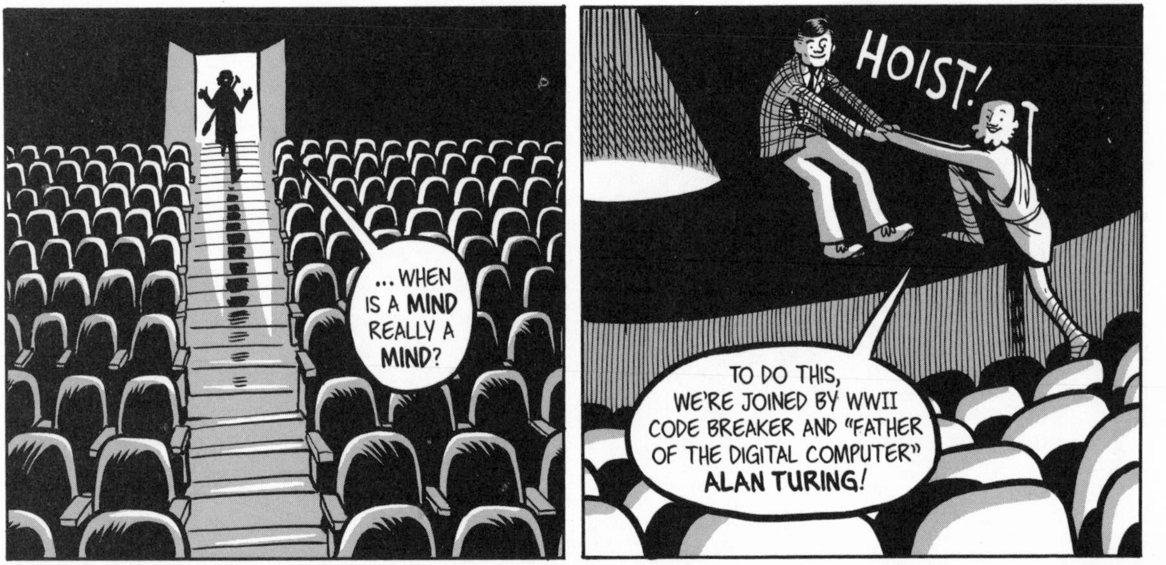
... WHEN IS A **MIND** REALLY A **MIND**?
HOIST!
TO DO THIS, WE'RE JOINED BY WWII CODE BREAKER AND "FATHER OF THE DIGITAL COMPUTER" **ALAN TURING**!

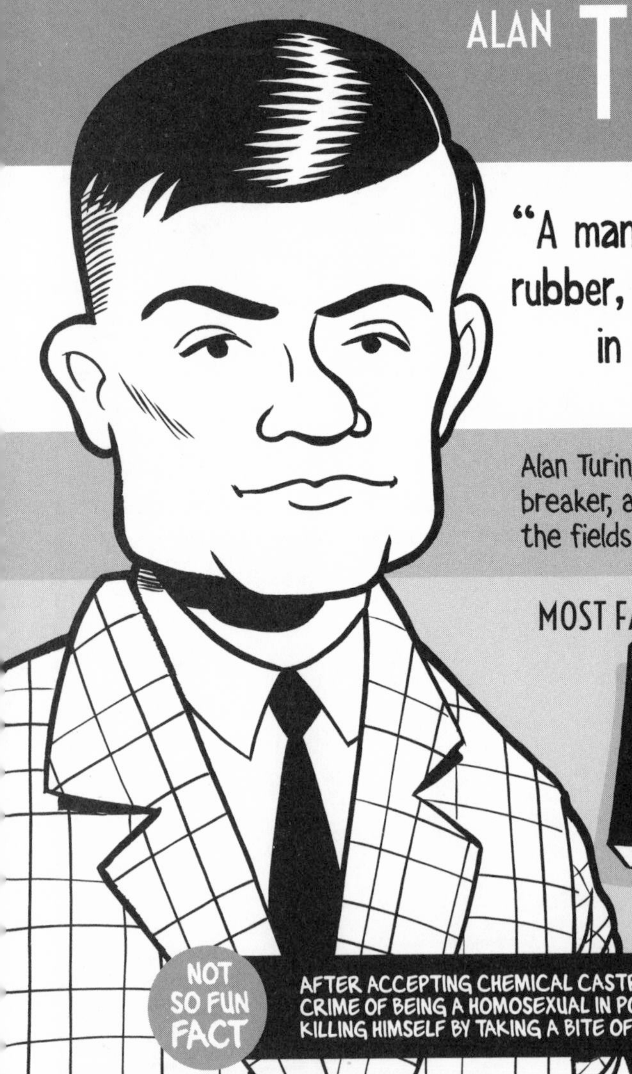

ALAN TURING

b. 1912
d. 1954
C.E.

"A man provided with paper, pencil, and rubber, and subject to strict discipline, is in effect a universal machine."

-- *Intelligent Machinery*

Alan Turing was a British mathematician, logician, code breaker, and philosopher. His work was foundational to the fields of computer science and artificial intelligence.

MOST FAMOUS WORK:

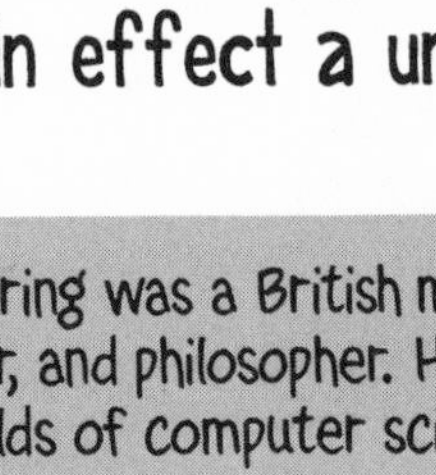
INTELLIGENT MACHINERY
1969*
*Originally published in 1948

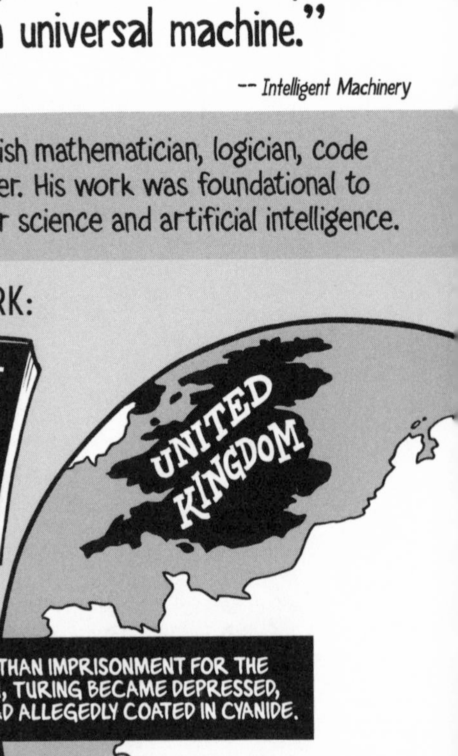
UNITED KINGDOM

NOT SO FUN FACT

AFTER ACCEPTING CHEMICAL CASTRATION RATHER THAN IMPRISONMENT FOR THE CRIME OF BEING A HOMOSEXUAL IN POSTWAR BRITAIN, TURING BECAME DEPRESSED, KILLING HIMSELF BY TAKING A BITE OF AN APPLE HE HAD ALLEGEDLY COATED IN CYANIDE.

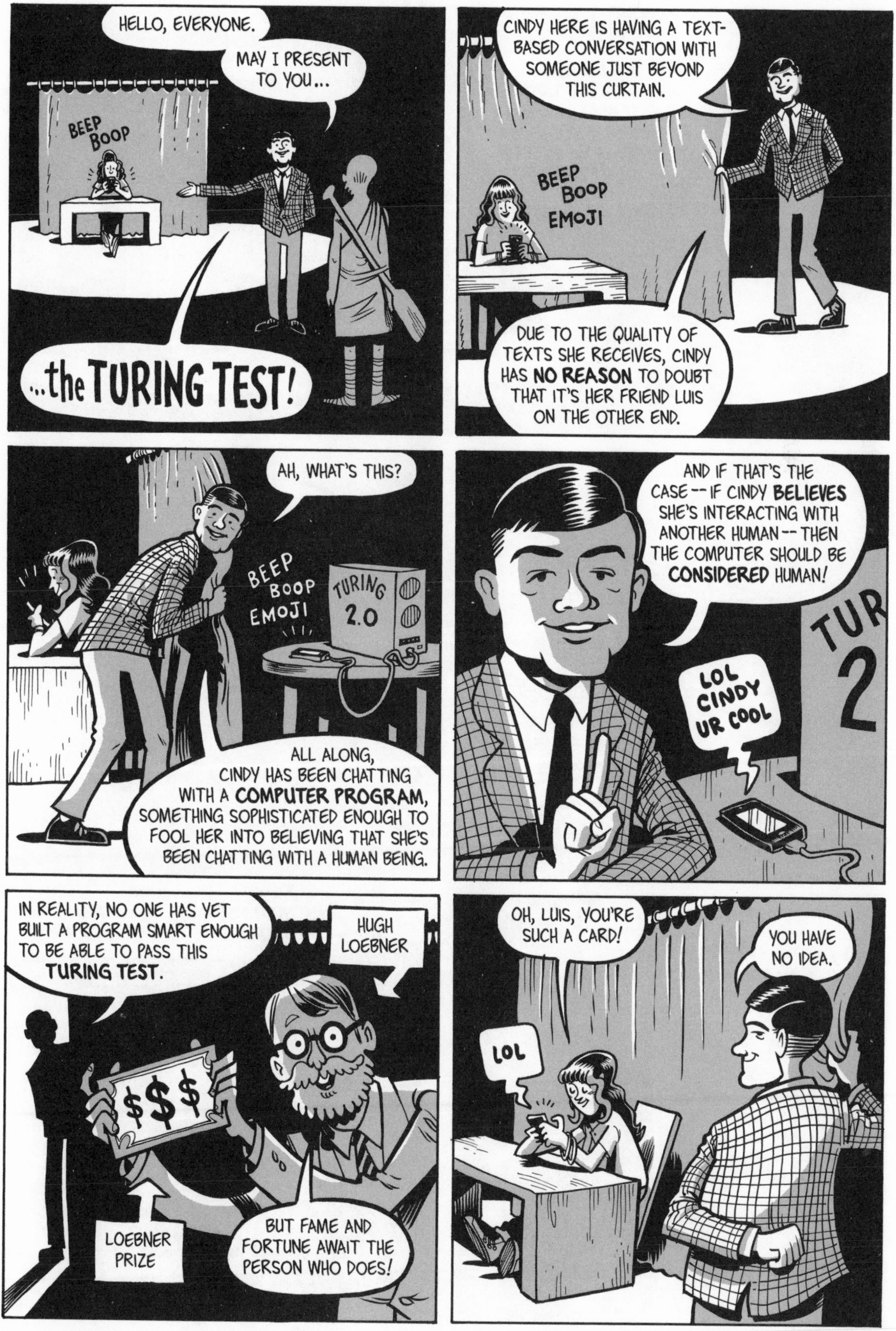
HELLO, EVERYONE.
MAY I PRESENT TO YOU...
BEEP BOOP
...the TURING TEST!
CINDY HERE IS HAVING A TEXT-BASED CONVERSATION WITH SOMEONE JUST BEYOND THIS CURTAIN.
BEEP BOOP EMOJI
DUE TO THE QUALITY OF TEXTS SHE RECEIVES, CINDY HAS NO REASON TO DOUBT THAT IT'S HER FRIEND LUIS ON THE OTHER END.
AH, WHAT'S THIS?
BEEP BOOP EMOJI
TURING 2.0
ALL ALONG, CINDY HAS BEEN CHATTING WITH A COMPUTER PROGRAM, SOMETHING SOPHISTICATED ENOUGH TO FOOL HER INTO BELIEVING THAT SHE'S BEEN CHATTING WITH A HUMAN BEING.
AND IF THAT'S THE CASE -- IF CINDY BELIEVES SHE'S INTERACTING WITH ANOTHER HUMAN -- THEN THE COMPUTER SHOULD BE CONSIDERED HUMAN!
TUR 2
LOL CINDY UR COOL
IN REALITY, NO ONE HAS YET BUILT A PROGRAM SMART ENOUGH TO BE ABLE TO PASS THIS TURING TEST.
HUGH LOEBNER
$$$
LOEBNER PRIZE
BUT FAME AND FORTUNE AWAIT THE PERSON WHO DOES!
OH, LUIS, YOU'RE SUCH A CARD!
YOU HAVE NO IDEA.
LOL

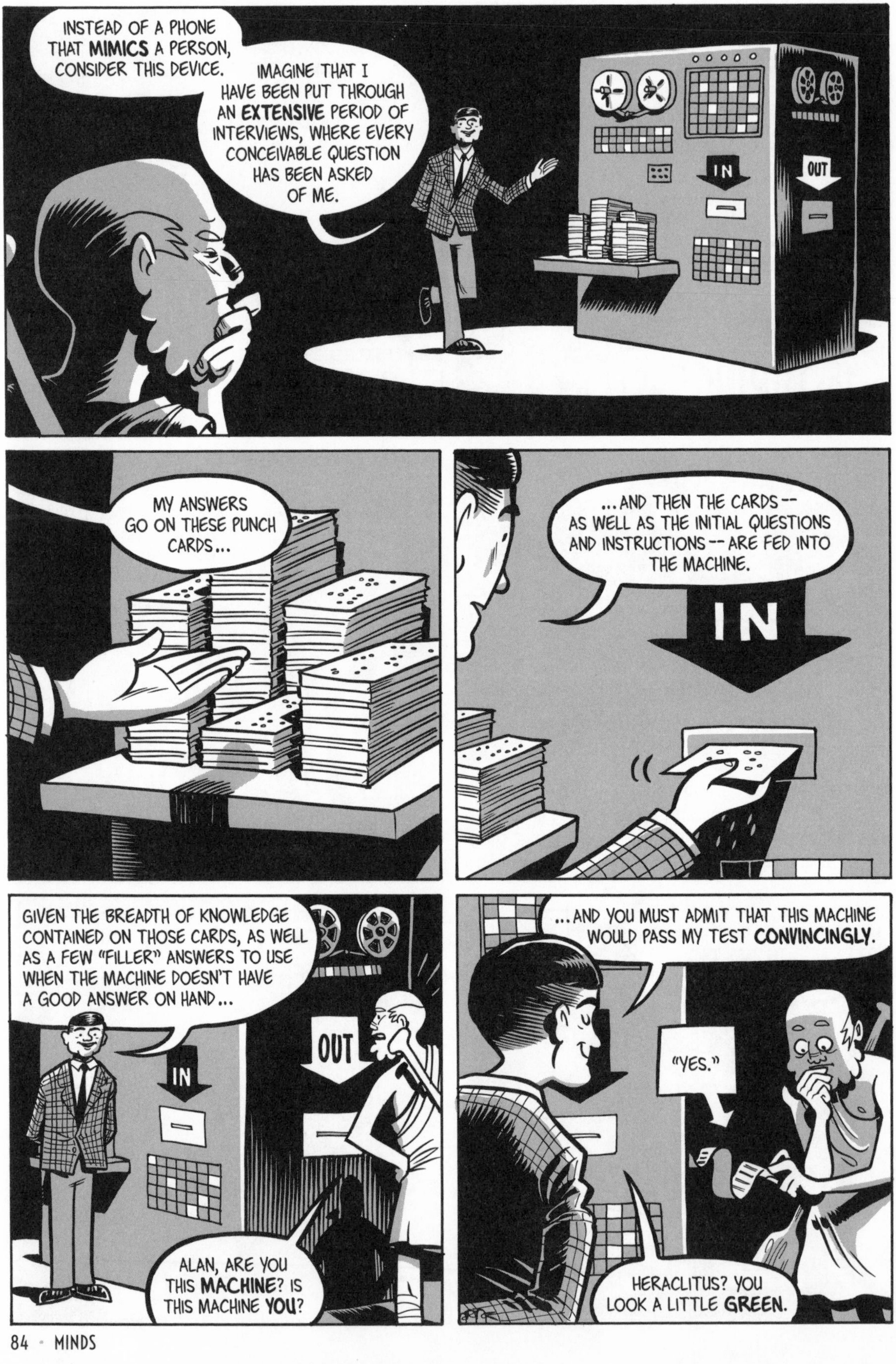
INSTEAD OF A PHONE THAT **MIMICS** A PERSON, CONSIDER THIS DEVICE.
IMAGINE THAT I HAVE BEEN PUT THROUGH AN **EXTENSIVE** PERIOD OF INTERVIEWS, WHERE EVERY CONCEIVABLE QUESTION HAS BEEN ASKED OF ME.
IN
OUT
MY ANSWERS GO ON THESE PUNCH CARDS...
...AND THEN THE CARDS -- AS WELL AS THE INITIAL QUESTIONS AND INSTRUCTIONS -- ARE FED INTO THE MACHINE.
IN
GIVEN THE BREADTH OF KNOWLEDGE CONTAINED ON THOSE CARDS, AS WELL AS A FEW "FILLER" ANSWERS TO USE WHEN THE MACHINE DOESN'T HAVE A GOOD ANSWER ON HAND...
OUT
IN
ALAN, ARE YOU THIS **MACHINE**? IS THIS MACHINE **YOU**?
...AND YOU MUST ADMIT THAT THIS MACHINE WOULD PASS MY TEST **CONVINCINGLY**.
"YES."
HERACLITUS? YOU LOOK A LITTLE **GREEN**.

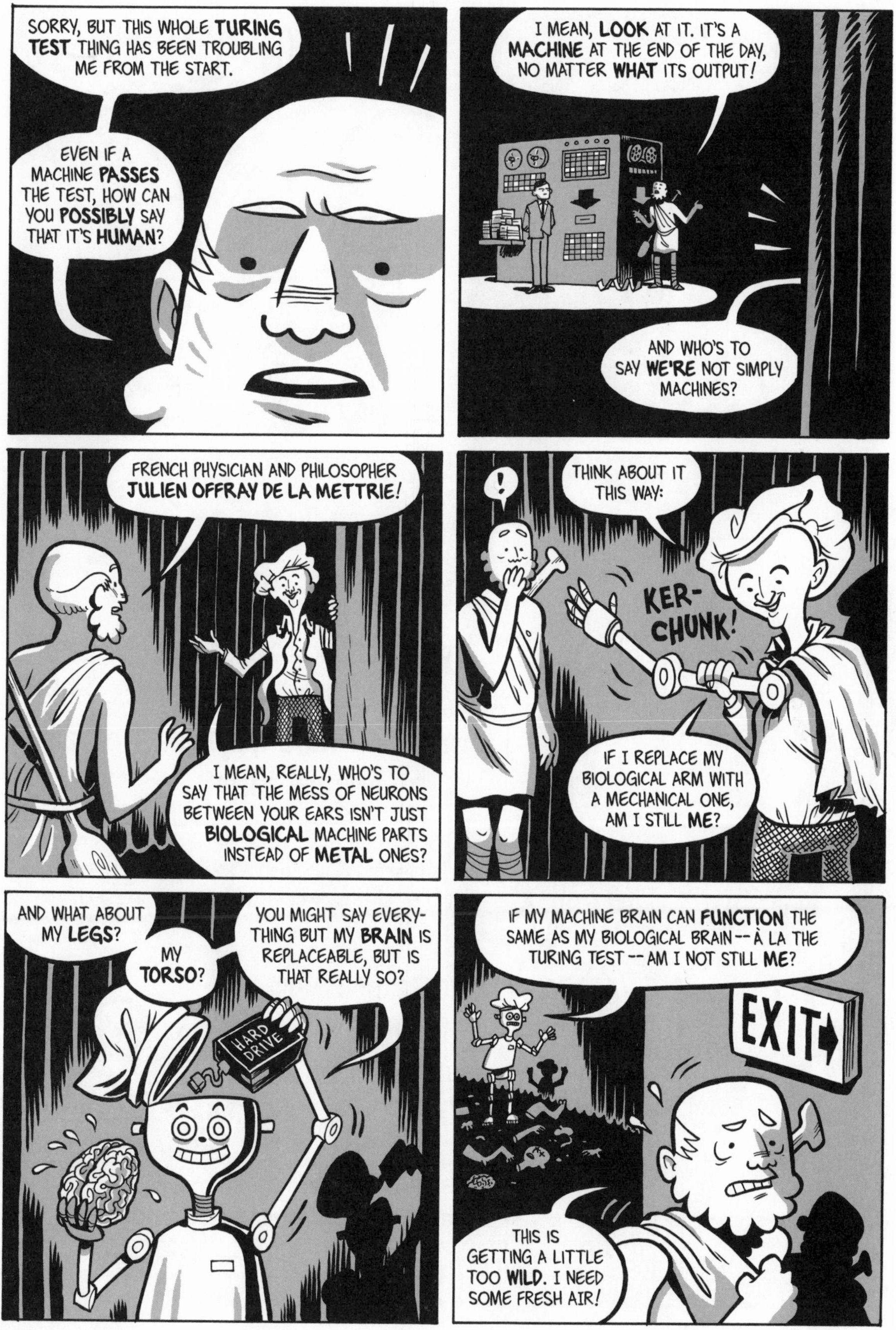
SORRY, BUT THIS WHOLE **TURING TEST** THING HAS BEEN TROUBLING ME FROM THE START.
EVEN IF A MACHINE **PASSES** THE TEST, HOW CAN YOU **POSSIBLY** SAY THAT IT'S **HUMAN**?
I MEAN, **LOOK** AT IT. IT'S A **MACHINE** AT THE END OF THE DAY, NO MATTER **WHAT** ITS OUTPUT!
AND WHO'S TO SAY **WE'RE** NOT SIMPLY MACHINES?
FRENCH PHYSICIAN AND PHILOSOPHER **JULIEN OFFRAY DE LA METTRIE**!
I MEAN, REALLY, WHO'S TO SAY THAT THE MESS OF NEURONS BETWEEN YOUR EARS ISN'T JUST **BIOLOGICAL** MACHINE PARTS INSTEAD OF **METAL** ONES?
!
THINK ABOUT IT THIS WAY:
KER-CHUNK!
IF I REPLACE MY BIOLOGICAL ARM WITH A MECHANICAL ONE, AM I STILL **ME**?
AND WHAT ABOUT MY **LEGS**?
MY **TORSO**?
YOU MIGHT SAY EVERY-THING BUT MY **BRAIN** IS REPLACEABLE, BUT IS THAT REALLY SO?
HARD DRIVE
IF MY MACHINE BRAIN CAN **FUNCTION** THE SAME AS MY BIOLOGICAL BRAIN--À LA THE TURING TEST--AM I NOT STILL **ME**?
EXIT
THIS IS GETTING A LITTLE TOO **WILD**. I NEED SOME FRESH AIR!

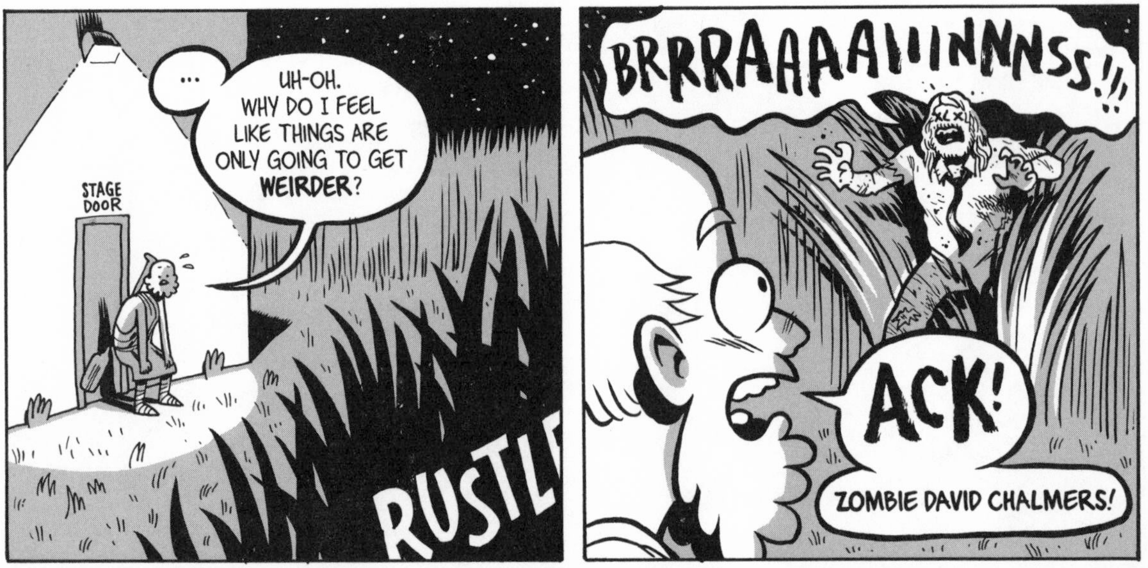
...
UH-OH. WHY DO I FEEL LIKE THINGS ARE ONLY GOING TO GET WEIRDER?
STAGE DOOR
RUSTLE
BRRRAAAAIIIINNNSS!!!
ACK!
ZOMBIE DAVID CHALMERS!

DAVID CHALMERS

b. 1966 C.E.

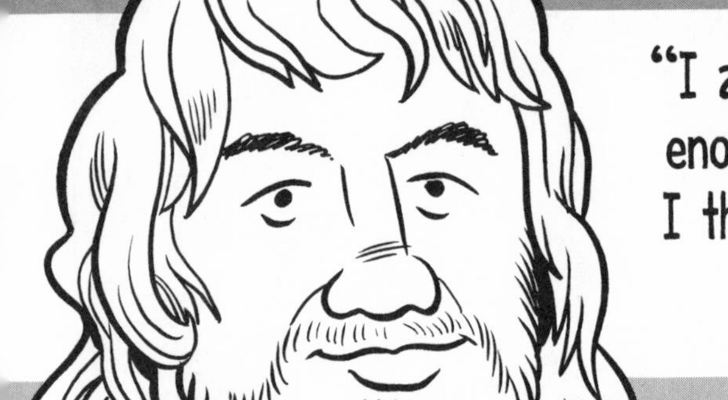

"I argue that neuroscience alone isn't enough to explain consciousness, but I think it will be a major part of an eventual theory."

-- Interview by Andrew Chrucky in *Philosophy Now*, 1998

David Chalmers is an Australian philosopher and cognitive scientist who studies the philosophy of mind and the philosophy of language.

MOST FAMOUS WORK:

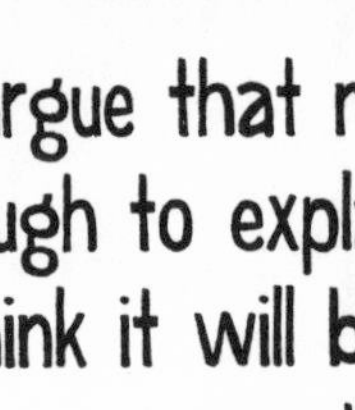
THE CONSCIOUS MIND
1996

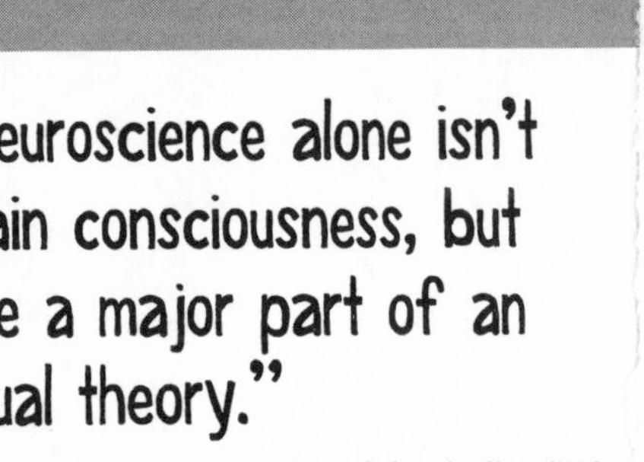
AUSTRALIA

FUN FACT

IN A RECENT "TED TALK," DAVID CHALMERS PROPOSED THAT WE SHOULD CONSIDER THE THEORY OF PANPSYCHISM TO EXPLAIN CONSCIOUSNESS. HE THINKS THAT EVERYTHING MIGHT BE CONSCIOUS AT SOME LEVEL: "PHOTONS [COULD CONCEIVABLY] HAVE SOME ELEMENT OF RAW SUBJECTIVE FEELING, A PRECURSOR TO CONSCIOUSNESS. THIS MIGHT SEEM CRAZY TO US BUT NOT TO PEOPLE FROM OTHER CULTURES."

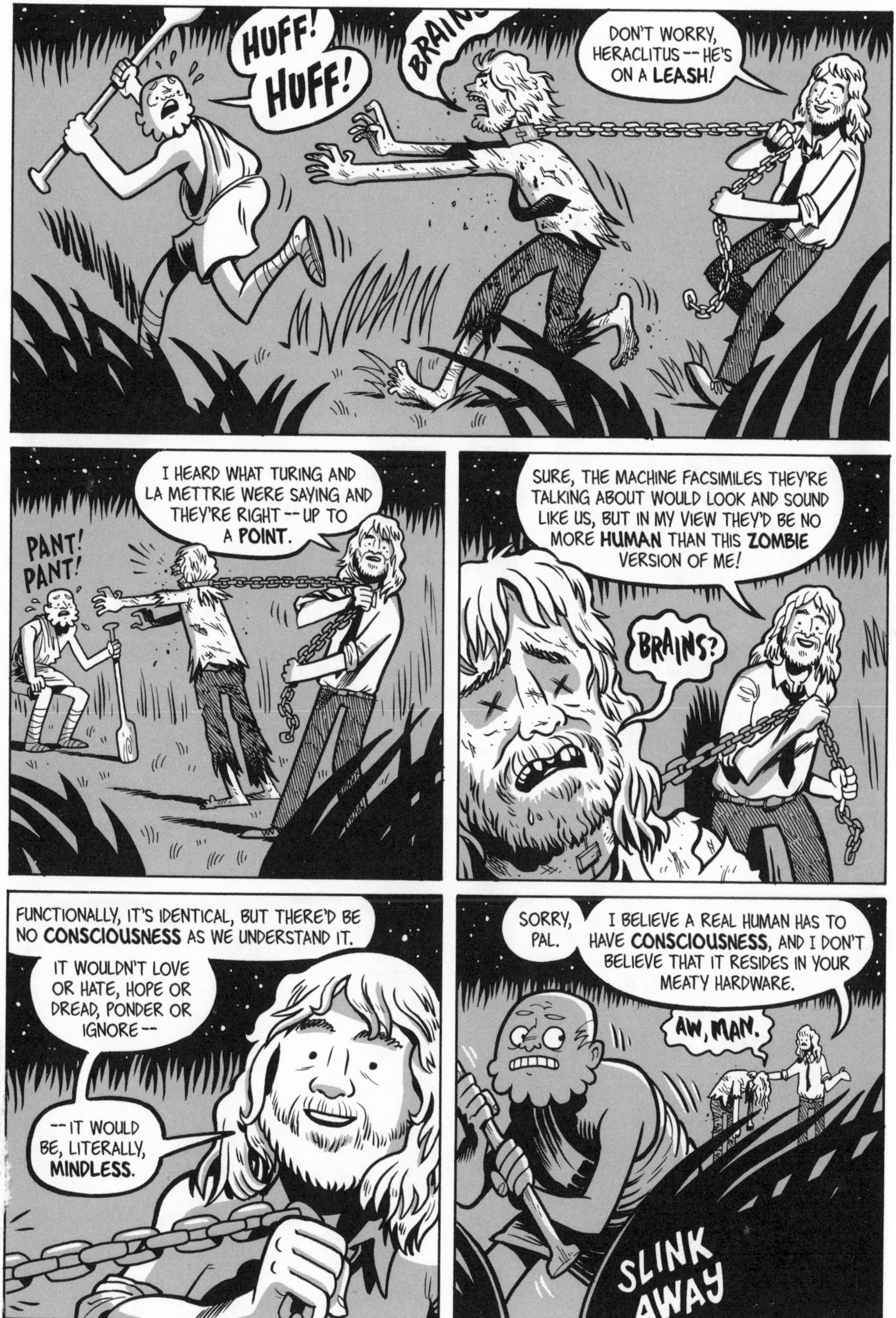
HUFF! HUFF!
BRAINS
DON'T WORRY, HERACLITUS -- HE'S ON A LEASH!
I HEARD WHAT TURING AND LA METTRIE WERE SAYING AND THEY'RE RIGHT -- UP TO A POINT.
PANT! PANT!
SURE, THE MACHINE FACSIMILES THEY'RE TALKING ABOUT WOULD LOOK AND SOUND LIKE US, BUT IN MY VIEW THEY'D BE NO MORE HUMAN THAN THIS ZOMBIE VERSION OF ME!
BRAINS?
FUNCTIONALLY, IT'S IDENTICAL, BUT THERE'D BE NO CONSCIOUSNESS AS WE UNDERSTAND IT.
IT WOULDN'T LOVE OR HATE, HOPE OR DREAD, PONDER OR IGNORE --
-- IT WOULD BE, LITERALLY, MINDLESS.
SORRY, PAL.
I BELIEVE A REAL HUMAN HAS TO HAVE CONSCIOUSNESS, AND I DON'T BELIEVE THAT IT RESIDES IN YOUR MEATY HARDWARE.
AW, MAN.
SLINK AWAY

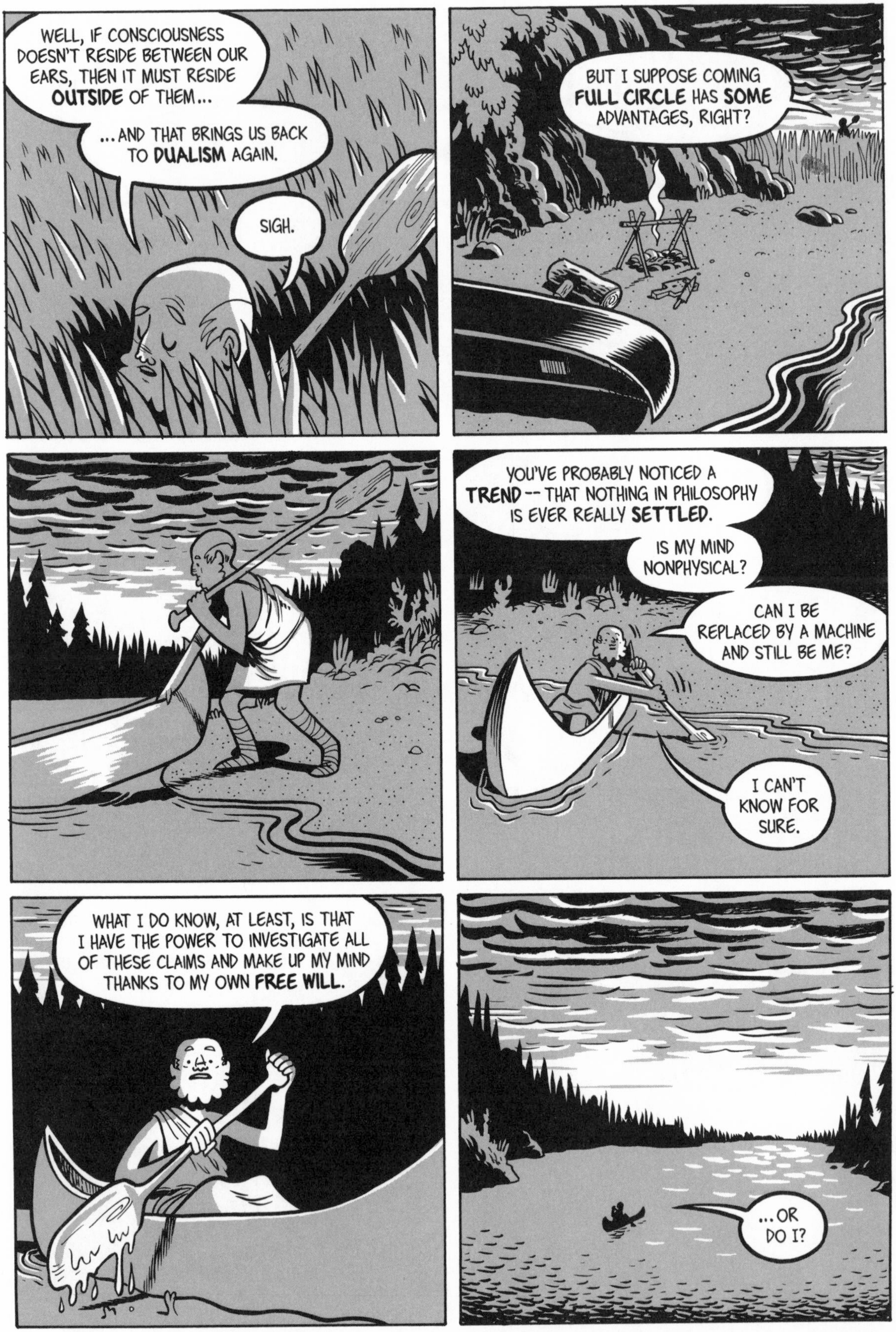
WELL, IF CONSCIOUSNESS DOESN'T RESIDE BETWEEN OUR EARS, THEN IT MUST RESIDE **OUTSIDE** OF THEM...
...AND THAT BRINGS US BACK TO **DUALISM** AGAIN.
SIGH.
BUT I SUPPOSE COMING **FULL CIRCLE** HAS **SOME** ADVANTAGES, RIGHT?
YOU'VE PROBABLY NOTICED A **TREND**-- THAT NOTHING IN PHILOSOPHY IS EVER REALLY **SETTLED**.
IS MY MIND NONPHYSICAL?
CAN I BE REPLACED BY A MACHINE AND STILL BE ME?
I CAN'T KNOW FOR SURE.
WHAT I DO KNOW, AT LEAST, IS THAT I HAVE THE POWER TO INVESTIGATE ALL OF THESE CLAIMS AND MAKE UP MY MIND THANKS TO MY OWN **FREE WILL**.
...OR DO I?

chapter 4
FREE WILL

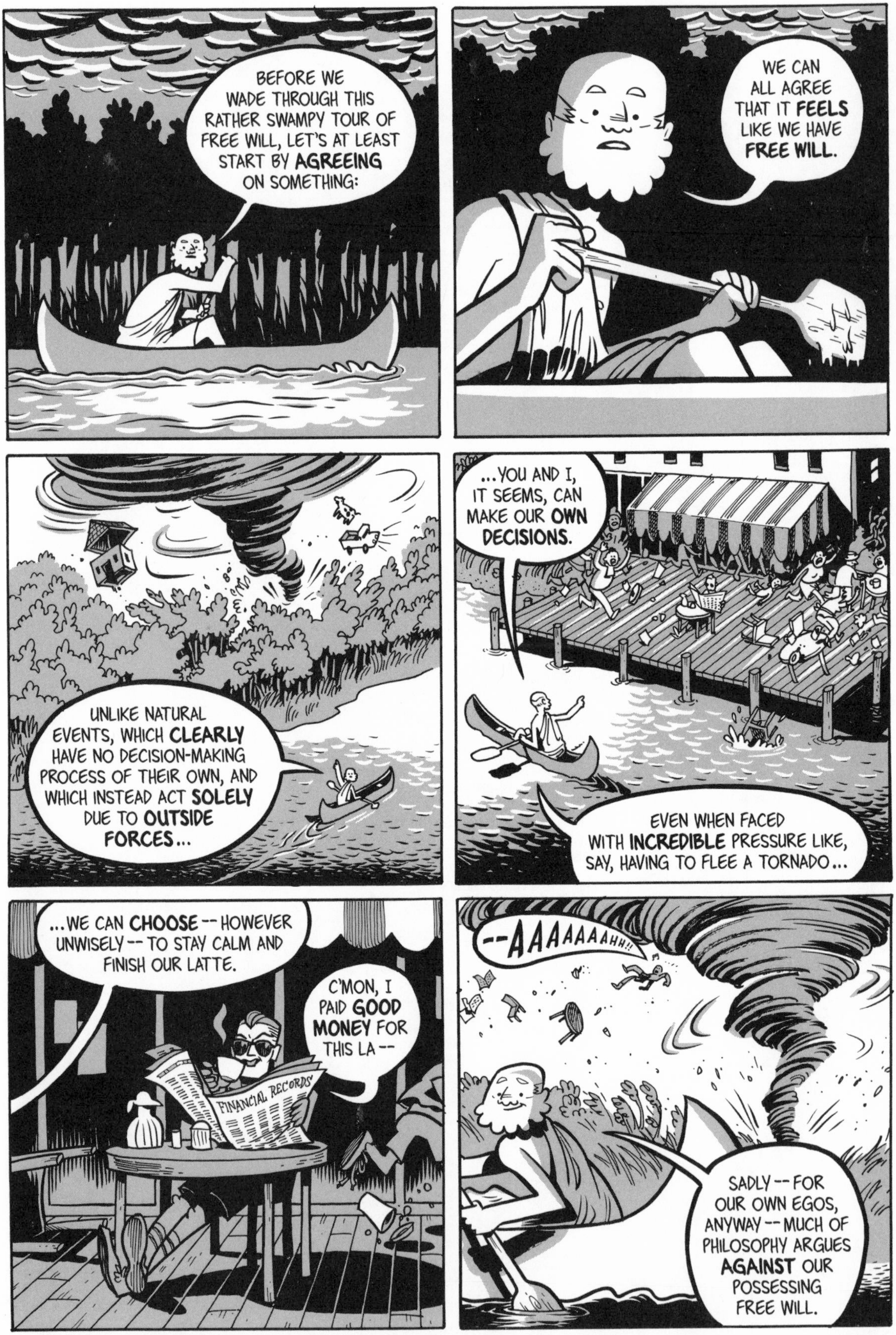
BEFORE WE WADE THROUGH THIS RATHER SWAMPY TOUR OF FREE WILL, LET'S AT LEAST START BY **AGREEING** ON SOMETHING:
WE CAN ALL AGREE THAT IT **FEELS** LIKE WE HAVE **FREE WILL**.
UNLIKE NATURAL EVENTS, WHICH **CLEARLY** HAVE NO DECISION-MAKING PROCESS OF THEIR OWN, AND WHICH INSTEAD ACT **SOLELY** DUE TO **OUTSIDE FORCES**...
...YOU AND I, IT SEEMS, CAN MAKE OUR **OWN DECISIONS**.
EVEN WHEN FACED WITH **INCREDIBLE** PRESSURE LIKE, SAY, HAVING TO FLEE A TORNADO...
...WE CAN **CHOOSE** -- HOWEVER UNWISELY -- TO STAY CALM AND FINISH OUR LATTE.
C'MON, I PAID **GOOD MONEY** FOR THIS LA --
FINANCIAL RECORDS
--AAAAAAAHH!!
SADLY -- FOR OUR OWN EGOS, ANYWAY -- MUCH OF PHILOSOPHY ARGUES **AGAINST** OUR POSSESSING FREE WILL.

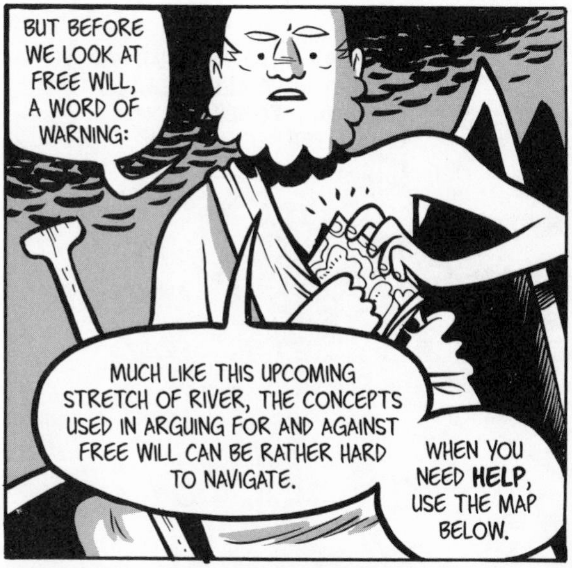
BUT BEFORE WE LOOK AT FREE WILL, A WORD OF WARNING:
MUCH LIKE THIS UPCOMING STRETCH OF RIVER, THE CONCEPTS USED IN ARGUING FOR AND AGAINST FREE WILL CAN BE RATHER HARD TO NAVIGATE.
WHEN YOU NEED **HELP**, USE THE MAP BELOW.

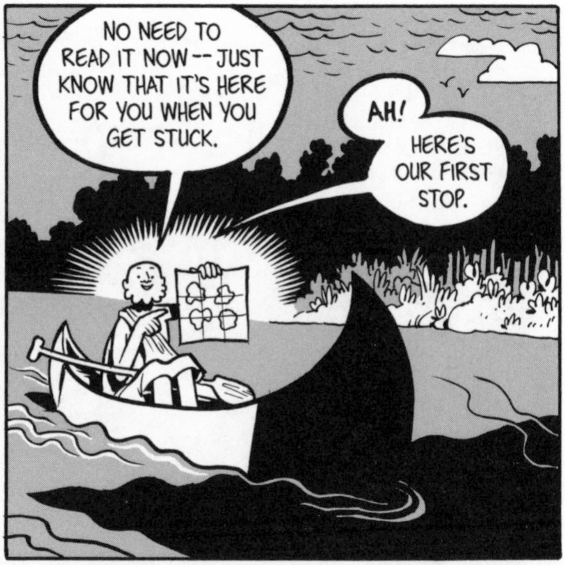
NO NEED TO READ IT NOW -- JUST KNOW THAT IT'S HERE FOR YOU WHEN YOU GET STUCK.
AH!
HERE'S OUR FIRST STOP.

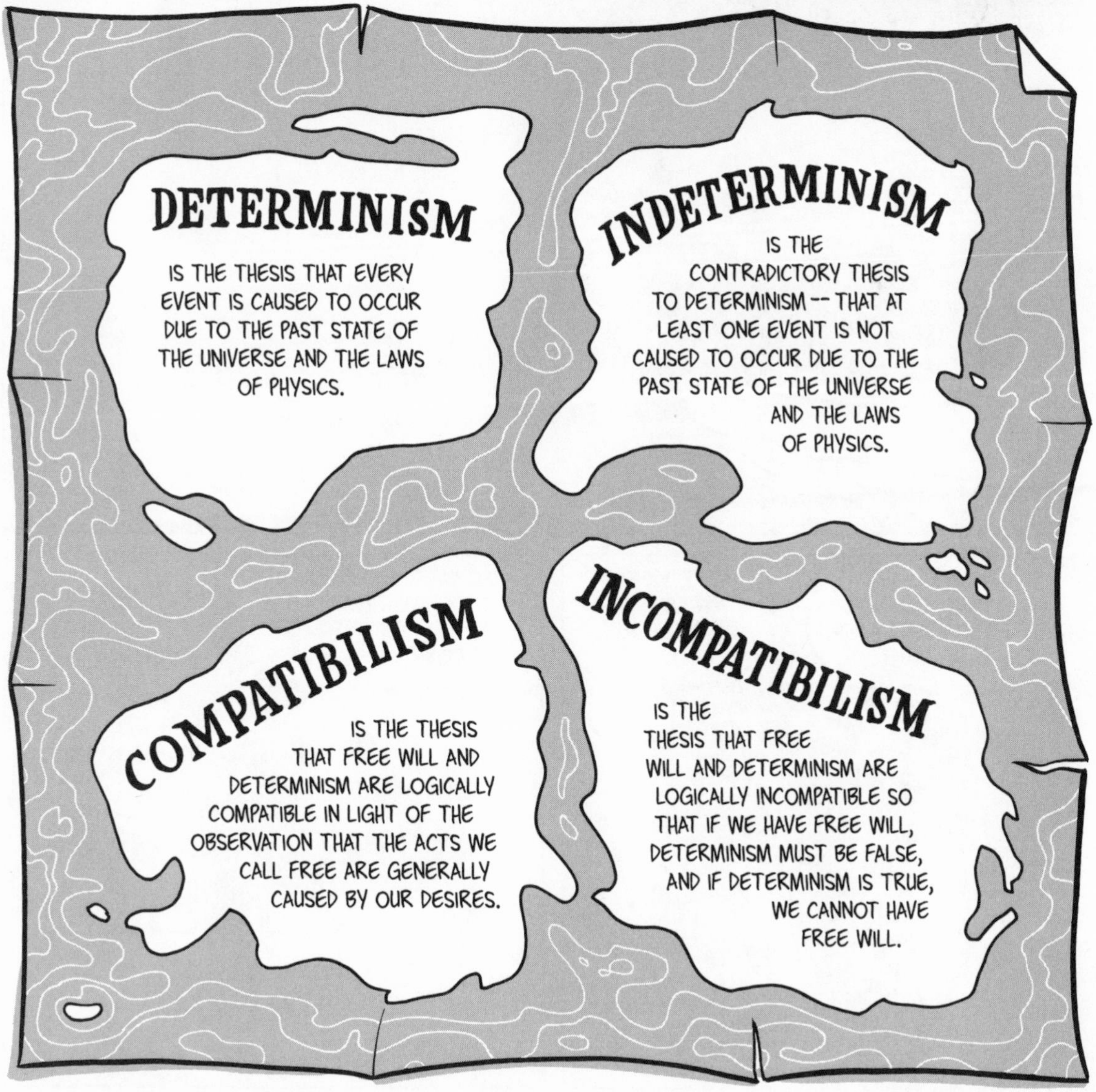
DETERMINISM
IS THE THESIS THAT EVERY EVENT IS CAUSED TO OCCUR DUE TO THE PAST STATE OF THE UNIVERSE AND THE LAWS OF PHYSICS.
INDETERMINISM
IS THE CONTRADICTORY THESIS TO DETERMINISM -- THAT AT LEAST ONE EVENT IS NOT CAUSED TO OCCUR DUE TO THE PAST STATE OF THE UNIVERSE AND THE LAWS OF PHYSICS.
COMPATIBILISM
IS THE THESIS THAT FREE WILL AND DETERMINISM ARE LOGICALLY COMPATIBLE IN LIGHT OF THE OBSERVATION THAT THE ACTS WE CALL FREE ARE GENERALLY CAUSED BY OUR DESIRES.
INCOMPATIBILISM
IS THE THESIS THAT FREE WILL AND DETERMINISM ARE LOGICALLY INCOMPATIBLE SO THAT IF WE HAVE FREE WILL, DETERMINISM MUST BE FALSE, AND IF DETERMINISM IS TRUE, WE CANNOT HAVE FREE WILL.

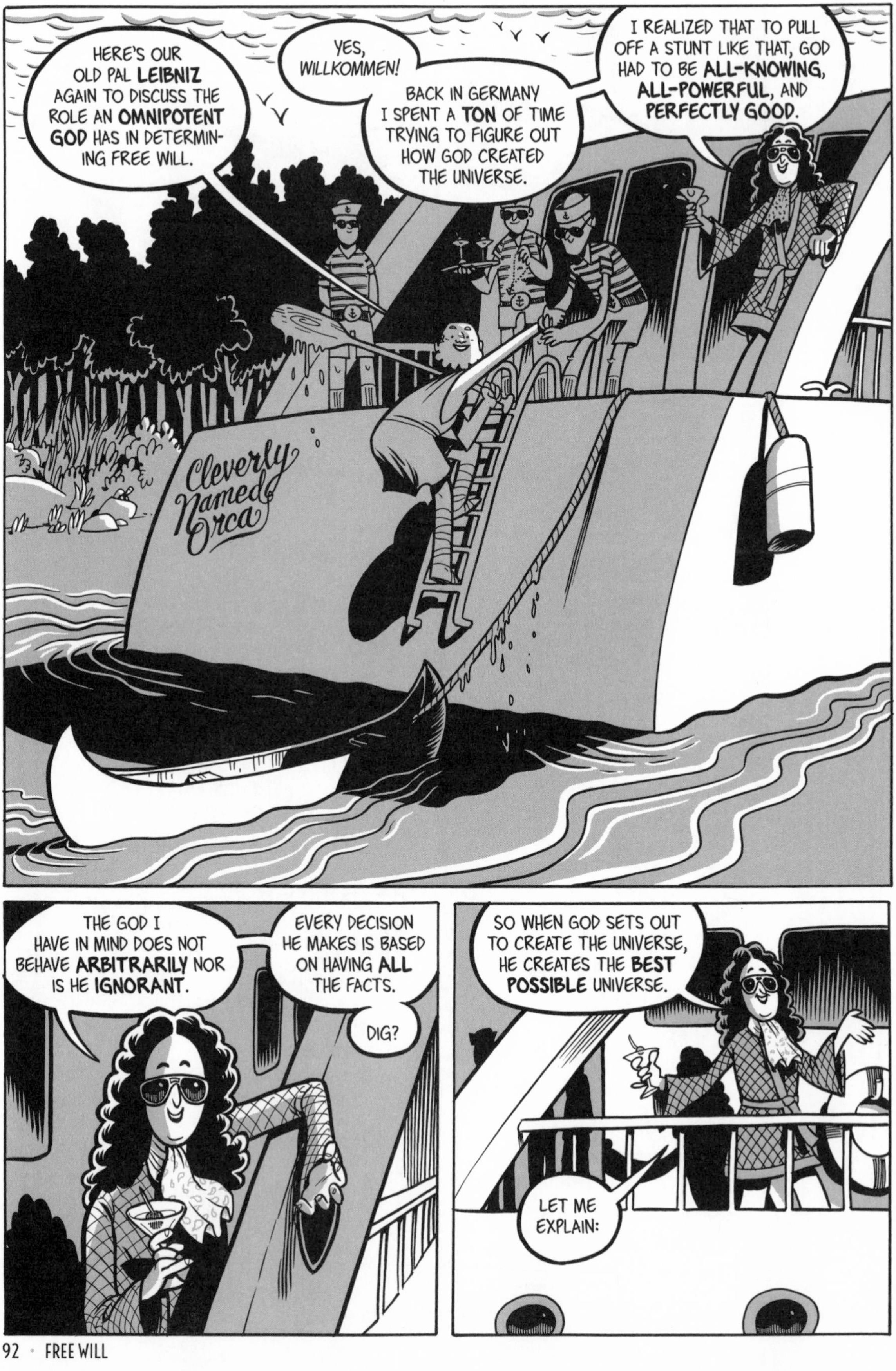
HERE'S OUR OLD PAL LEIBNIZ AGAIN TO DISCUSS THE ROLE AN OMNIPOTENT GOD HAS IN DETERMINING FREE WILL.
YES, WILLKOMMEN!
BACK IN GERMANY I SPENT A TON OF TIME TRYING TO FIGURE OUT HOW GOD CREATED THE UNIVERSE.
I REALIZED THAT TO PULL OFF A STUNT LIKE THAT, GOD HAD TO BE ALL-KNOWING, ALL-POWERFUL, AND PERFECTLY GOOD.
Cleverly Named Orca
THE GOD I HAVE IN MIND DOES NOT BEHAVE ARBITRARILY NOR IS HE IGNORANT.
EVERY DECISION HE MAKES IS BASED ON HAVING ALL THE FACTS.
DIG?
SO WHEN GOD SETS OUT TO CREATE THE UNIVERSE, HE CREATES THE BEST POSSIBLE UNIVERSE.
LET ME EXPLAIN:

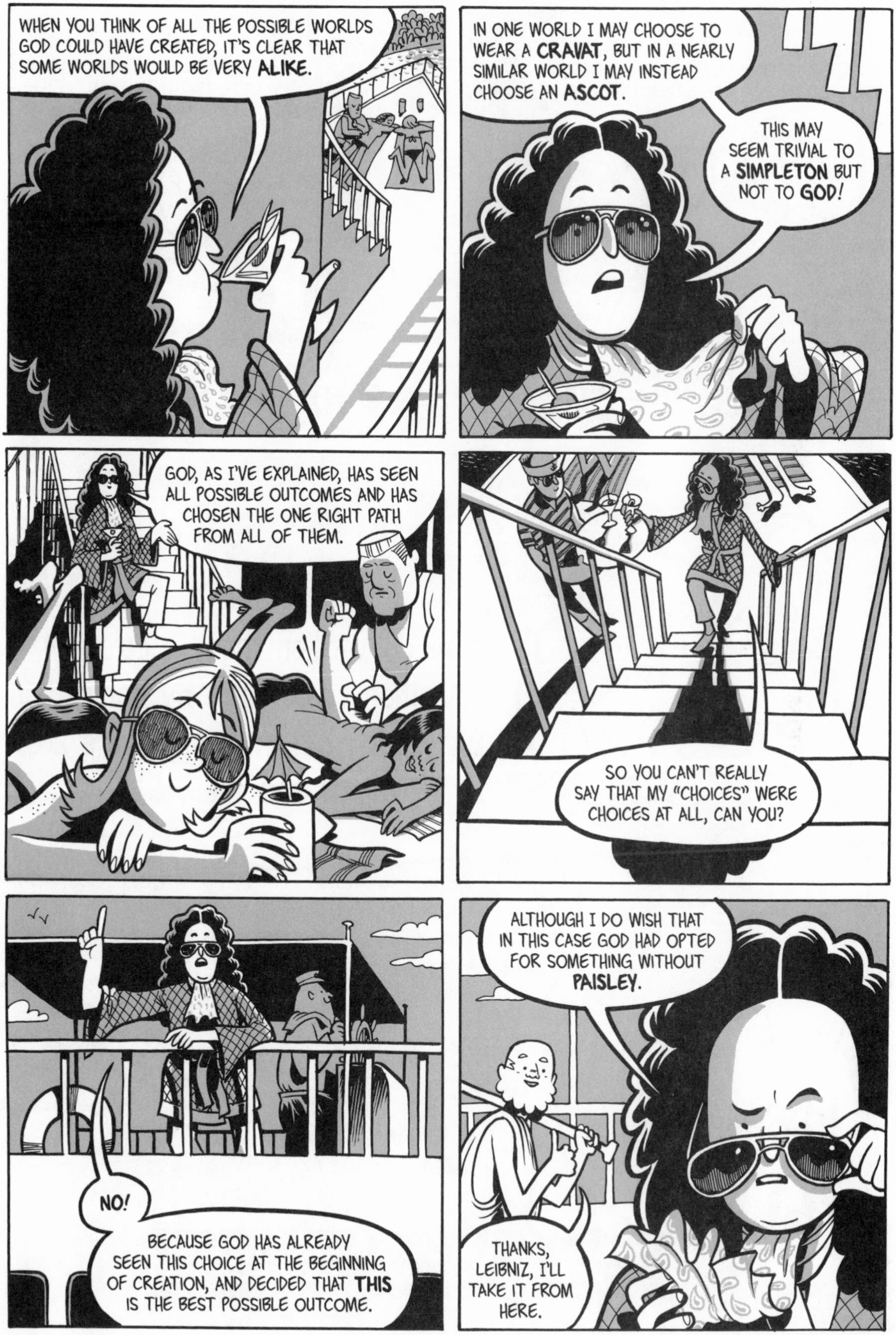
WHEN YOU THINK OF ALL THE POSSIBLE WORLDS GOD COULD HAVE CREATED, IT'S CLEAR THAT SOME WORLDS WOULD BE VERY **ALIKE**.
IN ONE WORLD I MAY CHOOSE TO WEAR A **CRAVAT**, BUT IN A NEARLY SIMILAR WORLD I MAY INSTEAD CHOOSE AN **ASCOT**.
THIS MAY SEEM TRIVIAL TO A **SIMPLETON** BUT NOT TO **GOD**!
GOD, AS I'VE EXPLAINED, HAS SEEN ALL POSSIBLE OUTCOMES AND HAS CHOSEN THE ONE RIGHT PATH FROM ALL OF THEM.
SO YOU CAN'T REALLY SAY THAT MY "CHOICES" WERE CHOICES AT ALL, CAN YOU?
NO!
BECAUSE GOD HAS ALREADY SEEN THIS CHOICE AT THE BEGINNING OF CREATION, AND DECIDED THAT **THIS** IS THE BEST POSSIBLE OUTCOME.
ALTHOUGH I DO WISH THAT IN THIS CASE GOD HAD OPTED FOR SOMETHING WITHOUT **PAISLEY**.
THANKS, LEIBNIZ, I'LL TAKE IT FROM HERE.

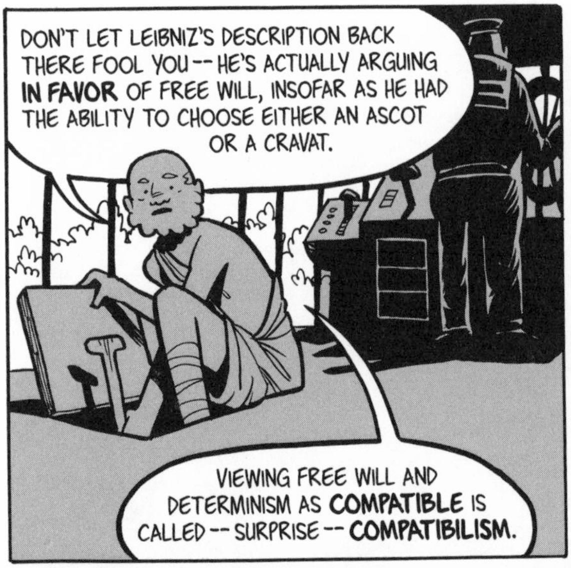
DON'T LET LEIBNIZ'S DESCRIPTION BACK THERE FOOL YOU -- HE'S ACTUALLY ARGUING IN FAVOR OF FREE WILL, INSOFAR AS HE HAD THE ABILITY TO CHOOSE EITHER AN ASCOT OR A CRAVAT.
VIEWING FREE WILL AND DETERMINISM AS COMPATIBLE IS CALLED -- SURPRISE -- COMPATIBILISM.

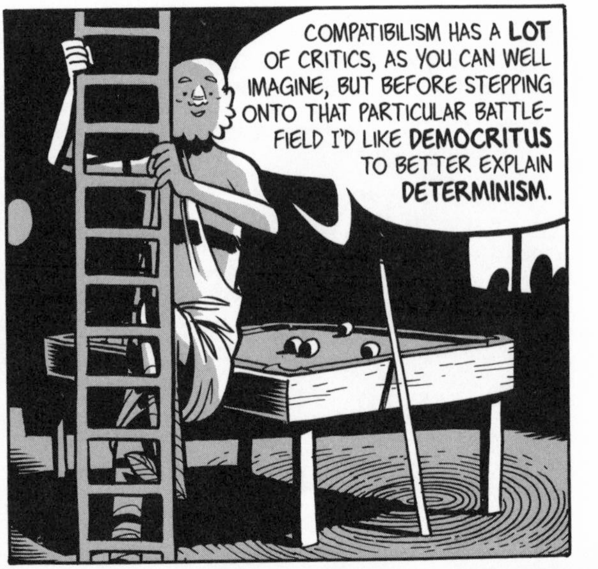
COMPATIBILISM HAS A LOT OF CRITICS, AS YOU CAN WELL IMAGINE, BUT BEFORE STEPPING ONTO THAT PARTICULAR BATTLE-FIELD I'D LIKE DEMOCRITUS TO BETTER EXPLAIN DETERMINISM.

DEMOCRITUS

b. 460
d. 370
B.C.E.

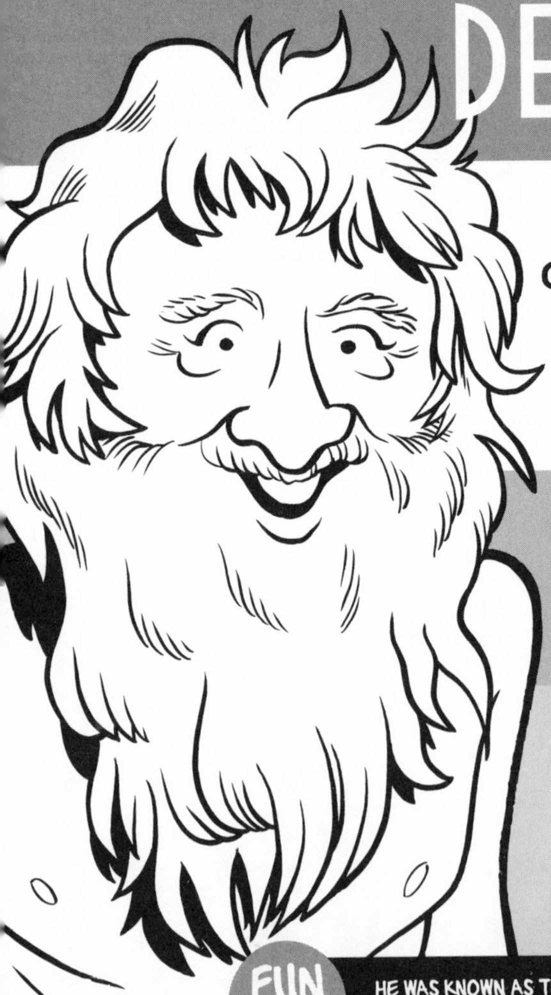

"By convention there is color, by convention sweetness, by convention bitterness, but in reality there are atoms and the void."

-- cited by Aristotle in *Metaphysics* (350 B.C.E.) and others

Democritus was a Greek philosopher whose atomic theory of the universe was quite influential. His ideas are known mainly through discussions of them in the works of others.

MOST FAMOUS WORK:

NO SURVIVING WORKS

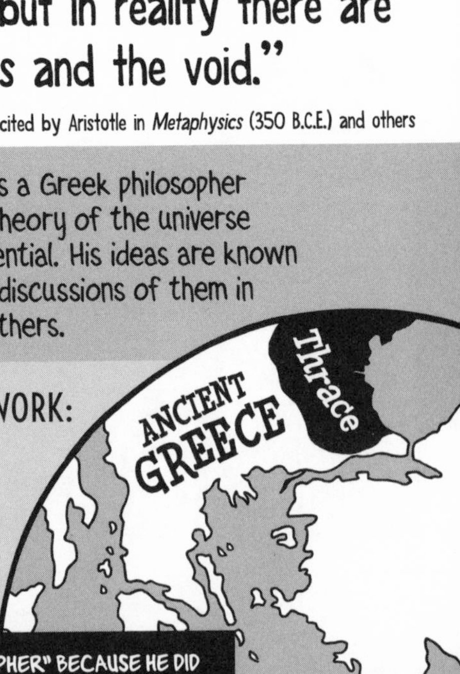
Thrace
ANCIENT GREECE

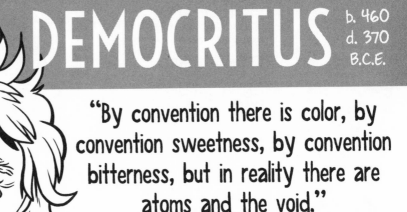

FUN FACT HE WAS KNOWN AS THE "LAUGHING PHILOSOPHER" BECAUSE HE DID NOT HESITATE TO MOCK HIS FELLOW CITIZENS FOR THEIR FOIBLES.

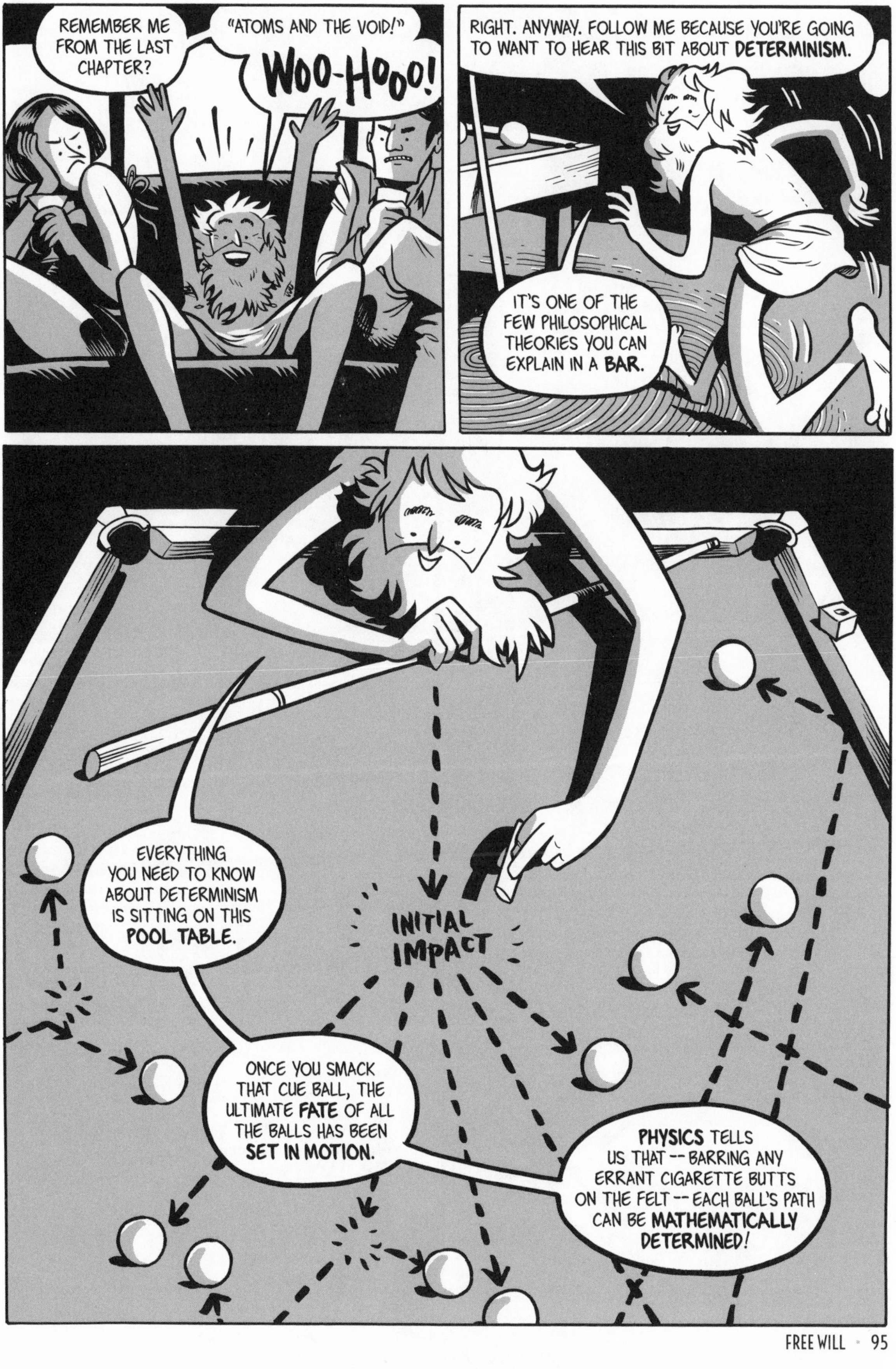
REMEMBER ME FROM THE LAST CHAPTER?
"ATOMS AND THE VOID!"
WOO-HOOO!
RIGHT. ANYWAY. FOLLOW ME BECAUSE YOU'RE GOING TO WANT TO HEAR THIS BIT ABOUT **DETERMINISM**.
IT'S ONE OF THE FEW PHILOSOPHICAL THEORIES YOU CAN EXPLAIN IN A **BAR**.
EVERYTHING YOU NEED TO KNOW ABOUT DETERMINISM IS SITTING ON THIS **POOL TABLE**.
INITIAL IMPACT
ONCE YOU SMACK THAT CUE BALL, THE ULTIMATE **FATE** OF ALL THE BALLS HAS BEEN **SET IN MOTION**.
PHYSICS TELLS US THAT -- BARRING ANY ERRANT CIGARETTE BUTTS ON THE FELT -- EACH BALL'S PATH CAN BE **MATHEMATICALLY DETERMINED**!

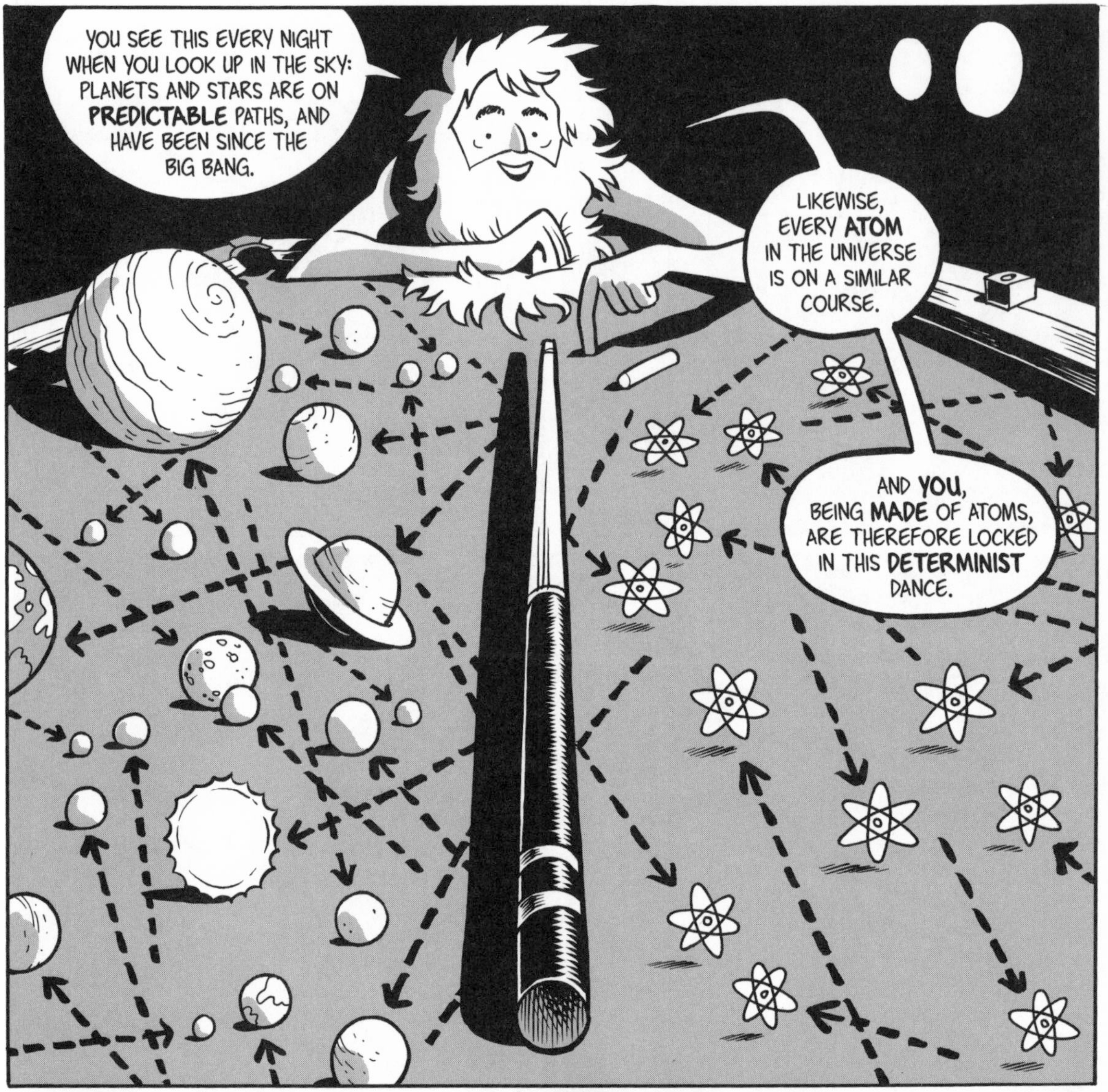
YOU SEE THIS EVERY NIGHT WHEN YOU LOOK UP IN THE SKY: PLANETS AND STARS ARE ON PREDICTABLE PATHS, AND HAVE BEEN SINCE THE BIG BANG.
LIKEWISE, EVERY ATOM IN THE UNIVERSE IS ON A SIMILAR COURSE.
AND YOU, BEING MADE OF ATOMS, ARE THEREFORE LOCKED IN THIS DETERMINIST DANCE.

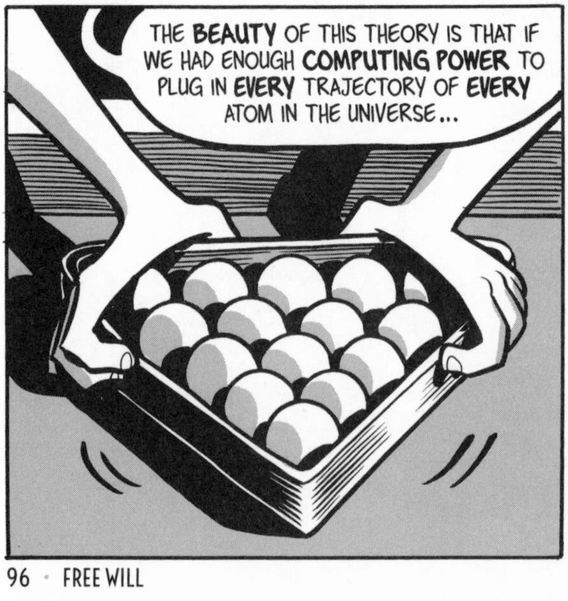
THE BEAUTY OF THIS THEORY IS THAT IF WE HAD ENOUGH COMPUTING POWER TO PLUG IN EVERY TRAJECTORY OF EVERY ATOM IN THE UNIVERSE...

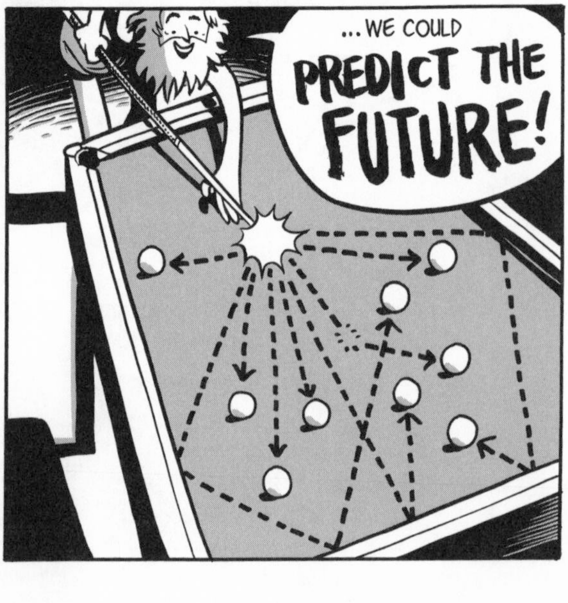
...WE COULD
PREDICT THE FUTURE!

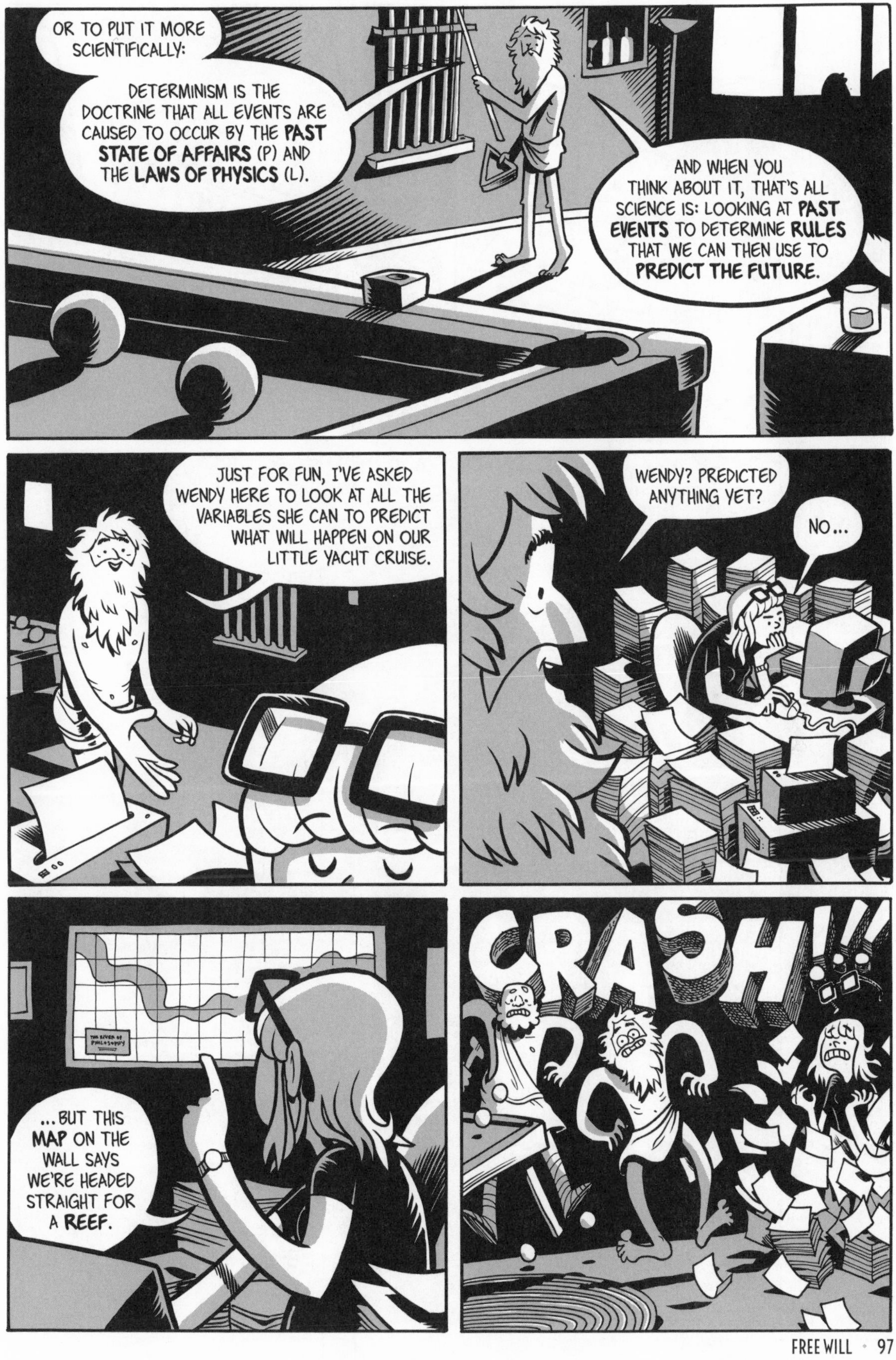
OR TO PUT IT MORE SCIENTIFICALLY:
DETERMINISM IS THE DOCTRINE THAT ALL EVENTS ARE CAUSED TO OCCUR BY THE **PAST STATE OF AFFAIRS** (P) AND THE **LAWS OF PHYSICS** (L).
AND WHEN YOU THINK ABOUT IT, THAT'S ALL SCIENCE IS: LOOKING AT **PAST EVENTS** TO DETERMINE **RULES** THAT WE CAN THEN USE TO **PREDICT THE FUTURE**.
JUST FOR FUN, I'VE ASKED WENDY HERE TO LOOK AT ALL THE VARIABLES SHE CAN TO PREDICT WHAT WILL HAPPEN ON OUR LITTLE YACHT CRUISE.
WENDY? PREDICTED ANYTHING YET?
NO...
THE RIVER OF PHILOSOPHY
...BUT THIS **MAP** ON THE WALL SAYS WE'RE HEADED STRAIGHT FOR A **REEF**.
CRASH!!!

SO. AS **AMAZING** AS DEMOCRITUS'S THEORY IS, THERE IS A **DOWNSIDE** TO DETERMINISM.

I'M TALKING ABOUT THE NECESSARY IMPLICATION THAT WE -- AS LUMPS OF ATOMS OURSELVES -- HAVE NO CHOICE BUT TO MOVE IN A PREDETERMINED WAY.

REMEMBER HOW LEIBNIZ THOUGHT THAT FREE WILL AND DETERMINISM COULD BE **COMPATIBLE**?

WELL, NOT HERE.

Premises:

1) IF DETERMINISM IS TRUE, THEN EVERY EVENT IS CAUSED BY THE PAST AND THE LAWS OF NATURE.

2) IF EVERY EVENT IS CAUSED BY THE PAST AND THE LAWS OF NATURE, THEN MY DOING ACT A IS CAUSED BY THE PAST AND THE LAWS OF NATURE.

3) IF MY DOING ACT A IS CAUSED BY THE PAST AND THE LAWS OF NATURE, THEN I COULD NOT HAVE DONE OTHERWISE THAN ACT A UNLESS I CAN CONTROL THE PAST OR THE LAWS OF NATURE.

4) I CANNOT CONTROL THE PAST.

5) I CANNOT CONTROL THE LAWS OF NATURE.

6) IF DETERMINISM IS TRUE, THEN I COULD NOT HAVE DONE OTHERWISE THAN ACT A.

7) IF I COULD NOT HAVE DONE OTHERWISE THAN ACT A, THEN I AM NOT FREE WITH RESPECT TO ACT A.

8) IF DETERMINISM IS TRUE, THEN I AM NOT FREE WITH RESPECT TO ACT A.

9) THEREFORE, NO ONE IS FREE WITH RESPECT TO HIS OR HER ACTIONS.

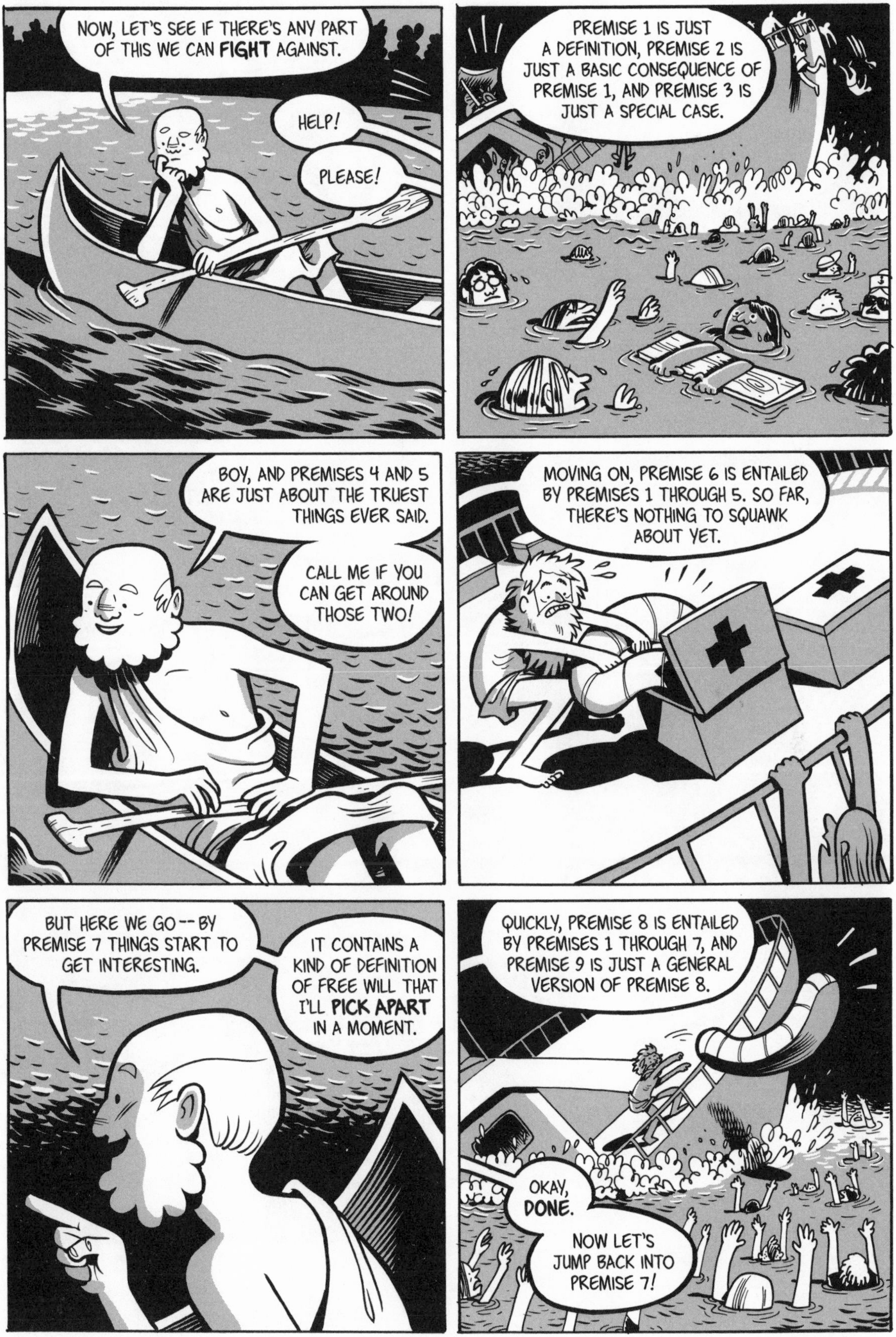

NOW, LET'S SEE IF THERE'S ANY PART OF THIS WE CAN **FIGHT** AGAINST.
HELP!
PLEASE!
PREMISE 1 IS JUST A DEFINITION, PREMISE 2 IS JUST A BASIC CONSEQUENCE OF PREMISE 1, AND PREMISE 3 IS JUST A SPECIAL CASE.
BOY, AND PREMISES 4 AND 5 ARE JUST ABOUT THE TRUEST THINGS EVER SAID.
CALL ME IF YOU CAN GET AROUND THOSE TWO!
MOVING ON, PREMISE 6 IS ENTAILED BY PREMISES 1 THROUGH 5. SO FAR, THERE'S NOTHING TO SQUAWK ABOUT YET.
BUT HERE WE GO-- BY PREMISE 7 THINGS START TO GET INTERESTING.
IT CONTAINS A KIND OF DEFINITION OF FREE WILL THAT I'LL **PICK APART** IN A MOMENT.
QUICKLY, PREMISE 8 IS ENTAILED BY PREMISES 1 THROUGH 7, AND PREMISE 9 IS JUST A GENERAL VERSION OF PREMISE 8.
OKAY, **DONE**.
NOW LET'S JUMP BACK INTO PREMISE 7!

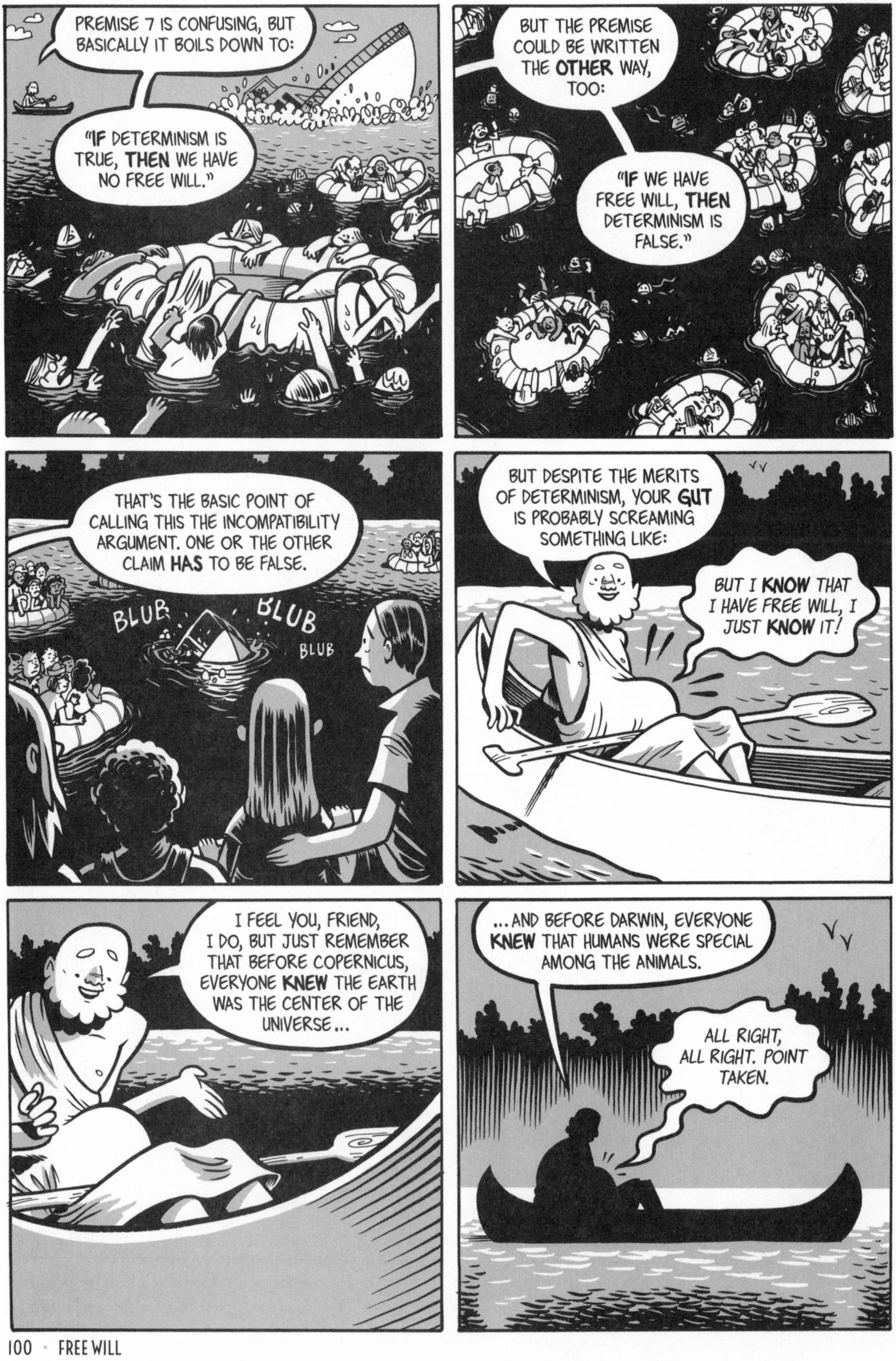
PREMISE 7 IS CONFUSING, BUT BASICALLY IT BOILS DOWN TO:
"IF DETERMINISM IS TRUE, THEN WE HAVE NO FREE WILL."
BUT THE PREMISE COULD BE WRITTEN THE OTHER WAY, TOO:
"IF WE HAVE FREE WILL, THEN DETERMINISM IS FALSE."
THAT'S THE BASIC POINT OF CALLING THIS THE INCOMPATIBILITY ARGUMENT. ONE OR THE OTHER CLAIM HAS TO BE FALSE.
BLUB
BLUB
BLUB
BUT DESPITE THE MERITS OF DETERMINISM, YOUR GUT IS PROBABLY SCREAMING SOMETHING LIKE:
BUT I KNOW THAT I HAVE FREE WILL, I JUST KNOW IT!
I FEEL YOU, FRIEND, I DO, BUT JUST REMEMBER THAT BEFORE COPERNICUS, EVERYONE KNEW THE EARTH WAS THE CENTER OF THE UNIVERSE...
...AND BEFORE DARWIN, EVERYONE KNEW THAT HUMANS WERE SPECIAL AMONG THE ANIMALS.
ALL RIGHT, ALL RIGHT. POINT TAKEN.

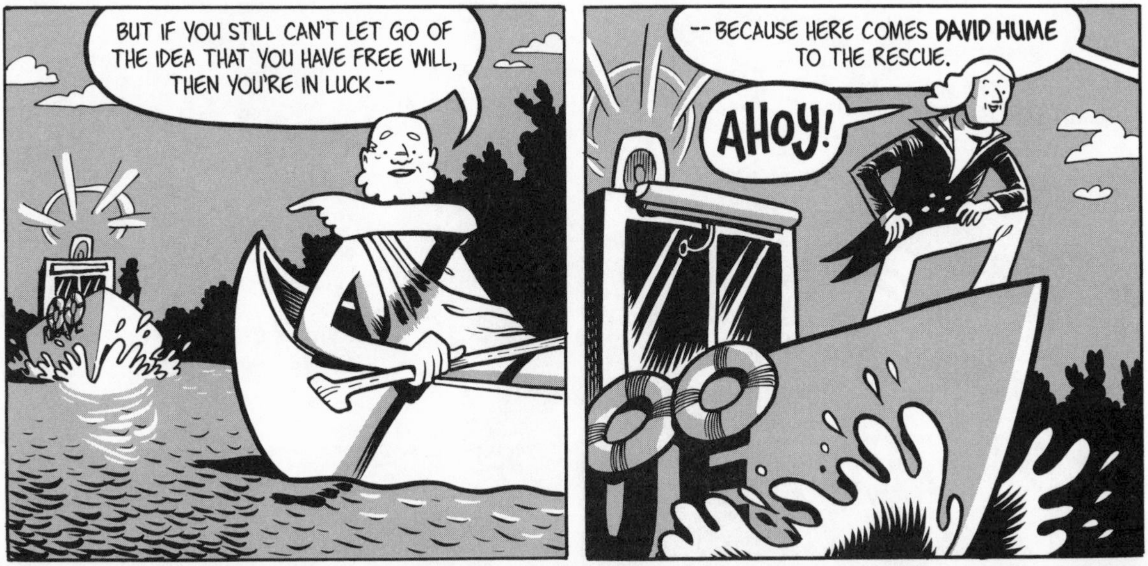
BUT IF YOU STILL CAN'T LET GO OF THE IDEA THAT YOU HAVE FREE WILL, THEN YOU'RE IN LUCK--
-- BECAUSE HERE COMES **DAVID HUME** TO THE RESCUE.
AHOY!

DAVID HUME

b. 1711
d. 1776
C.E.

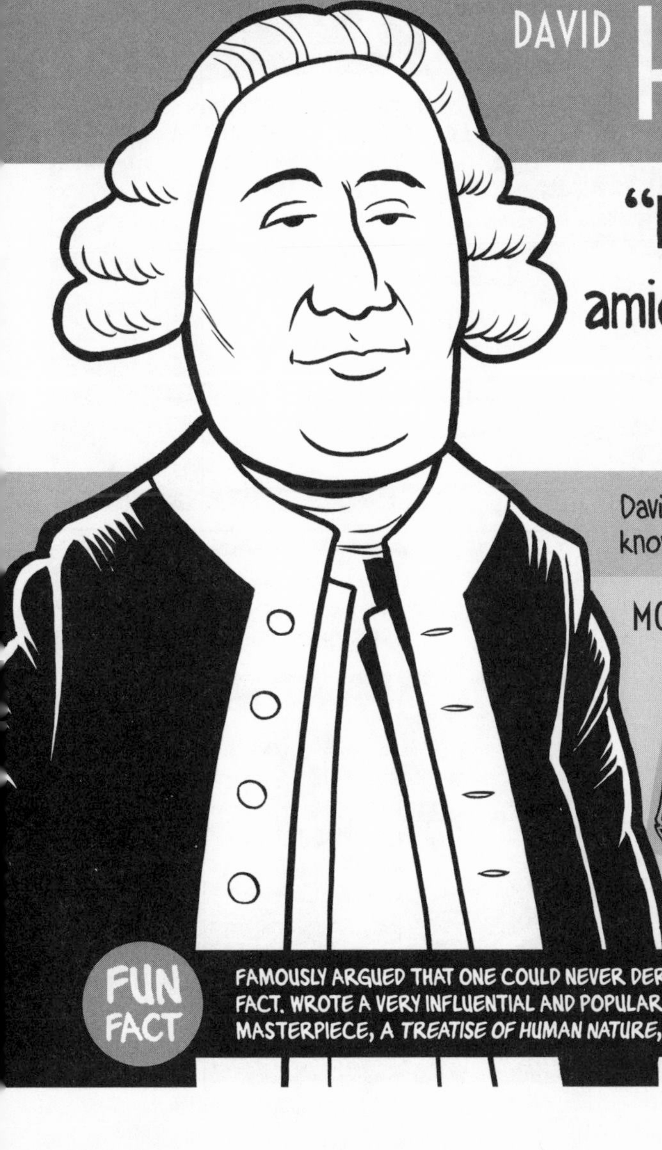

"Be a philosopher; but, amidst all your philosophy, be still a man."

-- *An Enquiry Concerning Human Understanding* (1748)

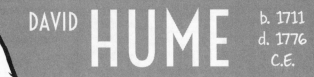

David Hume was a Scottish philosopher most known for his empiricism and skepticism.

MOST FAMOUS WORK:

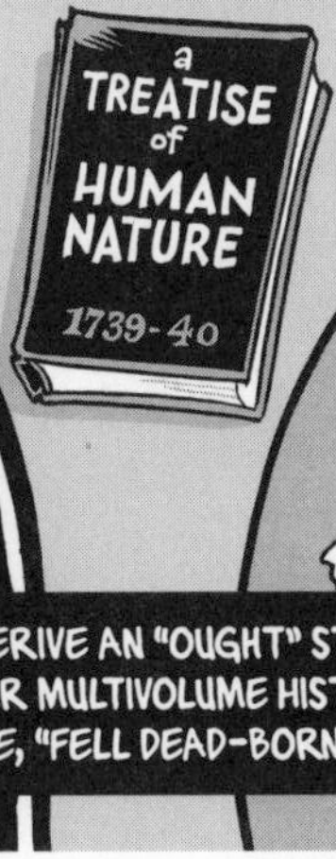
a
TREATISE
of
HUMAN
NATURE
1739-40

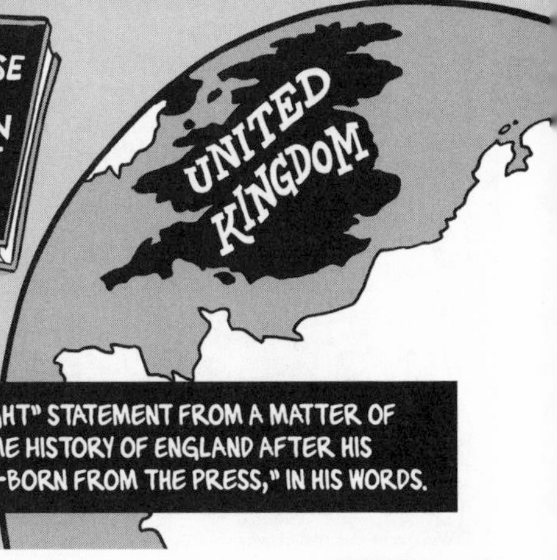
UNITED
KINGDOM

FUN FACT

FAMOUSLY ARGUED THAT ONE COULD NEVER DERIVE AN "OUGHT" STATEMENT FROM A MATTER OF FACT. WROTE A VERY INFLUENTIAL AND POPULAR MULTIVOLUME HISTORY OF ENGLAND AFTER HIS MASTERPIECE, *A TREATISE OF HUMAN NATURE*, "FELL DEAD-BORN FROM THE PRESS," IN HIS WORDS.

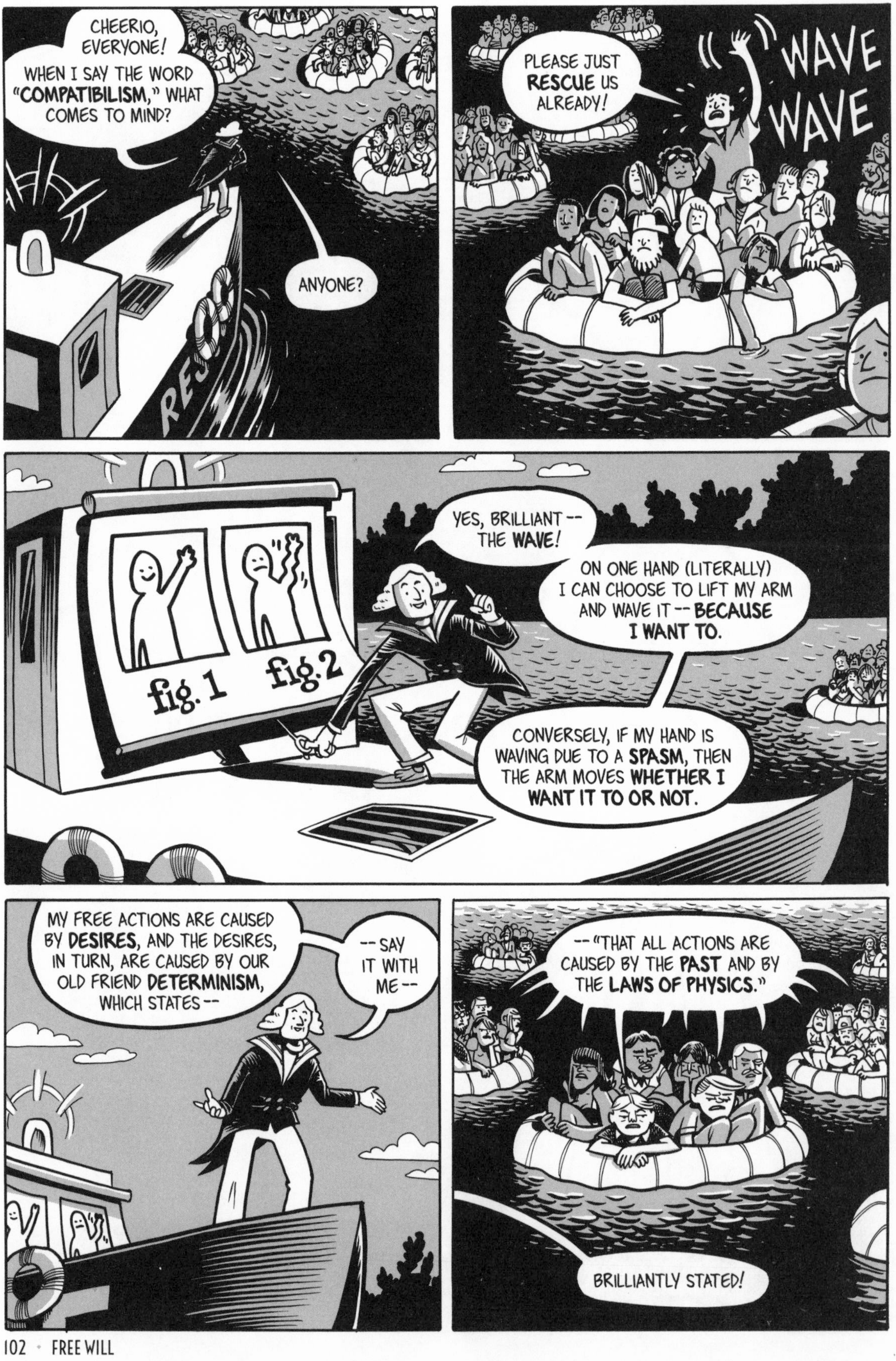
CHEERIO, EVERYONE!
WHEN I SAY THE WORD "COMPATIBILISM," WHAT COMES TO MIND?
ANYONE?
RES
PLEASE JUST RESCUE US ALREADY!
WAVE WAVE
YES, BRILLIANT -- THE WAVE!
fig. 1
fig. 2
ON ONE HAND (LITERALLY) I CAN CHOOSE TO LIFT MY ARM AND WAVE IT -- BECAUSE I WANT TO.
CONVERSELY, IF MY HAND IS WAVING DUE TO A SPASM, THEN THE ARM MOVES WHETHER I WANT IT TO OR NOT.
MY FREE ACTIONS ARE CAUSED BY DESIRES, AND THE DESIRES, IN TURN, ARE CAUSED BY OUR OLD FRIEND DETERMINISM, WHICH STATES --
-- SAY IT WITH ME --
-- "THAT ALL ACTIONS ARE CAUSED BY THE PAST AND BY THE LAWS OF PHYSICS."
BRILLIANTLY STATED!

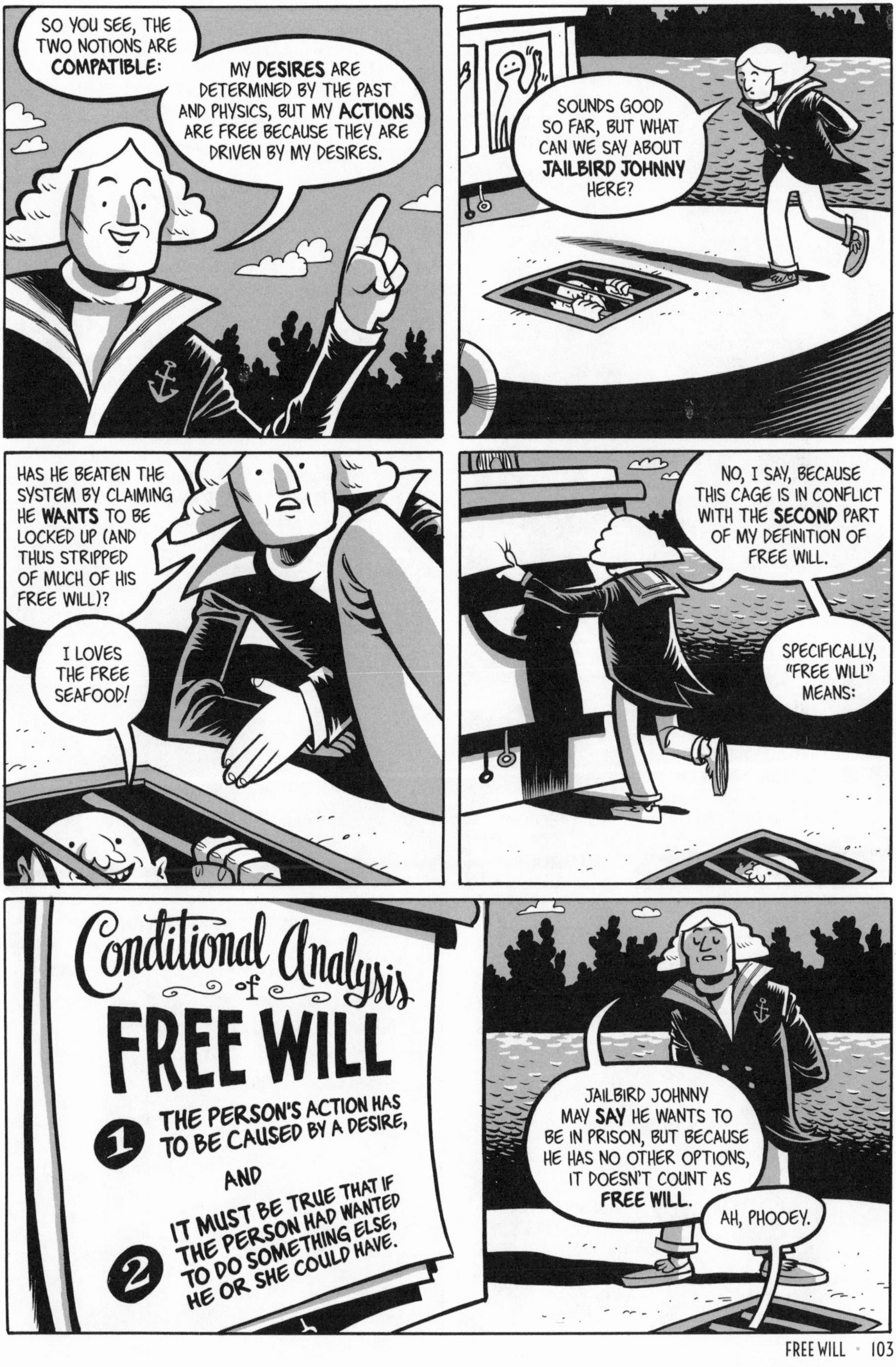
SO YOU SEE, THE TWO NOTIONS ARE **COMPATIBLE**:
MY **DESIRES** ARE DETERMINED BY THE PAST AND PHYSICS, BUT MY **ACTIONS** ARE FREE BECAUSE THEY ARE DRIVEN BY MY DESIRES.
SOUNDS GOOD SO FAR, BUT WHAT CAN WE SAY ABOUT **JAILBIRD JOHNNY** HERE?
HAS HE BEATEN THE SYSTEM BY CLAIMING HE **WANTS** TO BE LOCKED UP (AND THUS STRIPPED OF MUCH OF HIS FREE WILL)?
I LOVES THE FREE SEAFOOD!
NO, I SAY, BECAUSE THIS CAGE IS IN CONFLICT WITH THE **SECOND** PART OF MY DEFINITION OF FREE WILL.
SPECIFICALLY, "FREE WILL" MEANS:
Conditional Analysis of FREE WILL
1 THE PERSON'S ACTION HAS TO BE CAUSED BY A DESIRE,
AND
2 IT MUST BE TRUE THAT IF THE PERSON HAD WANTED TO DO SOMETHING ELSE, HE OR SHE COULD HAVE.
JAILBIRD JOHNNY MAY **SAY** HE WANTS TO BE IN PRISON, BUT BECAUSE HE HAS NO OTHER OPTIONS, IT DOESN'T COUNT AS **FREE WILL**.
AH, PHOOEY.

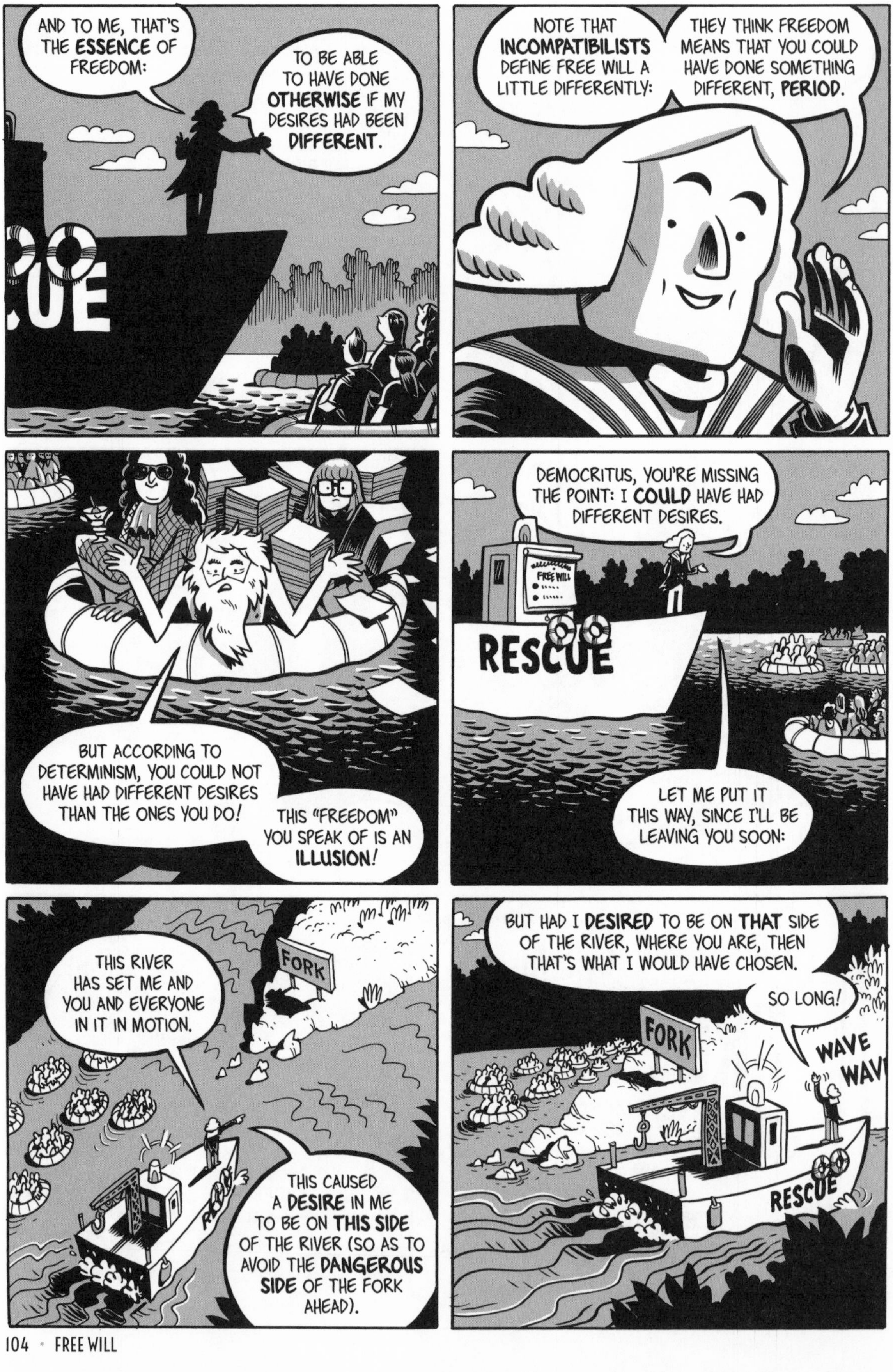
AND TO ME, THAT'S THE **ESSENCE** OF FREEDOM:
TO BE ABLE TO HAVE DONE **OTHERWISE** IF MY DESIRES HAD BEEN **DIFFERENT**.
RESCUE
NOTE THAT **INCOMPATIBILISTS** DEFINE FREE WILL A LITTLE DIFFERENTLY:
THEY THINK FREEDOM MEANS THAT YOU COULD HAVE DONE SOMETHING DIFFERENT, **PERIOD**.
BUT ACCORDING TO DETERMINISM, YOU COULD NOT HAVE HAD DIFFERENT DESIRES THAN THE ONES YOU DO!
THIS "FREEDOM" YOU SPEAK OF IS AN **ILLUSION**!
DEMOCRITUS, YOU'RE MISSING THE POINT: I **COULD** HAVE HAD DIFFERENT DESIRES.
FREE WILL
RESCUE
LET ME PUT IT THIS WAY, SINCE I'LL BE LEAVING YOU SOON:
THIS RIVER HAS SET ME AND YOU AND EVERYONE IN IT IN MOTION.
FORK
THIS CAUSED A **DESIRE** IN ME TO BE ON **THIS SIDE** OF THE RIVER (SO AS TO AVOID THE **DANGEROUS SIDE** OF THE FORK AHEAD).
BUT HAD I **DESIRED** TO BE ON **THAT** SIDE OF THE RIVER, WHERE YOU ARE, THEN THAT'S WHAT I WOULD HAVE CHOSEN.
SO LONG!
FORK
WAVE WAV
RESCUE

YIKES.

AHH!

SO... ARE YOU CONVINCED BY HUME'S ACCOUNT OF COMPATIBILISM?

A LOT OF PEOPLE ARE.

HURK!

BUT CONSIDER THIS:

CRITICS CONTEND THAT HYPNOTISTS COULD **PLANT** DESIRES IN THEIR SUBJECTS --

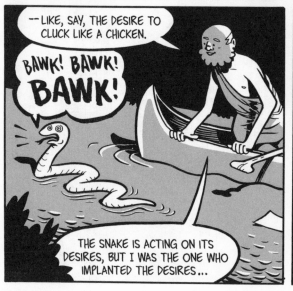

--LIKE, SAY, THE DESIRE TO CLUCK LIKE A CHICKEN.

BAWK! BAWK! BAWK!

THE SNAKE IS ACTING ON ITS DESIRES, BUT I WAS THE ONE WHO IMPLANTED THE DESIRES...

...SO EVEN THOUGH THIS SCENARIO **FITS** WITH COMPATIBILISM, WHO'S **REALLY** IN CONTROL OF THE SNAKE'S CHOICES HERE, ME OR THE SNAKE?

MODERN SCIENCE, TOO, HAS SOMETHING TO SAY ABOUT THIS.

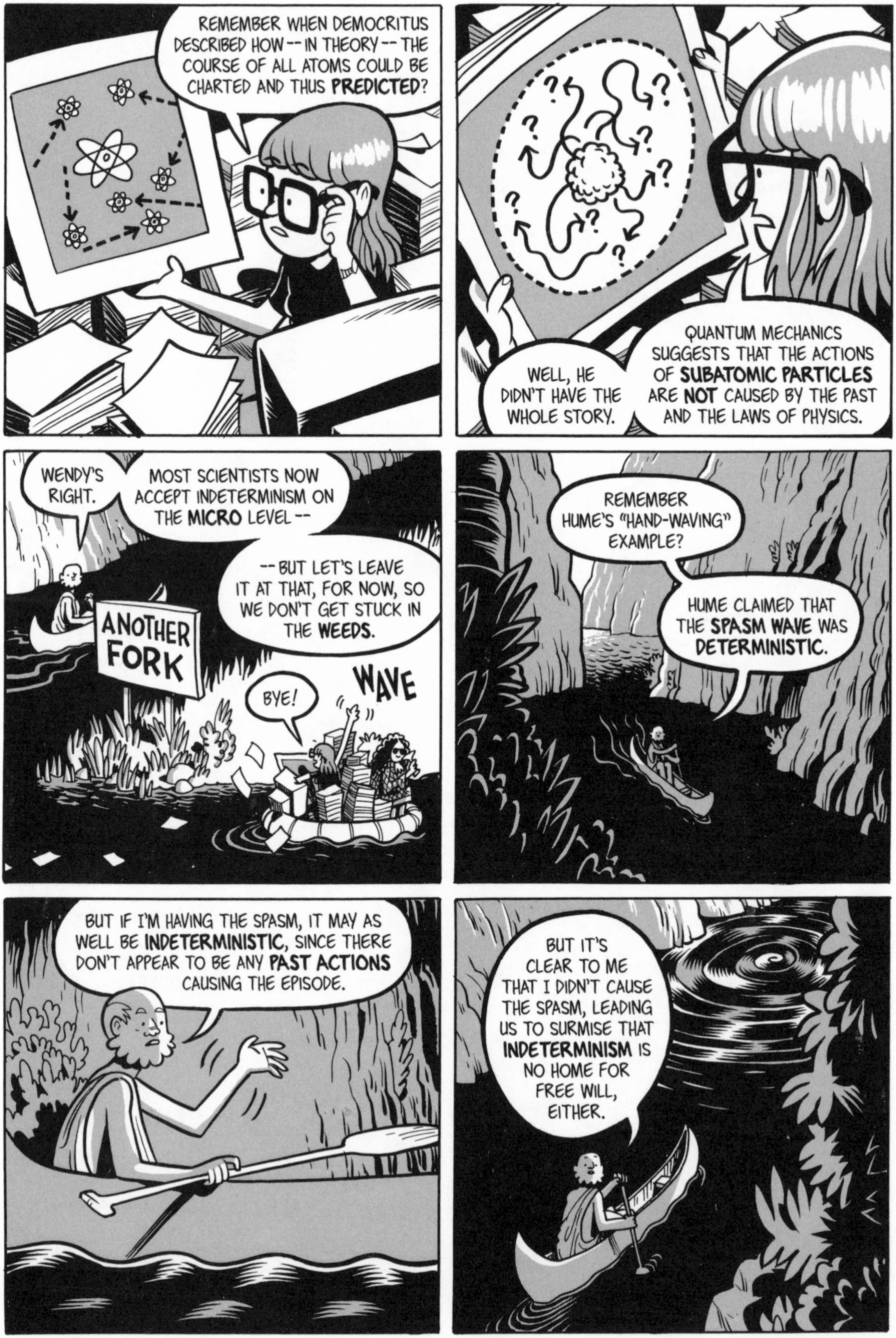

REMEMBER WHEN DEMOCRITUS DESCRIBED HOW -- IN THEORY -- THE COURSE OF ALL ATOMS COULD BE CHARTED AND THUS **PREDICTED**?
WELL, HE DIDN'T HAVE THE WHOLE STORY.
QUANTUM MECHANICS SUGGESTS THAT THE ACTIONS OF **SUBATOMIC PARTICLES** ARE **NOT** CAUSED BY THE PAST AND THE LAWS OF PHYSICS.
WENDY'S RIGHT.
MOST SCIENTISTS NOW ACCEPT INDETERMINISM ON THE **MICRO** LEVEL --
-- BUT LET'S LEAVE IT AT THAT, FOR NOW, SO WE DON'T GET STUCK IN THE **WEEDS**.
ANOTHER FORK
BYE!
WAVE
REMEMBER HUME'S "HAND-WAVING" EXAMPLE?
HUME CLAIMED THAT THE **SPASM WAVE** WAS **DETERMINISTIC**.
BUT IF I'M HAVING THE SPASM, IT MAY AS WELL BE **INDETERMINISTIC**, SINCE THERE DON'T APPEAR TO BE ANY **PAST ACTIONS** CAUSING THE EPISODE.
BUT IT'S CLEAR TO ME THAT I DIDN'T CAUSE THE SPASM, LEADING US TO SURMISE THAT **INDETERMINISM** IS NO HOME FOR FREE WILL, EITHER.

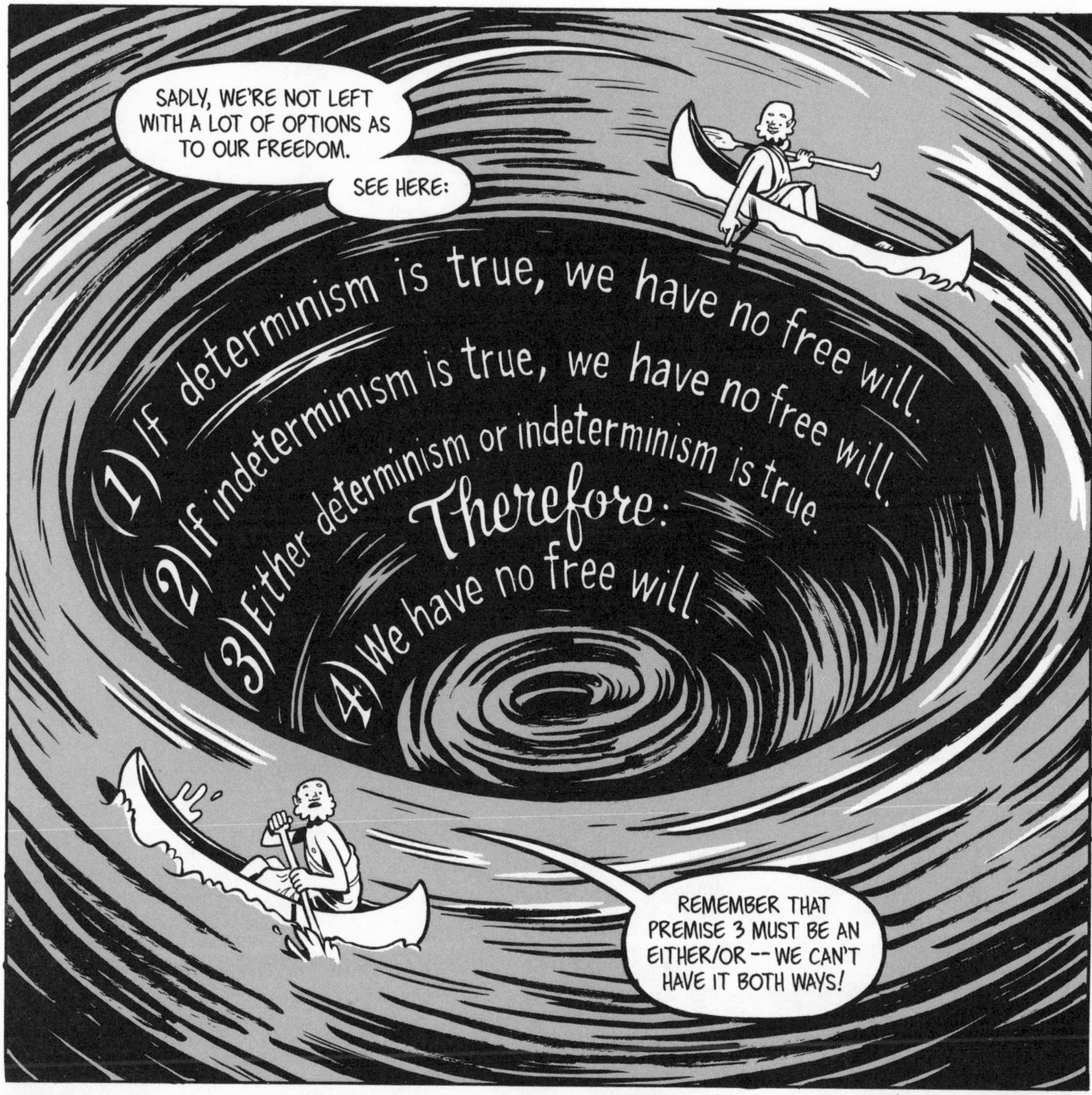
SADLY, WE'RE NOT LEFT WITH A LOT OF OPTIONS AS TO OUR FREEDOM.
SEE HERE:
(1) If determinism is true, we have no free will.
(2) If indeterminism is true, we have no free will.
(3) Either determinism or indeterminism is true.
Therefore:
(4) We have no free will.
REMEMBER THAT PREMISE 3 MUST BE AN EITHER/OR -- WE CAN'T HAVE IT BOTH WAYS!

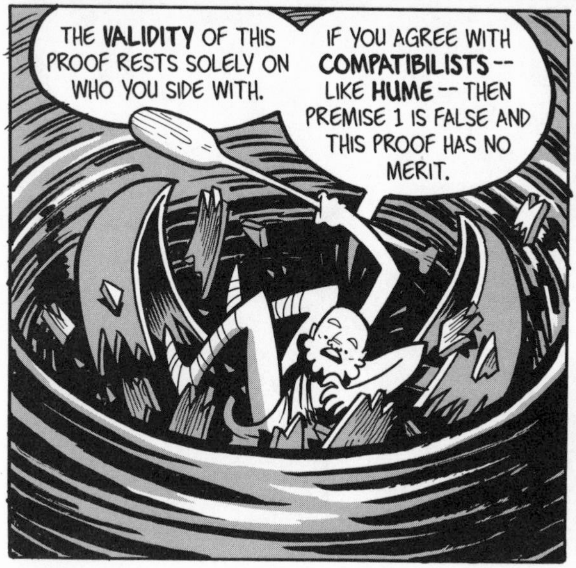
THE **VALIDITY** OF THIS PROOF RESTS SOLELY ON WHO YOU SIDE WITH.
IF YOU AGREE WITH **COMPATIBILISTS** -- LIKE **HUME** -- THEN PREMISE 1 IS FALSE AND THIS PROOF HAS NO MERIT.

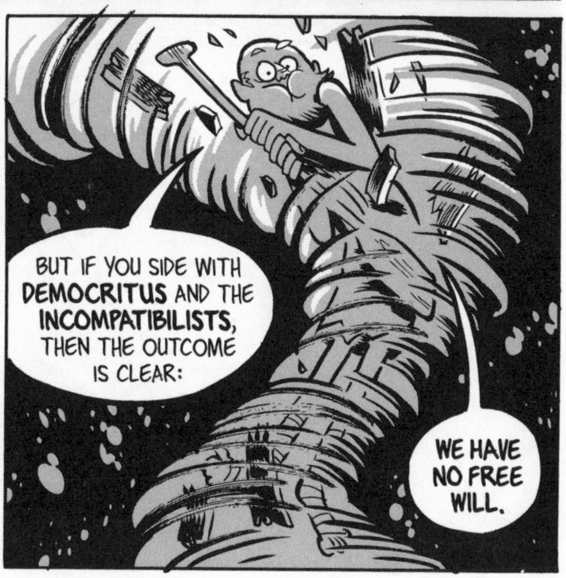
BUT IF YOU SIDE WITH **DEMOCRITUS** AND THE **INCOMPATIBILISTS**, THEN THE OUTCOME IS CLEAR:
WE HAVE NO FREE WILL.

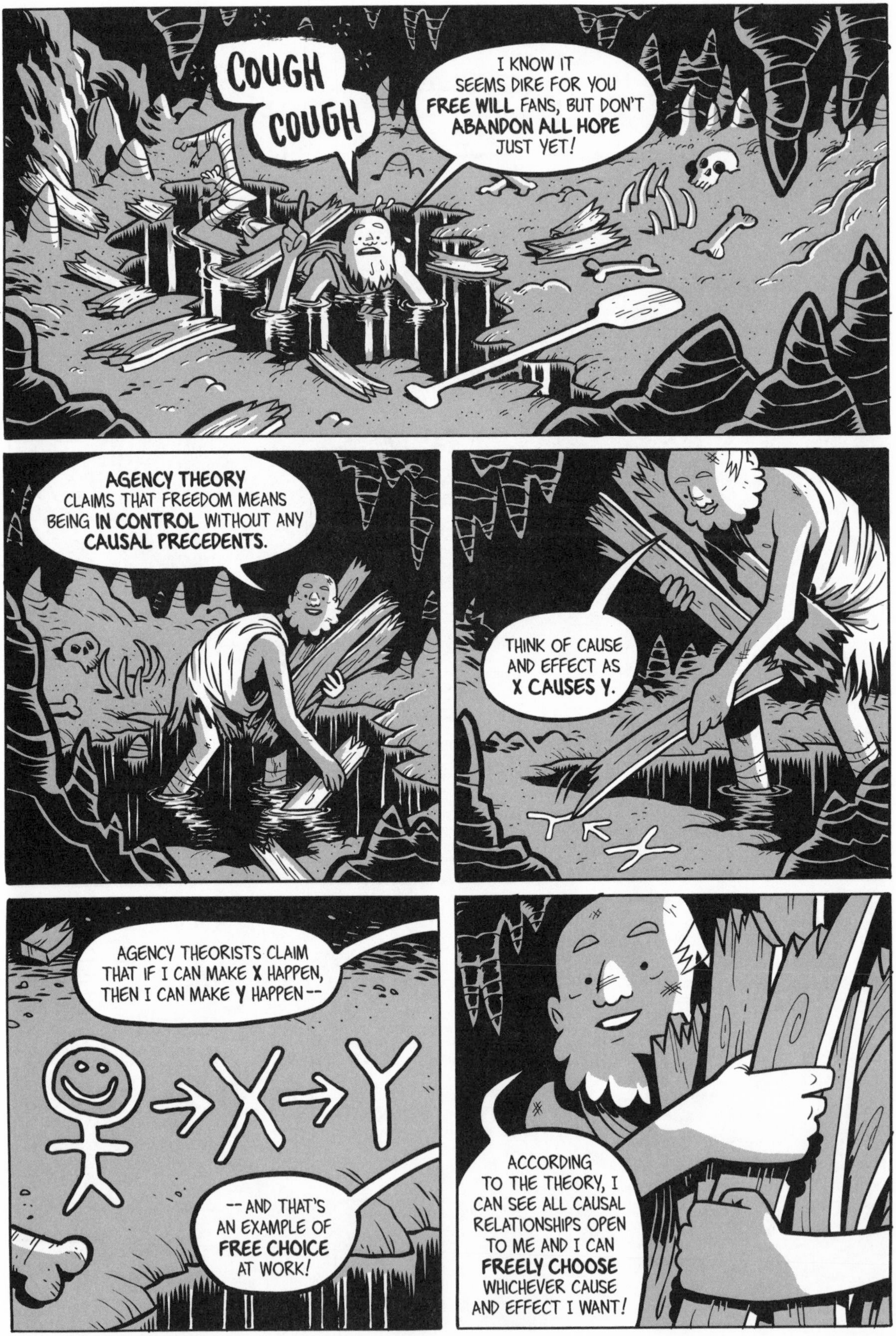
COUGH COUGH
I KNOW IT SEEMS DIRE FOR YOU FREE WILL FANS, BUT DON'T ABANDON ALL HOPE JUST YET!
AGENCY THEORY CLAIMS THAT FREEDOM MEANS BEING IN CONTROL WITHOUT ANY CAUSAL PRECEDENTS.
THINK OF CAUSE AND EFFECT AS X CAUSES Y.
Y
X
AGENCY THEORISTS CLAIM THAT IF I CAN MAKE X HAPPEN, THEN I CAN MAKE Y HAPPEN--
X
Y
--AND THAT'S AN EXAMPLE OF FREE CHOICE AT WORK!
ACCORDING TO THE THEORY, I CAN SEE ALL CAUSAL RELATIONSHIPS OPEN TO ME AND I CAN FREELY CHOOSE WHICHEVER CAUSE AND EFFECT I WANT!

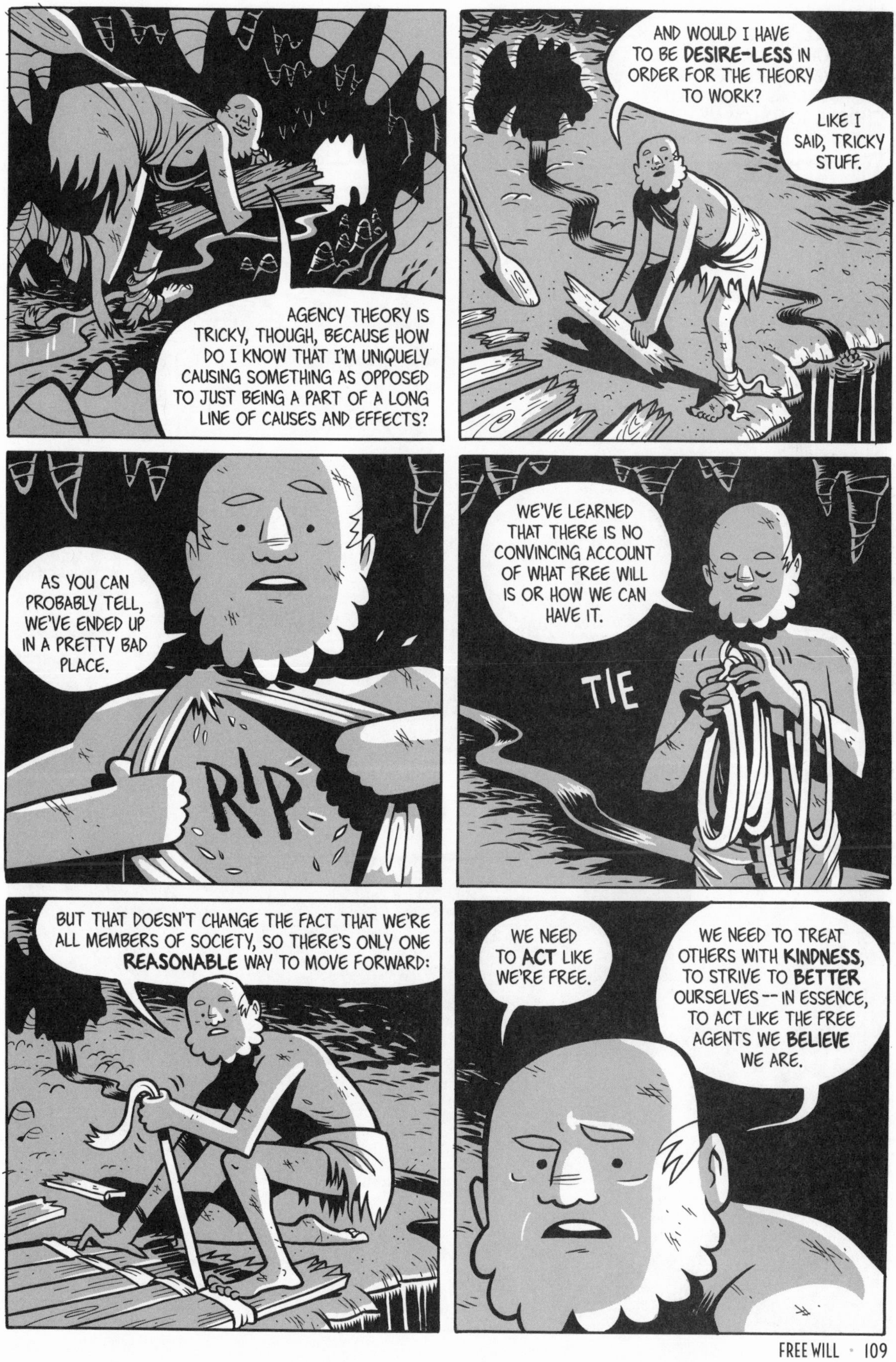
AGENCY THEORY IS TRICKY, THOUGH, BECAUSE HOW DO I KNOW THAT I'M UNIQUELY CAUSING SOMETHING AS OPPOSED TO JUST BEING A PART OF A LONG LINE OF CAUSES AND EFFECTS?
AND WOULD I HAVE TO BE **DESIRE-LESS** IN ORDER FOR THE THEORY TO WORK?
LIKE I SAID, TRICKY STUFF.
AS YOU CAN PROBABLY TELL, WE'VE ENDED UP IN A PRETTY BAD PLACE.
RIP
WE'VE LEARNED THAT THERE IS NO CONVINCING ACCOUNT OF WHAT FREE WILL IS OR HOW WE CAN HAVE IT.
TIE
BUT THAT DOESN'T CHANGE THE FACT THAT WE'RE ALL MEMBERS OF SOCIETY, SO THERE'S ONLY ONE **REASONABLE** WAY TO MOVE FORWARD:
WE NEED TO **ACT** LIKE WE'RE FREE.
WE NEED TO TREAT OTHERS WITH **KINDNESS**, TO STRIVE TO **BETTER** OURSELVES -- IN ESSENCE, TO ACT LIKE THE FREE AGENTS WE **BELIEVE** WE ARE.

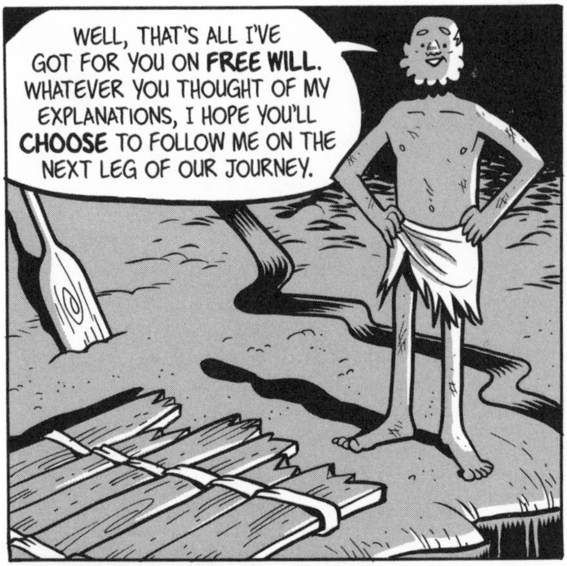
WELL, THAT'S ALL I'VE GOT FOR YOU ON **FREE WILL**. WHATEVER YOU THOUGHT OF MY EXPLANATIONS, I HOPE YOU'LL **CHOOSE** TO FOLLOW ME ON THE NEXT LEG OF OUR JOURNEY.

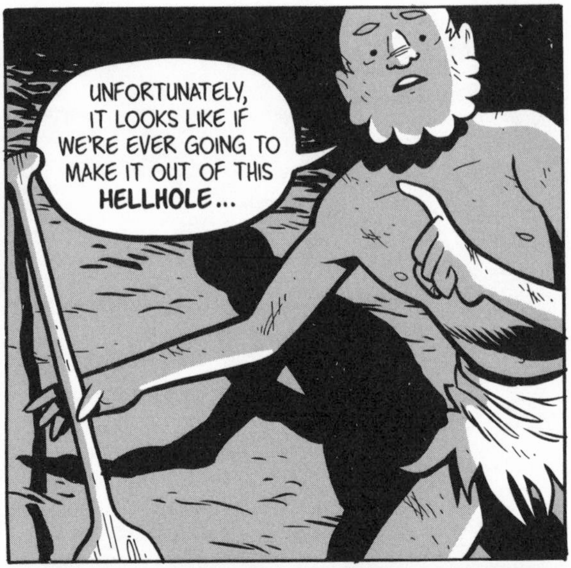
UNFORTUNATELY, IT LOOKS LIKE IF WE'RE EVER GOING TO MAKE IT OUT OF THIS **HELLHOLE**...

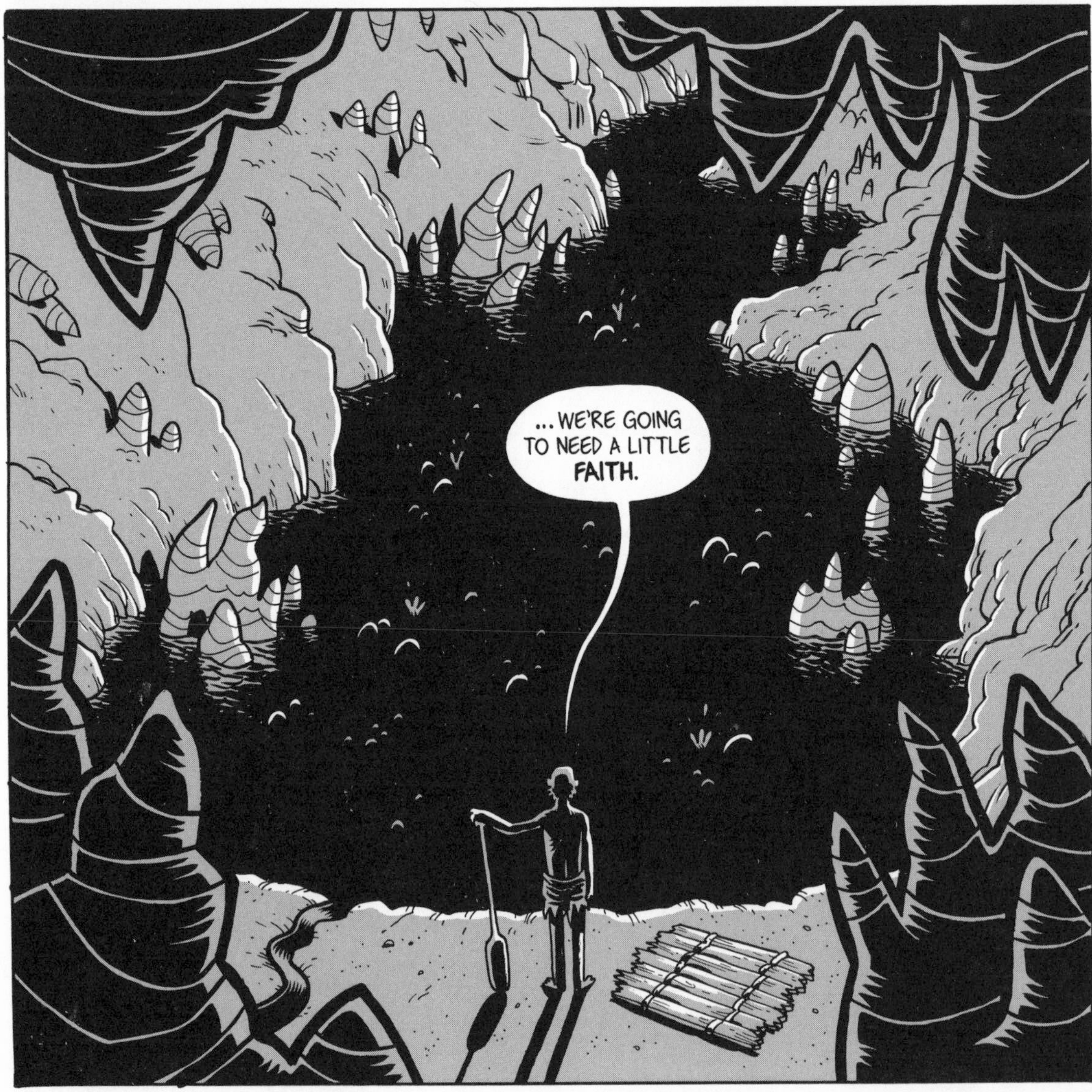
...WE'RE GOING TO NEED A LITTLE **FAITH**.

chapter 5

GOD

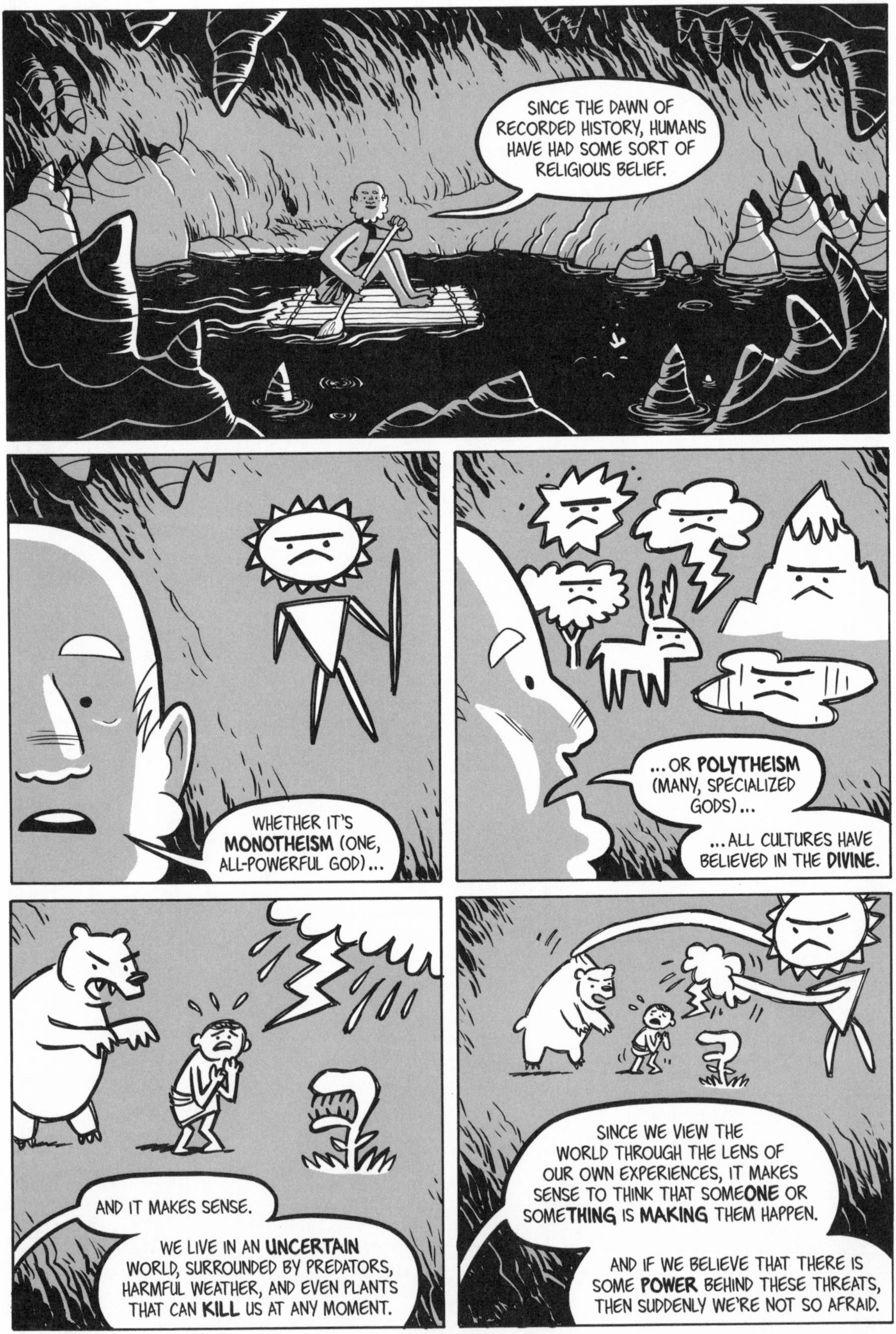
SINCE THE DAWN OF RECORDED HISTORY, HUMANS HAVE HAD SOME SORT OF RELIGIOUS BELIEF.
WHETHER IT'S **MONOTHEISM** (ONE, ALL-POWERFUL GOD)...
...OR **POLYTHEISM** (MANY, SPECIALIZED GODS)...
...ALL CULTURES HAVE BELIEVED IN THE **DIVINE**.
AND IT MAKES SENSE.
WE LIVE IN AN **UNCERTAIN** WORLD, SURROUNDED BY PREDATORS, HARMFUL WEATHER, AND EVEN PLANTS THAT CAN **KILL** US AT ANY MOMENT.
SINCE WE VIEW THE WORLD THROUGH THE LENS OF OUR OWN EXPERIENCES, IT MAKES SENSE TO THINK THAT SOME**ONE** OR SOME**THING** IS **MAKING** THEM HAPPEN.
AND IF WE BELIEVE THAT THERE IS SOME **POWER** BEHIND THESE THREATS, THEN SUDDENLY WE'RE NOT SO AFRAID.

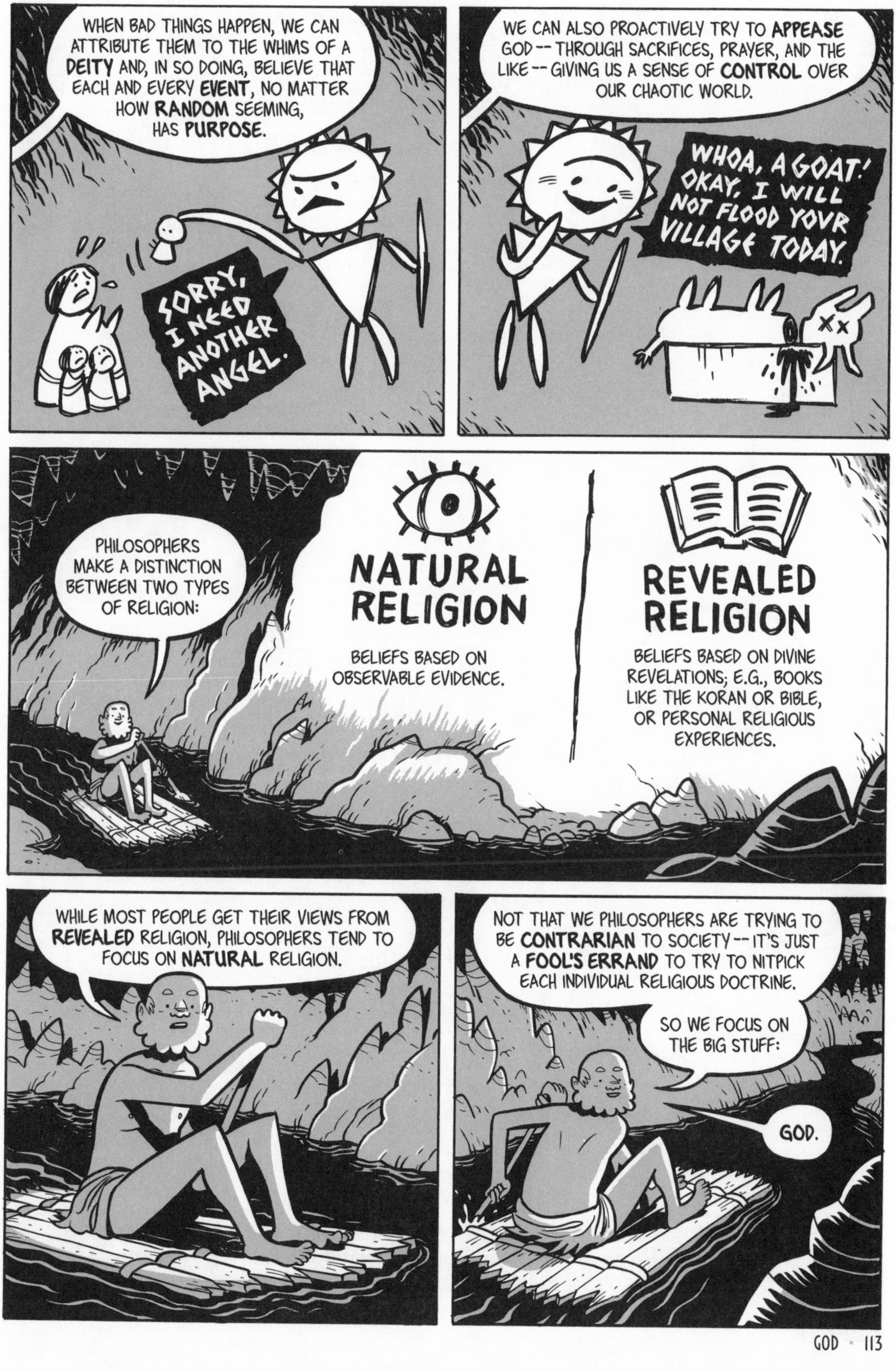
WHEN BAD THINGS HAPPEN, WE CAN ATTRIBUTE THEM TO THE WHIMS OF A DEITY AND, IN SO DOING, BELIEVE THAT EACH AND EVERY EVENT, NO MATTER HOW RANDOM SEEMING, HAS PURPOSE.
SORRY, I NEED ANOTHER ANGEL.
WE CAN ALSO PROACTIVELY TRY TO APPEASE GOD -- THROUGH SACRIFICES, PRAYER, AND THE LIKE -- GIVING US A SENSE OF CONTROL OVER OUR CHAOTIC WORLD.
WHOA, A GOAT! OKAY, I WILL NOT FLOOD YOUR VILLAGE TODAY.
PHILOSOPHERS MAKE A DISTINCTION BETWEEN TWO TYPES OF RELIGION:
NATURAL RELIGION
BELIEFS BASED ON OBSERVABLE EVIDENCE.
REVEALED RELIGION
BELIEFS BASED ON DIVINE REVELATIONS; E.G., BOOKS LIKE THE KORAN OR BIBLE, OR PERSONAL RELIGIOUS EXPERIENCES.
WHILE MOST PEOPLE GET THEIR VIEWS FROM REVEALED RELIGION, PHILOSOPHERS TEND TO FOCUS ON NATURAL RELIGION.
NOT THAT WE PHILOSOPHERS ARE TRYING TO BE CONTRARIAN TO SOCIETY -- IT'S JUST A FOOL'S ERRAND TO TRY TO NITPICK EACH INDIVIDUAL RELIGIOUS DOCTRINE.
SO WE FOCUS ON THE BIG STUFF:
GOD.

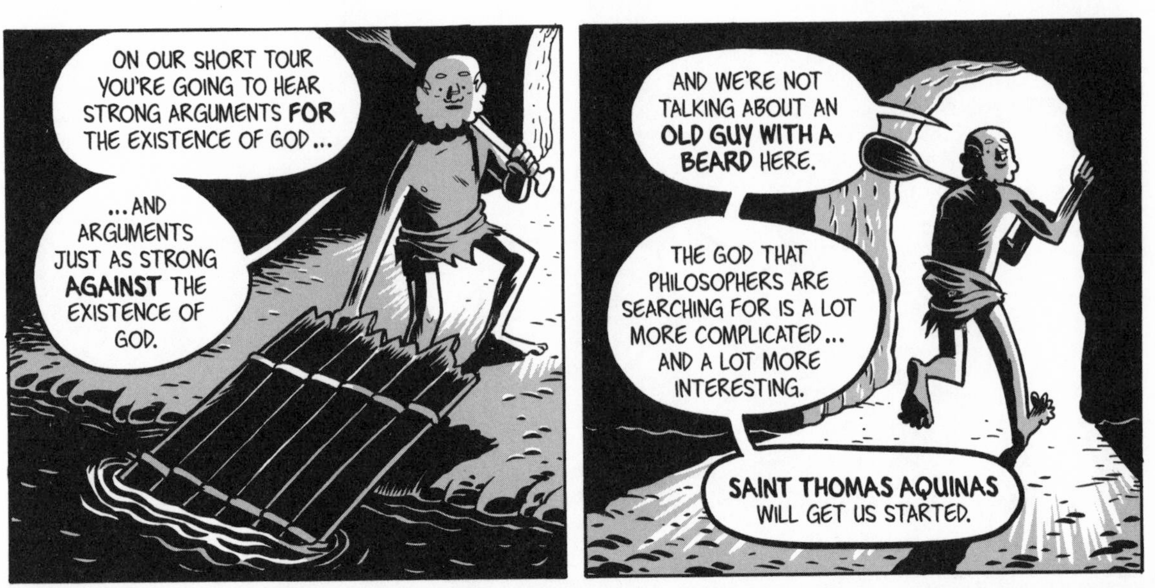
ON OUR SHORT TOUR YOU'RE GOING TO HEAR STRONG ARGUMENTS **FOR** THE EXISTENCE OF GOD...
...AND ARGUMENTS JUST AS STRONG **AGAINST** THE EXISTENCE OF GOD.
AND WE'RE NOT TALKING ABOUT AN **OLD GUY WITH A BEARD** HERE.
THE GOD THAT PHILOSOPHERS ARE SEARCHING FOR IS A LOT MORE COMPLICATED... AND A LOT MORE INTERESTING.
SAINT THOMAS AQUINAS WILL GET US STARTED.

THOMAS AQUINAS

b. 1225
d. 1274
C.E.

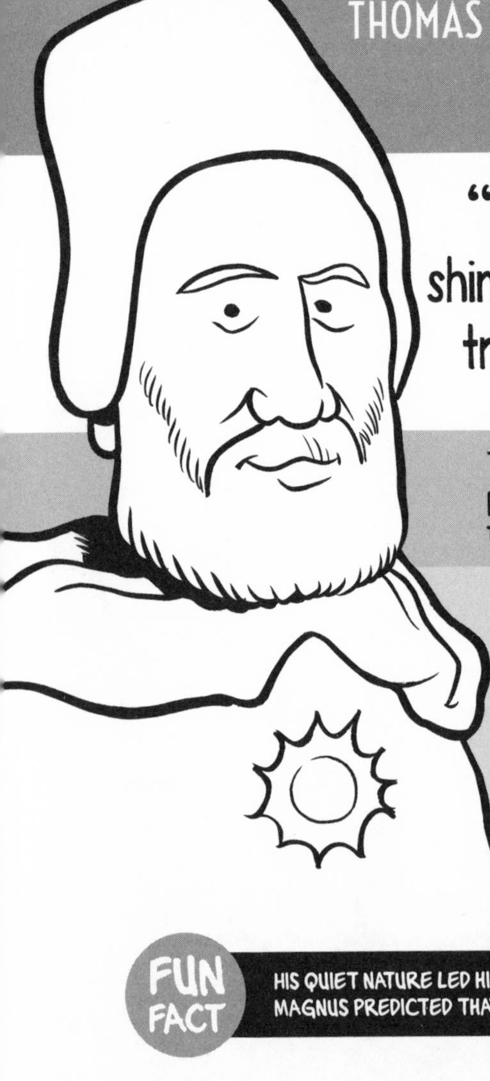

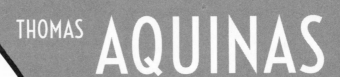

"Better to illuminate than merely to shine, to deliver to others contemplated truths than merely to contemplate."

-- *Summa Theologica*

Thomas Aquinas was an Italian Dominican friar and priest and an important philosopher and theologian in the tradition of scholasticism.

MOST FAMOUS WORK:

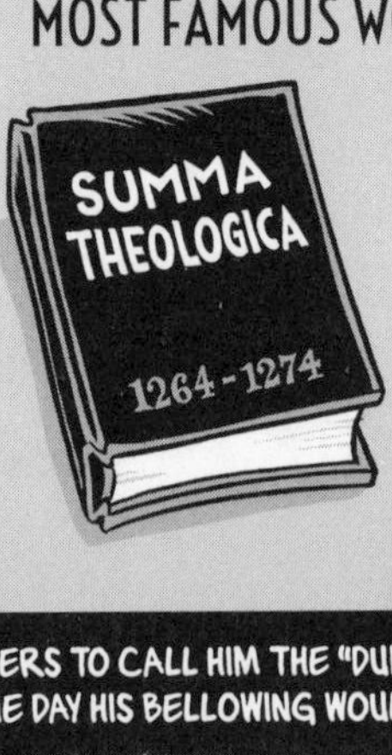
SUMMA THEOLOGICA
1264-1274

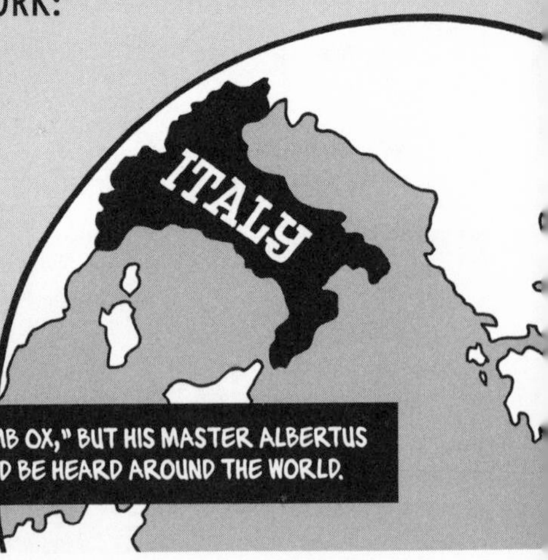
ITALY

FUN FACT HIS QUIET NATURE LED HIS PEERS TO CALL HIM THE "DUMB OX," BUT HIS MASTER ALBERTUS MAGNUS PREDICTED THAT ONE DAY HIS BELLOWING WOULD BE HEARD AROUND THE WORLD.

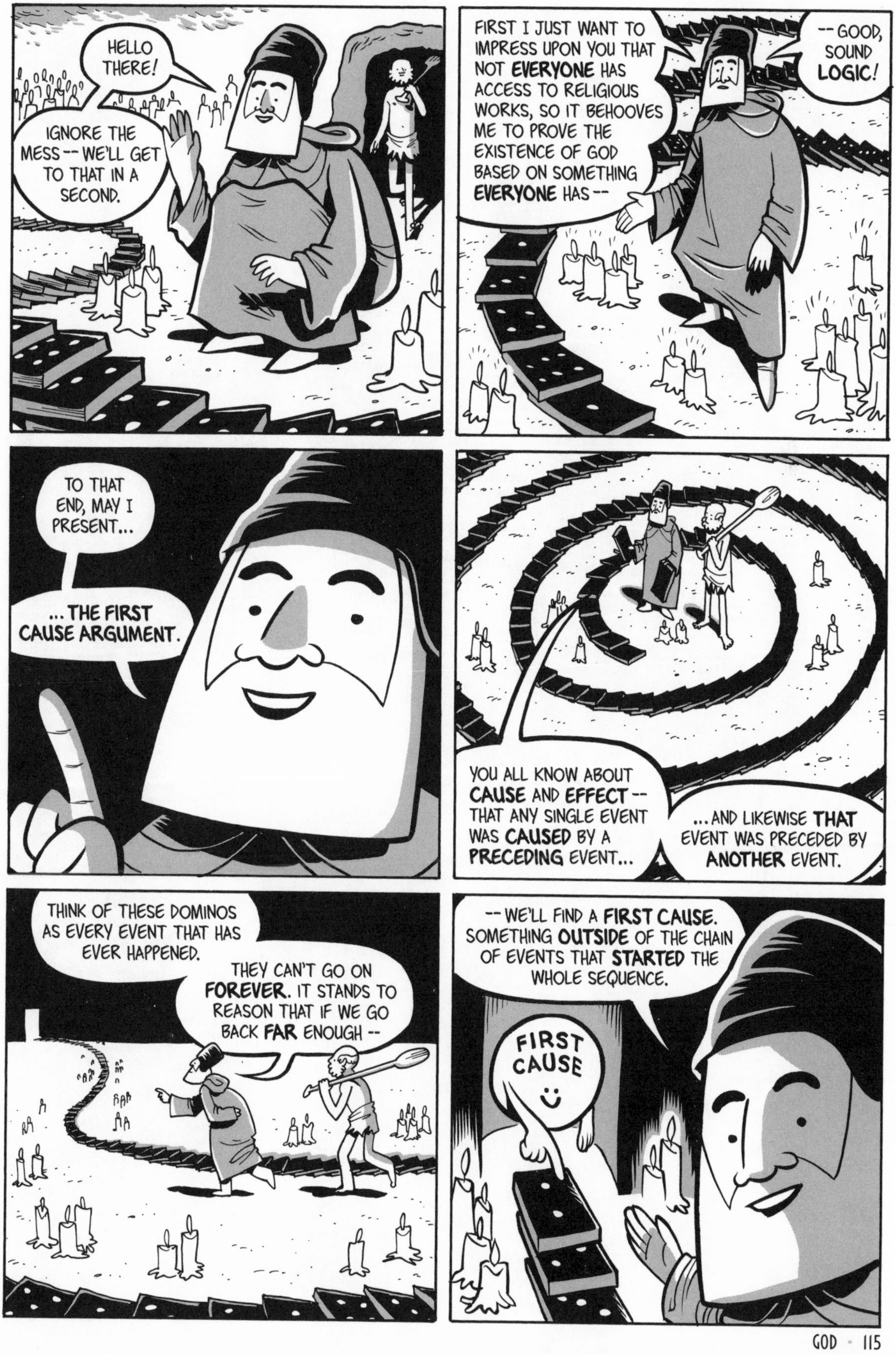
HELLO THERE!
IGNORE THE MESS -- WE'LL GET TO THAT IN A SECOND.
FIRST I JUST WANT TO IMPRESS UPON YOU THAT NOT **EVERYONE** HAS ACCESS TO RELIGIOUS WORKS, SO IT BEHOOVES ME TO PROVE THE EXISTENCE OF GOD BASED ON SOMETHING **EVERYONE** HAS --
-- GOOD, SOUND **LOGIC!**
TO THAT END, MAY I PRESENT...
... THE FIRST CAUSE ARGUMENT.
YOU ALL KNOW ABOUT **CAUSE** AND **EFFECT** -- THAT ANY SINGLE EVENT WAS **CAUSED** BY A **PRECEDING** EVENT...
... AND LIKEWISE **THAT** EVENT WAS PRECEDED BY **ANOTHER** EVENT.
THINK OF THESE DOMINOS AS EVERY EVENT THAT HAS EVER HAPPENED.
THEY CAN'T GO ON **FOREVER**. IT STANDS TO REASON THAT IF WE GO BACK **FAR** ENOUGH --
-- WE'LL FIND A **FIRST CAUSE**. SOMETHING **OUTSIDE** OF THE CHAIN OF EVENTS THAT **STARTED** THE WHOLE SEQUENCE.
FIRST CAUSE

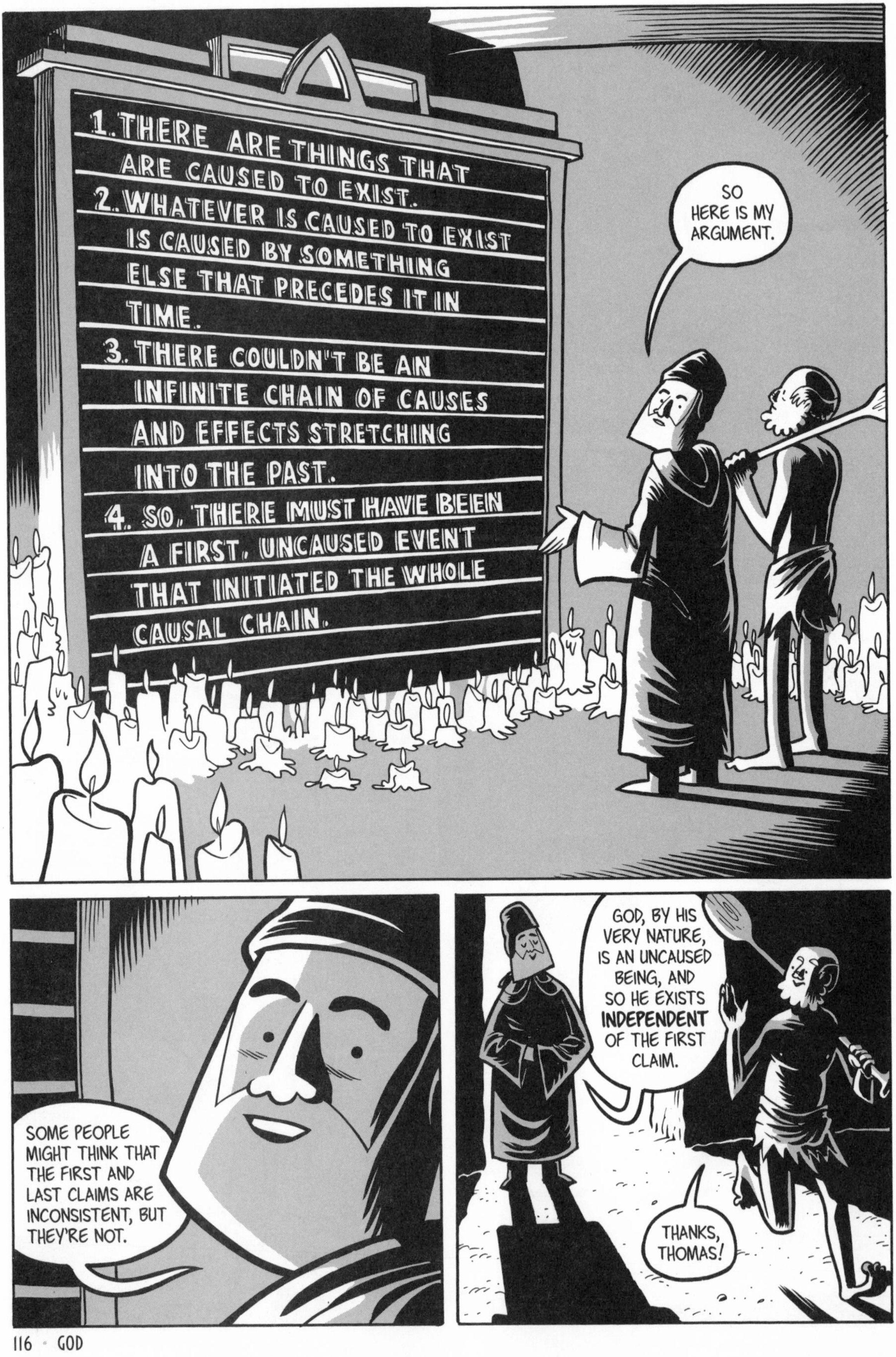
1. THERE ARE THINGS THAT ARE CAUSED TO EXIST.
2. WHATEVER IS CAUSED TO EXIST IS CAUSED BY SOMETHING ELSE THAT PRECEDES IT IN TIME.
3. THERE COULDN'T BE AN INFINITE CHAIN OF CAUSES AND EFFECTS STRETCHING INTO THE PAST.
4. SO, THERE MUST HAVE BEEN A FIRST, UNCAUSED EVENT THAT INITIATED THE WHOLE CAUSAL CHAIN.
SO HERE IS MY ARGUMENT.
SOME PEOPLE MIGHT THINK THAT THE FIRST AND LAST CLAIMS ARE INCONSISTENT, BUT THEY'RE NOT.
GOD, BY HIS VERY NATURE, IS AN UNCAUSED BEING, AND SO HE EXISTS **INDEPENDENT** OF THE FIRST CLAIM.
THANKS, THOMAS!

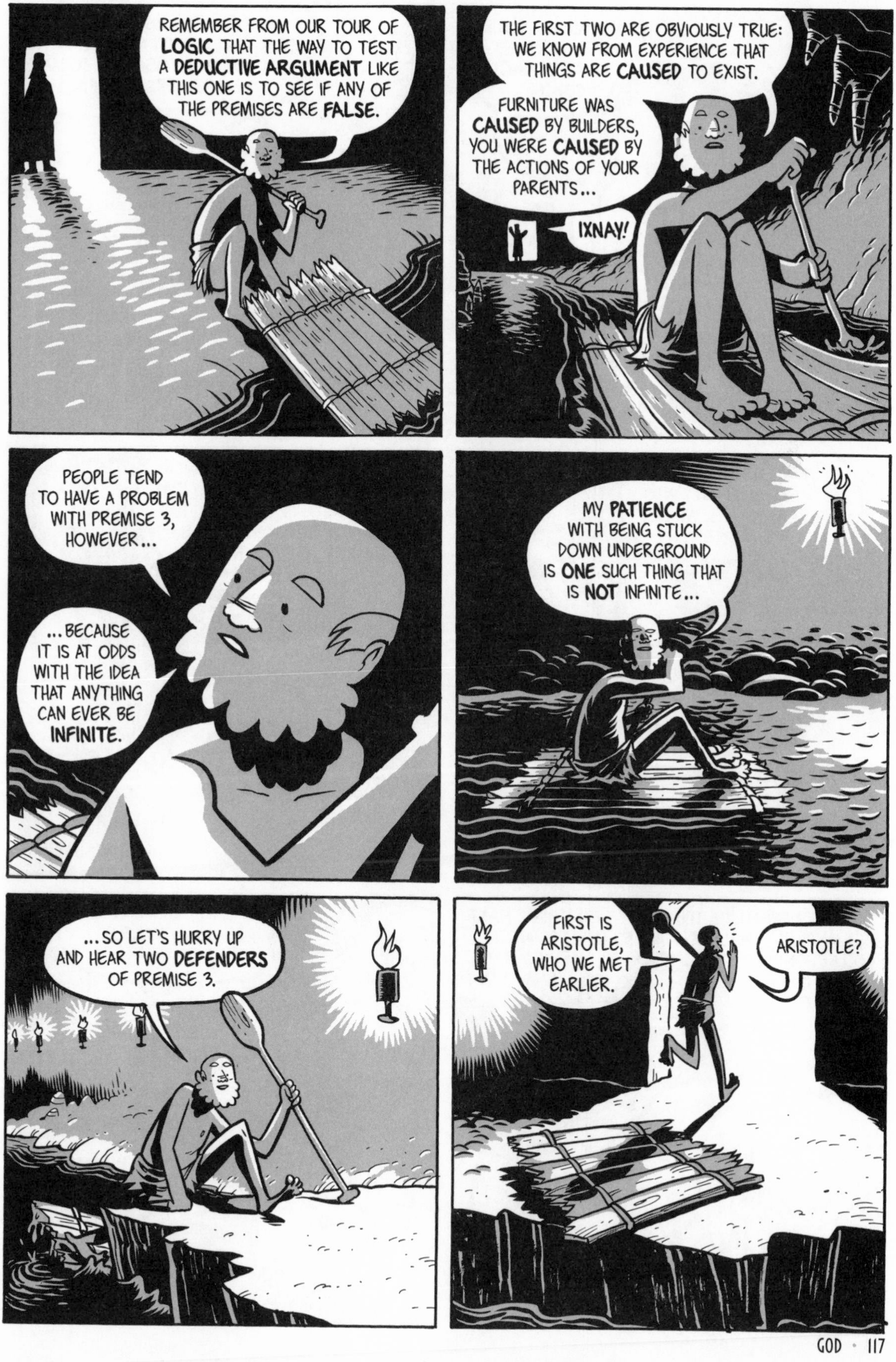
REMEMBER FROM OUR TOUR OF LOGIC THAT THE WAY TO TEST A DEDUCTIVE ARGUMENT LIKE THIS ONE IS TO SEE IF ANY OF THE PREMISES ARE FALSE.
THE FIRST TWO ARE OBVIOUSLY TRUE: WE KNOW FROM EXPERIENCE THAT THINGS ARE CAUSED TO EXIST.
FURNITURE WAS CAUSED BY BUILDERS, YOU WERE CAUSED BY THE ACTIONS OF YOUR PARENTS...
IXNAY!
PEOPLE TEND TO HAVE A PROBLEM WITH PREMISE 3, HOWEVER...
...BECAUSE IT IS AT ODDS WITH THE IDEA THAT ANYTHING CAN EVER BE INFINITE.
MY PATIENCE WITH BEING STUCK DOWN UNDERGROUND IS ONE SUCH THING THAT IS NOT INFINITE...
...SO LET'S HURRY UP AND HEAR TWO DEFENDERS OF PREMISE 3.
FIRST IS ARISTOTLE, WHO WE MET EARLIER.
ARISTOTLE?

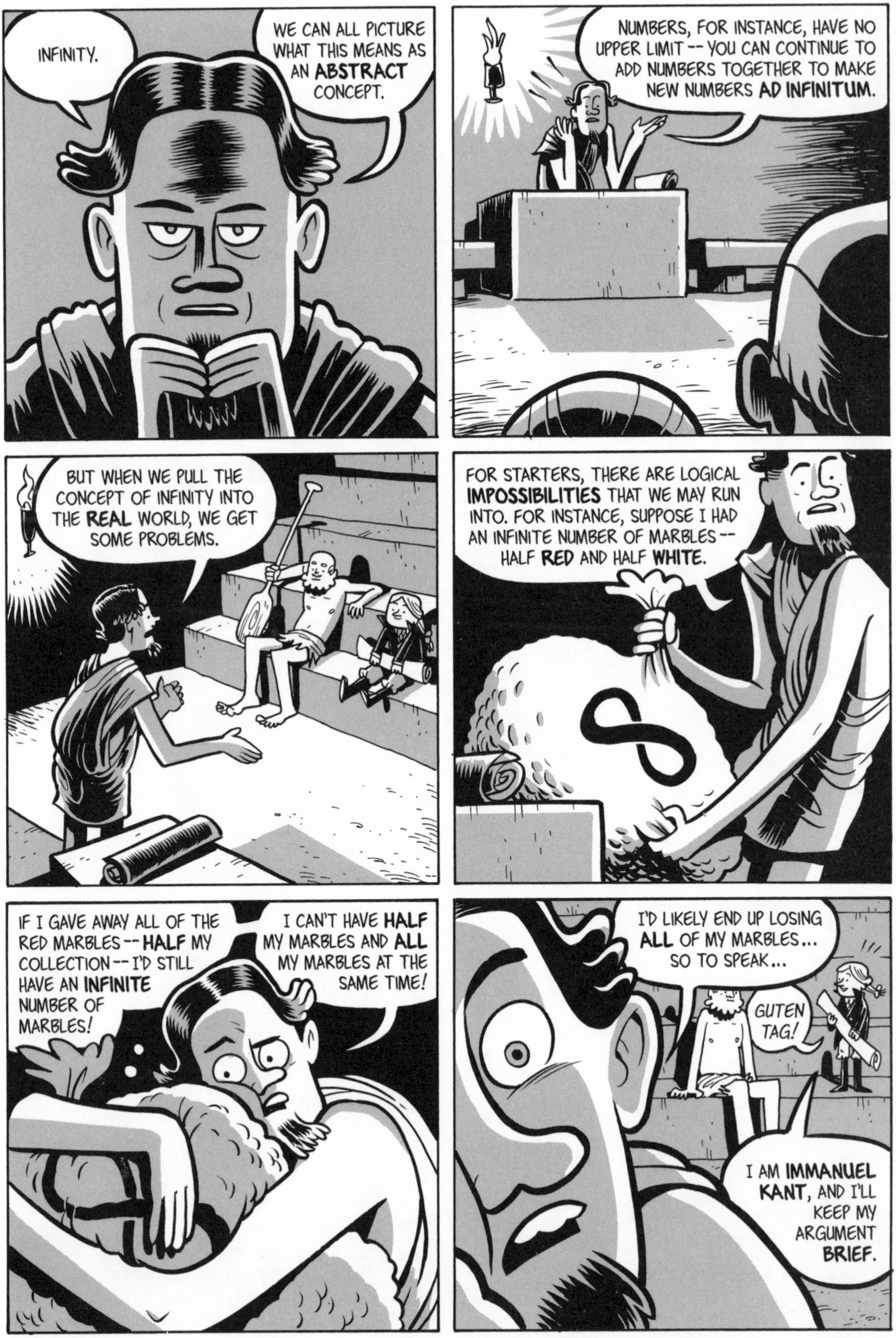
INFINITY.
WE CAN ALL PICTURE WHAT THIS MEANS AS AN ABSTRACT CONCEPT.
NUMBERS, FOR INSTANCE, HAVE NO UPPER LIMIT -- YOU CAN CONTINUE TO ADD NUMBERS TOGETHER TO MAKE NEW NUMBERS AD INFINITUM.
BUT WHEN WE PULL THE CONCEPT OF INFINITY INTO THE REAL WORLD, WE GET SOME PROBLEMS.
FOR STARTERS, THERE ARE LOGICAL IMPOSSIBILITIES THAT WE MAY RUN INTO. FOR INSTANCE, SUPPOSE I HAD AN INFINITE NUMBER OF MARBLES -- HALF RED AND HALF WHITE.
IF I GAVE AWAY ALL OF THE RED MARBLES -- HALF MY COLLECTION -- I'D STILL HAVE AN INFINITE NUMBER OF MARBLES!
I CAN'T HAVE HALF MY MARBLES AND ALL MY MARBLES AT THE SAME TIME!
I'D LIKELY END UP LOSING ALL OF MY MARBLES... SO TO SPEAK...
GUTEN TAG!
I AM IMMANUEL KANT, AND I'LL KEEP MY ARGUMENT BRIEF.

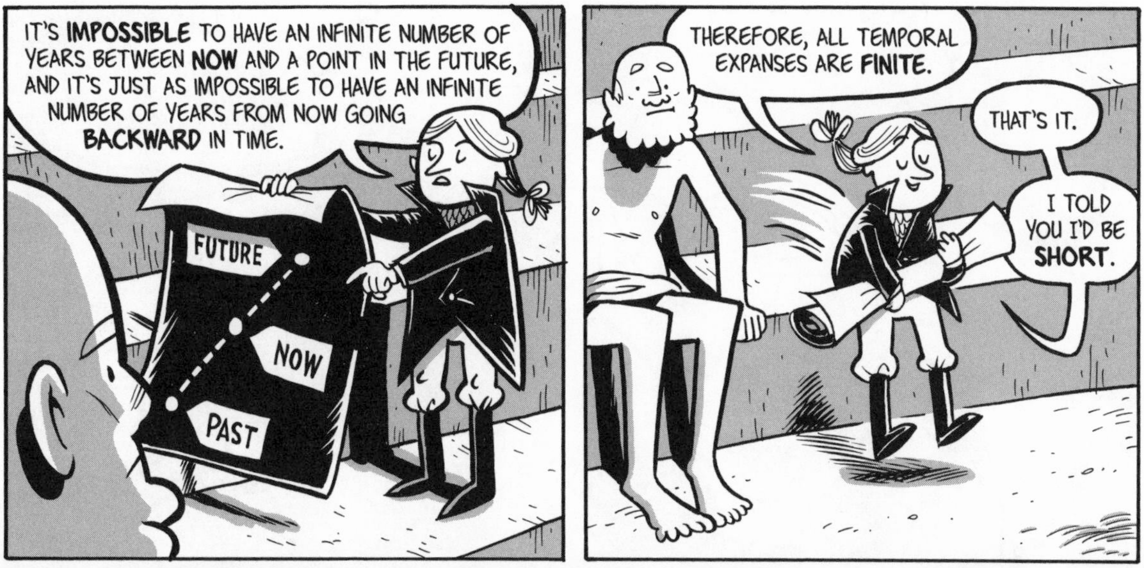
IT'S **IMPOSSIBLE** TO HAVE AN INFINITE NUMBER OF YEARS BETWEEN **NOW** AND A POINT IN THE FUTURE, AND IT'S JUST AS IMPOSSIBLE TO HAVE AN INFINITE NUMBER OF YEARS FROM NOW GOING **BACKWARD** IN TIME.
FUTURE
NOW
PAST
THEREFORE, ALL TEMPORAL EXPANSES ARE **FINITE**.
THAT'S IT.
I TOLD YOU I'D BE **SHORT**.

IMMANUEL KANT

b. 1724
d. 1804
C.E.

"Two things fill the mind with ever new and increasing admiration and awe, the oftener and the more steadily we reflect on them: the starry heavens above and the moral law within."

-- *Critique of Practical Reason* (1788)

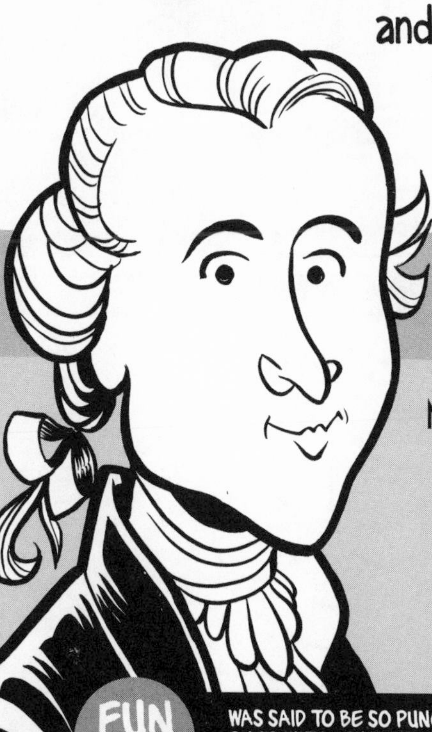

Immanuel Kant was a German philosopher who wrote influential works on metaphysics, ethics, and aesthetics.

MOST FAMOUS WORK:

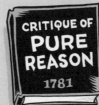

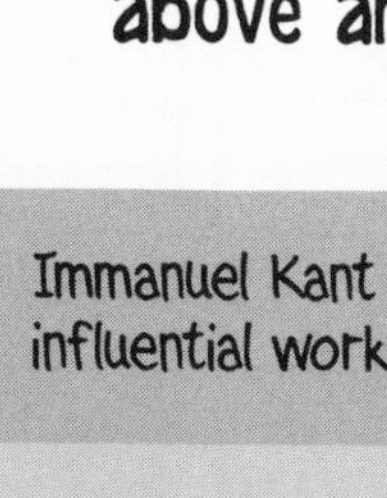
CRITIQUE OF
PURE
REASON
1781

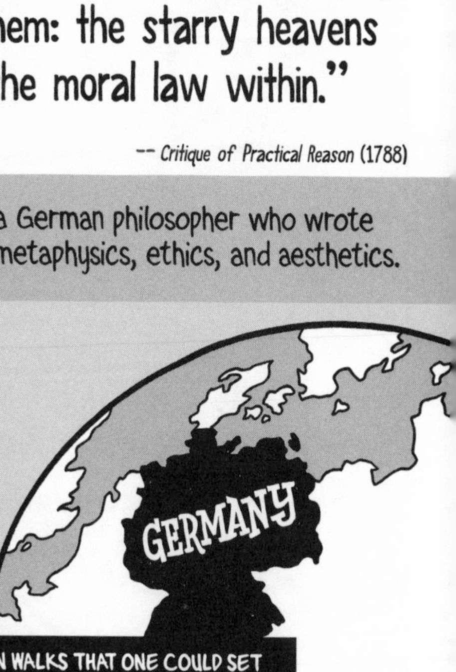
GERMANY

FUN FACT

WAS SAID TO BE SO PUNCTUAL DURING HIS AFTERNOON WALKS THAT ONE COULD SET ONE'S WATCH BY THEM. CLAIMED THAT READING HUME AWAKENED HIM FROM HIS "DOGMATIC SLUMBER" AND SET HIM ON THE ROAD TO HIS OWN PHILOSOPHICAL WORK.

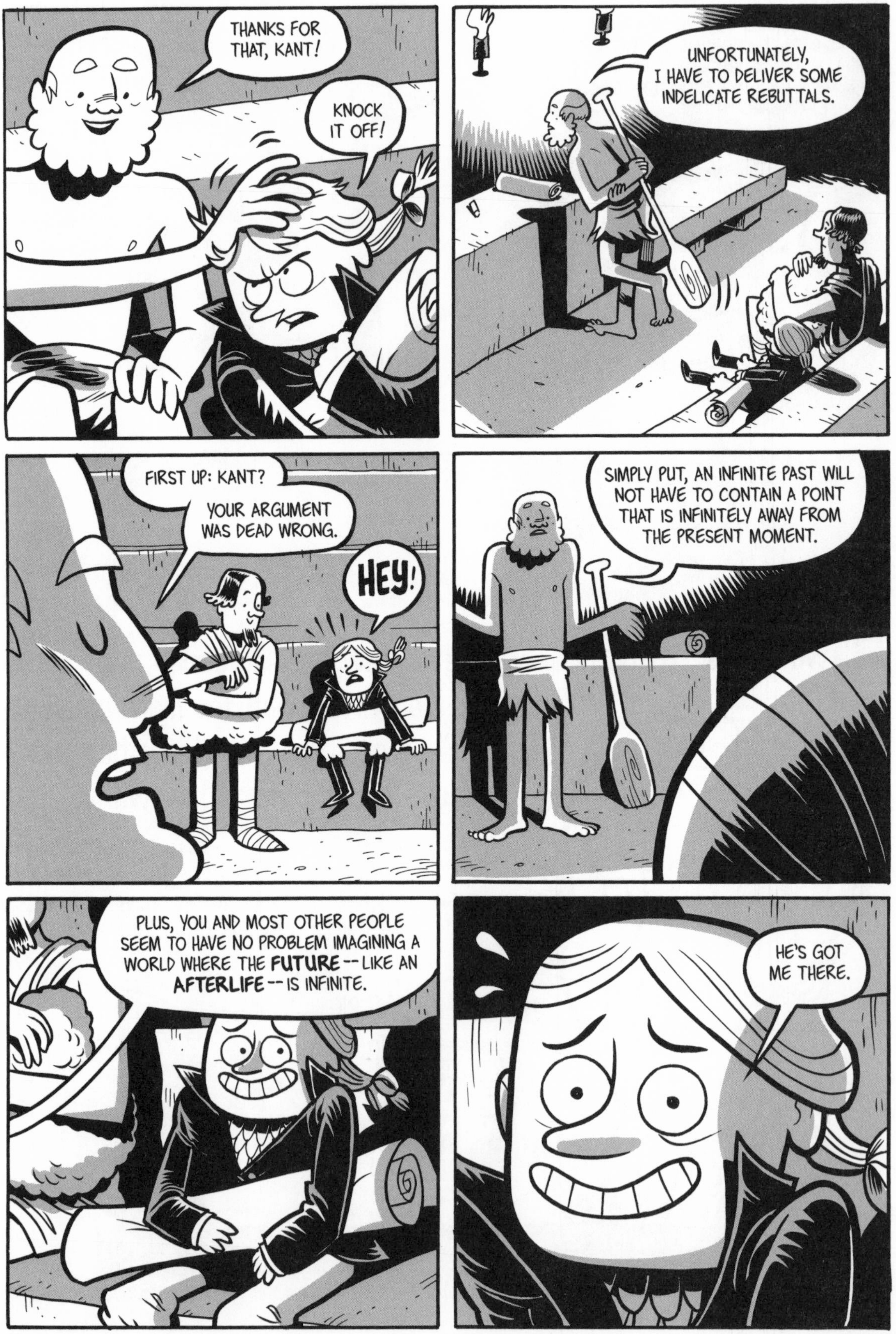
THANKS FOR THAT, KANT!
KNOCK IT OFF!
UNFORTUNATELY, I HAVE TO DELIVER SOME INDELICATE REBUTTALS.
FIRST UP: KANT?
YOUR ARGUMENT WAS DEAD WRONG.
HEY!
SIMPLY PUT, AN INFINITE PAST WILL NOT HAVE TO CONTAIN A POINT THAT IS INFINITELY AWAY FROM THE PRESENT MOMENT.
PLUS, YOU AND MOST OTHER PEOPLE SEEM TO HAVE NO PROBLEM IMAGINING A WORLD WHERE THE **FUTURE**--LIKE AN **AFTERLIFE**--IS INFINITE.
HE'S GOT ME THERE.

AND ARISTOTLE.

UHHH...YEAH?

THE ONLY THING WRONG WITH **YOUR** ARGUMENT IS THAT YOUR **MATH** IS A LITTLE OUTDATED.

MODERN MATHEMATICIANS HAVE **NO PROBLEM** GROUPING NUMBERS INTO INFINITE SETS.

IN FACT, CALCULUS WOULDN'T WORK **WITHOUT** THIS APPROACH!

$\{1, 2, 3, 4, 5, 6, 7, 8, 9, ...\}$
$\{2, 4, 6, 8, 10, 12, 14, 16, 18, ...\}$
$\{1, 3, 5, 7, 9, 11, 13, 15, 17, ...\}$
$\lim_{x \to \infty} \left(\frac{1}{x}\right) = 0$

AND EXPERTS, FOR THE MOST PART, ARE FINE WITH THE IDEA OF THE **PAST** AND **FUTURE** BEING INFINITE AS WELL.

WHICH IS ALL TO SAY THAT AQUINAS'S THIRD PREMISE DOESN'T HOLD A LOT OF WATER...

...AND BECAUSE WE CAN DOUBT **ONE** PREMISE, WE NO LONGER CLAIM THAT THE CONCLUSION **MUST** BE TRUE.

AW, MAN.

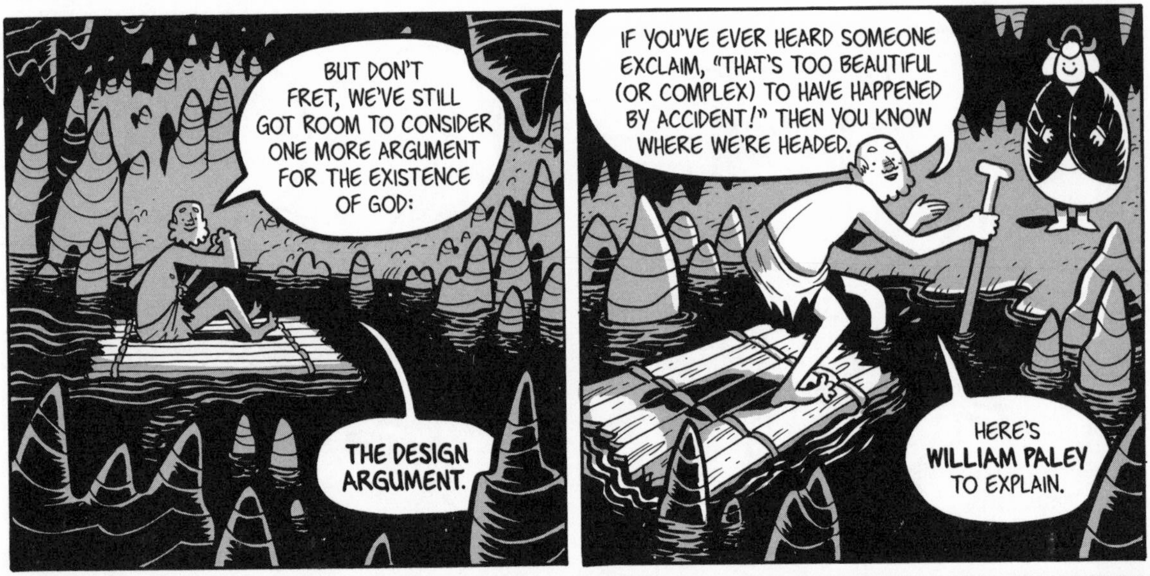
BUT DON'T FRET, WE'VE STILL GOT ROOM TO CONSIDER ONE MORE ARGUMENT FOR THE EXISTENCE OF GOD:
THE DESIGN ARGUMENT.
IF YOU'VE EVER HEARD SOMEONE EXCLAIM, "THAT'S TOO BEAUTIFUL (OR COMPLEX) TO HAVE HAPPENED BY ACCIDENT!" THEN YOU KNOW WHERE WE'RE HEADED.
HERE'S **WILLIAM PALEY** TO EXPLAIN.

WILLIAM PALEY

b. 1743
d. 1805
C.E.

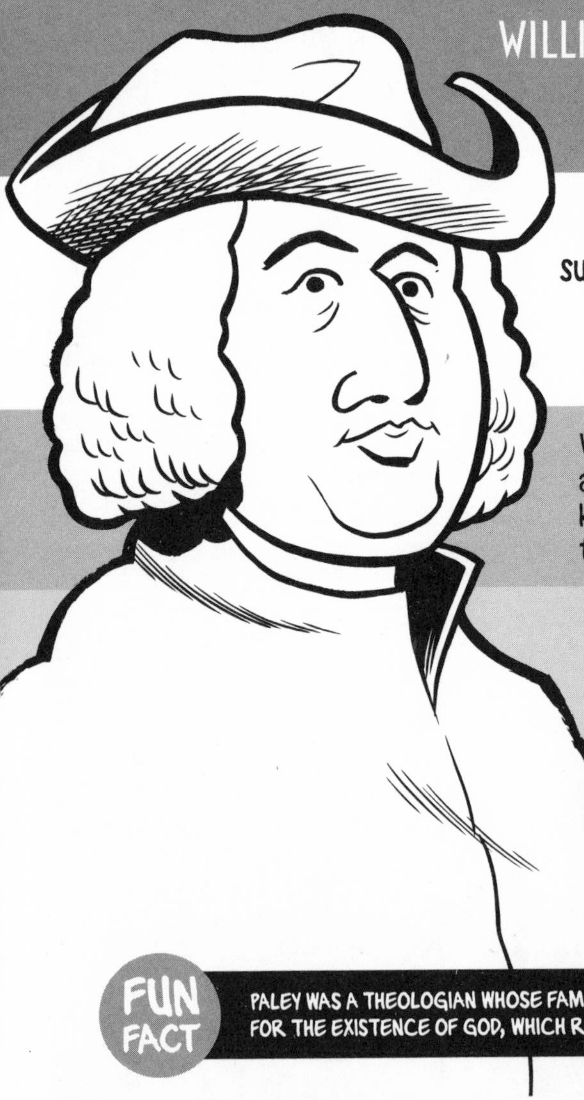

"Arrangement, disposition of parts, subserviency of means to an end, relation of instruments to use, imply the preference of intelligence and mind."

-- *Natural Theology*

William Paley was an English clergyman, Christian apologist, philosopher, and utilitarian. He is best known for his natural theology exposition of the teleological argument for the existence of God.

MOST FAMOUS WORK:

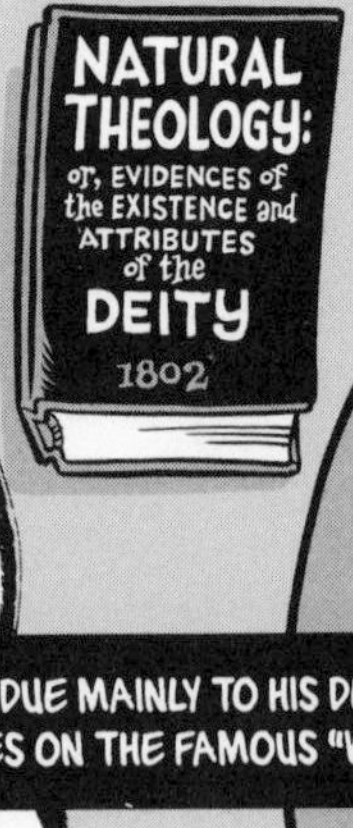
NATURAL THEOLOGY:
or, EVIDENCES of the EXISTENCE and ATTRIBUTES of the DEITY
1802

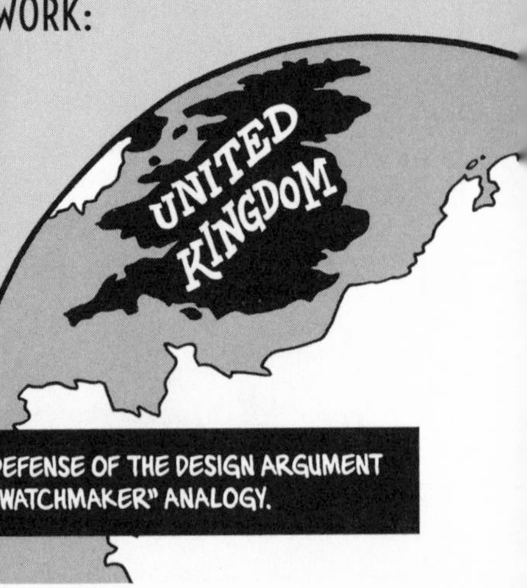
UNITED KINGDOM

FUN FACT

PALEY WAS A THEOLOGIAN WHOSE FAME IS DUE MAINLY TO HIS DEFENSE OF THE DESIGN ARGUMENT FOR THE EXISTENCE OF GOD, WHICH RELIES ON THE FAMOUS "WATCHMAKER" ANALOGY.

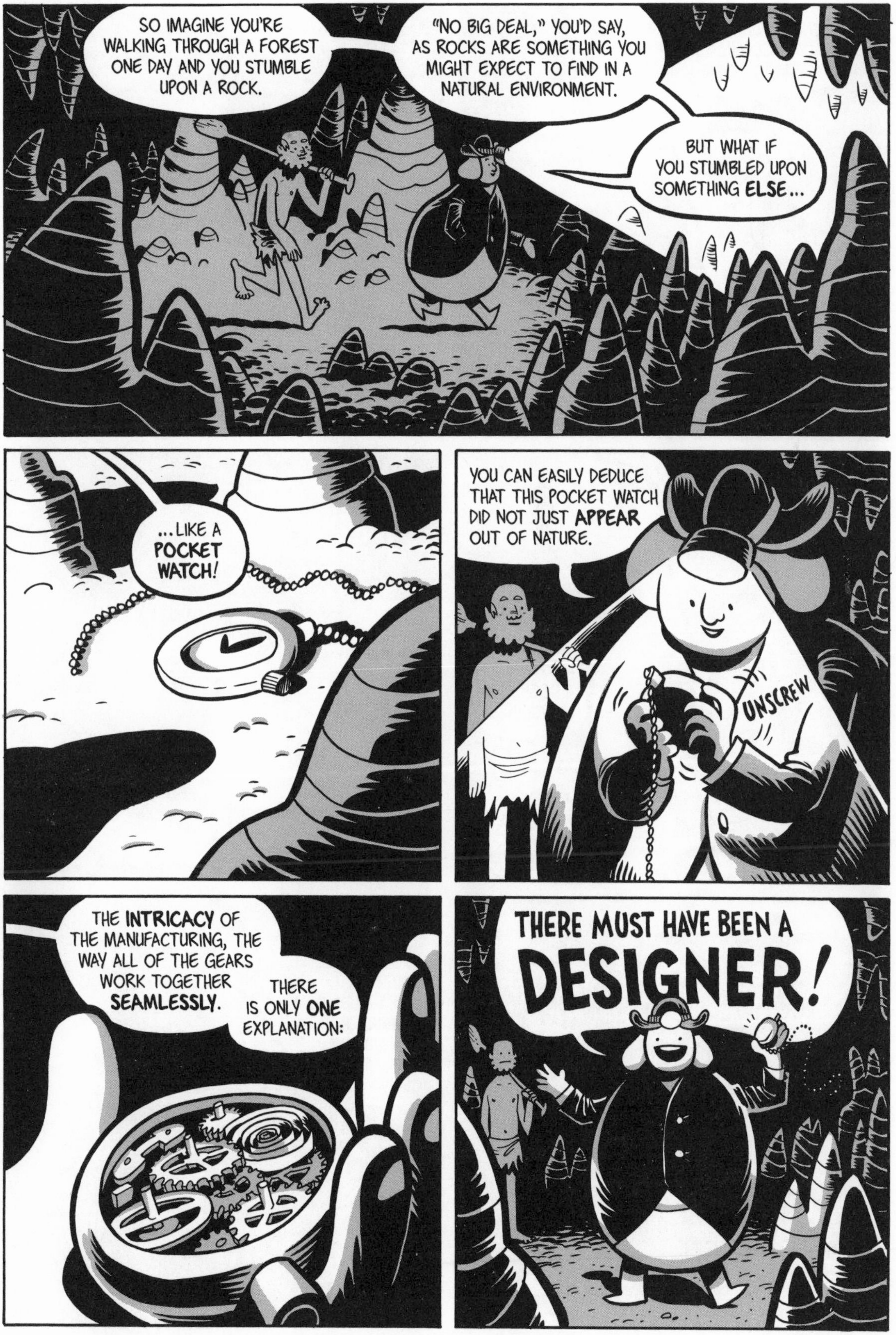

SO IMAGINE YOU'RE WALKING THROUGH A FOREST ONE DAY AND YOU STUMBLE UPON A ROCK.
"NO BIG DEAL," YOU'D SAY, AS ROCKS ARE SOMETHING YOU MIGHT EXPECT TO FIND IN A NATURAL ENVIRONMENT.
BUT WHAT IF YOU STUMBLED UPON SOMETHING **ELSE**...
...LIKE A **POCKET WATCH**!
YOU CAN EASILY DEDUCE THAT THIS POCKET WATCH DID NOT JUST **APPEAR** OUT OF NATURE.
UNSCREW
THE **INTRICACY** OF THE MANUFACTURING, THE WAY ALL OF THE GEARS WORK TOGETHER **SEAMLESSLY**.
THERE IS ONLY **ONE** EXPLANATION:
THERE MUST HAVE BEEN A DESIGNER!

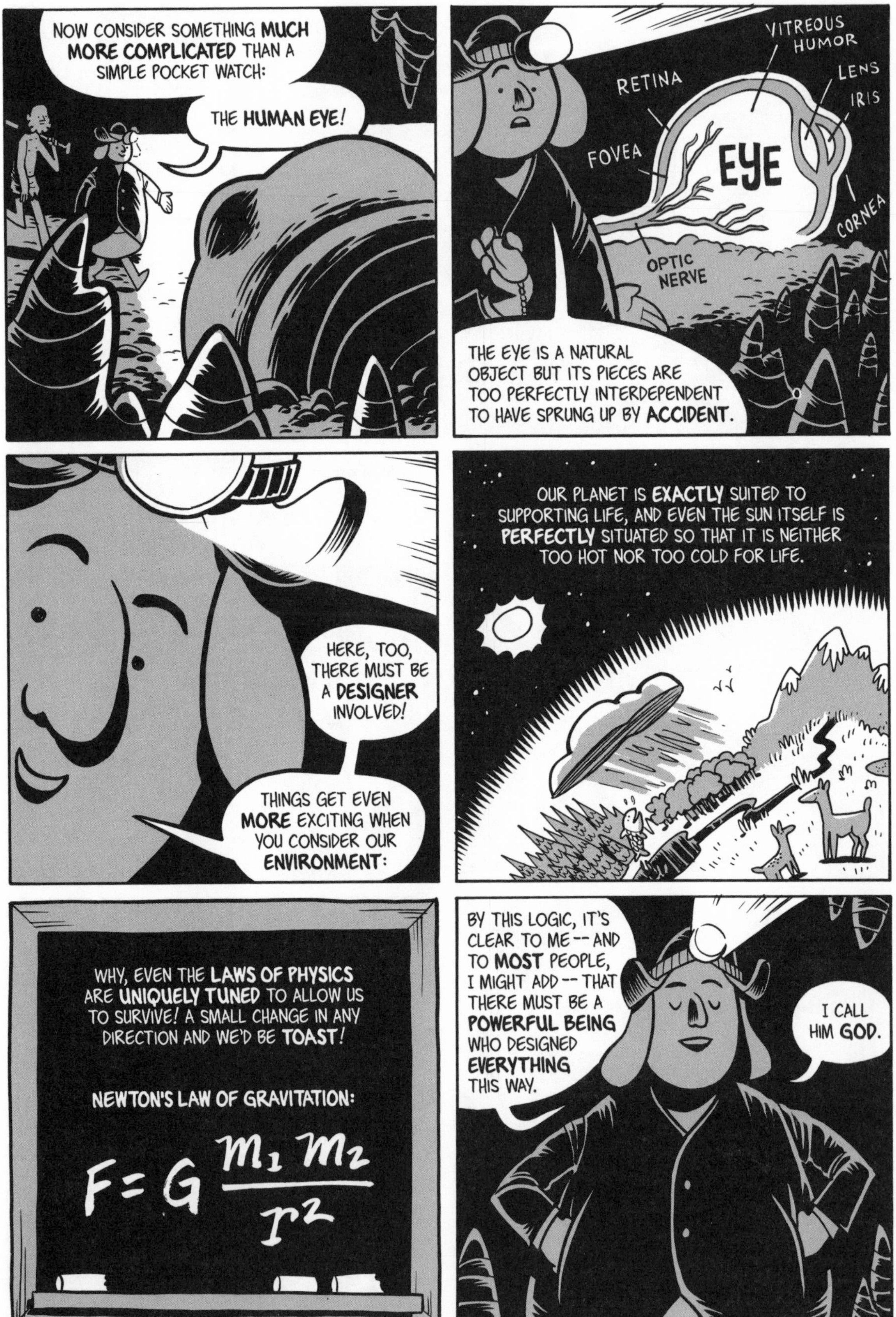
NOW CONSIDER SOMETHING MUCH MORE COMPLICATED THAN A SIMPLE POCKET WATCH:
THE HUMAN EYE!
VITREOUS HUMOR
RETINA
LENS
IRIS
FOVEA
EYE
CORNEA
OPTIC NERVE
THE EYE IS A NATURAL OBJECT BUT ITS PIECES ARE TOO PERFECTLY INTERDEPENDENT TO HAVE SPRUNG UP BY ACCIDENT.
HERE, TOO, THERE MUST BE A DESIGNER INVOLVED!
THINGS GET EVEN MORE EXCITING WHEN YOU CONSIDER OUR ENVIRONMENT:
OUR PLANET IS EXACTLY SUITED TO SUPPORTING LIFE, AND EVEN THE SUN ITSELF IS PERFECTLY SITUATED SO THAT IT IS NEITHER TOO HOT NOR TOO COLD FOR LIFE.
WHY, EVEN THE LAWS OF PHYSICS ARE UNIQUELY TUNED TO ALLOW US TO SURVIVE! A SMALL CHANGE IN ANY DIRECTION AND WE'D BE TOAST!
NEWTON'S LAW OF GRAVITATION:
$F = G\frac{m_1 m_2}{r^2}$
BY THIS LOGIC, IT'S CLEAR TO ME -- AND TO MOST PEOPLE, I MIGHT ADD -- THAT THERE MUST BE A POWERFUL BEING WHO DESIGNED EVERYTHING THIS WAY.
I CALL HIM GOD.

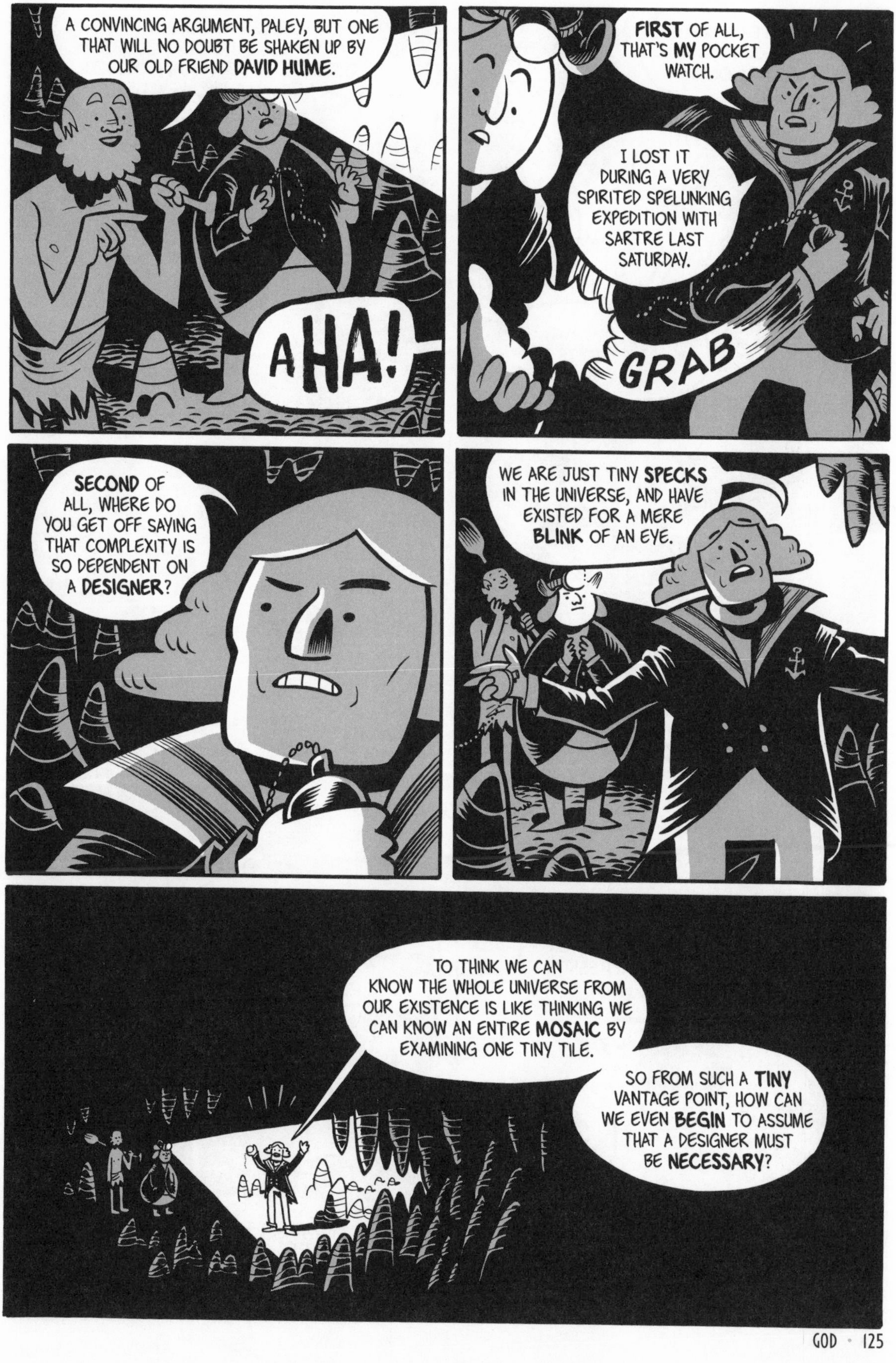
A CONVINCING ARGUMENT, PALEY, BUT ONE THAT WILL NO DOUBT BE SHAKEN UP BY OUR OLD FRIEND DAVID HUME.
AHA!
FIRST OF ALL, THAT'S MY POCKET WATCH.
I LOST IT DURING A VERY SPIRITED SPELUNKING EXPEDITION WITH SARTRE LAST SATURDAY.
GRAB
SECOND OF ALL, WHERE DO YOU GET OFF SAYING THAT COMPLEXITY IS SO DEPENDENT ON A DESIGNER?
WE ARE JUST TINY SPECKS IN THE UNIVERSE, AND HAVE EXISTED FOR A MERE BLINK OF AN EYE.
TO THINK WE CAN KNOW THE WHOLE UNIVERSE FROM OUR EXISTENCE IS LIKE THINKING WE CAN KNOW AN ENTIRE MOSAIC BY EXAMINING ONE TINY TILE.
SO FROM SUCH A TINY VANTAGE POINT, HOW CAN WE EVEN BEGIN TO ASSUME THAT A DESIGNER MUST BE NECESSARY?

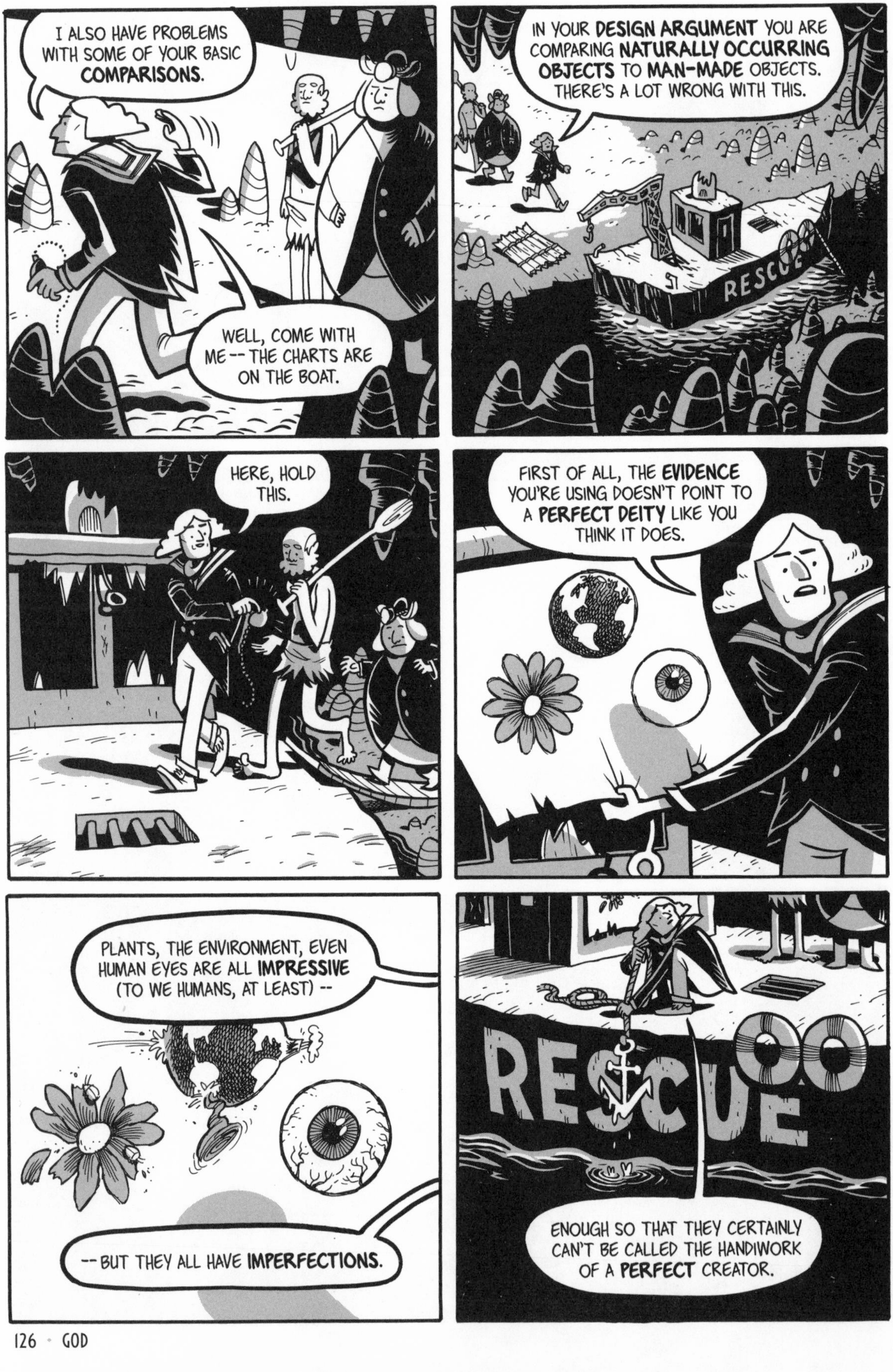
I ALSO HAVE PROBLEMS WITH SOME OF YOUR BASIC **COMPARISONS**.
WELL, COME WITH ME -- THE CHARTS ARE ON THE BOAT.
IN YOUR **DESIGN ARGUMENT** YOU ARE COMPARING **NATURALLY OCCURRING OBJECTS** TO **MAN-MADE** OBJECTS. THERE'S A LOT WRONG WITH THIS.
RESCUE
HERE, HOLD THIS.
FIRST OF ALL, THE **EVIDENCE** YOU'RE USING DOESN'T POINT TO A **PERFECT DEITY** LIKE YOU THINK IT DOES.
PLANTS, THE ENVIRONMENT, EVEN HUMAN EYES ARE ALL **IMPRESSIVE** (TO WE HUMANS, AT LEAST) --
-- BUT THEY ALL HAVE **IMPERFECTIONS**.
RESCUE
ENOUGH SO THAT THEY CERTAINLY CAN'T BE CALLED THE HANDIWORK OF A **PERFECT** CREATOR.

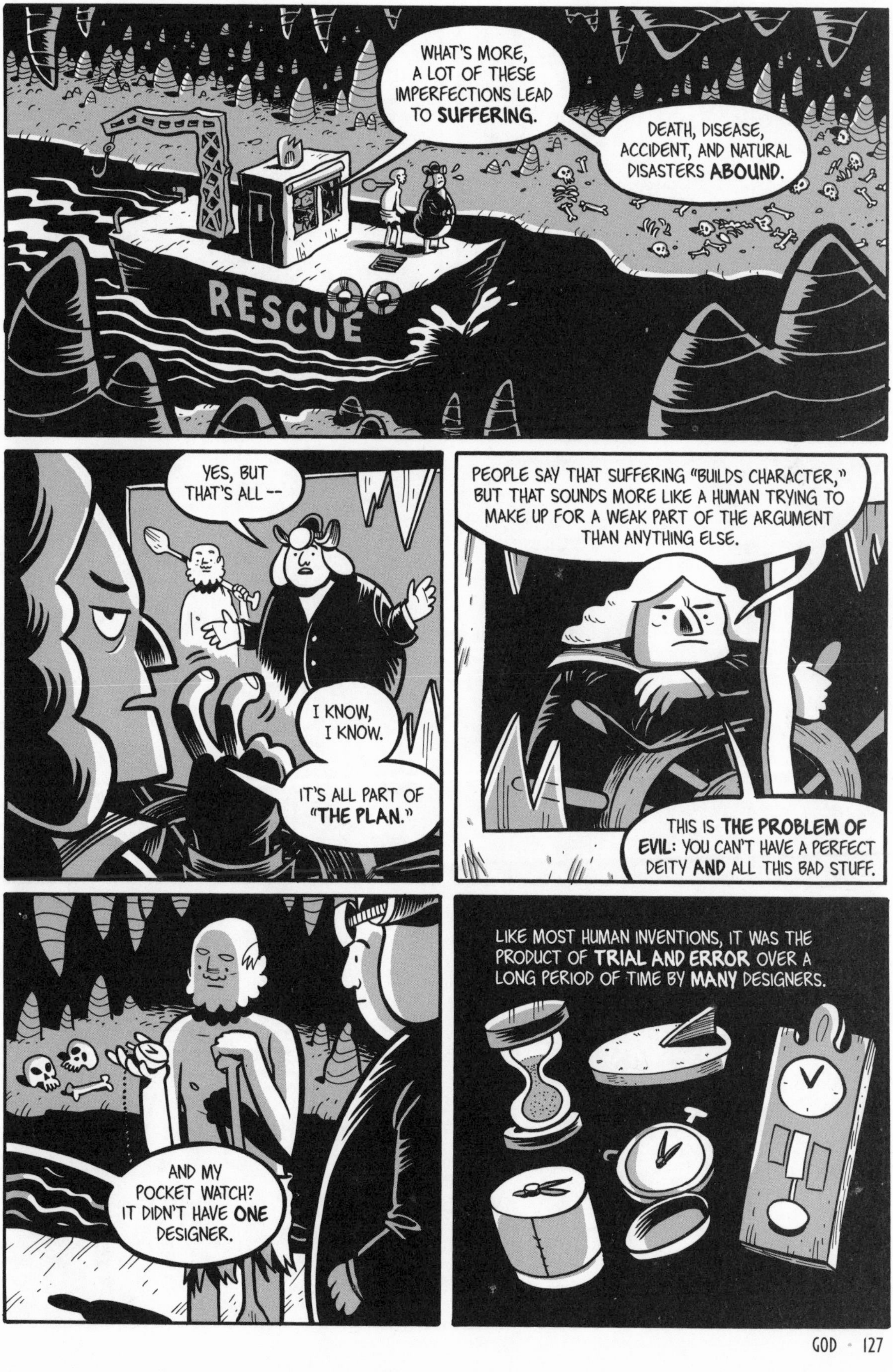
WHAT'S MORE, A LOT OF THESE IMPERFECTIONS LEAD TO SUFFERING.
DEATH, DISEASE, ACCIDENT, AND NATURAL DISASTERS ABOUND.
RESCUE
YES, BUT THAT'S ALL--
I KNOW, I KNOW.
IT'S ALL PART OF "THE PLAN."
PEOPLE SAY THAT SUFFERING "BUILDS CHARACTER," BUT THAT SOUNDS MORE LIKE A HUMAN TRYING TO MAKE UP FOR A WEAK PART OF THE ARGUMENT THAN ANYTHING ELSE.
THIS IS THE PROBLEM OF EVIL: YOU CAN'T HAVE A PERFECT DEITY AND ALL THIS BAD STUFF.
AND MY POCKET WATCH? IT DIDN'T HAVE ONE DESIGNER.
LIKE MOST HUMAN INVENTIONS, IT WAS THE PRODUCT OF TRIAL AND ERROR OVER A LONG PERIOD OF TIME BY MANY DESIGNERS.

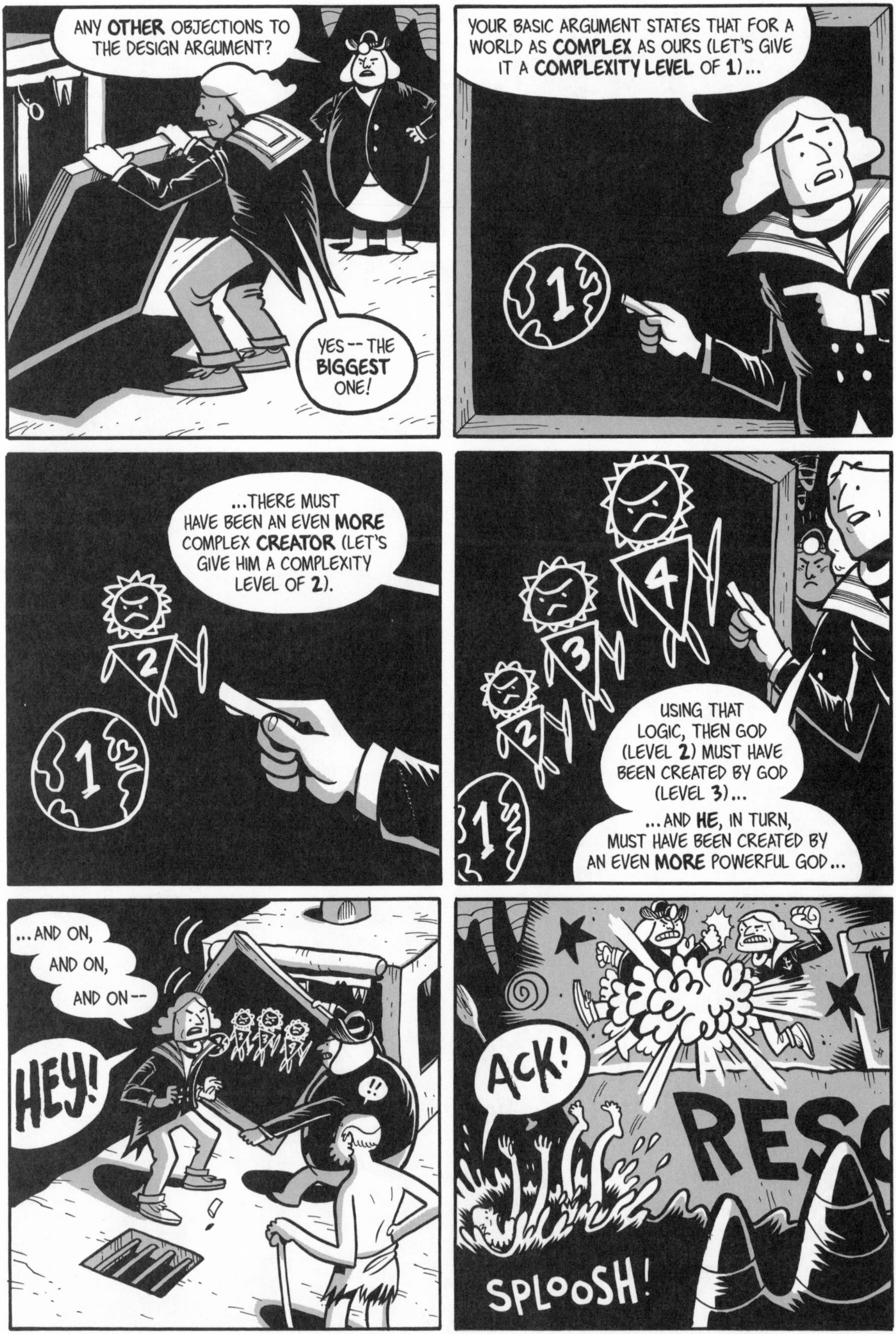
ANY **OTHER** OBJECTIONS TO THE DESIGN ARGUMENT?
YES -- THE **BIGGEST** ONE!
YOUR BASIC ARGUMENT STATES THAT FOR A WORLD AS **COMPLEX** AS OURS (LET'S GIVE IT A **COMPLEXITY LEVEL** OF **1**)...
1
...THERE MUST HAVE BEEN AN EVEN **MORE** COMPLEX **CREATOR** (LET'S GIVE HIM A COMPLEXITY LEVEL OF **2**).
2
1
4
3
2
1
USING THAT LOGIC, THEN GOD (LEVEL **2**) MUST HAVE BEEN CREATED BY GOD (LEVEL **3**)...
...AND **HE**, IN TURN, MUST HAVE BEEN CREATED BY AN EVEN **MORE** POWERFUL GOD...
...AND ON, AND ON, AND ON--
HEY!
!!
ACK!
RES
SPLOOSH!

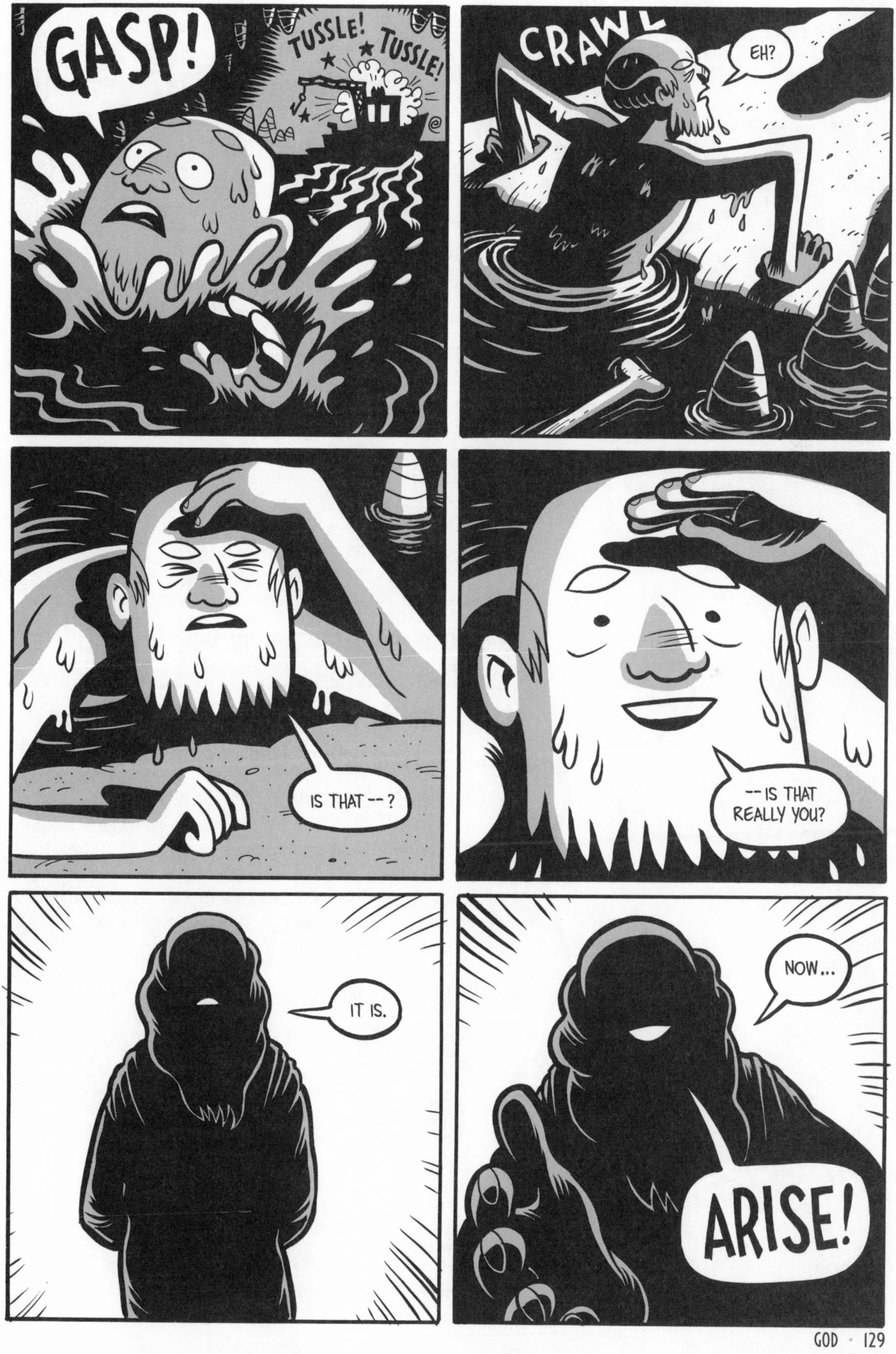
GASP!
TUSSLE! TUSSLE!
CRAWL
EH?
IS THAT -- ?
-- IS THAT REALLY YOU?
IT IS.
NOW...
ARISE!

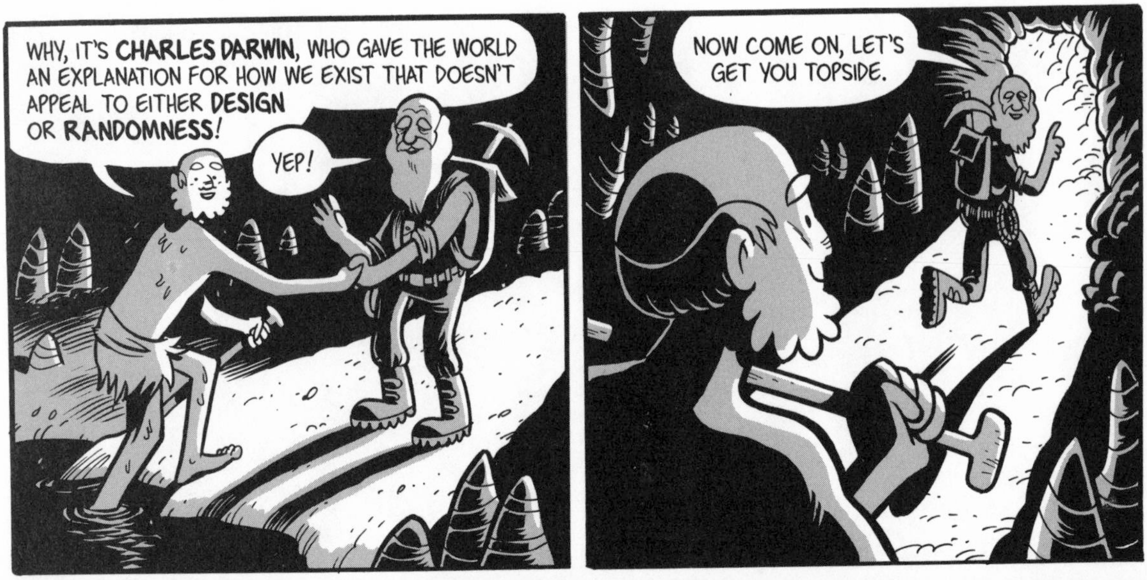
WHY, IT'S **CHARLES DARWIN**, WHO GAVE THE WORLD AN EXPLANATION FOR HOW WE EXIST THAT DOESN'T APPEAL TO EITHER **DESIGN** OR **RANDOMNESS**!
YEP!
NOW COME ON, LET'S GET YOU TOPSIDE.

CHARLES ROBERT DARWIN

b. 1809
d. 1882
C.E.

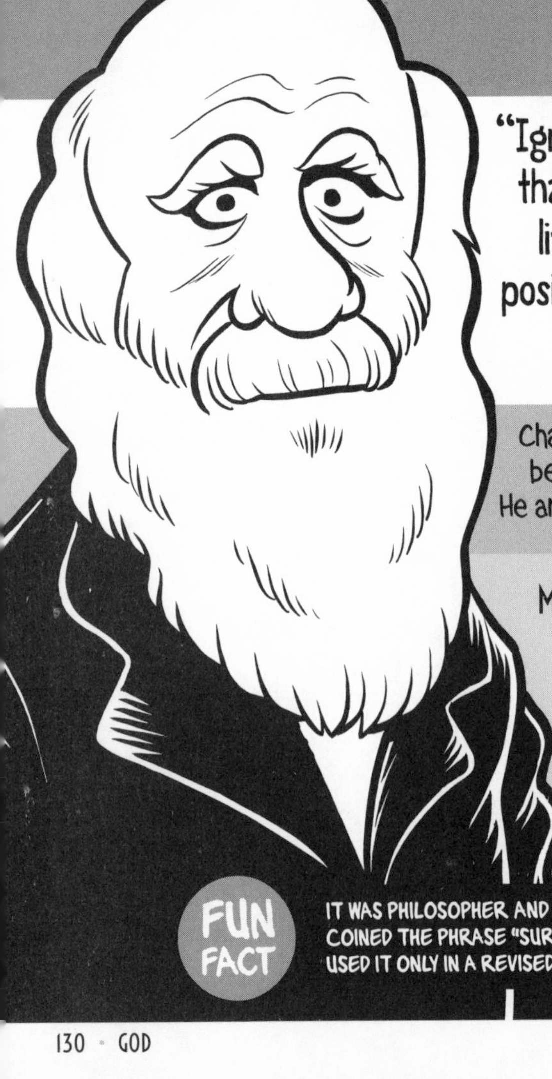

"Ignorance more frequently begets confidence than does knowledge: it is those who know little, not those who know much, who so positively assert that this or that problem will never be solved by science."

-- *The Descent of Man* (1871)

Charles Robert Darwin was an English naturalist and geologist best known for his contributions to evolutionary theory. He argued that all species descended from a common ancestor.

MOST FAMOUS WORK:

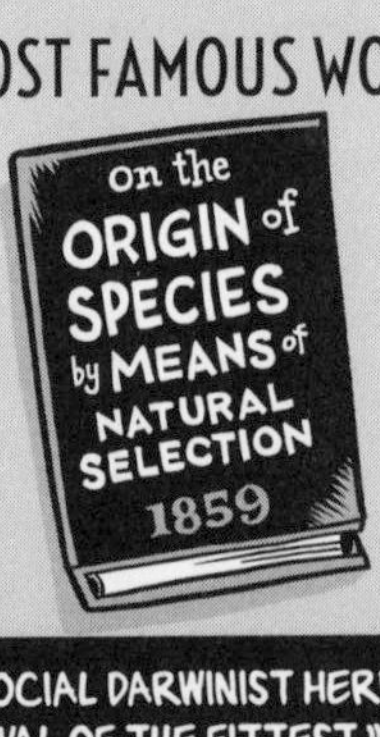
on the ORIGIN of SPECIES by MEANS of NATURAL SELECTION
1859

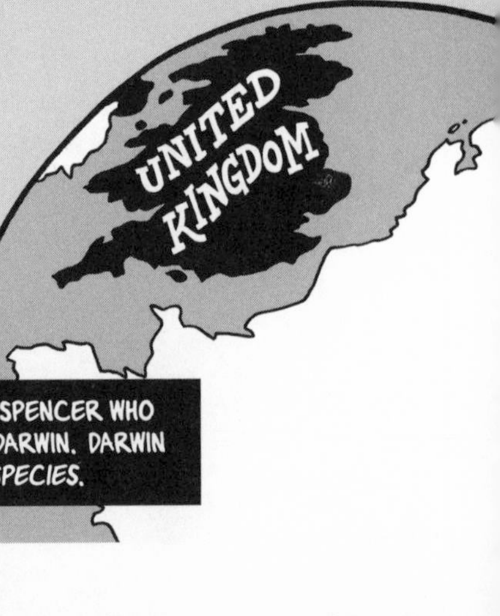
UNITED KINGDOM

FUN FACT

IT WAS PHILOSOPHER AND SOCIAL DARWINIST HERBERT SPENCER WHO COINED THE PHRASE "SURVIVAL OF THE FITTEST," NOT DARWIN. DARWIN USED IT ONLY IN A REVISED EDITION OF *THE ORIGIN OF SPECIES*.

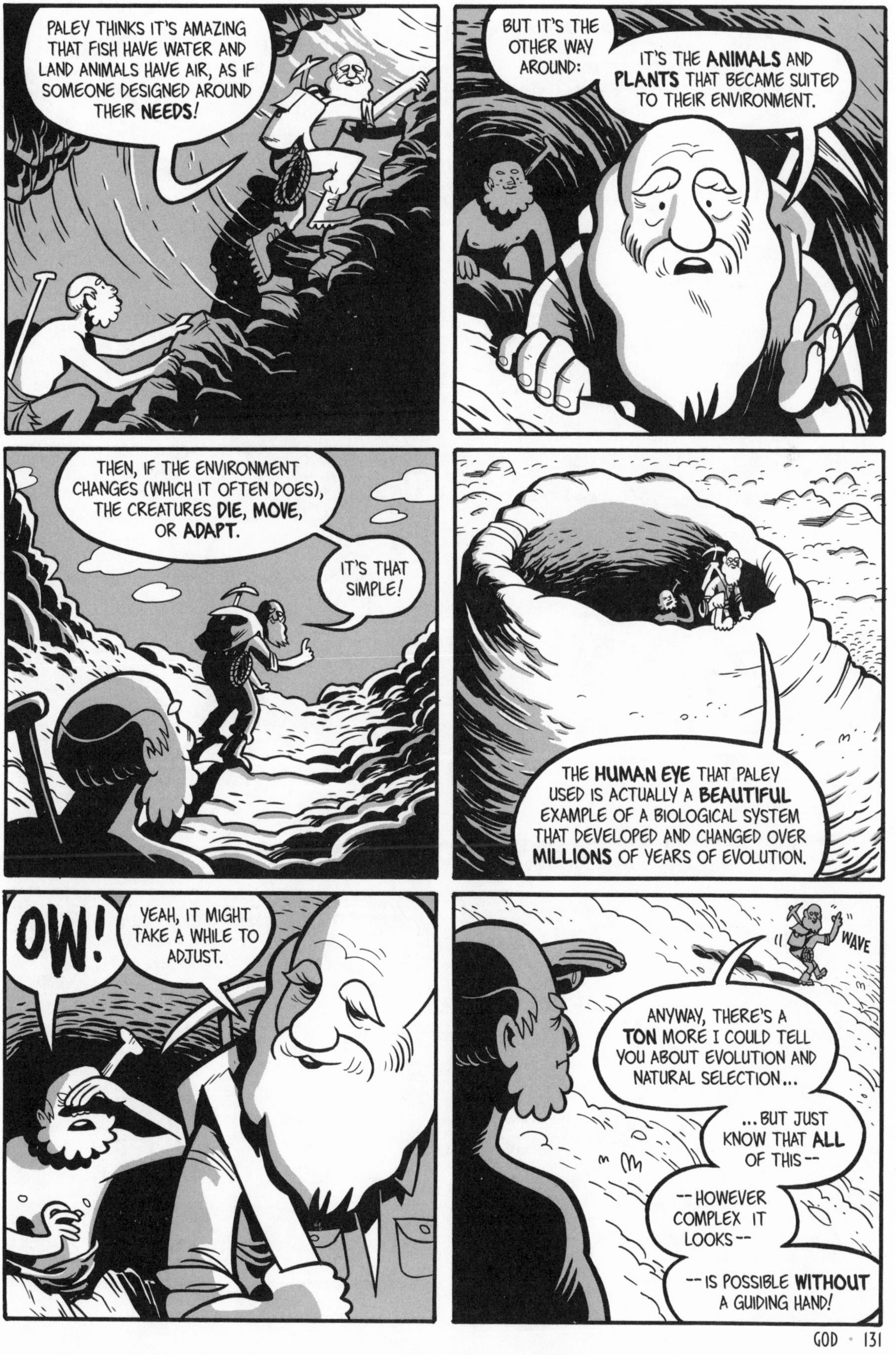
PALEY THINKS IT'S AMAZING THAT FISH HAVE WATER AND LAND ANIMALS HAVE AIR, AS IF SOMEONE DESIGNED AROUND THEIR **NEEDS**!
BUT IT'S THE OTHER WAY AROUND:
IT'S THE **ANIMALS** AND **PLANTS** THAT BECAME SUITED TO THEIR ENVIRONMENT.
THEN, IF THE ENVIRONMENT CHANGES (WHICH IT OFTEN DOES), THE CREATURES **DIE**, **MOVE**, OR **ADAPT**.
IT'S THAT SIMPLE!
THE **HUMAN EYE** THAT PALEY USED IS ACTUALLY A **BEAUTIFUL** EXAMPLE OF A BIOLOGICAL SYSTEM THAT DEVELOPED AND CHANGED OVER **MILLIONS** OF YEARS OF EVOLUTION.
OW!
YEAH, IT MIGHT TAKE A WHILE TO ADJUST.
WAVE
ANYWAY, THERE'S A **TON** MORE I COULD TELL YOU ABOUT EVOLUTION AND NATURAL SELECTION...
...BUT JUST KNOW THAT **ALL** OF THIS--
--HOWEVER COMPLEX IT LOOKS--
--IS POSSIBLE **WITHOUT** A GUIDING HAND!

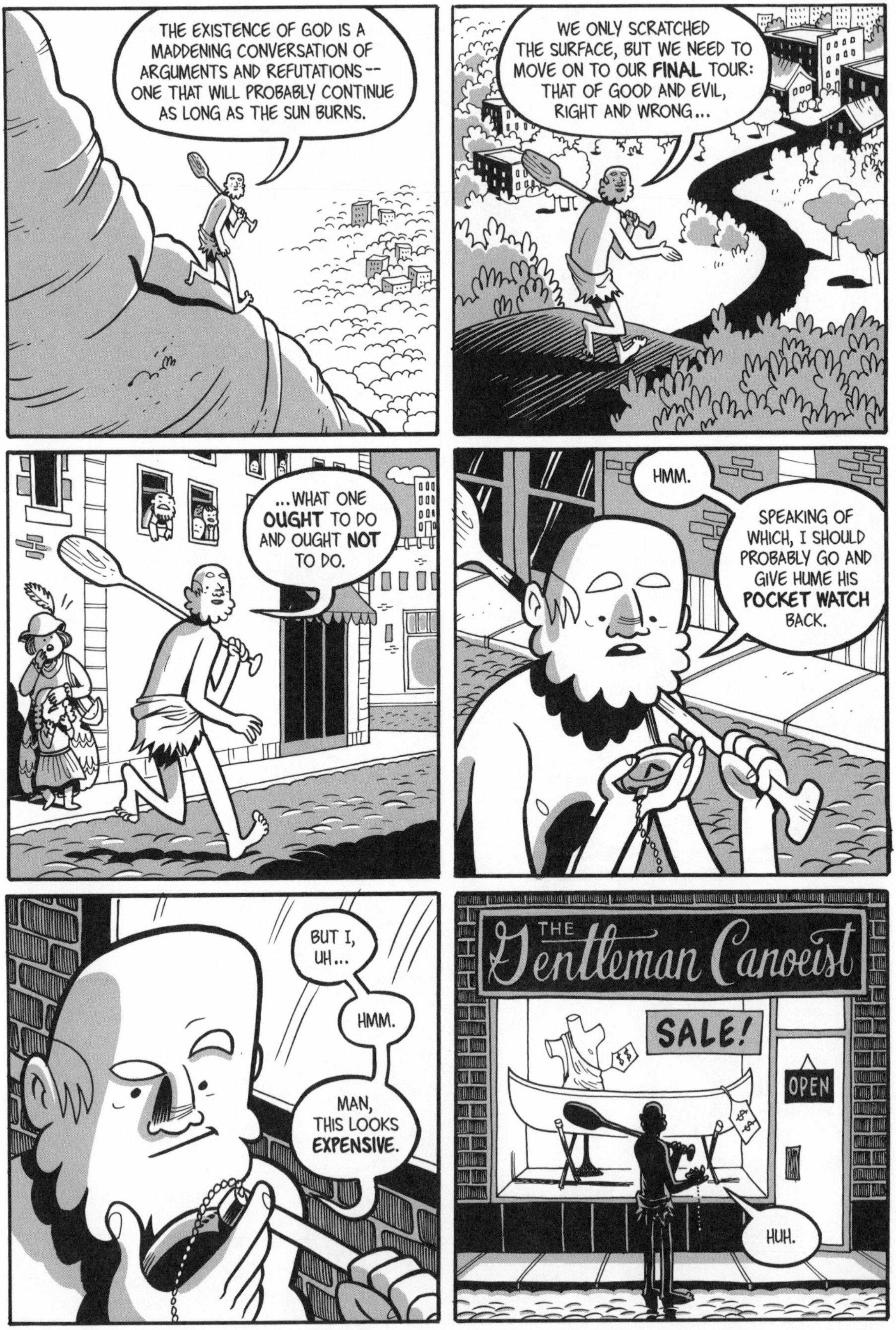

THE EXISTENCE OF GOD IS A MADDENING CONVERSATION OF ARGUMENTS AND REFUTATIONS-- ONE THAT WILL PROBABLY CONTINUE AS LONG AS THE SUN BURNS.
WE ONLY SCRATCHED THE SURFACE, BUT WE NEED TO MOVE ON TO OUR **FINAL** TOUR: THAT OF GOOD AND EVIL, RIGHT AND WRONG...
...WHAT ONE **OUGHT** TO DO AND OUGHT **NOT** TO DO.
HMM.
SPEAKING OF WHICH, I SHOULD PROBABLY GO AND GIVE HUME HIS **POCKET WATCH** BACK.
BUT I, UH...
HMM.
MAN, THIS LOOKS **EXPENSIVE**.
THE Gentleman Canoeist
SALE!
OPEN
HUH.

chapter 6
ETHICS

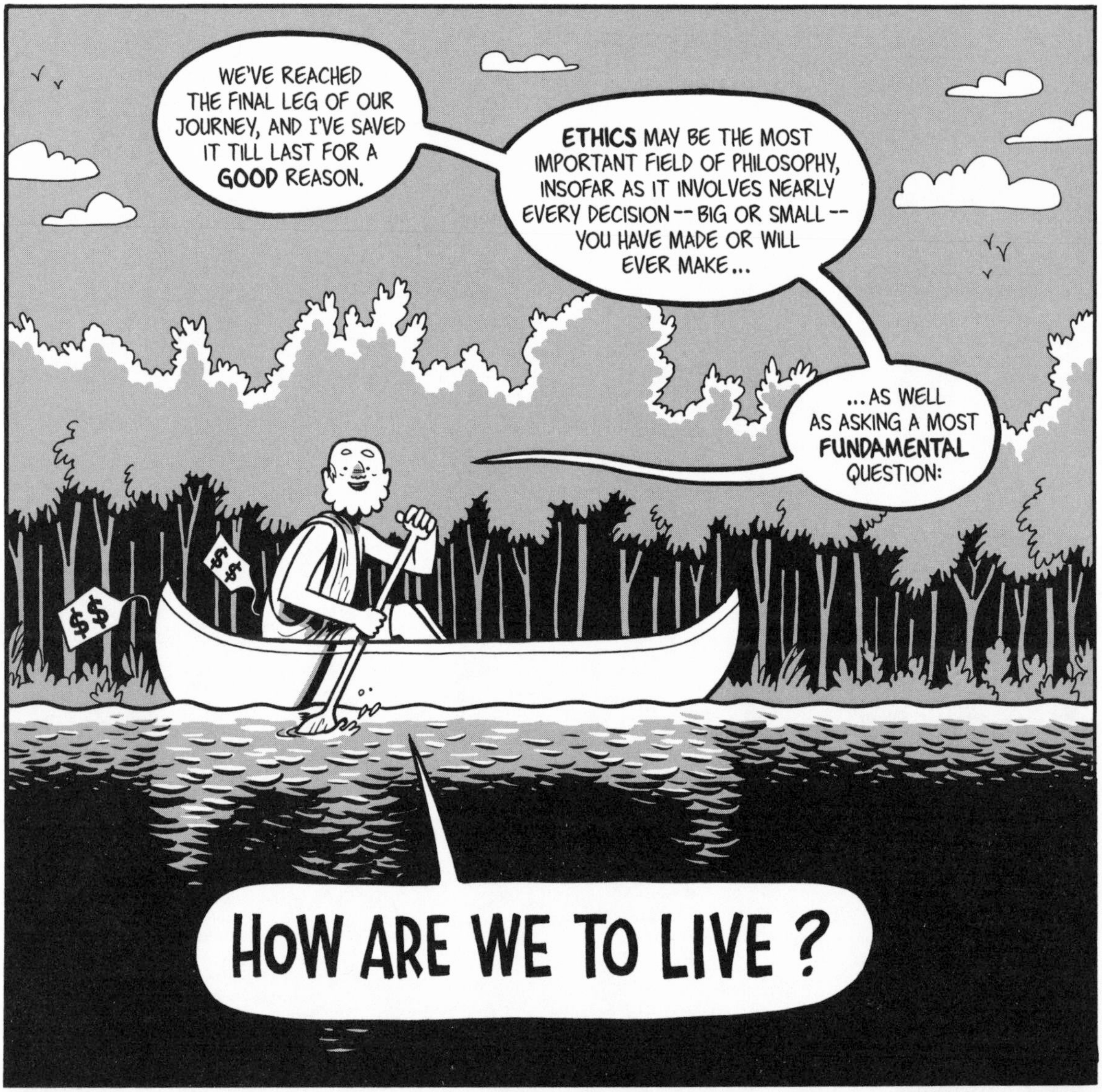
WE'VE REACHED THE FINAL LEG OF OUR JOURNEY, AND I'VE SAVED IT TILL LAST FOR A GOOD REASON.
ETHICS MAY BE THE MOST IMPORTANT FIELD OF PHILOSOPHY, INSOFAR AS IT INVOLVES NEARLY EVERY DECISION -- BIG OR SMALL -- YOU HAVE MADE OR WILL EVER MAKE...
...AS WELL AS ASKING A MOST FUNDAMENTAL QUESTION:
$$
$$
HOW ARE WE TO LIVE?

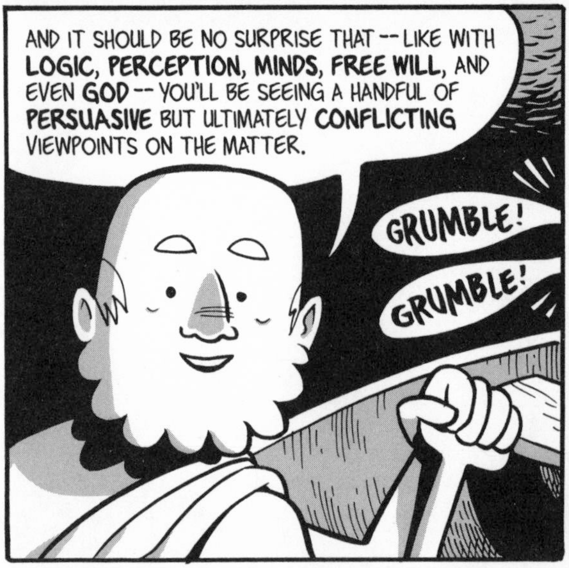
AND IT SHOULD BE NO SURPRISE THAT -- LIKE WITH LOGIC, PERCEPTION, MINDS, FREE WILL, AND EVEN GOD -- YOU'LL BE SEEING A HANDFUL OF PERSUASIVE BUT ULTIMATELY CONFLICTING VIEWPOINTS ON THE MATTER.
GRUMBLE!
GRUMBLE!

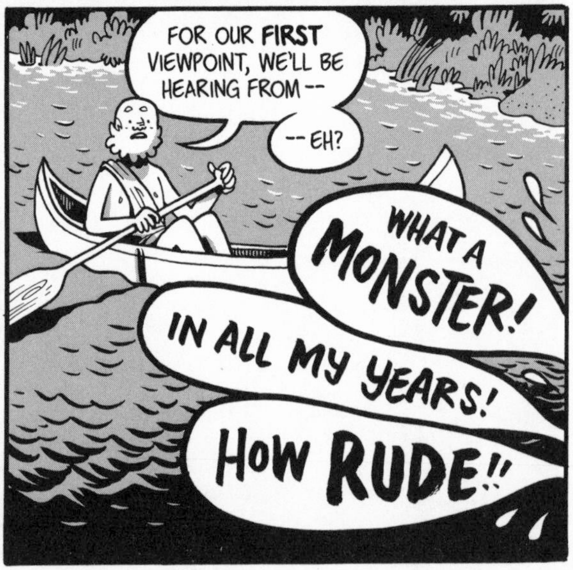
FOR OUR FIRST VIEWPOINT, WE'LL BE HEARING FROM --
-- EH?
WHAT A MONSTER!
IN ALL MY YEARS!
HOW RUDE!!

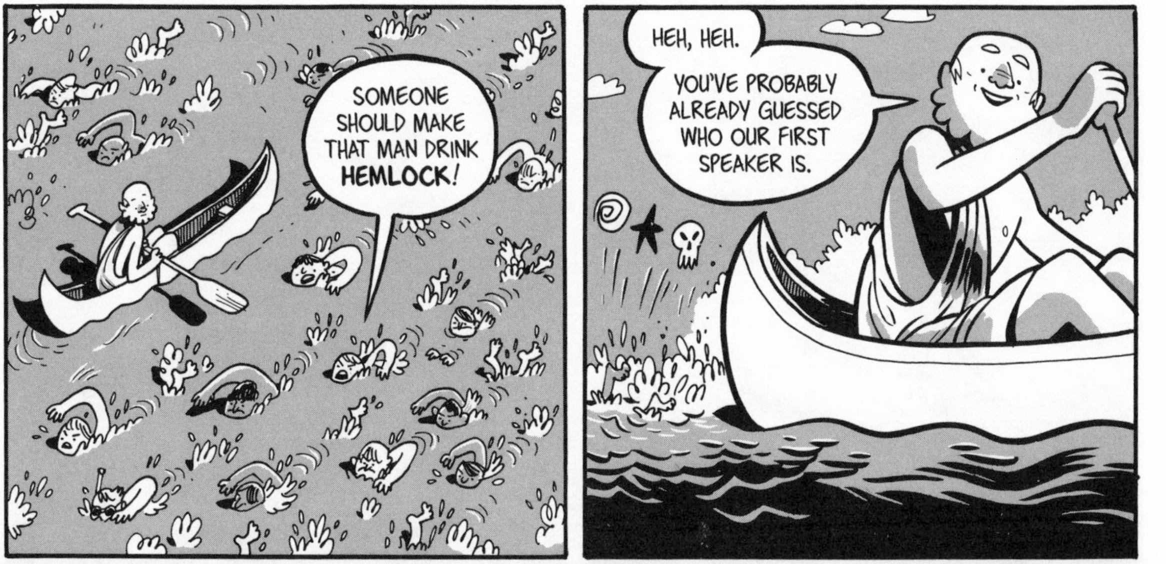
SOMEONE SHOULD MAKE THAT MAN DRINK **HEMLOCK**!
HEH, HEH.
YOU'VE PROBABLY ALREADY GUESSED WHO OUR FIRST SPEAKER IS.

SOCRATES

b. 469
d. 399
B.C.E.

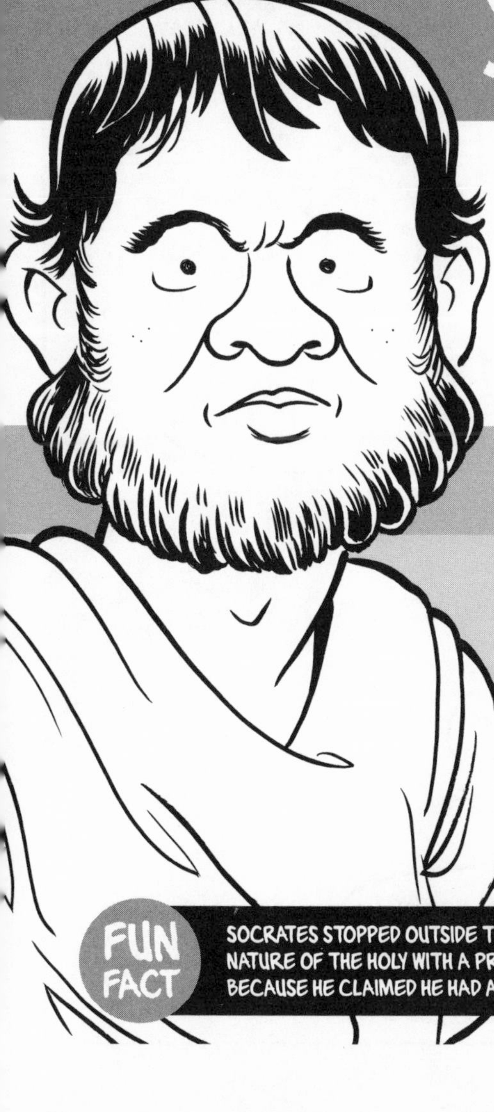

"The unexamined life is not worth living."

—Plato's *Apology* (unknown, ca. 360 B.C.E.?)

Socrates was a Greek philosopher. According to most, his thinking marks the beginning of Western philosophy.

MOST FAMOUS WORK:

Never having written any philosophy, he is known chiefly through the accounts of his students Plato and Xenophon.

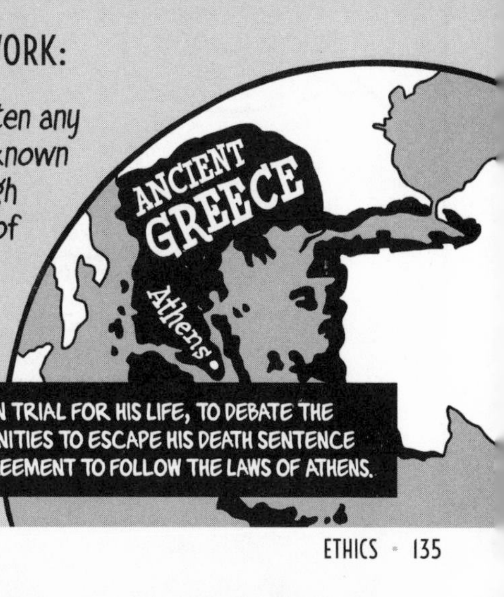
ANCIENT
GREECE
Athens

FUN FACT SOCRATES STOPPED OUTSIDE THE SENATE, WHERE HE WAS ON TRIAL FOR HIS LIFE, TO DEBATE THE NATURE OF THE HOLY WITH A PRIEST. HE REFUSED OPPORTUNITIES TO ESCAPE HIS DEATH SENTENCE BECAUSE HE CLAIMED HE HAD A DUTY TO OBEY HIS TACIT AGREEMENT TO FOLLOW THE LAWS OF ATHENS.

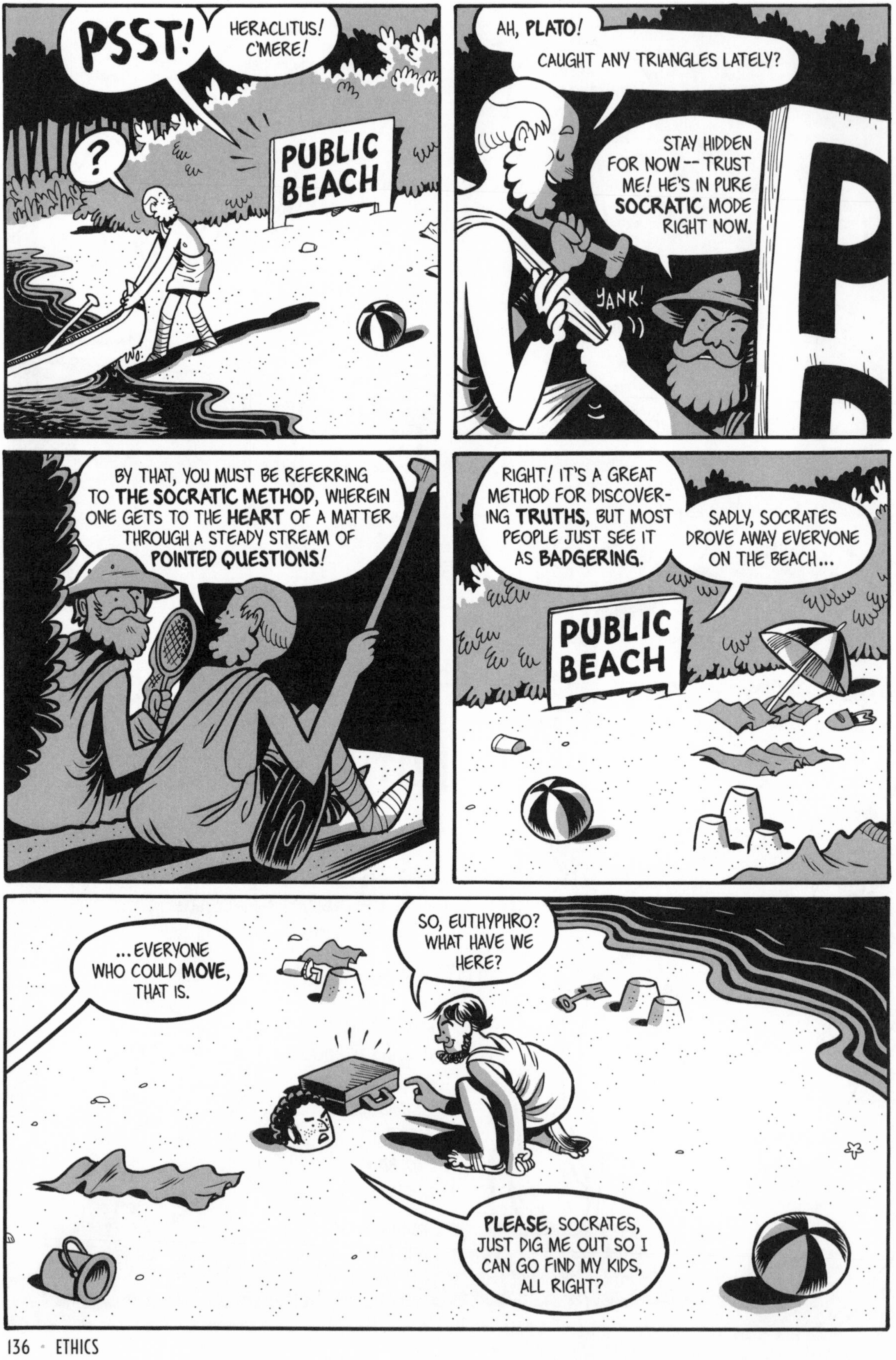
PSST!
HERACLITUS! C'MERE!
?
PUBLIC BEACH
AH, PLATO!
CAUGHT ANY TRIANGLES LATELY?
STAY HIDDEN FOR NOW -- TRUST ME! HE'S IN PURE SOCRATIC MODE RIGHT NOW.
YANK!
BY THAT, YOU MUST BE REFERRING TO THE SOCRATIC METHOD, WHEREIN ONE GETS TO THE HEART OF A MATTER THROUGH A STEADY STREAM OF POINTED QUESTIONS!
RIGHT! IT'S A GREAT METHOD FOR DISCOVERING TRUTHS, BUT MOST PEOPLE JUST SEE IT AS BADGERING.
SADLY, SOCRATES DROVE AWAY EVERYONE ON THE BEACH...
PUBLIC BEACH
...EVERYONE WHO COULD MOVE, THAT IS.
SO, EUTHYPHRO? WHAT HAVE WE HERE?
PLEASE, SOCRATES, JUST DIG ME OUT SO I CAN GO FIND MY KIDS, ALL RIGHT?

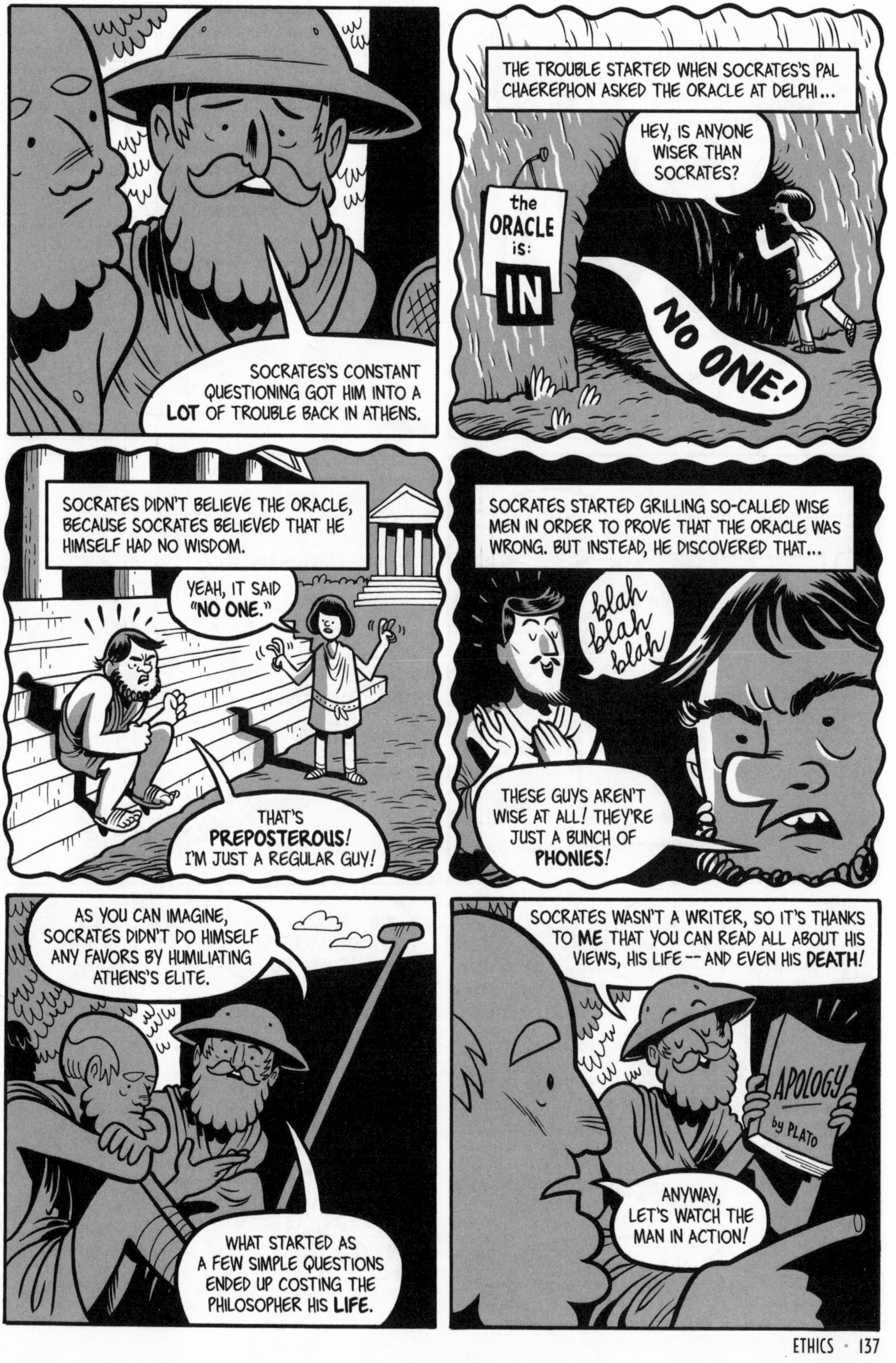

SOCRATES'S CONSTANT QUESTIONING GOT HIM INTO A LOT OF TROUBLE BACK IN ATHENS.
THE TROUBLE STARTED WHEN SOCRATES'S PAL CHAEREPHON ASKED THE ORACLE AT DELPHI...
HEY, IS ANYONE WISER THAN SOCRATES?
the ORACLE is: IN
NO ONE!
SOCRATES DIDN'T BELIEVE THE ORACLE, BECAUSE SOCRATES BELIEVED THAT HE HIMSELF HAD NO WISDOM.
YEAH, IT SAID "NO ONE."
THAT'S PREPOSTEROUS! I'M JUST A REGULAR GUY!
SOCRATES STARTED GRILLING SO-CALLED WISE MEN IN ORDER TO PROVE THAT THE ORACLE WAS WRONG. BUT INSTEAD, HE DISCOVERED THAT...
blah blah blah
THESE GUYS AREN'T WISE AT ALL! THEY'RE JUST A BUNCH OF PHONIES!
AS YOU CAN IMAGINE, SOCRATES DIDN'T DO HIMSELF ANY FAVORS BY HUMILIATING ATHENS'S ELITE.
WHAT STARTED AS A FEW SIMPLE QUESTIONS ENDED UP COSTING THE PHILOSOPHER HIS LIFE.
SOCRATES WASN'T A WRITER, SO IT'S THANKS TO ME THAT YOU CAN READ ALL ABOUT HIS VIEWS, HIS LIFE -- AND EVEN HIS DEATH!
APOLOGY by PLATO
ANYWAY, LET'S WATCH THE MAN IN ACTION!

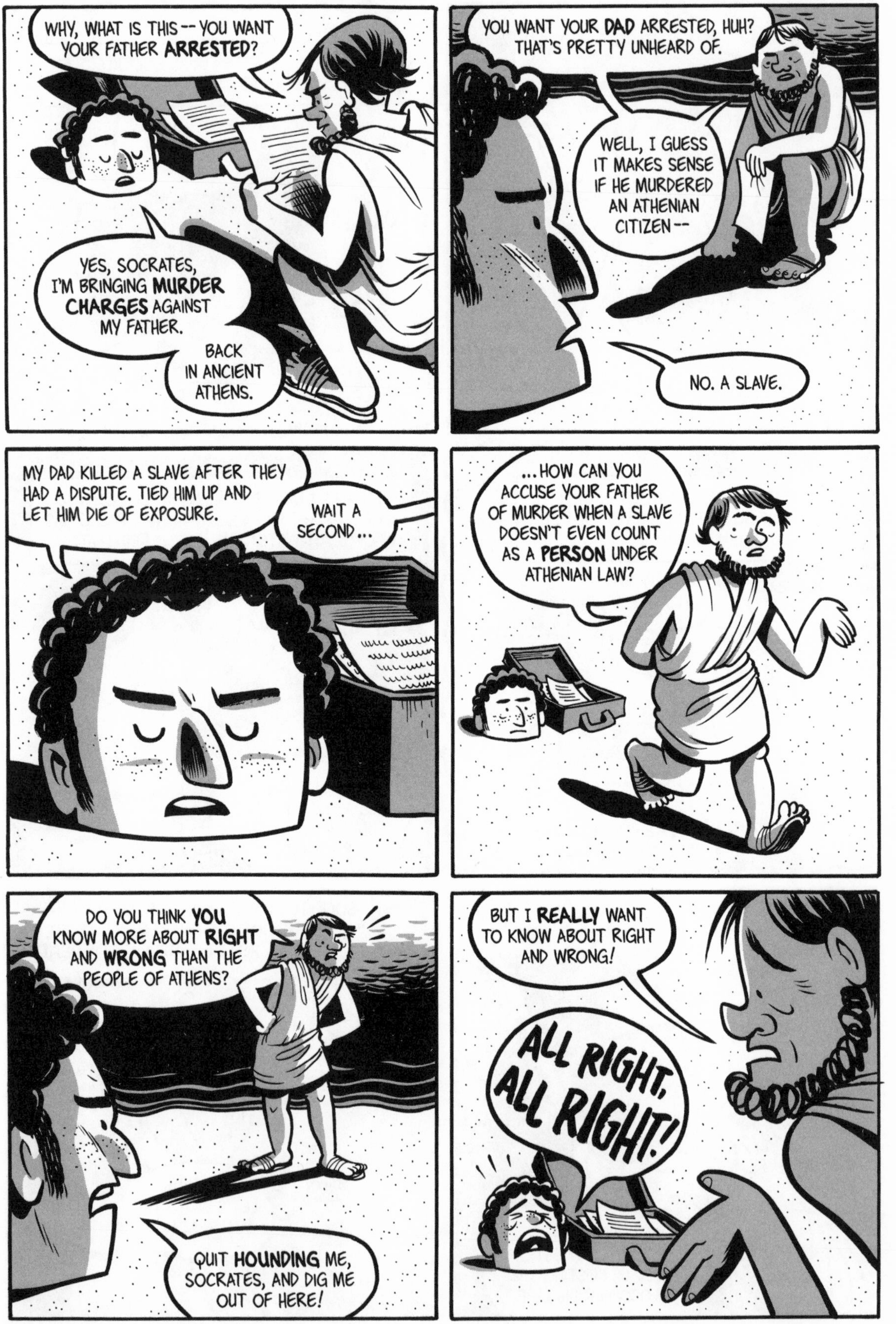
WHY, WHAT IS THIS -- YOU WANT YOUR FATHER ARRESTED?
YES, SOCRATES, I'M BRINGING MURDER CHARGES AGAINST MY FATHER.
BACK IN ANCIENT ATHENS.
YOU WANT YOUR DAD ARRESTED, HUH? THAT'S PRETTY UNHEARD OF.
WELL, I GUESS IT MAKES SENSE IF HE MURDERED AN ATHENIAN CITIZEN --
NO. A SLAVE.
MY DAD KILLED A SLAVE AFTER THEY HAD A DISPUTE. TIED HIM UP AND LET HIM DIE OF EXPOSURE.
WAIT A SECOND...
...HOW CAN YOU ACCUSE YOUR FATHER OF MURDER WHEN A SLAVE DOESN'T EVEN COUNT AS A PERSON UNDER ATHENIAN LAW?
DO YOU THINK YOU KNOW MORE ABOUT RIGHT AND WRONG THAN THE PEOPLE OF ATHENS?
QUIT HOUNDING ME, SOCRATES, AND DIG ME OUT OF HERE!
BUT I REALLY WANT TO KNOW ABOUT RIGHT AND WRONG!
ALL RIGHT, ALL RIGHT!

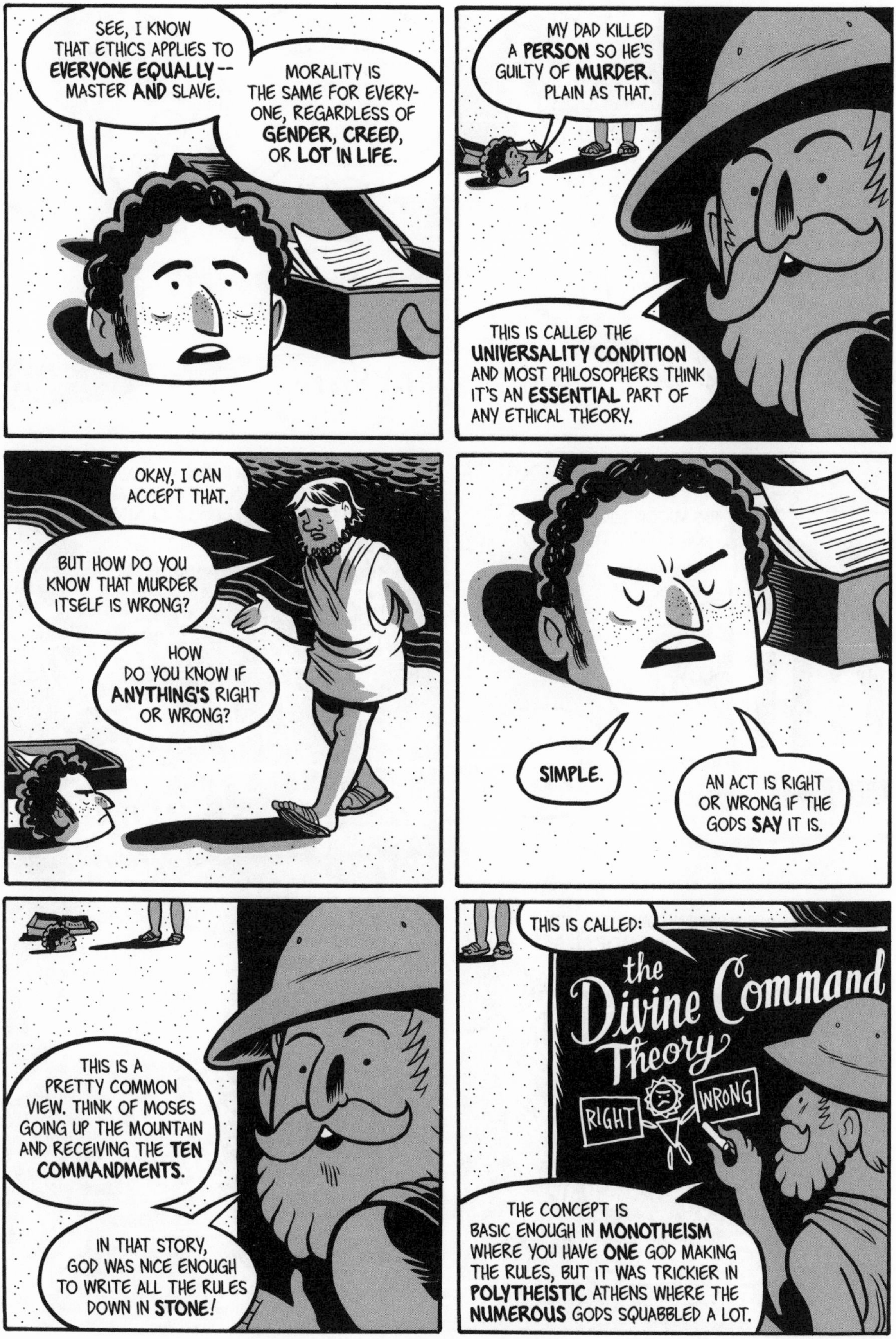

SEE, I KNOW THAT ETHICS APPLIES TO **EVERYONE EQUALLY** -- MASTER **AND** SLAVE.
MORALITY IS THE SAME FOR EVERYONE, REGARDLESS OF **GENDER**, **CREED**, OR **LOT IN LIFE**.
MY DAD KILLED A **PERSON** SO HE'S GUILTY OF **MURDER**. PLAIN AS THAT.
THIS IS CALLED THE **UNIVERSALITY CONDITION** AND MOST PHILOSOPHERS THINK IT'S AN **ESSENTIAL** PART OF ANY ETHICAL THEORY.
OKAY, I CAN ACCEPT THAT.
BUT HOW DO YOU KNOW THAT MURDER ITSELF IS WRONG?
HOW DO YOU KNOW IF **ANYTHING'S** RIGHT OR WRONG?
SIMPLE.
AN ACT IS RIGHT OR WRONG IF THE GODS **SAY** IT IS.
THIS IS A PRETTY COMMON VIEW. THINK OF MOSES GOING UP THE MOUNTAIN AND RECEIVING THE **TEN COMMANDMENTS**.
IN THAT STORY, GOD WAS NICE ENOUGH TO WRITE ALL THE RULES DOWN IN **STONE**!
THIS IS CALLED:
the Divine Command Theory
RIGHT
WRONG
THE CONCEPT IS BASIC ENOUGH IN **MONOTHEISM** WHERE YOU HAVE **ONE** GOD MAKING THE RULES, BUT IT WAS TRICKIER IN **POLYTHEISTIC** ATHENS WHERE THE **NUMEROUS** GODS SQUABBLED A LOT.

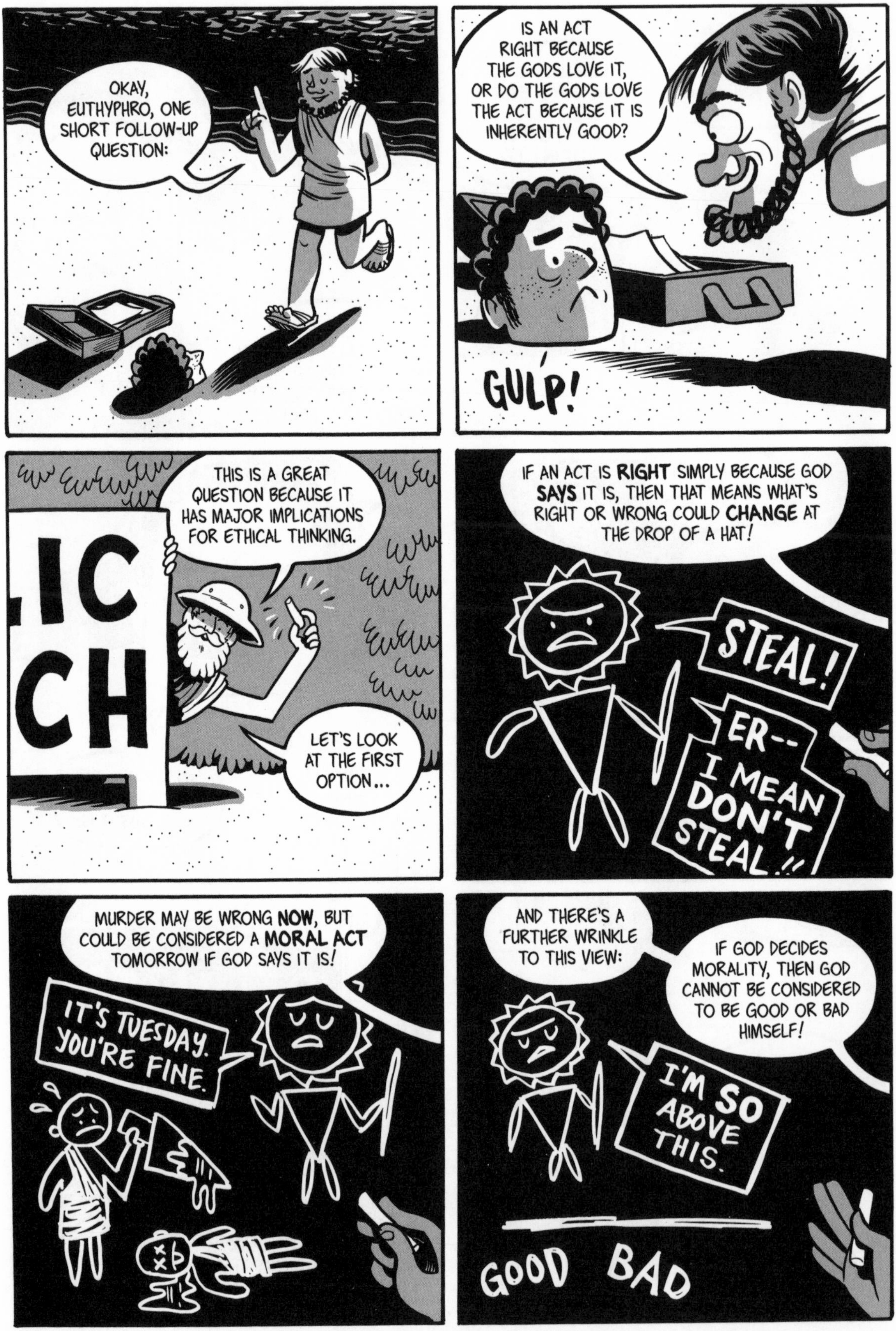
OKAY, EUTHYPHRO, ONE SHORT FOLLOW-UP QUESTION:
IS AN ACT RIGHT BECAUSE THE GODS LOVE IT, OR DO THE GODS LOVE THE ACT BECAUSE IT IS INHERENTLY GOOD?
GULP!
IC
CH
THIS IS A GREAT QUESTION BECAUSE IT HAS MAJOR IMPLICATIONS FOR ETHICAL THINKING.
LET'S LOOK AT THE FIRST OPTION...
IF AN ACT IS **RIGHT** SIMPLY BECAUSE GOD **SAYS** IT IS, THEN THAT MEANS WHAT'S RIGHT OR WRONG COULD **CHANGE** AT THE DROP OF A HAT!
STEAL!
ER-- I MEAN DON'T STEAL!!
MURDER MAY BE WRONG **NOW**, BUT COULD BE CONSIDERED A **MORAL ACT** TOMORROW IF GOD SAYS IT IS!
IT'S TUESDAY. YOU'RE FINE.
AND THERE'S A FURTHER WRINKLE TO THIS VIEW:
IF GOD DECIDES MORALITY, THEN GOD CANNOT BE CONSIDERED TO BE GOOD OR BAD HIMSELF!
I'M SO ABOVE THIS.
GOOD BAD

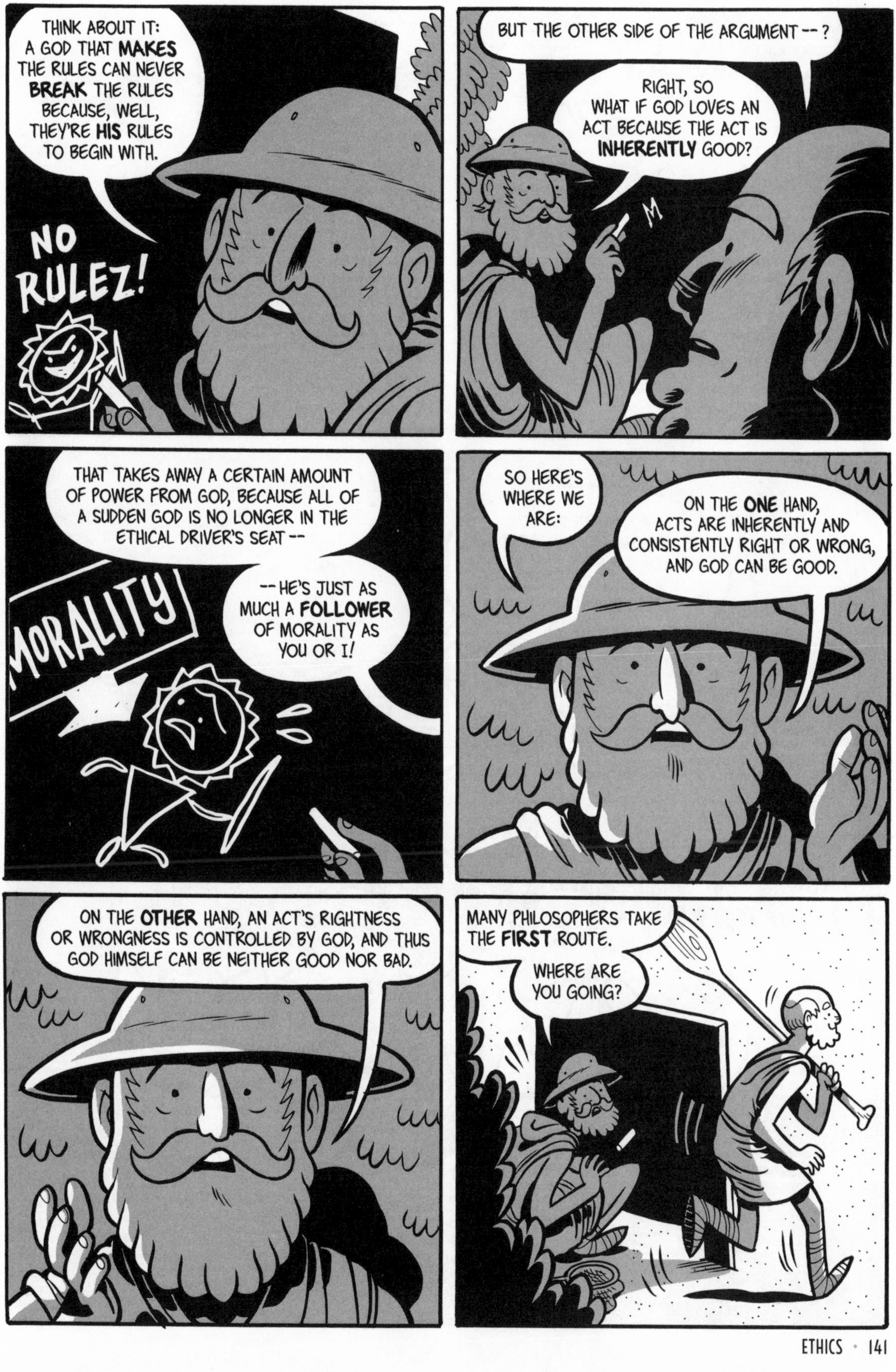
THINK ABOUT IT: A GOD THAT MAKES THE RULES CAN NEVER BREAK THE RULES BECAUSE, WELL, THEY'RE HIS RULES TO BEGIN WITH.
NO RULEZ!
BUT THE OTHER SIDE OF THE ARGUMENT -- ?
RIGHT, SO WHAT IF GOD LOVES AN ACT BECAUSE THE ACT IS INHERENTLY GOOD?
THAT TAKES AWAY A CERTAIN AMOUNT OF POWER FROM GOD, BECAUSE ALL OF A SUDDEN GOD IS NO LONGER IN THE ETHICAL DRIVER'S SEAT --
MORALITY
-- HE'S JUST AS MUCH A FOLLOWER OF MORALITY AS YOU OR I!
SO HERE'S WHERE WE ARE:
ON THE ONE HAND, ACTS ARE INHERENTLY AND CONSISTENTLY RIGHT OR WRONG, AND GOD CAN BE GOOD.
ON THE OTHER HAND, AN ACT'S RIGHTNESS OR WRONGNESS IS CONTROLLED BY GOD, AND THUS GOD HIMSELF CAN BE NEITHER GOOD NOR BAD.
MANY PHILOSOPHERS TAKE THE FIRST ROUTE.
WHERE ARE YOU GOING?

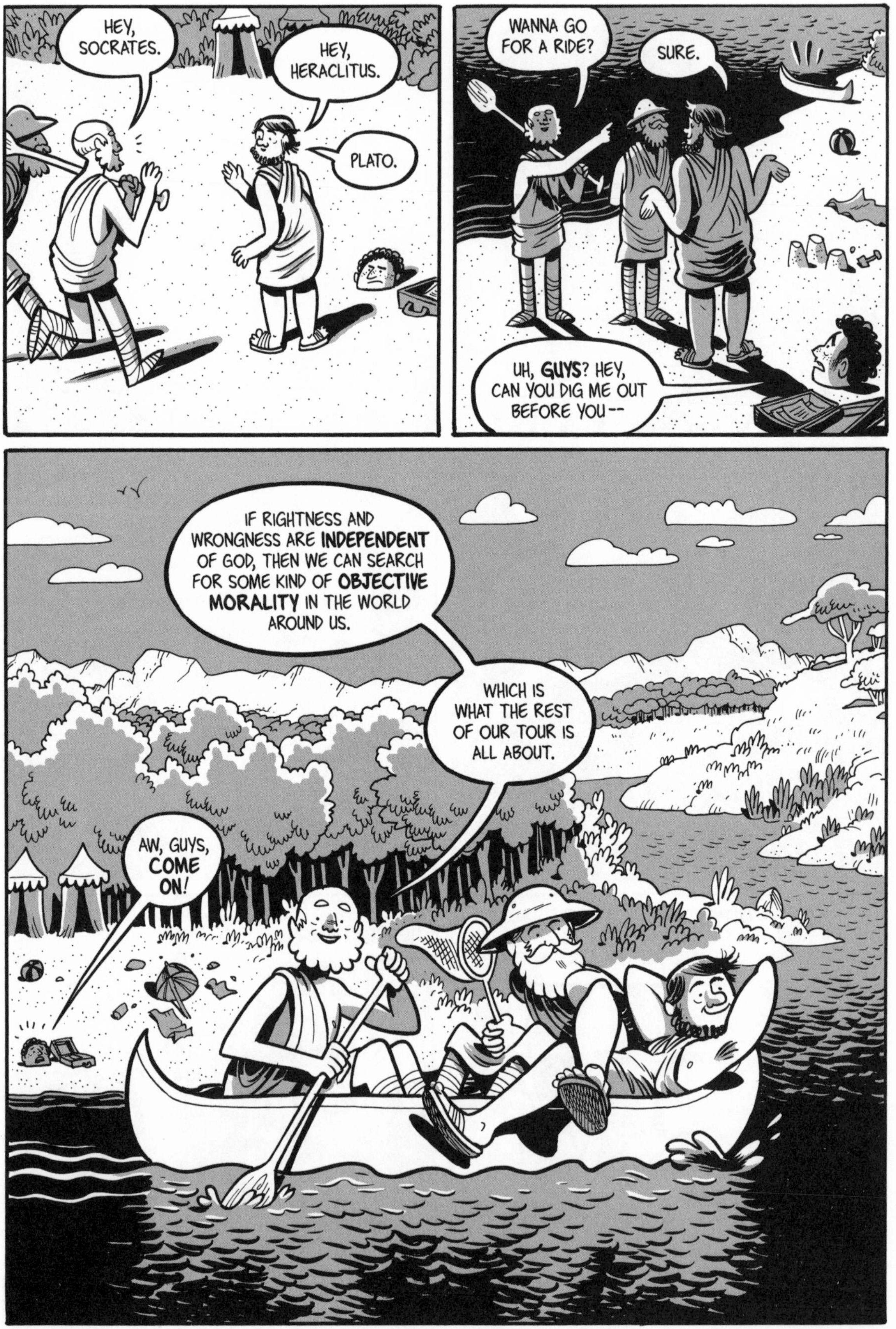
HEY, SOCRATES.
HEY, HERACLITUS.
PLATO.
WANNA GO FOR A RIDE?
SURE.
UH, **GUYS**? HEY, CAN YOU DIG ME OUT BEFORE YOU--
IF RIGHTNESS AND WRONGNESS ARE **INDEPENDENT** OF GOD, THEN WE CAN SEARCH FOR SOME KIND OF **OBJECTIVE MORALITY** IN THE WORLD AROUND US.
WHICH IS WHAT THE REST OF OUR TOUR IS ALL ABOUT.
AW, GUYS, **COME ON**!

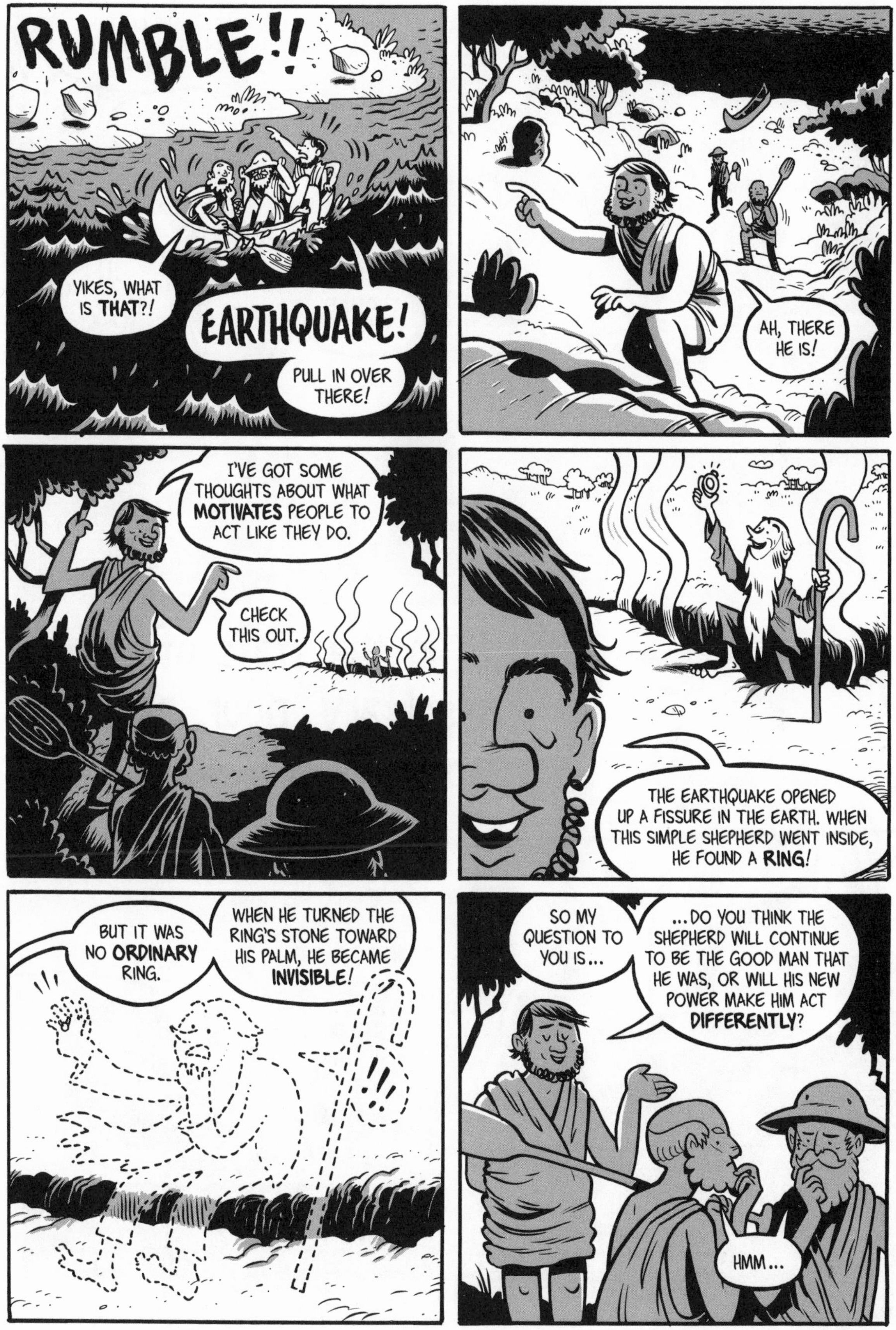
RUMBLE!!
YIKES, WHAT IS THAT?!
EARTHQUAKE!
PULL IN OVER THERE!
AH, THERE HE IS!
I'VE GOT SOME THOUGHTS ABOUT WHAT MOTIVATES PEOPLE TO ACT LIKE THEY DO.
CHECK THIS OUT.
THE EARTHQUAKE OPENED UP A FISSURE IN THE EARTH. WHEN THIS SIMPLE SHEPHERD WENT INSIDE, HE FOUND A RING!
BUT IT WAS NO ORDINARY RING.
WHEN HE TURNED THE RING'S STONE TOWARD HIS PALM, HE BECAME INVISIBLE!
!!
SO MY QUESTION TO YOU IS...
...DO YOU THINK THE SHEPHERD WILL CONTINUE TO BE THE GOOD MAN THAT HE WAS, OR WILL HIS NEW POWER MAKE HIM ACT DIFFERENTLY?
HMM...

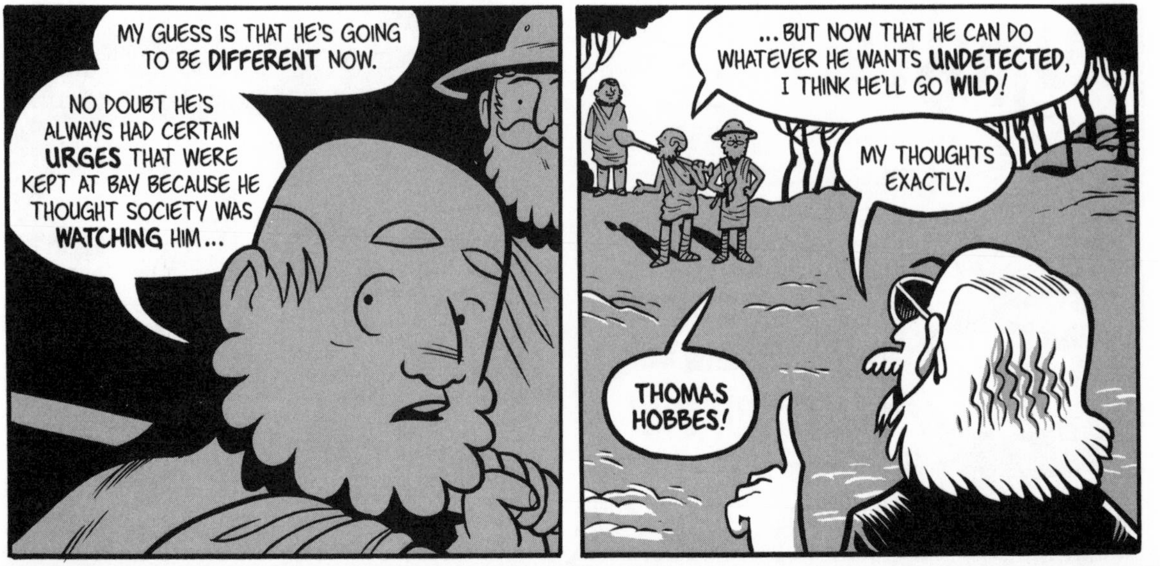
MY GUESS IS THAT HE'S GOING TO BE **DIFFERENT** NOW.
NO DOUBT HE'S ALWAYS HAD CERTAIN **URGES** THAT WERE KEPT AT BAY BECAUSE HE THOUGHT SOCIETY WAS **WATCHING** HIM...
...BUT NOW THAT HE CAN DO WHATEVER HE WANTS **UNDETECTED**, I THINK HE'LL GO **WILD**!
MY THOUGHTS EXACTLY.
THOMAS HOBBES!

THOMAS HOBBES

b. 1588
d. 1679
C.E.

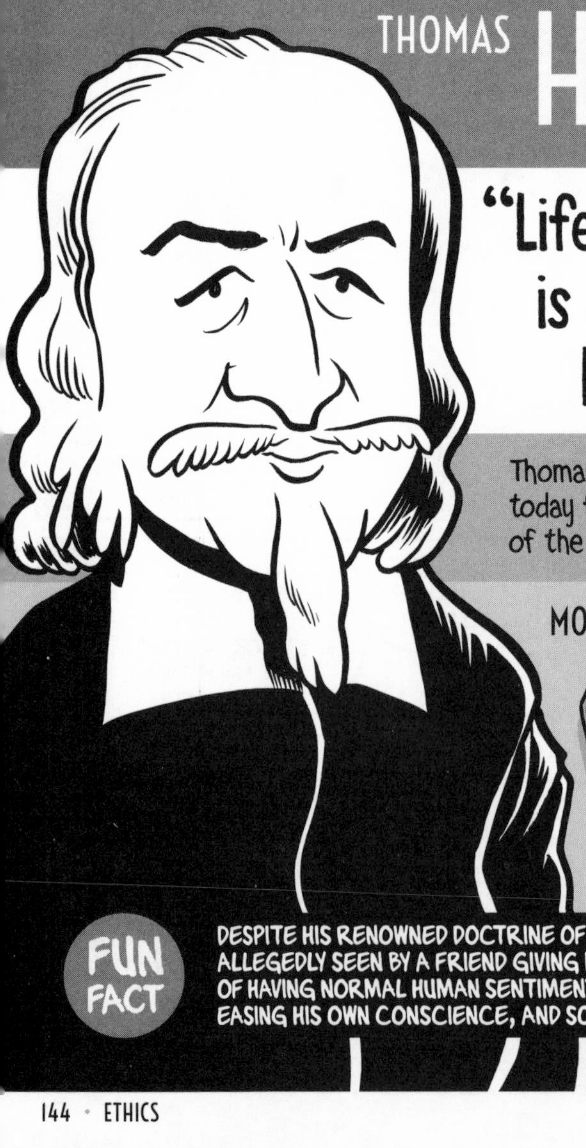

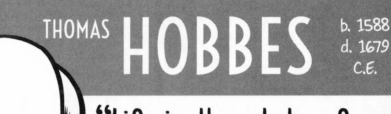

"Life in the state of nature is solitary, poor, nasty, brutish, and short."

-- *Leviathan*

Thomas Hobbes was an English philosopher, best known today for his political philosophy, which stressed the role of the social contract.

MOST FAMOUS WORK:

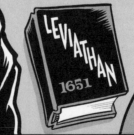

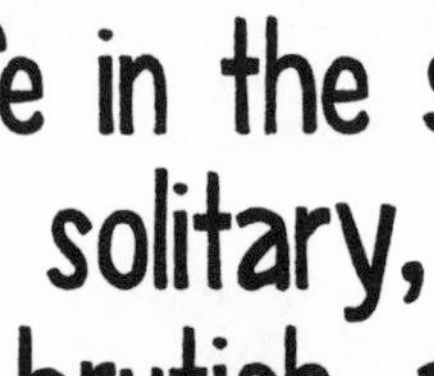
LEVIATHAN
1651

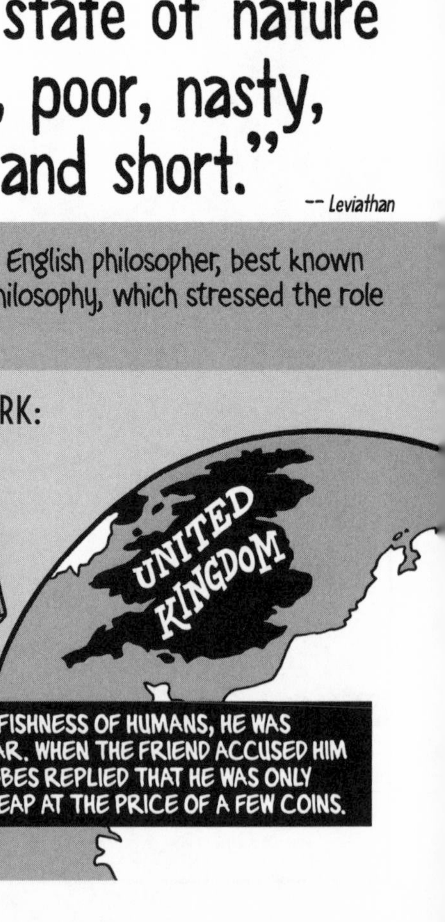
UNITED KINGDOM

FUN FACT

DESPITE HIS RENOWNED DOCTRINE OF THE INTRINSIC SELFISHNESS OF HUMANS, HE WAS ALLEGEDLY SEEN BY A FRIEND GIVING MONEY TO A BEGGAR. WHEN THE FRIEND ACCUSED HIM OF HAVING NORMAL HUMAN SENTIMENTS AFTER ALL, HOBBES REPLIED THAT HE WAS ONLY EASING HIS OWN CONSCIENCE, AND SOUND SLEEP WAS CHEAP AT THE PRICE OF A FEW COINS.

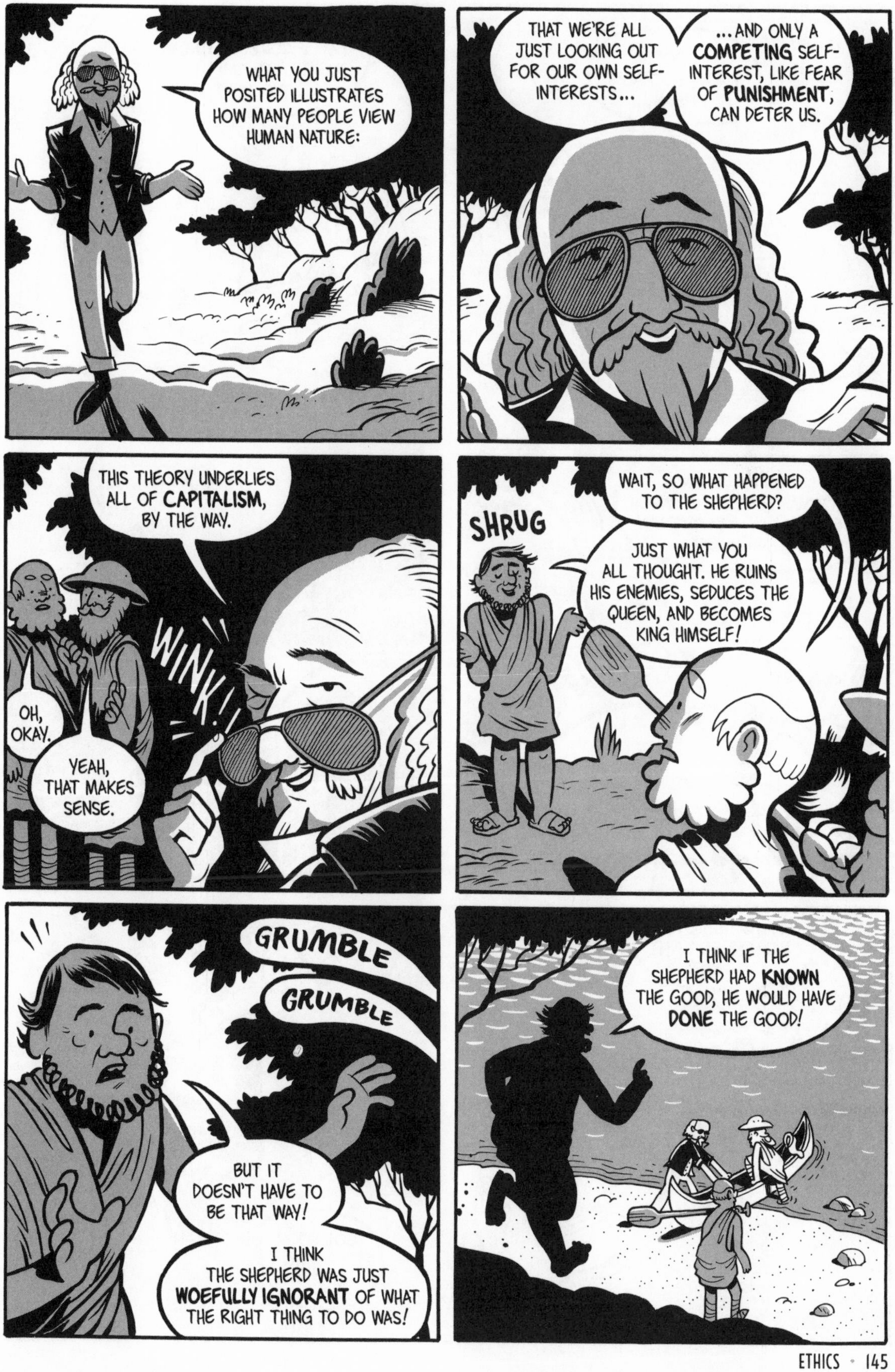
WHAT YOU JUST POSITED ILLUSTRATES HOW MANY PEOPLE VIEW HUMAN NATURE:
THAT WE'RE ALL JUST LOOKING OUT FOR OUR OWN SELF-INTERESTS...
...AND ONLY A COMPETING SELF-INTEREST, LIKE FEAR OF PUNISHMENT, CAN DETER US.
THIS THEORY UNDERLIES ALL OF CAPITALISM, BY THE WAY.
WINK!
OH, OKAY.
YEAH, THAT MAKES SENSE.
WAIT, SO WHAT HAPPENED TO THE SHEPHERD?
SHRUG
JUST WHAT YOU ALL THOUGHT. HE RUINS HIS ENEMIES, SEDUCES THE QUEEN, AND BECOMES KING HIMSELF!
GRUMBLE
GRUMBLE
BUT IT DOESN'T HAVE TO BE THAT WAY!
I THINK THE SHEPHERD WAS JUST WOEFULLY IGNORANT OF WHAT THE RIGHT THING TO DO WAS!
I THINK IF THE SHEPHERD HAD KNOWN THE GOOD, HE WOULD HAVE DONE THE GOOD!

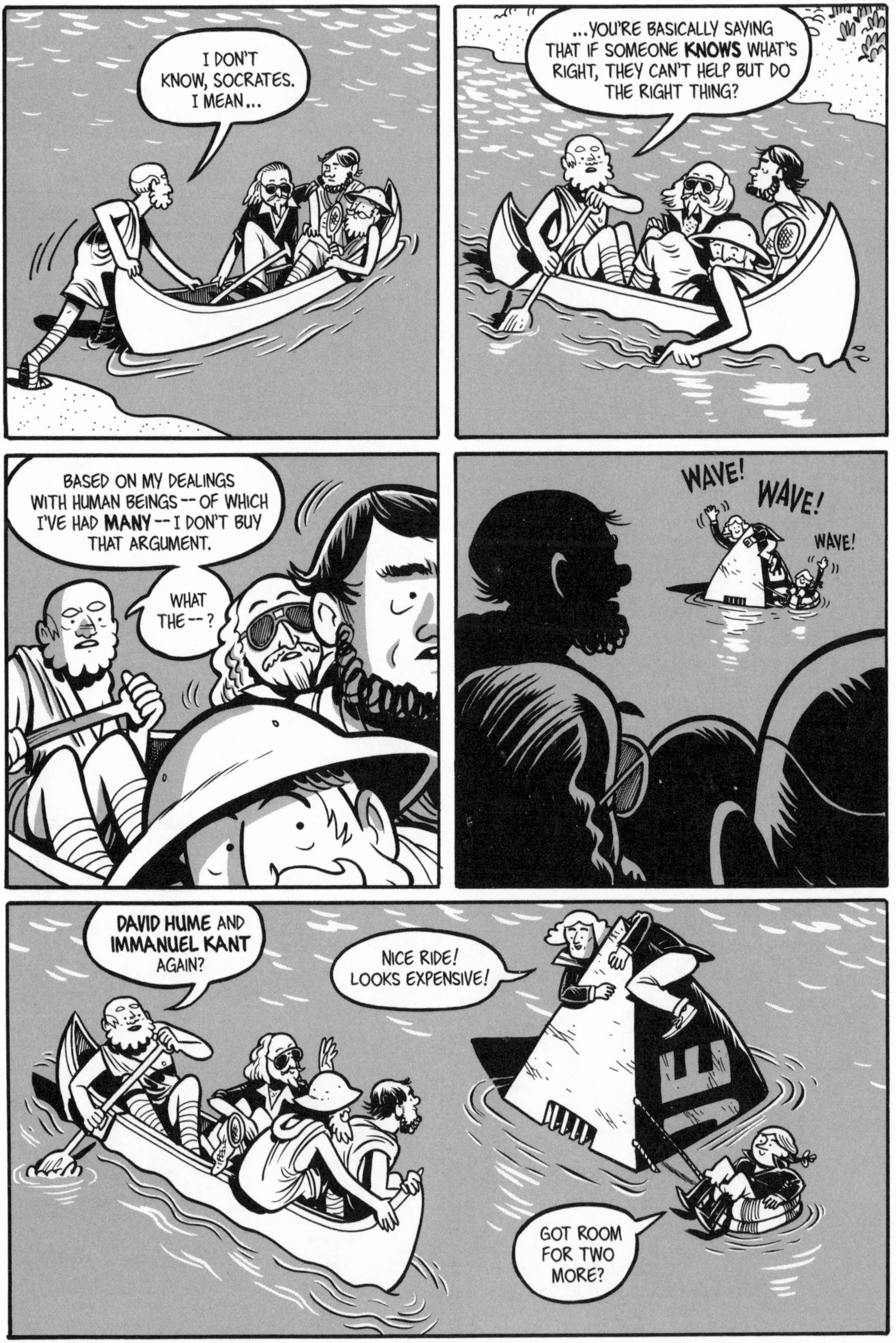
I DON'T KNOW, SOCRATES. I MEAN...
...YOU'RE BASICALLY SAYING THAT IF SOMEONE **KNOWS** WHAT'S RIGHT, THEY CAN'T HELP BUT DO THE RIGHT THING?
BASED ON MY DEALINGS WITH HUMAN BEINGS -- OF WHICH I'VE HAD **MANY** -- I DON'T BUY THAT ARGUMENT.
WHAT THE -- ?
WAVE!
WAVE!
WAVE!
DAVID HUME AND **IMMANUEL KANT** AGAIN?
NICE RIDE! LOOKS EXPENSIVE!
GOT ROOM FOR TWO MORE?

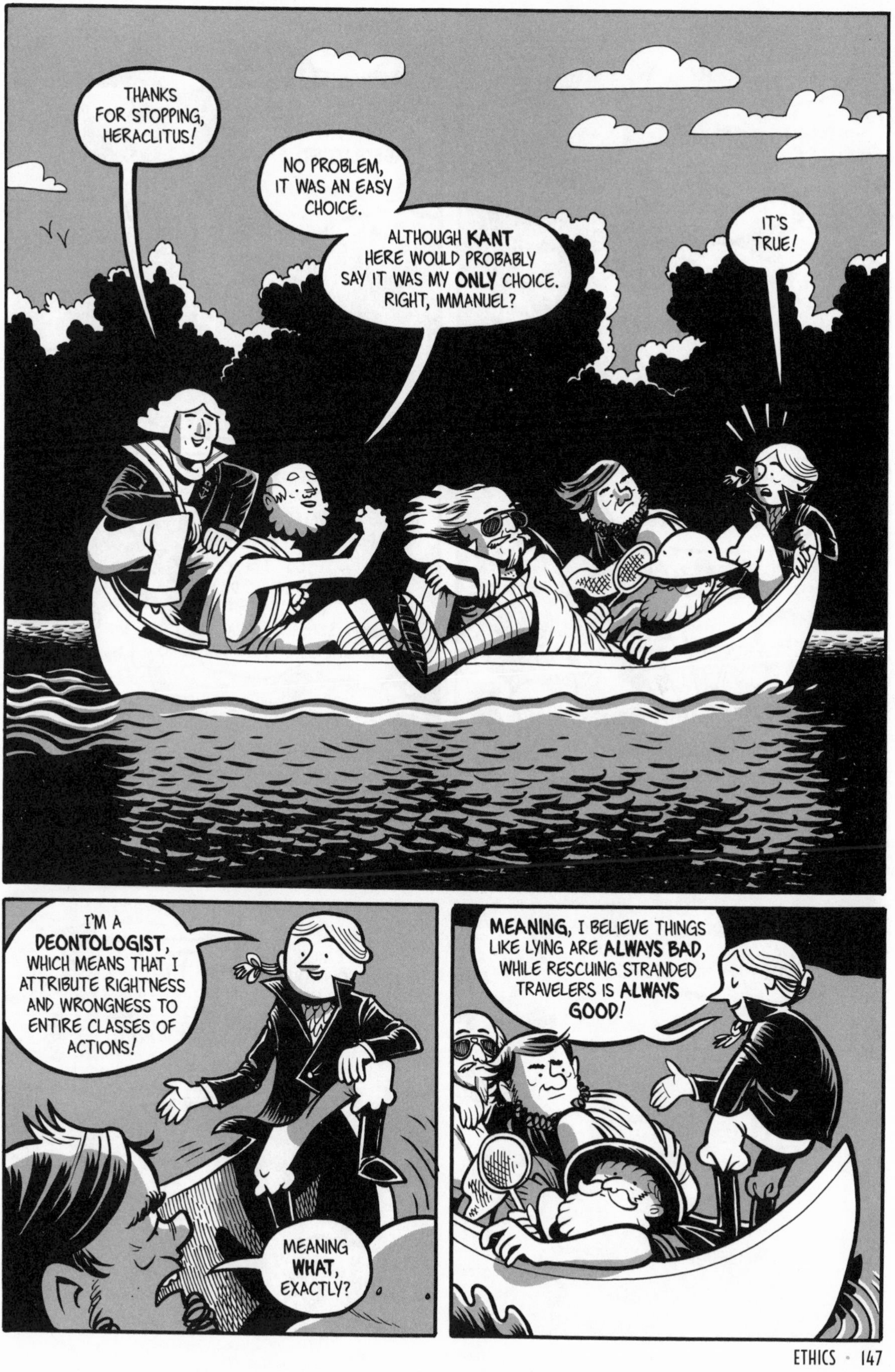
THANKS FOR STOPPING, HERACLITUS!
NO PROBLEM, IT WAS AN EASY CHOICE.
ALTHOUGH KANT HERE WOULD PROBABLY SAY IT WAS MY ONLY CHOICE. RIGHT, IMMANUEL?
IT'S TRUE!
I'M A DEONTOLOGIST, WHICH MEANS THAT I ATTRIBUTE RIGHTNESS AND WRONGNESS TO ENTIRE CLASSES OF ACTIONS!
MEANING WHAT, EXACTLY?
MEANING, I BELIEVE THINGS LIKE LYING ARE ALWAYS BAD, WHILE RESCUING STRANDED TRAVELERS IS ALWAYS GOOD!

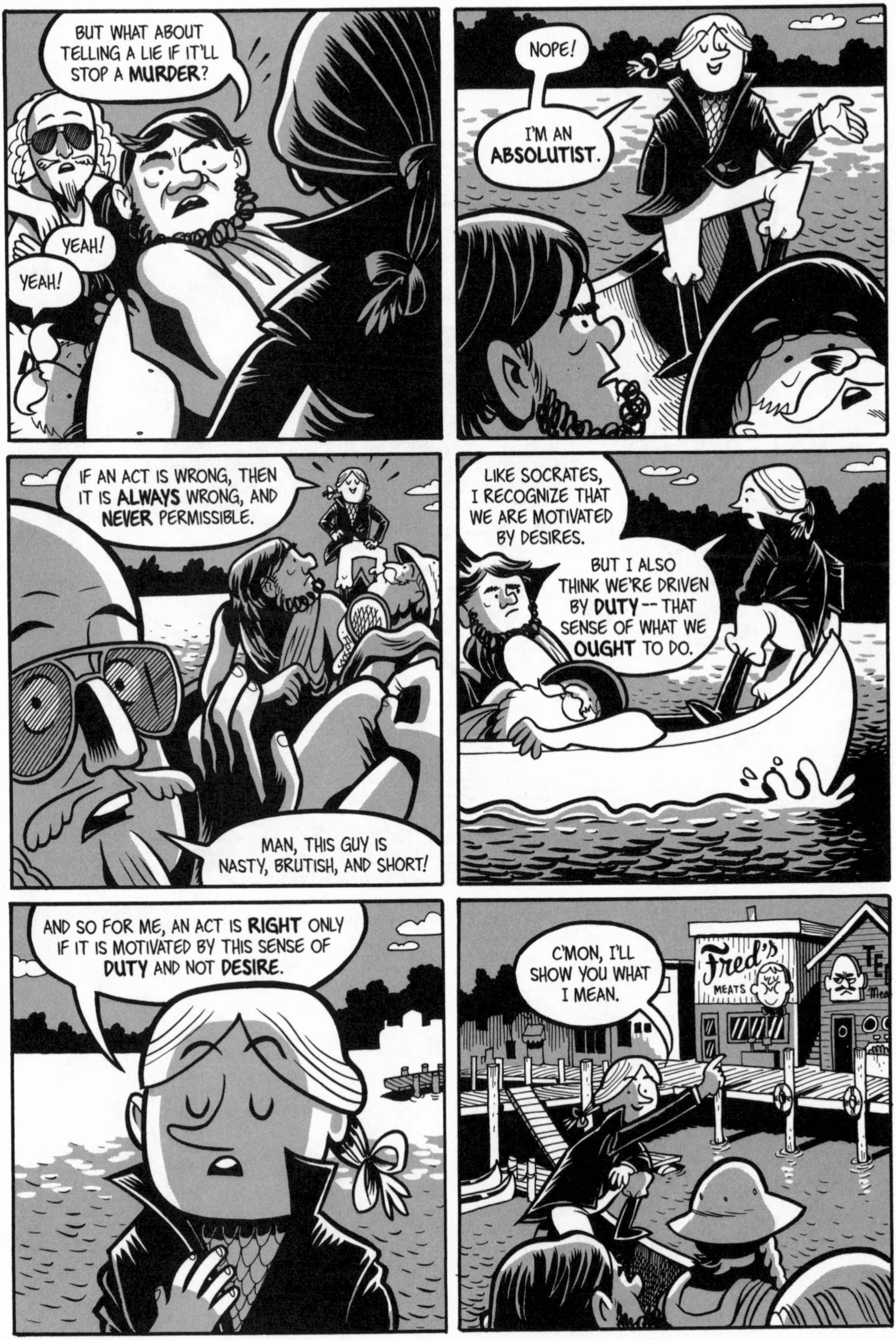
BUT WHAT ABOUT TELLING A LIE IF IT'LL STOP A MURDER?
YEAH!
YEAH!
NOPE!
I'M AN ABSOLUTIST.
IF AN ACT IS WRONG, THEN IT IS ALWAYS WRONG, AND NEVER PERMISSIBLE.
MAN, THIS GUY IS NASTY, BRUTISH, AND SHORT!
LIKE SOCRATES, I RECOGNIZE THAT WE ARE MOTIVATED BY DESIRES.
BUT I ALSO THINK WE'RE DRIVEN BY DUTY -- THAT SENSE OF WHAT WE OUGHT TO DO.
AND SO FOR ME, AN ACT IS RIGHT ONLY IF IT IS MOTIVATED BY THIS SENSE OF DUTY AND NOT DESIRE.
C'MON, I'LL SHOW YOU WHAT I MEAN.
Fred's
MEATS

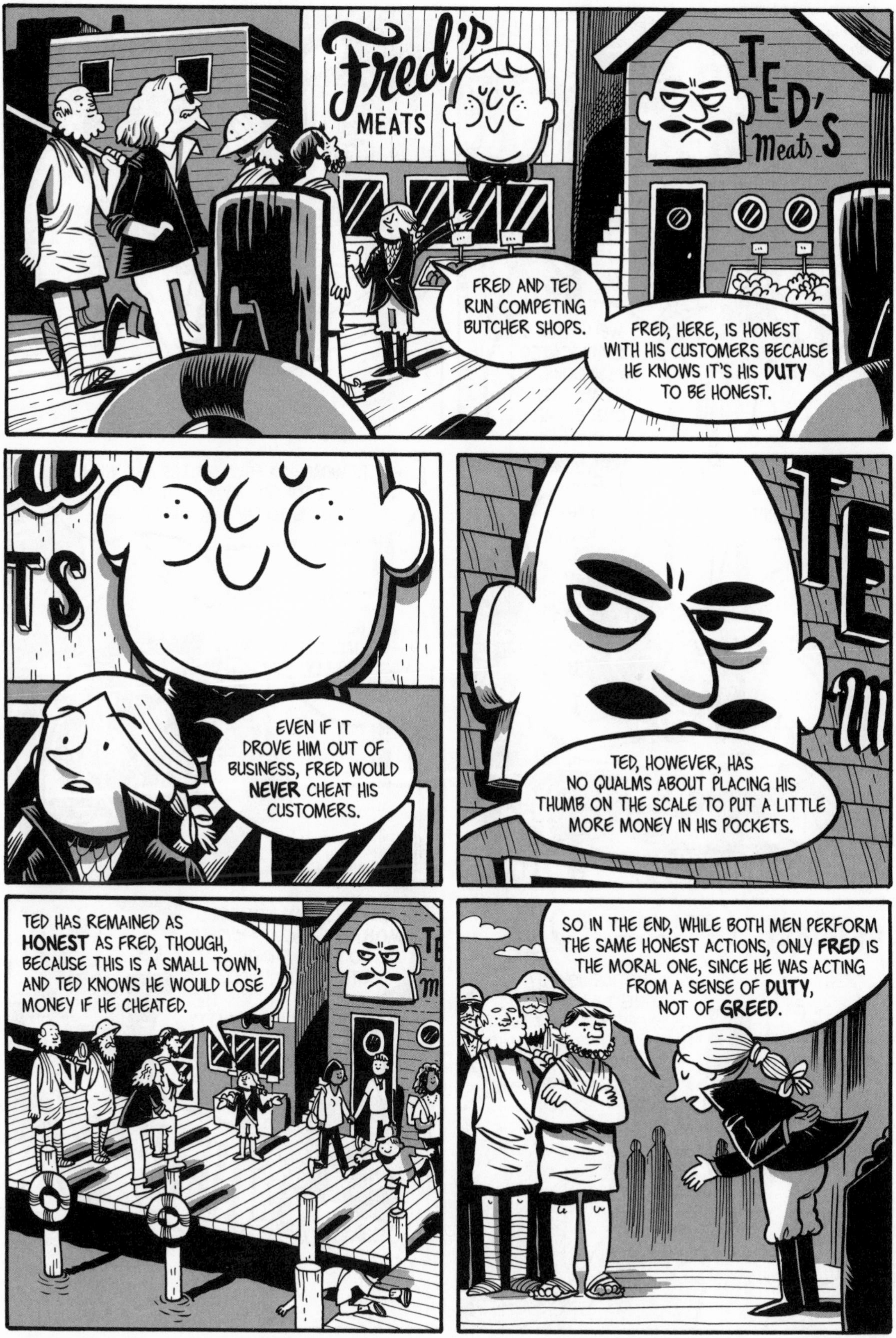
Fred's
MEATS
TED'S
Meats
FRED AND TED RUN COMPETING BUTCHER SHOPS.
FRED, HERE, IS HONEST WITH HIS CUSTOMERS BECAUSE HE KNOWS IT'S HIS **DUTY** TO BE HONEST.
EVEN IF IT DROVE HIM OUT OF BUSINESS, FRED WOULD **NEVER** CHEAT HIS CUSTOMERS.
TED, HOWEVER, HAS NO QUALMS ABOUT PLACING HIS THUMB ON THE SCALE TO PUT A LITTLE MORE MONEY IN HIS POCKETS.
TED HAS REMAINED AS **HONEST** AS FRED, THOUGH, BECAUSE THIS IS A SMALL TOWN, AND TED KNOWS HE WOULD LOSE MONEY IF HE CHEATED.
SO IN THE END, WHILE BOTH MEN PERFORM THE SAME HONEST ACTIONS, ONLY **FRED** IS THE MORAL ONE, SINCE HE WAS ACTING FROM A SENSE OF **DUTY**, NOT OF **GREED**.

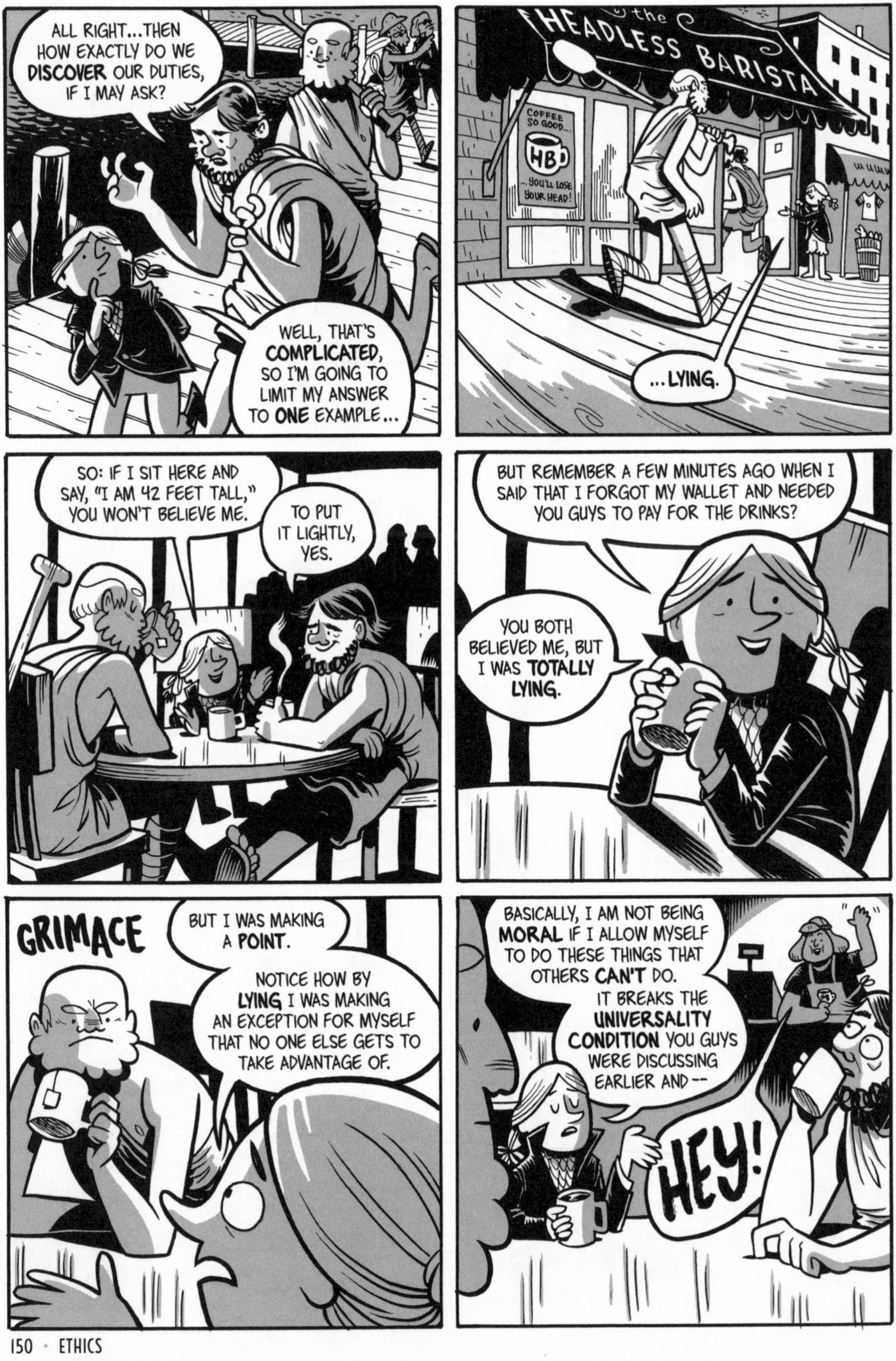
ALL RIGHT...THEN HOW EXACTLY DO WE DISCOVER OUR DUTIES, IF I MAY ASK?
WELL, THAT'S COMPLICATED, SO I'M GOING TO LIMIT MY ANSWER TO ONE EXAMPLE...
the HEADLESS BARISTA
COFFEE SO GOOD... HB ...YOU'LL LOSE YOUR HEAD!
...LYING.
SO: IF I SIT HERE AND SAY, "I AM 42 FEET TALL," YOU WON'T BELIEVE ME.
TO PUT IT LIGHTLY, YES.
BUT REMEMBER A FEW MINUTES AGO WHEN I SAID THAT I FORGOT MY WALLET AND NEEDED YOU GUYS TO PAY FOR THE DRINKS?
YOU BOTH BELIEVED ME, BUT I WAS TOTALLY LYING.
GRIMACE
BUT I WAS MAKING A POINT.
NOTICE HOW BY LYING I WAS MAKING AN EXCEPTION FOR MYSELF THAT NO ONE ELSE GETS TO TAKE ADVANTAGE OF.
BASICALLY, I AM NOT BEING MORAL IF I ALLOW MYSELF TO DO THESE THINGS THAT OTHERS CAN'T DO.
IT BREAKS THE UNIVERSALITY CONDITION YOU GUYS WERE DISCUSSING EARLIER AND--
HEY!

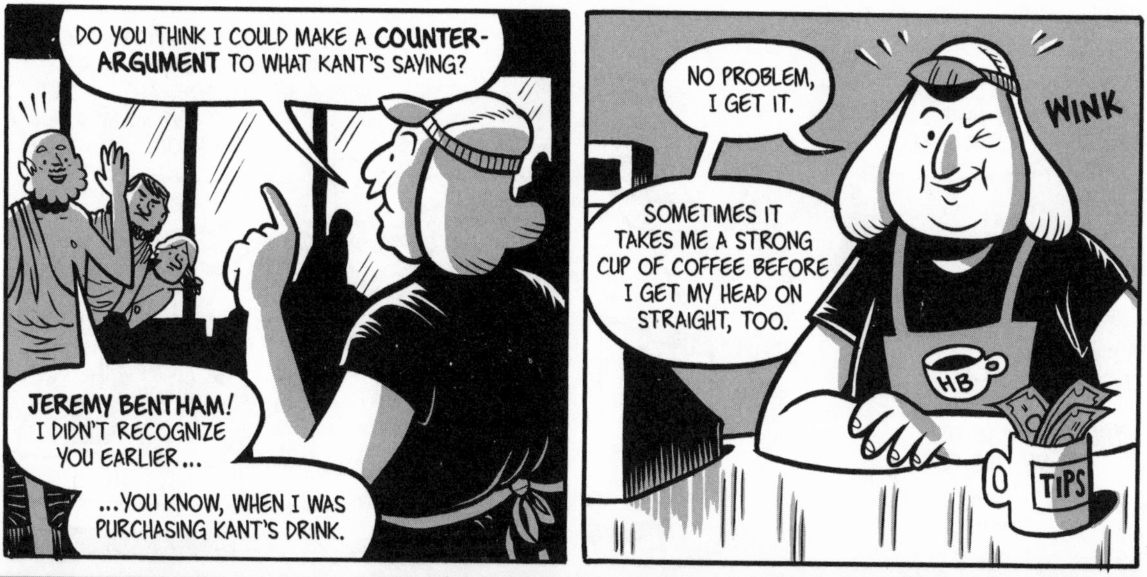
DO YOU THINK I COULD MAKE A **COUNTER-ARGUMENT** TO WHAT KANT'S SAYING?
JEREMY BENTHAM! I DIDN'T RECOGNIZE YOU EARLIER...
...YOU KNOW, WHEN I WAS PURCHASING KANT'S DRINK.
NO PROBLEM, I GET IT.
SOMETIMES IT TAKES ME A STRONG CUP OF COFFEE BEFORE I GET MY HEAD ON STRAIGHT, TOO.
WINK
HB
TIPS

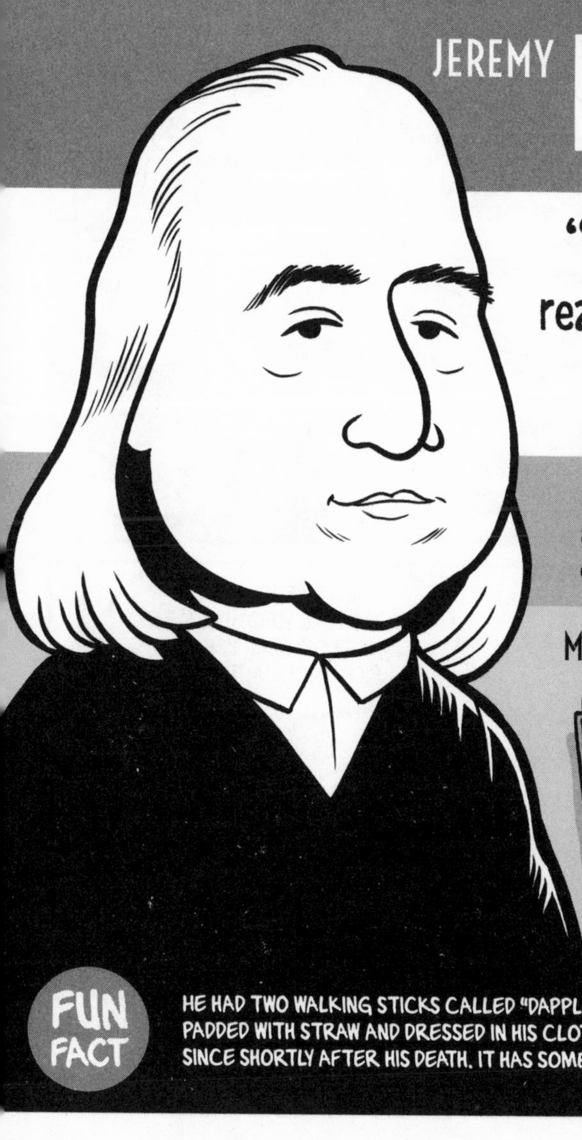

JEREMY BENTHAM

b. 1748
d. 1832
C.E.

"The question is not, 'Can they reason?' nor, 'Can they talk?' but 'Can they suffer?'"

-- *The Principles of Morals and Legislation*

Jeremy Bentham was a British philosopher, jurist, and social reformer. He is regarded as the founder of modern utilitarianism.

MOST FAMOUS WORK:

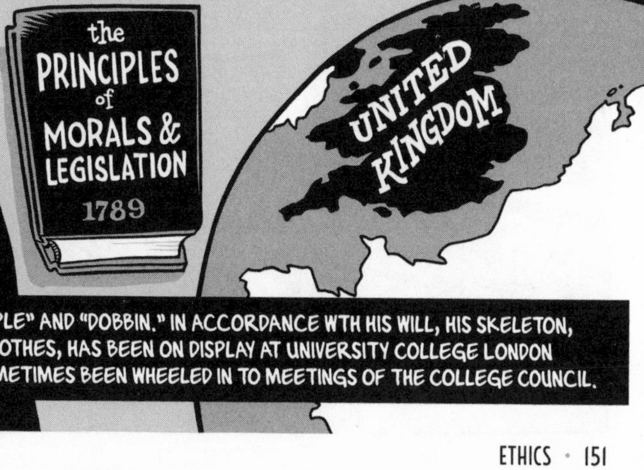
the PRINCIPLES of MORALS & LEGISLATION
1789
UNITED KINGDOM

FUN FACT HE HAD TWO WALKING STICKS CALLED "DAPPLE" AND "DOBBIN." IN ACCORDANCE WTH HIS WILL, HIS SKELETON, PADDED WITH STRAW AND DRESSED IN HIS CLOTHES, HAS BEEN ON DISPLAY AT UNIVERSITY COLLEGE LONDON SINCE SHORTLY AFTER HIS DEATH. IT HAS SOMETIMES BEEN WHEELED IN TO MEETINGS OF THE COLLEGE COUNCIL.

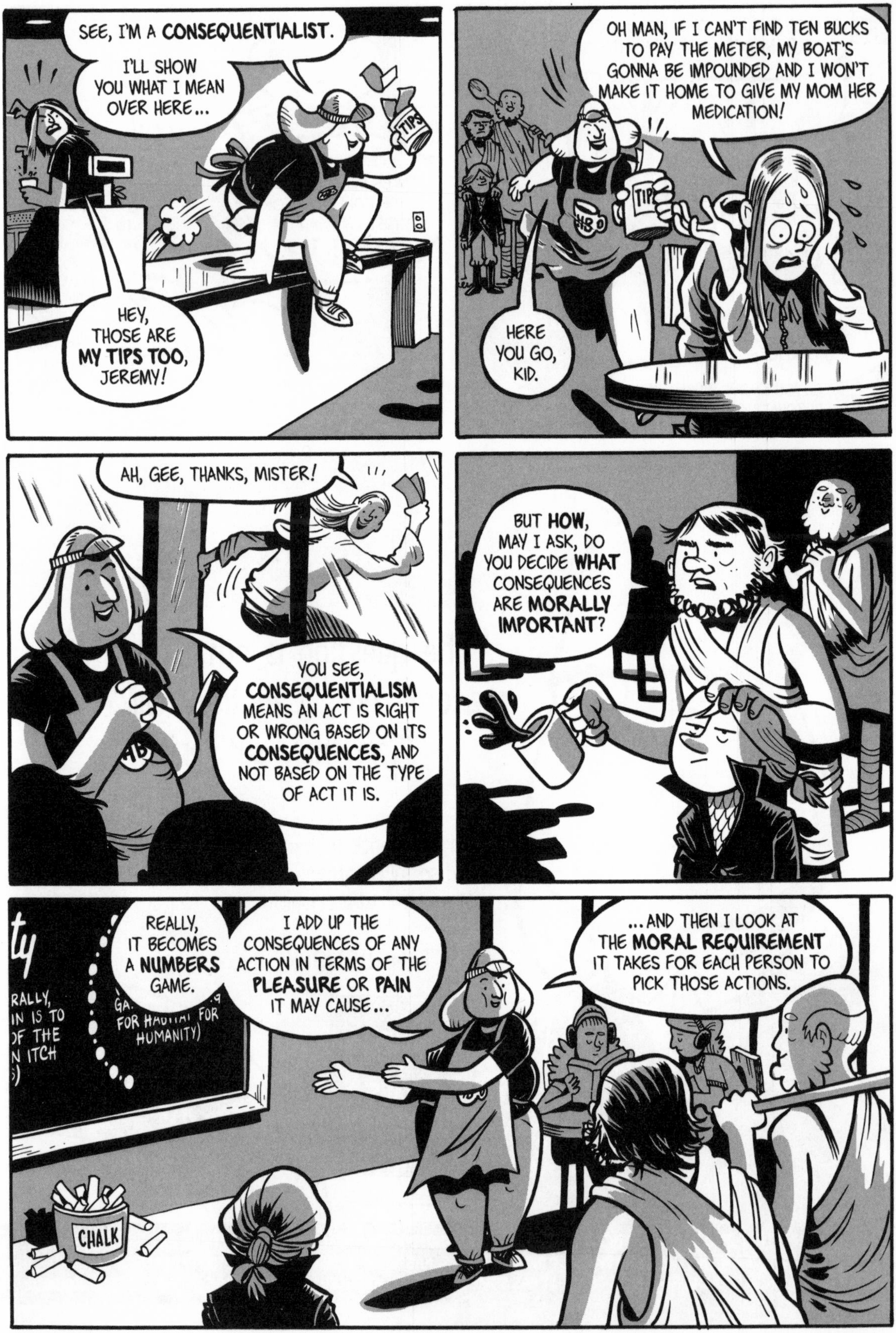
SEE, I'M A **CONSEQUENTIALIST**.
I'LL SHOW YOU WHAT I MEAN OVER HERE...
TIPS
HEY, THOSE ARE **MY TIPS TOO**, JEREMY!
OH MAN, IF I CAN'T FIND TEN BUCKS TO PAY THE METER, MY BOAT'S GONNA BE IMPOUNDED AND I WON'T MAKE IT HOME TO GIVE MY MOM HER MEDICATION!
HERE YOU GO, KID.
AH, GEE, THANKS, MISTER!
YOU SEE, **CONSEQUENTIALISM** MEANS AN ACT IS RIGHT OR WRONG BASED ON ITS **CONSEQUENCES**, AND NOT BASED ON THE TYPE OF ACT IT IS.
BUT **HOW**, MAY I ASK, DO YOU DECIDE **WHAT** CONSEQUENCES ARE **MORALLY IMPORTANT**?
REALLY, IT BECOMES A **NUMBERS** GAME.
I ADD UP THE CONSEQUENCES OF ANY ACTION IN TERMS OF THE **PLEASURE** OR **PAIN** IT MAY CAUSE...
...AND THEN I LOOK AT THE **MORAL REQUIREMENT** IT TAKES FOR EACH PERSON TO PICK THOSE ACTIONS.
CHALK

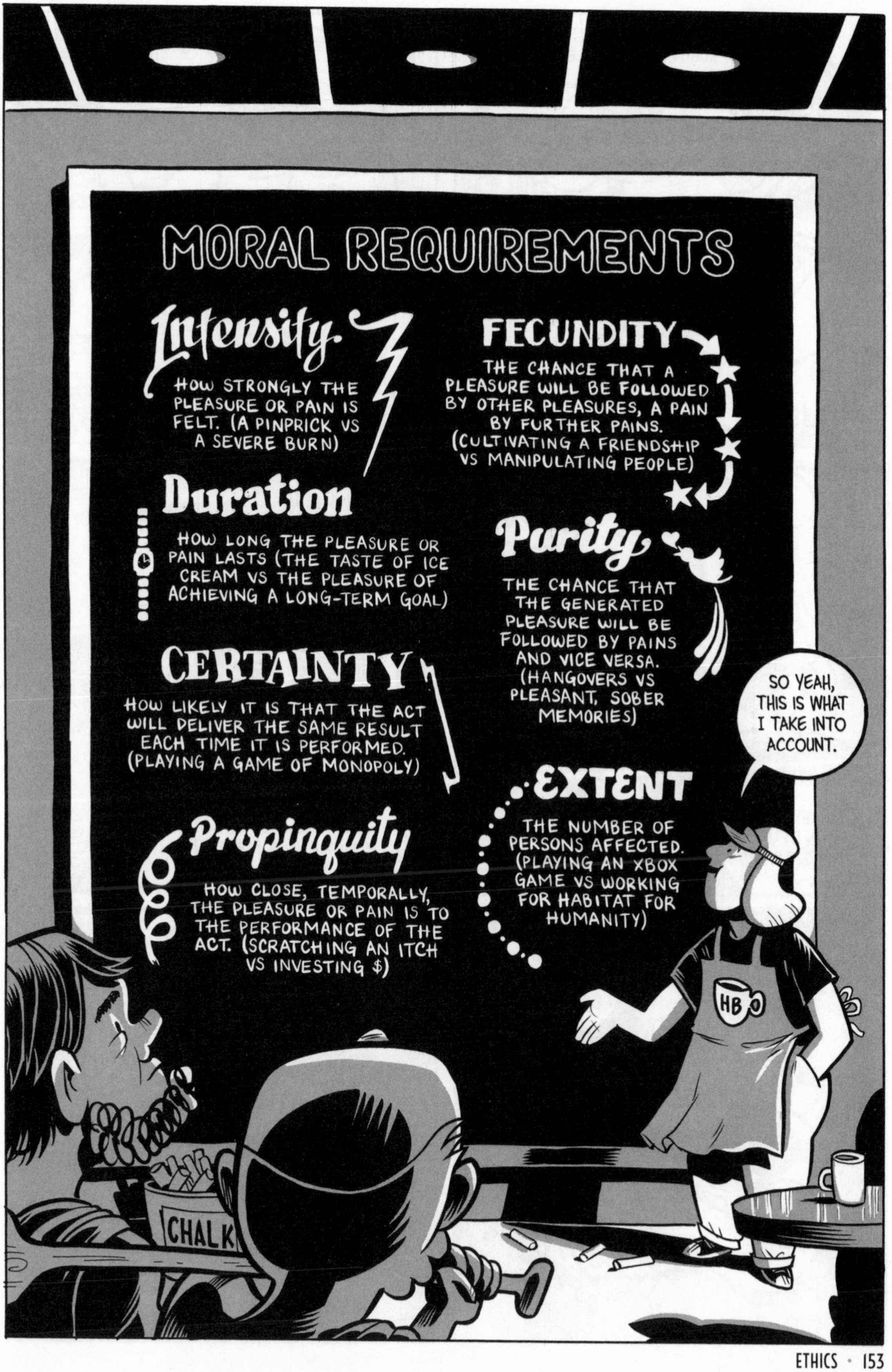
MORAL REQUIREMENTS
Intensity
HOW STRONGLY THE PLEASURE OR PAIN IS FELT. (A PINPRICK VS A SEVERE BURN)
Duration
HOW LONG THE PLEASURE OR PAIN LASTS (THE TASTE OF ICE CREAM VS THE PLEASURE OF ACHIEVING A LONG-TERM GOAL)
CERTAINTY
HOW LIKELY IT IS THAT THE ACT WILL DELIVER THE SAME RESULT EACH TIME IT IS PERFORMED. (PLAYING A GAME OF MONOPOLY)
Propinquity
HOW CLOSE, TEMPORALLY, THE PLEASURE OR PAIN IS TO THE PERFORMANCE OF THE ACT. (SCRATCHING AN ITCH VS INVESTING $)
FECUNDITY
THE CHANCE THAT A PLEASURE WILL BE FOLLOWED BY OTHER PLEASURES, A PAIN BY FURTHER PAINS. (CULTIVATING A FRIENDSHIP VS MANIPULATING PEOPLE)
Purity
THE CHANCE THAT THE GENERATED PLEASURE WILL BE FOLLOWED BY PAINS AND VICE VERSA. (HANGOVERS VS PLEASANT, SOBER MEMORIES)
EXTENT
THE NUMBER OF PERSONS AFFECTED. (PLAYING AN XBOX GAME VS WORKING FOR HABITAT FOR HUMANITY)
SO YEAH, THIS IS WHAT I TAKE INTO ACCOUNT.
HB
CHALK

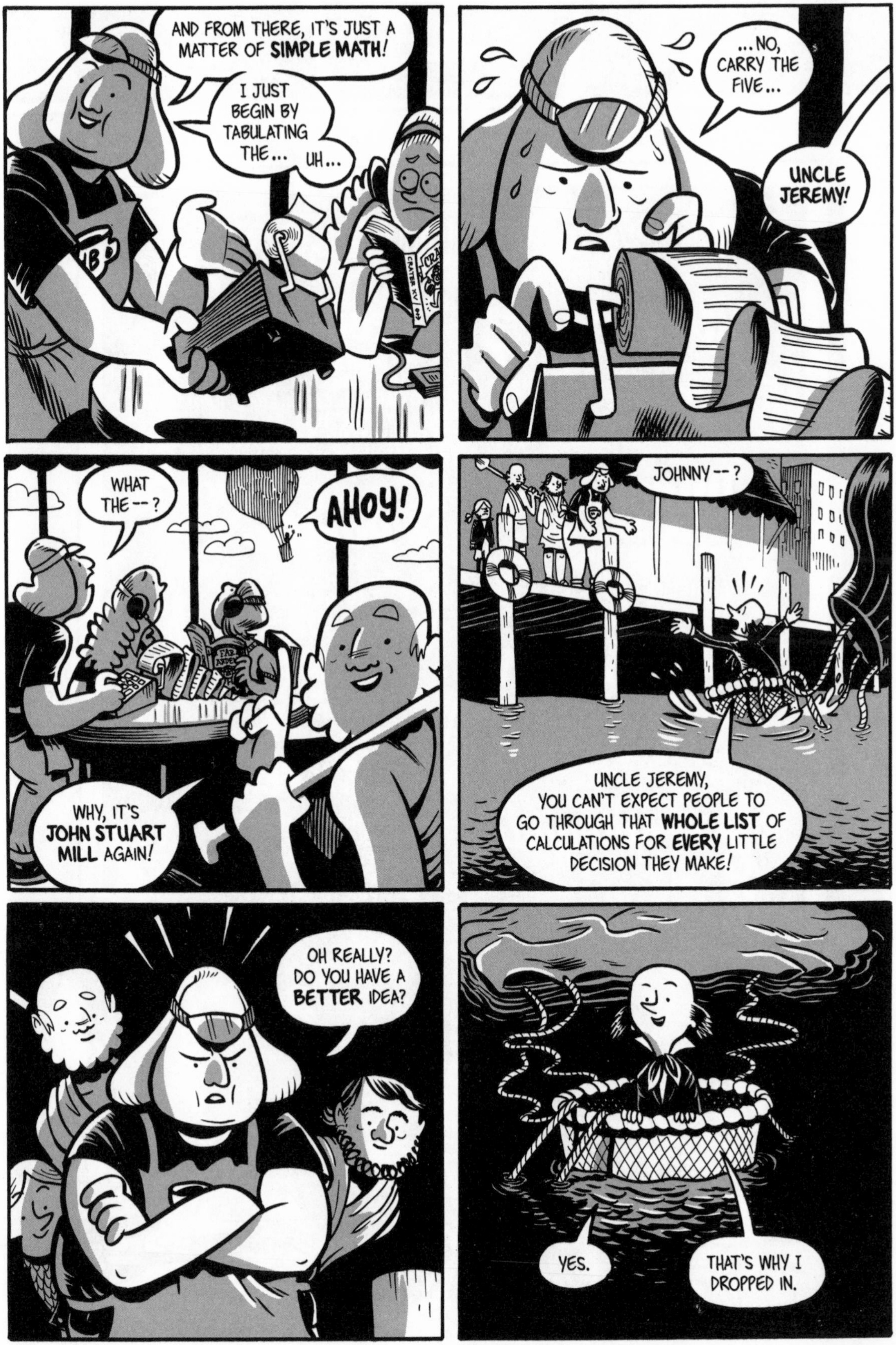
AND FROM THERE, IT'S JUST A MATTER OF **SIMPLE MATH**!
I JUST BEGIN BY TABULATING THE... UH...
...NO, CARRY THE FIVE...
UNCLE JEREMY!
WHAT THE--?
AHOY!
WHY, IT'S **JOHN STUART MILL** AGAIN!
JOHNNY--?
UNCLE JEREMY, YOU CAN'T EXPECT PEOPLE TO GO THROUGH THAT **WHOLE LIST** OF CALCULATIONS FOR **EVERY** LITTLE DECISION THEY MAKE!
OH REALLY? DO YOU HAVE A **BETTER** IDEA?
YES.
THAT'S WHY I DROPPED IN.

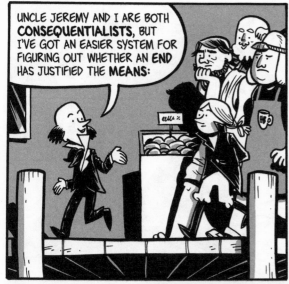

UNCLE JEREMY AND I ARE BOTH **CONSEQUENTIALISTS**, BUT I'VE GOT AN EASIER SYSTEM FOR FIGURING OUT WHETHER AN **END** HAS JUSTIFIED THE **MEANS**:

ASK THE PEOPLE INVOLVED.

ONE PERSON, ONE VOTE?

WELL, BASICALLY. BUT THERE ARE **EXCEPTIONS**.

IF THE VOTING COMES DOWN TO **SOCRATES** AND A **TALKING PIG**, FOR EXAMPLE...

...I MIGHT GIVE SOCRATES'S VOTE A LITTLE MORE **WEIGHT**.

MUCH OBLIGED!

I SHOULD NOTE THAT WE RUN INTO SOME INTERESTING ISSUES WITH CLASSIFYING **GOOD** OR **BAD** OUTCOMES OF **GOOD** OR **BAD** ACTIONS.

MEANING WHAT?

HELP!!

HELP ME!!

HERE, I'LL SHOW YOU!

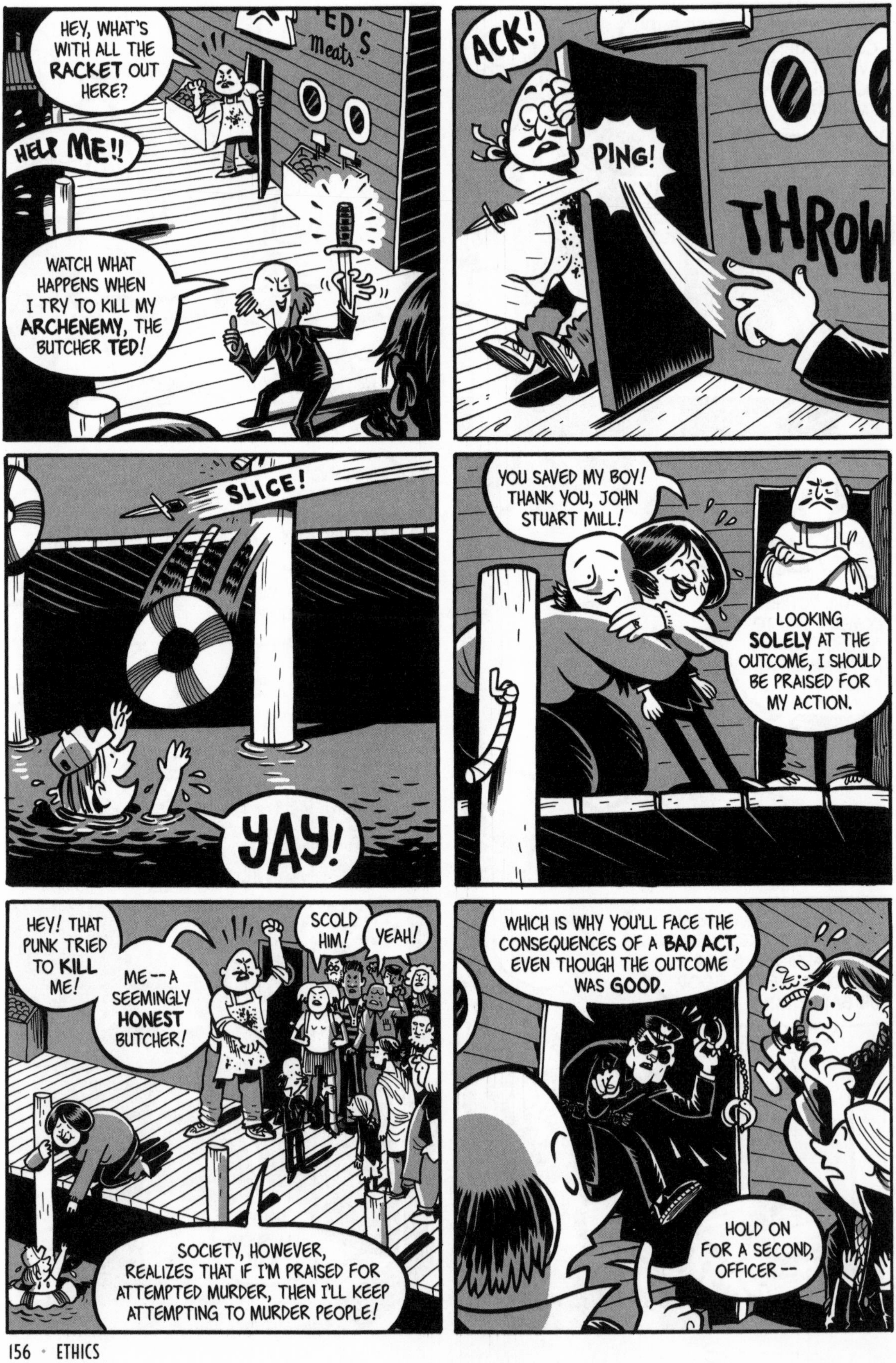
HEY, WHAT'S WITH ALL THE RACKET OUT HERE?
TED'S meats
HELP ME!!
WATCH WHAT HAPPENS WHEN I TRY TO KILL MY ARCHENEMY, THE BUTCHER TED!
ACK!
PING!
THROW
SLICE!
YAY!
YOU SAVED MY BOY! THANK YOU, JOHN STUART MILL!
LOOKING SOLELY AT THE OUTCOME, I SHOULD BE PRAISED FOR MY ACTION.
HEY! THAT PUNK TRIED TO KILL ME!
ME--A SEEMINGLY HONEST BUTCHER!
SCOLD HIM!
YEAH!
SOCIETY, HOWEVER, REALIZES THAT IF I'M PRAISED FOR ATTEMPTED MURDER, THEN I'LL KEEP ATTEMPTING TO MURDER PEOPLE!
WHICH IS WHY YOU'LL FACE THE CONSEQUENCES OF A BAD ACT, EVEN THOUGH THE OUTCOME WAS GOOD.
HOLD ON FOR A SECOND, OFFICER--

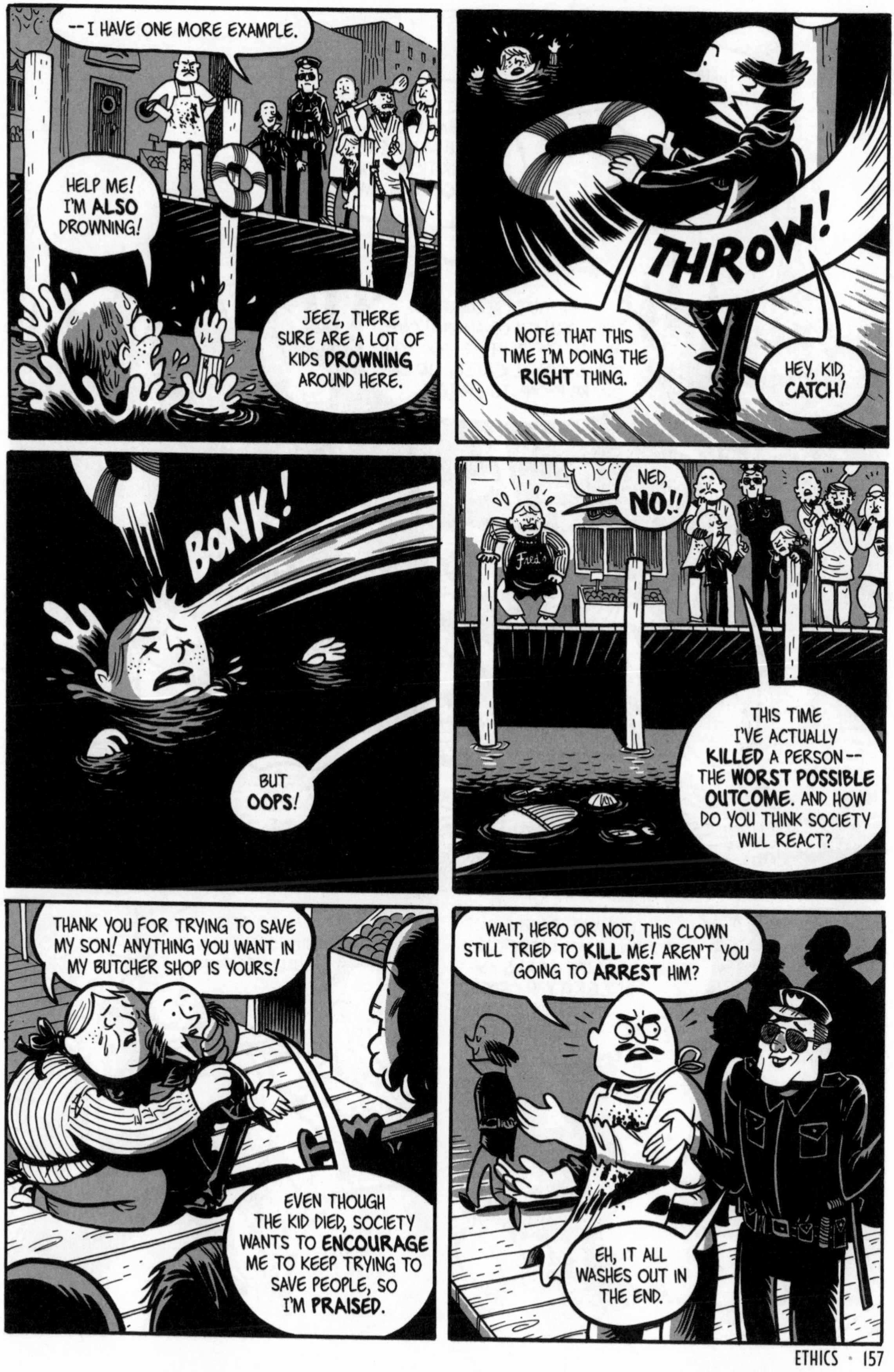
--I HAVE ONE MORE EXAMPLE.
HELP ME! I'M **ALSO** DROWNING!
JEEZ, THERE SURE ARE A LOT OF KIDS **DROWNING** AROUND HERE.
THROW!
NOTE THAT THIS TIME I'M DOING THE **RIGHT** THING.
HEY, KID, **CATCH**!
BONK!
BUT **OOPS**!
NED, **NO!!**
THIS TIME I'VE ACTUALLY **KILLED** A PERSON--THE **WORST POSSIBLE OUTCOME**. AND HOW DO YOU THINK SOCIETY WILL REACT?
THANK YOU FOR TRYING TO SAVE MY SON! ANYTHING YOU WANT IN MY BUTCHER SHOP IS YOURS!
EVEN THOUGH THE KID DIED, SOCIETY WANTS TO **ENCOURAGE** ME TO KEEP TRYING TO SAVE PEOPLE, SO I'M **PRAISED**.
WAIT, HERO OR NOT, THIS CLOWN STILL TRIED TO **KILL** ME! AREN'T YOU GOING TO **ARREST** HIM?
EH, IT ALL WASHES OUT IN THE END.

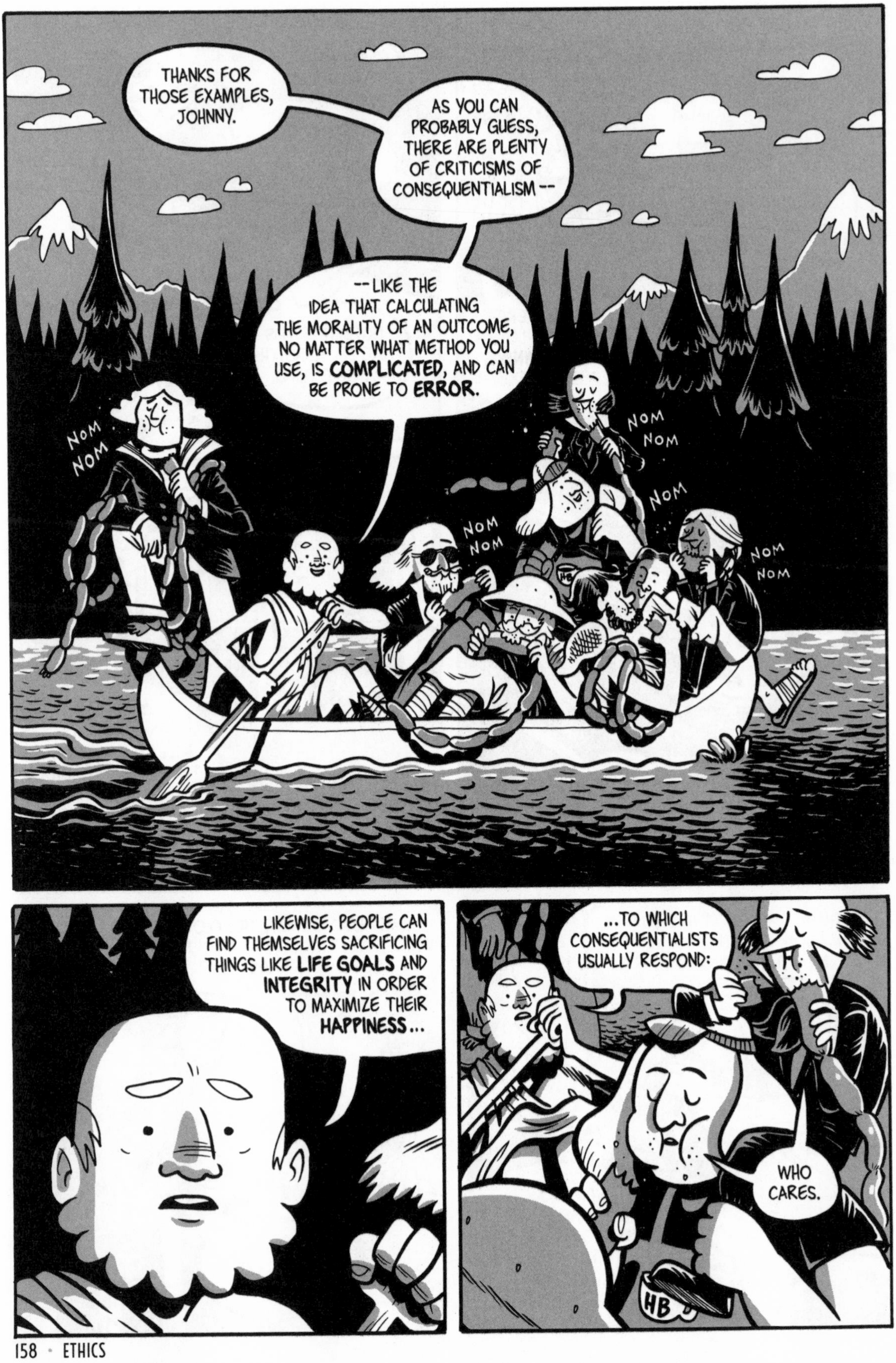
THANKS FOR THOSE EXAMPLES, JOHNNY.
AS YOU CAN PROBABLY GUESS, THERE ARE PLENTY OF CRITICISMS OF CONSEQUENTIALISM --
-- LIKE THE IDEA THAT CALCULATING THE MORALITY OF AN OUTCOME, NO MATTER WHAT METHOD YOU USE, IS **COMPLICATED**, AND CAN BE PRONE TO **ERROR**.
NOM NOM
NOM NOM
NOM NOM
NOM
NOM NOM
LIKEWISE, PEOPLE CAN FIND THEMSELVES SACRIFICING THINGS LIKE **LIFE GOALS** AND **INTEGRITY** IN ORDER TO MAXIMIZE THEIR **HAPPINESS**...
...TO WHICH CONSEQUENTIALISTS USUALLY RESPOND:
WHO CARES.

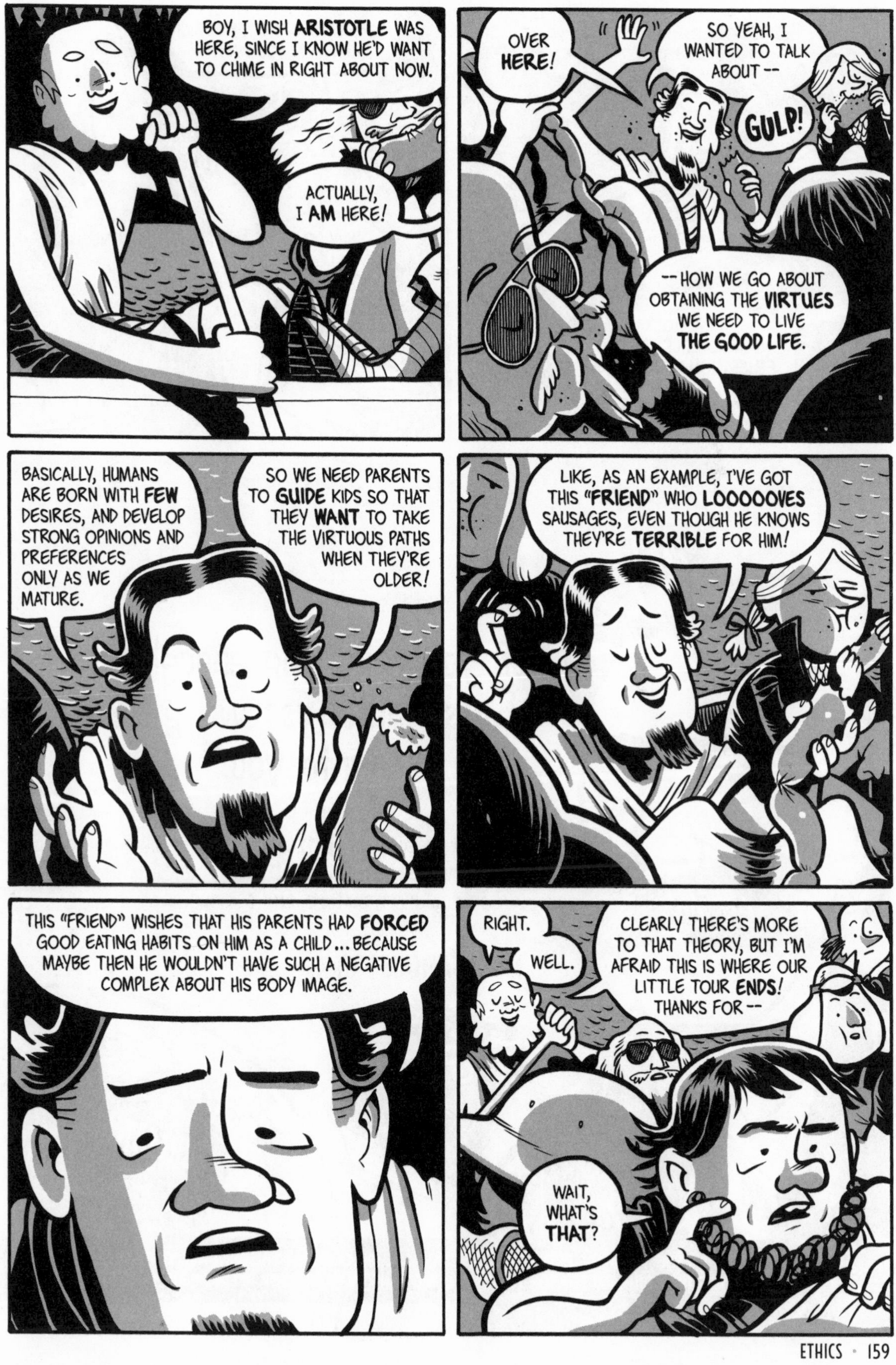
BOY, I WISH **ARISTOTLE** WAS HERE, SINCE I KNOW HE'D WANT TO CHIME IN RIGHT ABOUT NOW.
ACTUALLY, I **AM** HERE!
OVER **HERE**!
SO YEAH, I WANTED TO TALK ABOUT --
GULP!
-- HOW WE GO ABOUT OBTAINING THE **VIRTUES** WE NEED TO LIVE **THE GOOD LIFE**.
BASICALLY, HUMANS ARE BORN WITH **FEW** DESIRES, AND DEVELOP STRONG OPINIONS AND PREFERENCES ONLY AS WE MATURE.
SO WE NEED PARENTS TO **GUIDE** KIDS SO THAT THEY **WANT** TO TAKE THE VIRTUOUS PATHS WHEN THEY'RE OLDER!
LIKE, AS AN EXAMPLE, I'VE GOT THIS "**FRIEND**" WHO **LOOOOOVES** SAUSAGES, EVEN THOUGH HE KNOWS THEY'RE **TERRIBLE** FOR HIM!
THIS "FRIEND" WISHES THAT HIS PARENTS HAD **FORCED** GOOD EATING HABITS ON HIM AS A CHILD... BECAUSE MAYBE THEN HE WOULDN'T HAVE SUCH A NEGATIVE COMPLEX ABOUT HIS BODY IMAGE.
RIGHT.
WELL.
CLEARLY THERE'S MORE TO THAT THEORY, BUT I'M AFRAID THIS IS WHERE OUR LITTLE TOUR **ENDS**! THANKS FOR --
WAIT, WHAT'S **THAT**?

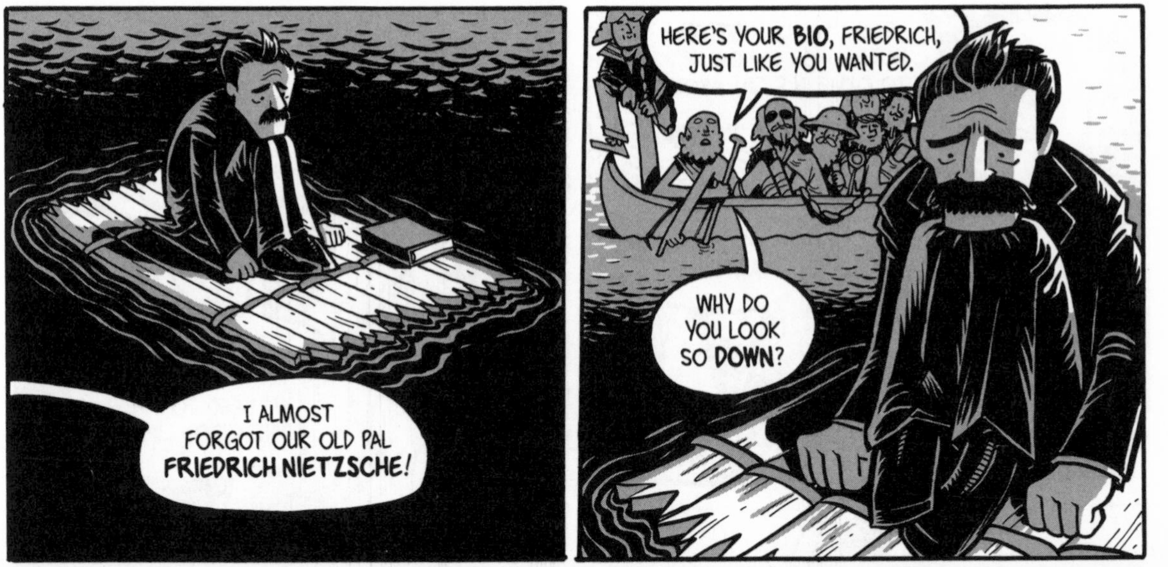
I ALMOST FORGOT OUR OLD PAL FRIEDRICH NIETZSCHE!
HERE'S YOUR BIO, FRIEDRICH, JUST LIKE YOU WANTED.
WHY DO YOU LOOK SO DOWN?

FRIEDRICH WILHELM **NIETZSCHE** b. 1844 d. 1900 C.E.

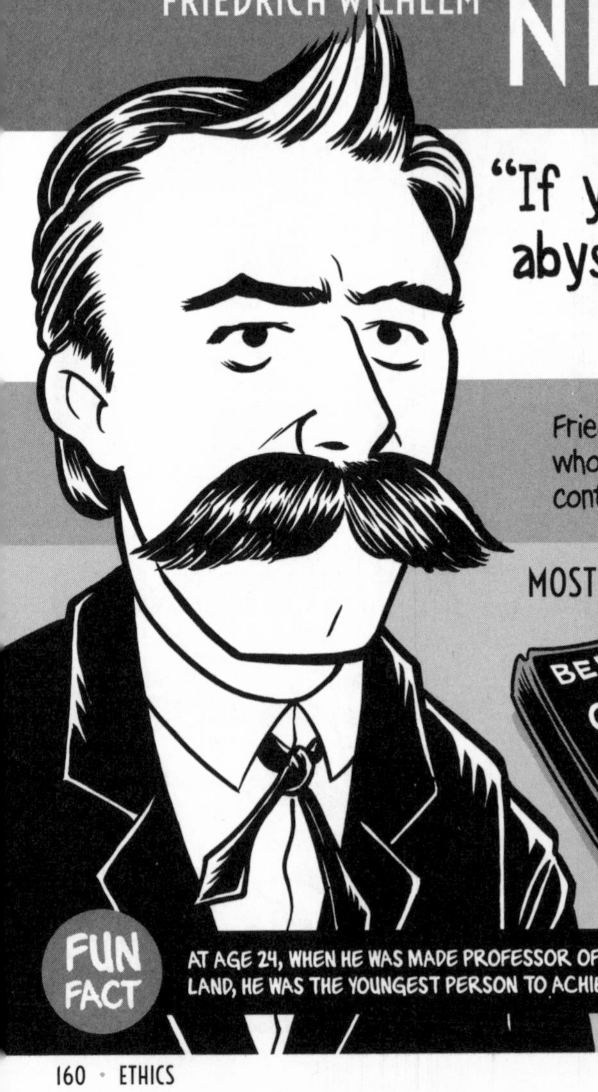

"If you gaze long enough into the abyss, the abyss will gaze back into you."

-- *Beyond Good and Evil*

Friedrich Wilhelm Nietzsche was a German philosopher who notably wrote about truth, morality, power, contemporary culture, and science.

MOST FAMOUS WORK:

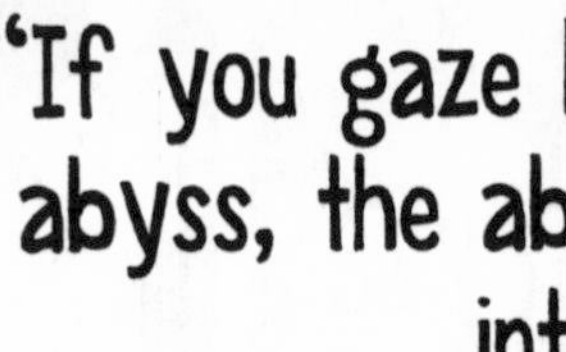
BEYOND GOOD & EVIL
1886

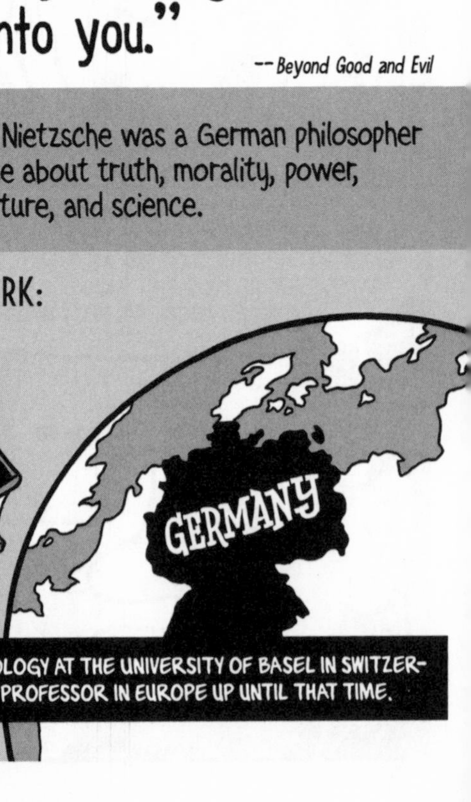
GERMANY

FUN FACT AT AGE 24, WHEN HE WAS MADE PROFESSOR OF CLASSICAL PHILOLOGY AT THE UNIVERSITY OF BASEL IN SWITZERLAND, HE WAS THE YOUNGEST PERSON TO ACHIEVE THE RANK OF PROFESSOR IN EUROPE UP UNTIL THAT TIME.

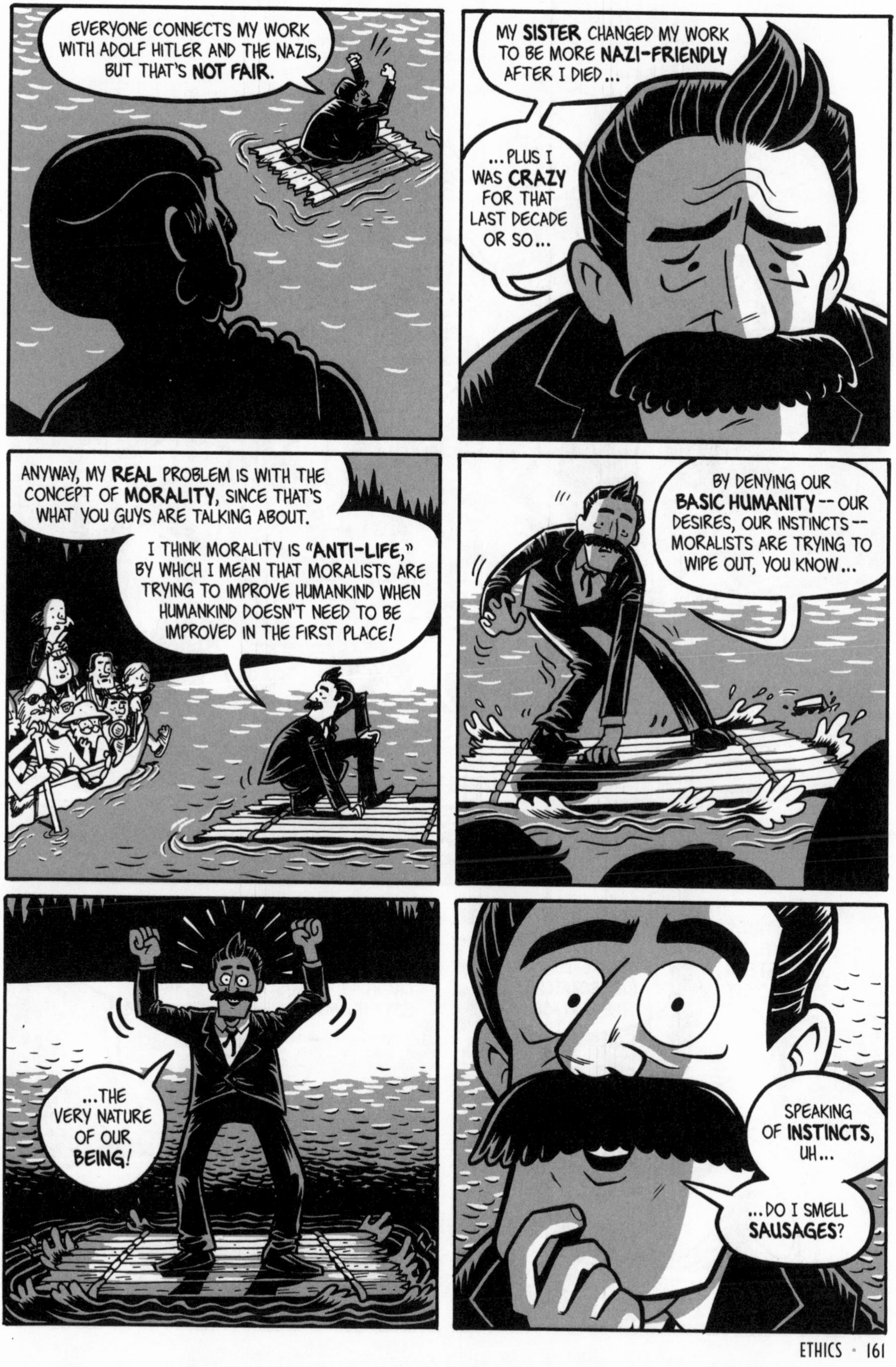
EVERYONE CONNECTS MY WORK WITH ADOLF HITLER AND THE NAZIS, BUT THAT'S **NOT FAIR**.
MY **SISTER** CHANGED MY WORK TO BE MORE **NAZI-FRIENDLY** AFTER I DIED...
...PLUS I WAS **CRAZY** FOR THAT LAST DECADE OR SO...
ANYWAY, MY **REAL** PROBLEM IS WITH THE CONCEPT OF **MORALITY**, SINCE THAT'S WHAT YOU GUYS ARE TALKING ABOUT.
I THINK MORALITY IS **"ANTI-LIFE,"** BY WHICH I MEAN THAT MORALISTS ARE TRYING TO IMPROVE HUMANKIND WHEN HUMANKIND DOESN'T NEED TO BE IMPROVED IN THE FIRST PLACE!
BY DENYING OUR **BASIC HUMANITY**--OUR DESIRES, OUR INSTINCTS--MORALISTS ARE TRYING TO WIPE OUT, YOU KNOW...
...THE VERY NATURE OF OUR **BEING**!
SPEAKING OF **INSTINCTS**, UH...
...DO I SMELL **SAUSAGES**?

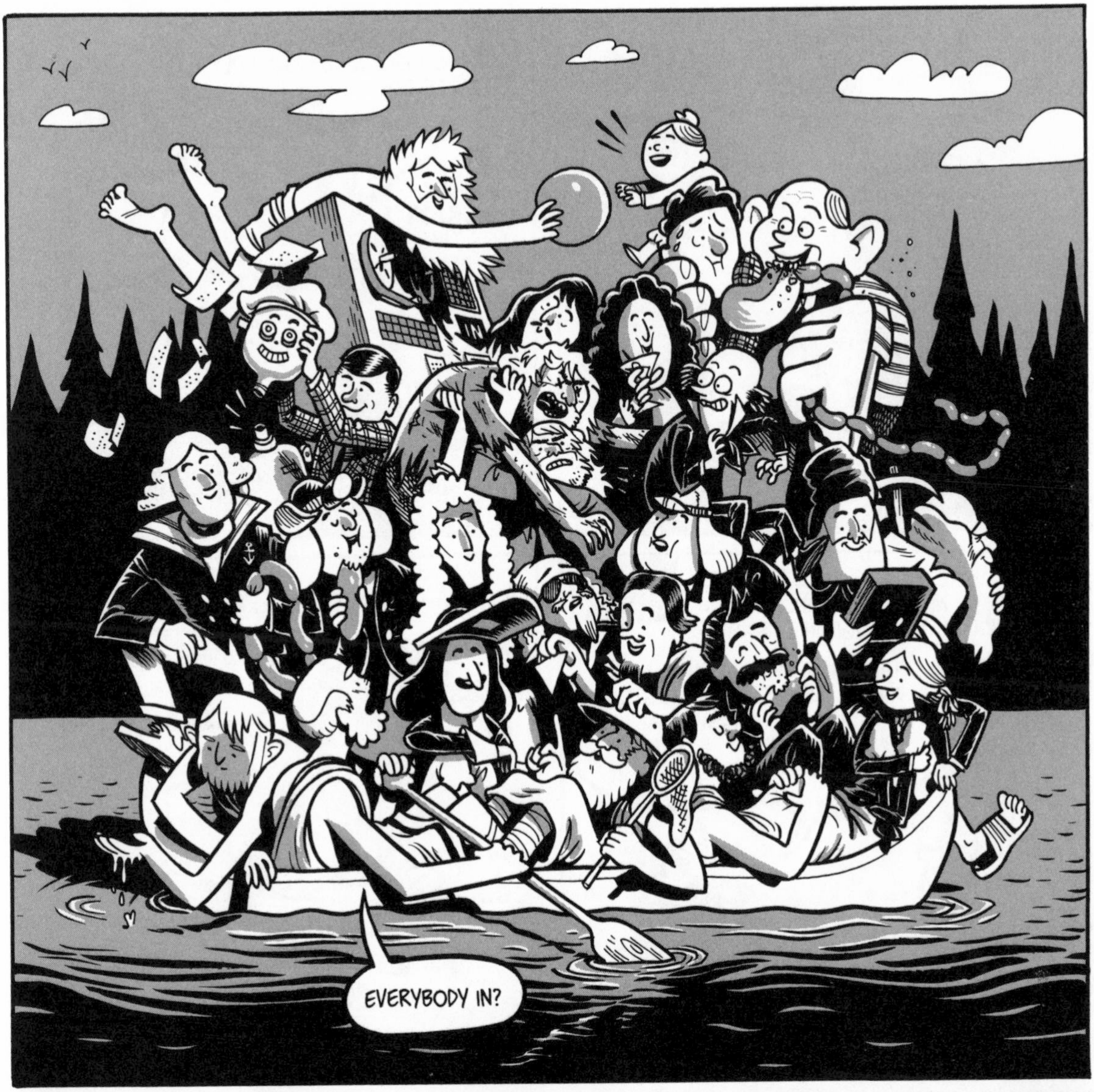
EVERYBODY IN?

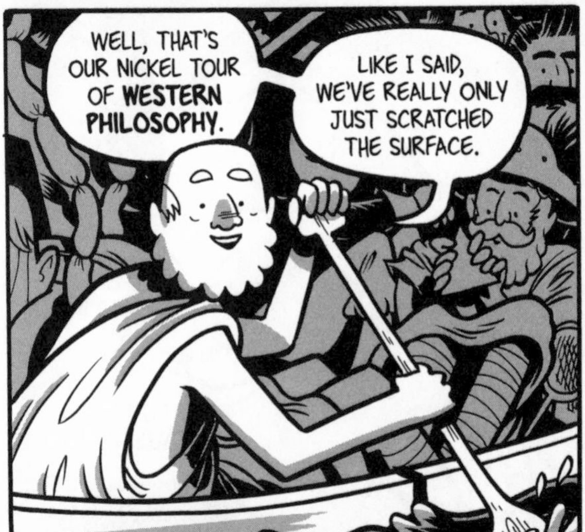
WELL, THAT'S OUR NICKEL TOUR OF **WESTERN PHILOSOPHY**.
LIKE I SAID, WE'VE REALLY ONLY JUST SCRATCHED THE SURFACE.

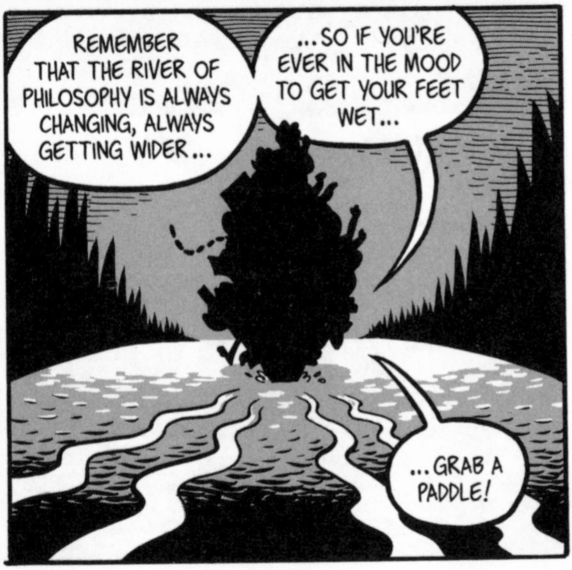
REMEMBER THAT THE RIVER OF PHILOSOPHY IS ALWAYS CHANGING, ALWAYS GETTING WIDER...
...SO IF YOU'RE EVER IN THE MOOD TO GET YOUR FEET WET...
...GRAB A PADDLE!

GLOSSARY

A

ABSOLUTISM
IN ETHICS, ANY THEORY THAT HOLDS SOME ACTIONS TO BE GOOD OR BAD NO MATTER WHAT. FOR EXAMPLE, WHILE SOME MIGHT HOLD THAT TELLING A LIE IS PERMISSIBLE IN ORDER TO STOP A MURDER (OR SOME OTHER GREATER WRONG), AN ABSOLUTIST WOULD HOLD THAT A LIE IS BAD NO MATTER WHAT.

C

CARTESIAN INTERACTIONISM
THE THEORY THAT THE NONPHYSICAL MIND AND THE PHYSICAL BODY CAN CAUSALLY AFFECT ONE ANOTHER. FOR EXAMPLE, MY STEPPING ON A NAIL CAUSES ALL SORTS OF PHYSICAL EVENTS, BUT MY CONSCIOUS SUFFERING TAKES PLACE SOLELY IN MY NONPHYSICAL MIND. MY SUFFERING MAY THEN CAUSE ME TO CRY OUT VIA MY PHYSICAL BODY.

COMPATIBILISM
THE THEORY THAT SINCE MY FREE ACTIONS ARE CAUSED BY MY DESIRES, MY HAVING FREE WILL IS NOT NECESSARILY INCOMPATIBLE WITH DETERMINISM'S TRUTH. COMPATIBILISTS CALL AN ACT FREE IF AND ONLY IF (1) IT WAS THE RESULT OF ONE OF MY DESIRES AND (2) IT IS TRUE THAT IF I'D HAD A DIFFERENT DESIRE, I WOULD HAVE PERFORMED A DIFFERENT ACT.

CONSEQUENTIALISM
IN ETHICS, ANY THEORY THAT ASSESSES THE MORAL STATUS OF AN ACTION BASED ON ITS CONSEQUENCES RATHER THAN ON OTHER FEATURES SUCH AS ORIGINS, MOTIVES, OR INTENTIONS.

D

DEDUCTIVE ARGUMENT
AN ARGUMENT THAT IS INTENDED TO PROVIDE SUPPORT FOR ITS CONCLUSION SUCH THAT IF THE PREMISES ARE TRUE, THEN THE CONCLUSION MUST BE TRUE.

DEONTOLOGY
IN ETHICS, ANY THEORY THAT ASSESSES ACTIONS ON THE BASIS OF THEIR ACTION TYPE RATHER THAN ON AN ACT-BY-ACT BASIS. FOR EXAMPLE, A DEONTOLOGIST MIGHT HOLD THAT ALL LIES ARE WRONG, WHEREAS A CONSEQUENTIALIST COULD SAY THAT ONE LIE WAS PERMISSIBLE WHILE ANOTHER LIE WAS IMPERMISSIBLE.

DETERMINISM
THE THEORY THAT EVERY EVENT IS CAUSED BY THE PRIOR STATES OF THE UNIVERSE AND THE LAWS OF PHYSICS.

DIVINE COMMAND THEORY
IN ITS SIMPLEST FORM, THE THEORY THAT AN ACTION'S MORAL STATUS IS DETERMINED BY THE WILL OF SOME GOD OR GODS.

DOGMATISM
AN UNWILLINGNESS TO CHANGE ONE'S BELIEFS DESPITE ANY AND ALL EVIDENCE TO THE CONTRARY.

DUALISM

ANY THEORY THAT HOLDS THAT MINDS AND BODIES ARE TWO DIFFERENT KINDS OF THING. DESCARTES, FOR EXAMPLE, HELD THAT THE MIND WAS A NONPHYSICAL SUBSTANCE WHILE THE BODY WAS A PHYSICAL SUBSTANCE. SPINOZA, BY CONTRAST, HELD THAT THE MENTAL AND THE PHYSICAL WERE SIMPLY TWO DIFFERENT PROPERTIES OF A SINGLE, UNDERLYING SUBSTANCE.

E

EMPIRICISM

THE DOCTRINE THAT ALL OF HUMAN KNOWLEDGE HAS ITS ORIGINS IN SENSORY EXPERIENCE.

F

FOUNDATIONALISM

THE THEORY THAT THE JUSTIFICATION OF A BELIEF MUST ULTIMATELY TERMINATE WITH A SELF-EVIDENT OR NECESSARILY TRUE CLAIM.

FREE WILL

THE ABILITY TO DETERMINE SOME OF ONE'S ACTIONS, OFTEN ASSUMED TO BE A PREREQUISITE FOR HAVING MORAL RESPONSIBILITY.

G

GENETIC ACCOUNT

ANY JUSTIFICATION OF A BELIEF THAT APPEALS ONLY TO THE BELIEF'S ORIGIN OR GENESIS INSTEAD OF TO ITS JUSTIFICATION.

I

IDEALISM

THE THEORY THAT ONLY MINDS AND THEIR IDEAS EXIST.

INDETERMINISM

THE THEORY THAT AT LEAST ONE EVENT IS NOT CAUSED BY THE PRIOR CONDITIONS OF THE UNIVERSE AND THE LAWS OF PHYSICS.

INDUCTIVE ARGUMENT

AN ARGUMENT THAT IS INTENDED TO PROVIDE SUPPORT FOR ITS CONCLUSION SUCH THAT THE TRUTH OF THE PREMISES MAKE THE CONCLUSION TO SOME (PREFERABLY HIGH) DEGREE LIKELY TO BE TRUE.

L

LOEBNER PRIZE

A PRIZE ESTABLISHED IN 1990 TO BE AWARDED TO THE FIRST COMPUTER TO PASS THE TURING TEST, THAT IS, TO GENERATE RESPONSES TO QUESTIONS THAT ARE INDISCERNIBLE FROM THE RESPONSES OF A HUMAN BEING.

M

MIND

A GENERIC TERM FOR WHATEVER IT IS THAT THINKS. A MIND MIGHT BE A NONPHYSICAL THING, A PHYSICAL THING, OR SOMETHING ELSE ENTIRELY, SUCH AS A PROPERTY OF SOME OTHER THING.

P

PARALLELISM

THE THEORY THAT THE MIND AND BODY ARE SEPARATE SUBSTANCES THAT ARE SYNCHRONIZED BUT THAT DO NOT INTERACT CAUSALLY WITH ONE ANOTHER.

PHYSICALISM

THE THEORY THAT ONLY PHYSICAL THINGS EXIST.

PROPERTY DUALISM

THE THEORY THAT THE MIND AND THE BODY ARE DISTINCT PROPERTIES OF A SINGLE SUBSTANCE AS OPPOSED TO BEING DISTINCT SUBSTANCES.

T

TURING TEST

A TEST PROPOSED BY ALAN TURING IN 1950 TO DETERMINE WHETHER A GIVEN COMPUTER SHOULD BE CONSIDERED TO BE THINKING IN THE HUMAN SENSE. TURING CONCEIVED OF AN INTERROGATOR INTERACTING WITH TWO UNKNOWN RESPONDENTS. IF, AFTER EXTENSIVE INTERROGATION, THE INTERROGATOR COULD NOT TELL WITH GREATER THAN 70 PERCENT ACCURACY WHICH RESPONDENT WAS THE PERSON AND WHICH WAS THE MACHINE, THE MACHINE, HE THOUGHT, COULD BE SAID TO BE THINKING.

V

VALIDITY

A PROPERTY OF SOME DEDUCTIVE ARGUMENTS. A DEDUCTIVE ARGUMENT IS VALID WHEN THE TRUTH OF ITS PREMISES GUARANTEES OR ESTABLISHES THE TRUTH OF ITS CONCLUSION.

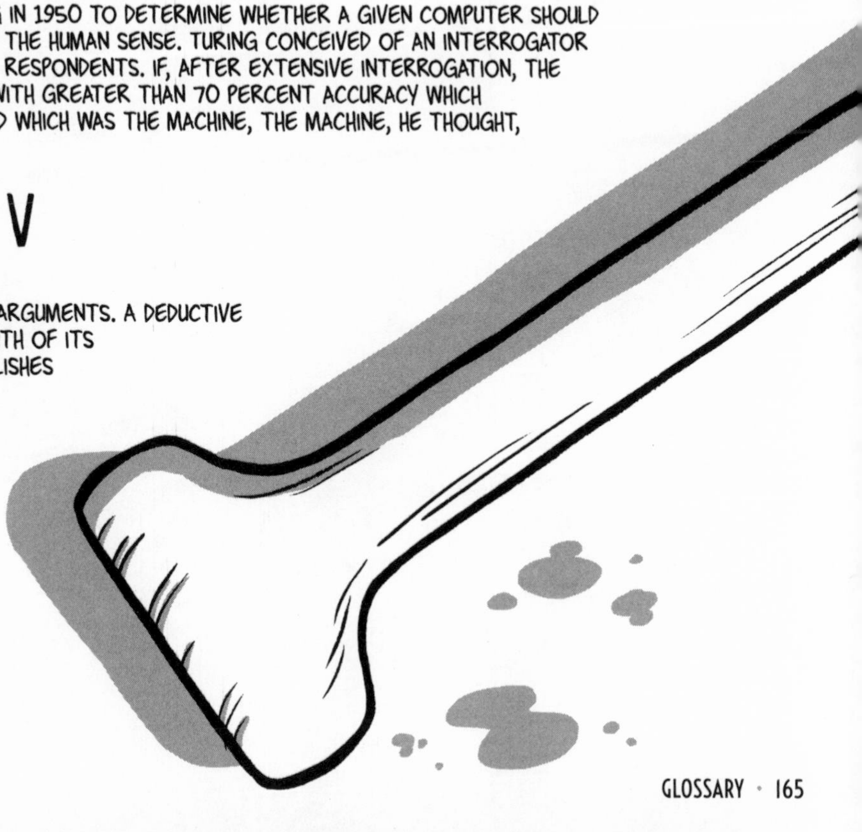

BIBLIOGRAPHY

AQUINAS, ST. THOMAS. *SUMMA THEOLOGICA*. TRANSLATED BY THE FATHERS OF THE ENGLISH DOMINICAN PROVINCE. WESTMINSTER, MD: CHRISTIAN CLASSICS, 1981.

BENTHAM, JEREMY. *THE PRINCIPLES OF MORALS AND LEGISLATION*. AMHERST, NY: PROMETHEUS BOOKS, 1988.

BERKELEY, GEORGE. *A TREATISE CONCERNING THE PRINCIPLES OF HUMAN KNOWLEDGE*. EDITED BY KENNETH WINKLER. INDIANAPOLIS: HACKETT PUB. CO., 1982.

CHALMERS, DAVID. "MUCH ADO ABOUT CONSCIOUSNESS," INTERVIEW BY ANDREW CHRUCKY. *PHILOSOPHY NOW* 21 (SUMMER/AUTUMN 1998). HTTPS://PHILOSOPHYNOW.ORG/ISSUES/21/MUCH_ADO_ABOUT_CONSCIOUSNESS.

COHEN, S. MARC, PATRICIA CURD, AND C. D. C. REEVE, EDS. *READINGS IN ANCIENT GREEK PHILOSOPHY: FROM THALES TO ARISTOTLE*. INDIANAPOLIS: HACKETT PUB. CO., 1995.

DARWIN, CHARLES. *THE DESCENT OF MAN*. EDITED AND WITH AN INTRODUCTION BY JAMES MOORE AND ADRIAN J. DESMOND. LONDON: PENGUIN, 2004.

DESCARTES, RENÉ. *THE PHILOSOPHICAL WRITINGS OF DESCARTES*. TRANSLATED BY JOHN COTTINGHAM, ROBERT STOOTHOFF, AND DUGALD MURDOCH. CAMBRIDGE, UK: CAMBRIDGE UNIVERSITY PRESS, 1985.

DESCARTES, RENÉ, BENEDICT DE SPINOZA, AND GOTTFRIED WILHELM FREIHERR VON LEIBNIZ. *THE RATIONALISTS*. NEW YORK: ANCHOR BOOKS, 1974.

HOBBES, THOMAS. *LEVIATHAN*. EDITED BY CRAWFORD B. MACPHERSON. HARMONDSWORTH, UK: PENGUIN BOOKS, 1982.

HUME, DAVID. *AN ENQUIRY CONCERNING HUMAN UNDERSTANDING*. EDITED BY TOM L. BEAUCHAMP. OXFORD, UK: OXFORD UNIVERSITY PRESS, 1999.

KANT, IMMANUEL. *CRITIQUE OF PRACTICAL REASON*. TRANSLATED BY LEWIS WHITE BECK. 3RD ED. NEW YORK: MACMILLAN PUB. CO., 1993.

LA METTRIE, JULIEN OFFRAY DE. *MAN A MACHINE*. 7TH ED. LA SALLE, IL: OPEN COURT, 1993.

LOCKE, JOHN. *AN ESSAY CONCERNING HUMAN UNDERSTANDING*. EDITED BY R. S. WOOLHOUSE. NEW YORK: PENGUIN, 1997.

MILL, JOHN STUART. *UTILITARIANISM*. EDITED BY GEORGE SHER. 2ND ED. INDIANAPOLIS: HACKETT PUB. CO., 2001.

NIETZSCHE, FRIEDRICH WILHELM. *BEYOND GOOD AND EVIL: PRELUDE TO A PHILOSOPHY OF THE FUTURE*. TRANSLATED BY WALTER KAUFMANN. NEW YORK: VINTAGE BOOKS, 1989.

PALEY, WILLIAM. *NATURAL THEOLOGY, OR, EVIDENCES OF THE EXISTENCE AND ATTRIBUTES OF THE DEITY*. LANDISVILLE, PA: COACHWHIP PUBLICATIONS, 2005.

SCHEUTZ, MATTHIAS. *COMPUTATIONALISM: NEW DIRECTIONS*. CAMBRIDGE, MA: MIT PRESS, 2002.

SPINOZA, BENEDICTUS DE. *ETHICS*. EDITED AND TRANSLATED BY EDWIN CURLEY WITH AN INTRODUCTION BY STUART HAMPSHIRE. LONDON: PENGUIN BOOKS, 1996.

A NOTE ABOUT THE AUTHORS

MICHAEL F. PATTON IS A PROFESSOR OF PHILOSOPHY AND THE COORDINATOR OF THE PHILOSOPHY AND RELIGION PROGRAM AT THE UNIVERSITY OF MONTEVALLO. HE LIVES IN MONTEVALLO, ALABAMA, WITH HIS WIFE, CHERYL.

KEVIN CANNON IS AN AWARD-WINNING ILLUSTRATOR WHO HAS CONTRIBUTED TO SEVERAL NONFICTION GRAPHIC NOVELS, INCLUDING *EVOLUTION* AND *THE STUFF OF LIFE* (BOTH PUBLISHED BY HILL AND WANG). HE LIVES IN MINNEAPOLIS, MINNESOTA.